Lecture Notes in Computer Scie

T0238346

Commenced Publication in 1973
Founding and Former Series Editors:
Gerhard Goos, Juris Hartmanis, and Jan van Leeuwen

András Horváth   Miklós Telek (Eds.)

Formal Methods and Stochastic Models for Performance Evaluation

Third European Performance Engineering Workshop, EPEW 2006
Budapest, Hungary, June 21-22, 2006
Proceedings

 Springer

Volume Editors

András Horváth
Università di Torino, Dipartimento di Informatica
Corso Svizzera 185, 10149 Torino, Italy
E-mail: horvath@di.unito.it

Miklós Telek
Budapest University of Technology and Economics, Department of Telecommunications
P.O. Box 91, 1521 Budapest, Hungary
E-mail: telek@hit.bme.hu

Library of Congress Control Number: 2006927343

CR Subject Classification (1998): D.2.4, C.2.4, F.3, D.4, C.4

LNCS Sublibrary: SL 2 – Programming and Software Engineering

ISSN   0302-9743
ISBN-10   3-540-35362-3 Springer Berlin Heidelberg New York
ISBN-13   978-3-540-35362-1 Springer Berlin Heidelberg New York

Springer is a part of Springer Science+Business Media

springer.com

© Springer-Verlag Berlin Heidelberg 2006
Printed in Germany

Typesetting: Camera-ready by author, data conversion by Scientific Publishing Services, Chennai, India
Printed on acid-free paper   SPIN: 11777830   06/3142   5 4 3 2 1 0

Preface

The idea to establish a European forum for academic and industrial researchers working on various aspects of performance modeling and analysis of manufacturing and information systems gave rise to an annual series of workshops, referred to as European Performance Engineering Workshop (EPEW). The first two EPEW workshops were held in Toledo, Spain, October 1-2, 2004, and Versailles, France, September 1-3, 2005. This volume contains the proceedings of the third EPEW workshop held at the Technical University of Budapest, Budapest, Hungary, June 21-22, 2006.

These proceedings comprise the 16 accepted contributed papers of EPEW 2006. To ensure the high-quality evaluation of the submitted papers we extended the Program Committee of EPEW 2006 with international experts from all over the world. Each submitted papers went through a rigorous review by at least three international reviewers. Based on the reviews, the subsequent discussions of reviewers with different judgement and an Internet-based Program Committee meeting held on March 30, 2006, we selected 40% of the submitted papers. We therefore owe special thanks to all members of the Program Committee and to all external referees for the excellent work they did for the proper evaluation of the papers.

The final workshop program, as well as this volume, are made up of five thematic sessions:

- Stochastic process algebra
- Workloads and benchmarks
- Theory of stochastic processes
- Formal dependability and performance evaluation
- Queues, theory and practice

These sessions cover a wide range of performance evaluation methods and compose an overview of the current research directions in performance evaluation. Some papers focus on a particular research field (e.g., convergence rate of specific Markov chains) while others provide a combination of research methodologies from essentially different fields (e.g., model checking and stochastic fluid models). We hope that these proceedings offer interesting research results for everyone dealing with performance evaluation.

Last, but not least, we would like to thank the publication chair and the local organizers of the workshops for their work. A special thanks to Levente Bodrog for creating and maintaining the website of the conference.

April 2007

András Horváth
Miklós Telek

Organization

Workshop Chair

Miklós Telek, Technical University of Budapest (Hungary)

Program Chair

András Horváth, University of Torino (Italy)

Publication Chair

Katinka Wolter, Humboldt University (Germany)

Local Organizers

Levente Bodrog, Technical University of Budapest (Hungary)
Gábor Horváth, Technical University of Budapest (Hungary)

Program Committee

Jeremy Bradley	András Horváth	András Pataricza
Mario Bravetti	Alain Jean-Marie	Brigitte Plateau
Peter Buchholz	Carlos Juiz	Antonio Puliafito
Gianfranco Ciardo	Helen Karatza	Marina Ribaudo
Tadeusz Czachórski	Leïla Kloul	Evgenia Smirni
Jean-Michel Fourneau	Kim G. Larsen	Mark Squillante
Reinard German	Fernando Lopez Pelayo	Miklós Telek
Stephen Gilmore	Raymond Marie	Nigel Thomas
Boudewijn Haverkort	Andrew Miner	Katinka Wolter
Holger Hermanns	Manuel Núñez	Wlodek M. Zuberek

External Referees

Salvador Alcaraz	H. Kalatunga	Ismael Rodríguez
Ashok Argent-Katwala	Matthias Kuntz	Pere Pau Sancho
Matteo Baldoni	Jenny Liu	Ihab Sbeity
Pieter-Tjerk de Boer	Daniele Manini	Marco Scarpa
Leonardo Brenner	Mercedes G. Merayo	Matteo Sereno
Katja Gilly	Miklós Molnár	Jean-Marc Vincent
Gábor Horváth	Zsolt Pándi	

Table of Contents

Formal Dependability and Performance Evaluation

Queues, Theory and Practice

A Precedence PEPA Model for Performance and Reliability Analysis

Jean-Michel Fourneau and Leïla Kloul

PRiSM, Université de Versailles Saint-Quentin,
45 Av. des Etats Unis, 78000 Versailles, France
{jmf, kle}@prism.uvsq.fr

Abstract. We propose new techniques to simplify the computation of the cycle times and the absorption times for a large class of PEPA models. These techniques allow us to simplify the model description to reduce the number of states of the underlying Markov chain. The simplification processes are associated with stochastic comparisons of random variables. Thus the simplified models are stochastic bounds for the original ones.

1 Introduction

In the recent years, several researchers have investigated ways to solve steady-state distributions for Stochastic Process Algebra models with exponential duration of activities such as PEPA models [10]. The tensor based representation [11] allows us to build large state spaces in a very efficient manner. However solving the steady-state distribution remains a difficult problem even if the bisimulation technique allows us to reduce the state space. Recently the process algebra formalism has also been used to solve transient problems [7], still under the Markovian assumption.

Here, we advocate a completely different approach which is not totally related to this Markovian assumption. First, we want to compute the distribution of the cycle time (if the model is well defined) or the distribution of the absorption time (if the model has an absorbing state) instead of the steady-state distribution. The cycle time is the delay between two successive visits to a specific state while the absorption time is the time until absorption. Cycle time is closely related to the throughput of the system while the distribution of the absorption time allows us to define the reliability of a system. By taking the average of these distributions, one can obtain the mean throughput and the average population with Little's formula or the mean time to failure. These quantities are in general significant for models based on customer's point of view rather than server's states.

We propose a two-level hierarchical approach. At the higher level, we consider a precedence PEPA model. Each component of the precedence model is a sub-model isolated from the other components. Because of the exponential duration of the activities in a PEPA component, these sub-models can be associated with continuous time Phase type distributions.

A. Horváth and M. Telek (Eds.): EPEW 2006, LNCS 4054, pp. 1–15, 2006.

Computing absorption time distribution is usually done by uniformization and analysis of transient discrete-time Markov chains. This technique requires a large number of vector-matrix multiplications. The matrix size is the number of states in the Markov chain. So it is important to find techniques which can be used to reduce this number of states. Cycle times computation are not necessarily based on Markovian assumption, even if exponential delays of individual activities may lead to the usual Markovian numerical analysis. For a class of decision-free Petri nets, cycle times are defined by recurrence relations [3]. Furthermore these relations are linear but on the max-plus semigroup. Such structures have been studied extensively in the context of random variables (see for instance Baccelli et al [1]). For more general systems, the computation of the cycle times is a complex problem. The stochastic comparison appears to be a promising technique to cope with this complexity.

If we need to compute the cycle time of a PEPA model which is too complex to analyse numerically, we design automatically a new model such that its cycle time is a bound for the exact one. This bound is stochastic: we do not compare reals but distribution functions. Thus stochastic bounds are far more accurate than worst-case analysis. If the new model has a reduced state space, we may then use numerical methods (or even analytical results) to efficiently solve the problem. Note that bounding some performance measures is often sufficient as quite often we only need to verify the requirements in terms of threshold. Stochastic bounds may also be applied to Markov chains (see [8] for a survey of the various techniques involved and [12] for an example of delays due to a Fair Queueing discipline).

Here we propose high level techniques which transform a PEPA model into simpler PEPA model. These techniques are based on stochastic bounds. They allow us to divide the problem into sub-problems or to replace a complete PEPA sub-model by a single activity. Here we just give some theoretical results, we will present in a sequel paper the algorithms we need and some numerical results.

The rest of the paper is organised as follows. In Section 2, we present some concepts of stochastic comparison while Section 3 gives a simple introduction to PEPA, the SPA we consider. Section 4 is devoted to the precedence PEPA model. Section 5 contains the main results of the paper. Finally in Section 6, we conclude our work with some remarks and future work.

2   A Simple Introduction to Stochastic Comparison

We restrict ourselves to finite Continuous Time Markov Chains (CTMC). Stoyan [14] defined the strong stochastic ordering ("st" ordering for short) by the set of non-decreasing functions. Bounds on the distribution imply bounds on these functions as well. Important performance measures such as average population, loss rates or tail probabilities are non decreasing functions. The second part of the definition for discrete random variables is much more convenient for an algebraic formulation and an algorithmic setting.

Definition 1. *Let X and Y be random variables taking values on a totally ordered space. Then X is said to be less than Y in the strong stochastic sense, that is, $X <_{st} Y$ iff $E[f(X)] \leq E[f(Y)]$ for all non decreasing functions f whenever the expectations exist.*

If X and Y take values on the finite state space $\{1, 2, \ldots, n\}$ with p and q as probability distribution vectors, then X is said to be less than Y in the strong stochastic sense, that is, $X <_{st} Y$ iff $\sum_{j=k}^{n} p_j \leq \sum_{j=k}^{n} q_j$ for $k = 1, 2, \ldots, n$.

Example 1. *Let $a = (0.1, 0.3, 0.4, 0.2)$ and $b = (0.1, 0.1, 0.5, 0.3)$. We have $a <_{st} b$ as:*

$$\begin{bmatrix} 0.2 & \leq 0.3 \\ 0.2 + 0.4 & \leq 0.3 + 0.5 \\ 0.2 + 0.4 + 0.3 \leq 0.3 + 0.5 + 0.1 \end{bmatrix}$$

Sufficient conditions for comparison for CTMC are known for a long time [14]. The stochastic comparison of CTMC implies that their steady-state and transient distributions are also ordered.

Theorem 1 (Stoyan [14], page 193). *Let us consider two CTMC $Z1$ and $Z2$ on the same state space whose transition rate matrix are respectively $Q1$ and $Q2$. If*

1. *$Z1_0 <_{st} Z2_0$*
2. *$\sum_{k \geq l} Q1(i, k) \leq \sum_{k \geq l} Q2(j, k)$ for all $i \leq j$ and for all l which satisfy $l \leq i$ or $l \geq j$.*

then $Z1 <_{st} Z2$.

It may be important to compare Phase type random variables with exponential ones because it allows building a smaller Markov chain. Let us first define a family of random variables well known in reliability modelling [4].

Definition 2 (New Better than Used in Expectation). *Let X_t be the residual time of X, given that $X > t$. X is said to be NBUE if $E(X_t) \leq E(X)$ for all t.*

For instance, Erlang, uniform and constant random variables are NBUE. This family leads to another stochastic ordering: the increasing convex ordering which is used to compare random variables with exponentials.

Definition 3. *Let X and Y be two random variables on the same space ϵ, X is smaller in increasing convex order than Y, if and only if $E(f(X)) \leq E(f(Y))$ for all convex and non decreasing functions f on ϵ, provided that the expectations exist. The relation is denoted by $X <_{icx} Y$.*

Property 1 ([14]). *If X is NBUE of mean m, then X is smaller in increasing convex ordering than an exponentially distributed random variable of mean m.*

The icx ordering also provides a very intuitive lower bound.

Property 2 ([14]). *For any arbitrary positive random variable X, $E(X) <_{icx} X$.*

We also have two very simple properties which will be used to derive bounds at the higher level of a model from bounds obtained at the lower level.

Property 3. *The Max and Plus operators are convex and non decreasing functions.*

Property 4. *Let X and Y be two r.v. such that $X <_{icx} Y$, then for all convex and non decreasing function f, we have $f(X) <_{icx} f(Y)$.*

Finally, we can compare the absorption time of Markov chains [5] as stated in the following property.

Property 5. *Let $Z1$ and $Z2$ be two homogeneous Markov chains with an absorbing state n and let $T_a(Z1)$ and $T_a(Z2)$ denote absorption times for the two chains. If $Z1 <_{st} Z2$ or $Z1 <_{icx} Z2$ then $T_a(Z2) <_{st} T_a(Z1)$.*

Note that the "st" comparison of absorption times is now on random variables T_a defined on the time instants, not on the states.

3   PEPA

In PEPA, a system is viewed as a set of *components* which carry out *activities*. Each activity is characterised by an *action type* and a duration which is exponentially distributed. Thus each activity is defined by a couple (α, r) where α is the action type and r is the *activity rate*. Because of the exponential distribution of the activity duration, the underlying Markov process of a PEPA model is a continuous time Markov process.

PEPA formalism provides a set of combinators which allows expressions to be built, defining the behaviour of components, via the activities they engage in. Below, we present informally the combinators we are interested in and which are necessary to our model. For more details about the formalism, see [10].

Constant: noted $S \stackrel{def}{=} P$, it allows us to assign names to components. To component S, we assign the behaviour of component P.

Prefix: noted $(\alpha, r).P$, this combinator is the basic mechanism by which the behaviours of components are constructed. The component carries out activity (α, r) and subsequently behaves as component P.

Choice: noted $P_1 + P_2$, this combinator represents competition between components. The system may behave either as component P_1 or as P_2. All current activities of the components are enabled. The first activity to complete, determined by the race condition, distinguishes one of these components, the other is discarded.

Cooperation: noted $P_1 \bowtie_L P_2$, it allows the synchronisation of components P_1 and P_2 over the activities in the cooperation set L. Components may proceed independently with activities whose types do not belong to this set. A particular case of the cooperation is when $L = \emptyset$. In this case, components proceed with activities independently and are noted $P_1 || P_2$.

In a cooperation, the rate of a shared activity is defined as the rate of the slowest component. For a component P_1 and an action type α, the working capacity is termed the *apparent rate* of α in P_1. It is the sum of the rates of the α type activities enabled in P_1. The apparent rate of α in a cooperation between P_1 and P_2 over α will be the minimum of the apparent rate of α in P_1 and the apparent rate of α in P_2.

The rate of an activity may be unspecified for a component and is noted $\top$. Such a component is said to be *passive* with respect to this action type and the rate of this shared activity is defined by the other component in cooperation.

In PEPA, when a component C carries out an activity (α, r) and subsequently behaves as component C', this one is said to be a *derivative* of C. From any PEPA component C, the *derivative set*, denoted $ds(C)$, is the set of derivatives (behaviours) which can evolve from the component. This set is defined recursively.

The evolution of a PEPA model is governed by the Structured Operational Semantics (SOS) rules of the language [10]. These rules define the admissible transitions or state changes associated with each combinator.

Necessary (but not sufficient) conditions for the ergodicity of the Markov process in terms of the structure of the PEPA model have been identified and can be readily checked [10]. These conditions imply that the model must be a *cyclic* PEPA component. The model should be constructed as a cooperation of *sequential* components, i.e. components constructed using only prefix, choice and constants. This leads to formally define the syntax of PEPA expressions in terms of *model components* P and *sequential components* S:

$$P ::= A \mid P \bowtie_L P \mid P/L \qquad\qquad S ::= (\alpha, r).S \mid S + S \mid A_s$$

where A denotes a constant which is either a model or a sequential component and A_s denotes a constant which is a sequential component. Thus the compositional structure of PEPA models is at the level of the cooperating components; such models are considered as *well-defined*.

4   The Precedence PEPA Model

We consider that a system is represented by a set of components which have the same general behaviour as they wake up, proceed with their activities and then make other components wake up. The components are assumed to be initially asleep (off) and cannot proceed with the execution of their activities unless they are woken up. We assume a precedence relation between the enabling of the components in the set as the results of some components can be used as an input by other components. The components are labelled to allow a representation of this precedence relation. We assume the following properties for the set of labels:

1. the set is totally ordered,
2. the set has a unique minimal element which is denoted by $Comp_0$ for convenience,
3. and the set has a unique maximal element which is denoted by $Comp_n$.

We assume that $Comp_0$ constitutes the starting component of the system and $Comp_n$ the last one to be enabled. When $Comp_n$ completes, the system is assumed to have the same behaviour, restarting from the beginning, i.e. $Comp_0$ (Figure 1). Furthermore, we assume that the precedence relation between the components is a Directed Acyclic Graph (DAG) modified by this return arc from $Comp_n$ to $Comp_0$.

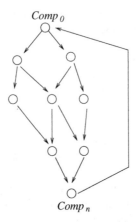

Fig. 1. The precedence relation between the components

Our system specifications allow us to consider two kinds of analysis, performance analysis and reliability analysis. The former exploits the presence of the return arc from $Comp_n$ to $Comp_0$ to compute performance measures such as the cycle times. The latter is only possible if we have in our system an absorbing state, that is the precedence relation between the components is a real DAG. Moreover, $Comp_n$ must contain an absorbing state.

4.1   Formal Description of the System

To represent the precedence relation characterising our system, we define two families of sets P_i and S_i. P_i is the set of components which must complete their activities before $Comp_i$ is woken up and S_i represents the set of components which are enabled when $Comp_i$ has completed its activities. Note that the two families of sets have to be consistent.

We describe the system using $n + 1$ components. Each component $Comp_k$, $k = 0 \ldots n$, is woken up thanks to activity $wake\_up_{jk}$ where j is a predecessor of $Comp_k$, that is $j \in P_k$. Once awake, the component can then proceed with its own activities $\alpha_{k,l}$, $l = 1..m_k$, where m_k is the number of activities of $Comp_k$. Note that these activities ($\alpha_{k,l}$) are all individual activities and once $Comp_k$ has finished executing them, it will wake up the components which are in its set of successors S_k.

The behaviour of the components of the system are modelled using the following equations:

$$Comp_0 \stackrel{def}{=} (start, w_1).(\alpha_{0,1}, r_{0,1})...(\alpha_{0,m_0}, r_{0,m_0}). \prod_{i \in S_0} (wake\_up_{0i}, s).Comp_0$$

$$Comp_i \stackrel{def}{=} (wake\_up_{0i}, \top).(\alpha_{i,1}, r_{i,1})...(\alpha_{i,m_i}, r_{i,m_i}). \prod_{k \in S_i} (wake\_up_{ik}, s).Comp_i$$

$$\forall i \in S_0$$

$$Comp_k \stackrel{def}{=} \prod_{j \in P_k} (wake\_up_{jk}, \top).(\alpha_{0,k}, r_{0,k})...(\alpha_{k,m_k}, r_{k,m_k}). \prod_{j \in S_k} (wake\_up_{kj}, s).Comp_k$$

$$\forall k \in S_i$$

$$Comp_n \stackrel{def}{=} \prod_{j \in P_n} (wake\_up_{jn}, \top).(\alpha_{n,1}, r_{n,1})...(\alpha_{n,m_n}, r_{n,m_n}).(end, w_2).Comp_n$$

where the notation of the form $\prod_{k \in A_i} (\beta_{ik}, r)$ refers to $(\beta_{ii_1}, r).(\beta_{ii_2}, r).\cdots.(\beta_{i_{|A_i|}}, r)$.

The use of $\prod_{k \in S_i} (wake\_up_{ik}, s)$ allows us to model the case where $Comp_i$ wakes up all the components in its successors set one by one. Whereas the use of $\prod_{j \in P_n} (wake\_up_{jn}, \top)$ like in $Comp_n$ models the case where a component has to wait for several predecessors to complete their activities before proceeding with its own activities.

Additionally, we consider another component $Clock$, which allows starting, and restarting the system only once $Comp_n$ has completed its activities. This additional component has to synchronise with $Comp_0$ on activity $start$ then on activity end with $Comp_n$.

$$Clock \stackrel{def}{=} (start, \top).Clock_0$$
$$Clock_0 \stackrel{def}{=} (end, \top).Clock$$

The behaviour of the complete system is modelled as the interaction of its components as follows:

$$System \stackrel{def}{=} Clock \underset{\{start,end\}}{\bowtie} (\ldots (Comp_0 \underset{\{wake\_up_{0i}/i \in S_0\}}{\bowtie} (\ldots ||Comp_i|| \ldots)_{i \in S_0})$$
$$\underset{\{wake\_up_{ik}/k \in S_i\}}{\bowtie} (\ldots ||Comp_k|| \ldots) \ldots)_{k \in S_i} \ldots (\ldots ||Comp_j|| \ldots)_{j \in P_n}$$
$$\underset{\{wake\_up_{jn}/j \in P_n\}}{\bowtie} Comp_n) \ldots)$$

4.2 Reliability Analysis Using the PEPA Model

Component $Clock$ is only necessary in the case where a performance analysis is targeted as it allows modelling the return arc of the precedence relation between the components. Reciprocally, whenever reliability analysis is the objective, component $Clock$ is not only unnecessary, but has to be removed from the model. As all its activities have an unspecified rate ($\top$), its removal from the model has no impact on the remaining components.

Moreover, to ensure that the underlying Markov chain of the model has an absorbing state, we need the last component $Comp_n$ to not return to its initial state once activity end has been completed. Therefore, we have to redefine $Comp_n$ as follows:

$$Comp_n \stackrel{def}{=} \prod_{j \in P_n} (wake\_up_{jn}, \top).(\alpha_{n,1}, r_{n,1})...(\alpha_{n,m_n}, r_{n,m_n}).(end, w_2).Comp_n^*$$

In the first definition of $Comp_n$, the first and the last derivatives (states) were the same, that is $Comp_n$. In the new definition, the first derivative is still $Comp_n$, but the last one is different. It is denoted by $Comp_n^*$ and models the absorbing state of the system.   □

As explained above, finding the absorption times and the cycle times for our class of systems are connected problems. The former assumes that the durations of the activities are independent, which is the case in our model. Thus the delays from successive beginnings of the first component form a renewal process. In the case of the latter, once the last component has completed its activities, the first component is woken up.

In the following we only consider the absorption times. The computation of the cycle times can be easily deduced from the results developed for the absorption times.

5   Reliability Analysis: Computing the Absorption Times

The PEPA model is a two-level hierarchy model, the component level and the model level. Therefore the computation of the bounds on the absorption times rely on two different classes of techniques according to the hierarchy level considered. However, all these techniques are based on the recurrence equations we can obtain at the higher level of our hierarchy.

In the following, once we show how to obtain the recurrence equations, we first propose techniques which can be applied on the PEPA sub-models (components). Then we show how we can modify the precedence relation between the PEPA components to derive simpler models.

The bounds on the absorption times are obtained from the recurrence equations which can be established on instants of transition. Let (t_i) (resp. (b_i)) be the completion time (resp. the wake up time) of component $Comp_i$. The main results come from the type of equations connecting instants t_i to other instants t_j if $Comp_j$ is a predecessor of $Comp_i$ in the precedence model.

Let d_i be the service time of $Comp_i$, that is the time required for $Comp_i$ to proceed with all its activities $\alpha_{i,l}$, $l = 1..m_i$. As $Comp_i$ is a PEPA component where all the activities have exponential durations, the total duration of $Comp_i$ has a continuous Phase type distribution (PH in the following).

Clearly for all i, we have $t_i = b_i + d_i$. Now it is important to note that $Comp_i$ wakes up as soon as all the components in its predecessors set P_i have completed all their activities. Thus

$$b_i = max_{j \in P_i}(t_j)$$

After substitution, we get:

$$t_i = d_i + max_{j \in P_i}(t_j) \tag{5.1}$$

Thus we obtain a linear equation on vector (t_i) using two operators: the addition and the maximum. Such linear equations have been extensively studied as they allow new types of analytical or numerical methods which are not based on exponential delays or embedded Markov chains. In this paper we assume that activities have exponential durations, but as the random variables d_i model a PEPA sub-model $(Comp_i)$ duration, d_i has a PH distribution.

5.1   Bounds Due to Service-Time of Activities

Using equation 5.1 and properties 3 and 4 we obtain the first comparison results if all the random variables d_i are New Better than Used in Expectation (NBUE). Indeed, the NBUE property implies the relation between a single random variable and an exponential one with the same mean. Equation 5.1 and property 3 show that t_i is defined using two increasing and convex operators. Property 4 states that the relation holds for the absorption time.

Property 6. *Consider a precedence PEPA model such that the PH distribution associated with $Comp_i$, a component of the model, is NBUE. The absorption time is upper bounded in the increasing convex sense by the absorption time of the same model where $Comp_i$ is replaced by a single activity with rate $E(d_i)$.*

Similarly, we have a lower bound provided by constant random variable with the same mean using property 1.

Property 7. *Consider a precedence PEPA model with arbitrary random variables. The absorption time is lower bounded in the increasing convex sense by the absorption time of the same model where the PH distribution associated with $Comp_i$, a component of the model, is replaced by a constant with the same mean.*

Note that, in this case, the resulting model is not a usual PEPA model anymore as we have a component with a non exponential duration. One can also obtain a lower bound of the completion time by a very simple argument on the duration of any component. This is stated in the following property.

Property 8. *For all positive random variables X, we have zero $\leq_{st} X$ where zero is considered as the constant r.v. with mean 0.*

Finally,

Property 9. *Consider a precedence PEPA model. The absorption time is lower bounded in the strong stochastic sense by the absorption time of the same model where $Comp_i$, a component of the model, has been removed and where we have added arcs (C_1, C_2) in the precedence model for all components C_1 and C_2 such that arcs $(C_1, Comp_i)$ and $(Comp_i, C_2)$ were in the initial precedence model.*

So the main question remaining now is whether a PH distribution is NBUE or not. To the best of our knowledge such a problem has never been studied before.

5.1.1 Phase Type and NBUE Distributions

A Phase type distribution is the absorption time of a transient Markov chain on state space $1..N$. It is defined by the initial distribution (say σ) and the transition rate matrix Q. Let Y be this chain and X the absorption time of Y knowing σ. Without loss of generality we assume that there exists only one absorbing state which is the last one (i.e N). Thus

$$
Q = \begin{bmatrix} T & t \\ \hline 0 & 0 \end{bmatrix}
$$

with $t = -Te$, e being a column of 1. Without loss of generality we assume that the initial distribution σ is $(1, 0, \ldots, 0)$. Indeed, a general distribution can be considered if we add an extra state at the beginning.

Let X_t be the residual time before absorption, given that $X \geq t$. Remember that the distribution of X is NBUE iff $E(X_t) \leq E(X)$ for all t.

At time t, chain Y is in state j with probability $Pr(Y_t = j | Y_0 = 1)$. Let μ_k be the rate of activity k. The expectation of the remaining time before absorption in Y can be computed using the mean number of passages in any state of Y before being absorbed. Of course these quantities depend on the initial state of the chain. Let $a_{i,j}$ be the average number of visits to state i when the initial state of chain Y is j. Clearly, we have:

$$
E(X) = \sum_{i=1}^{N-1} \frac{a_{i,1}}{\mu_i}
$$

Similarly because of the memoryless property, the remaining time after t is obtained by conditioning on the state reached at time t as follows:

$$
E(X_t) = \sum_{j=1}^{N-1} Pr(Y_t = j | Y_0 = 1) \sum_{i=1}^{N-1} \frac{a_{i,j}}{\mu_i}
$$

Now, we must compare E and $E(X_t)$ to check if a distribution is NBUE. First we obtain a very simple result which is quite useful.

Property 10. *If, for all state i, we have for all state j, $a_{i,j} \leq a_{i,1}$ then the PH distribution is NBUE.*

Proof: If $a_{i,j} \leq a_{i,1}$ for all j, then any convex sum of $a_{i,j}$ is smaller than $a_{i,1}$. And $\sum_{j=1}^{N-1} Pr(Y_t = j | Y_0 = 1) a_{i,j}$ is such a convex sum. Finally we get $E(X_t) \leq E(X)$.

Property 10 allows us to derive the following one:

Property 11. *The hypoexponential distribution is NBUE.*

Remember that the hypoexponential distribution is a generalisation of the Erlang distribution where the exponential stages do not have the same rate. For an hypoexponential distribution we get $a_{i,1} = 1$ as we visit every stage exactly once. If we begin at stage j, the number of visits is 1 or 0 depending if the stage to visit is after j or before j. Thus $a_{i,j} \leq a_{i,1}$ for all i, j.

The hypoexponential distribution is easy to detect from a PEPA specification of a component. It is a set of successive individual activities without any choice operator.

Theorem 2. *If a PEPA component C is constructed using only the prefix operator, the rates of successive individual activities of C are the rates of the stages of an hypoexponential distribution and the completion time of C is NBUE. These individual activities of C can therefore be aggregated into a single individual activity with the same mean.*

Proof: Consider a PEPA component which consists of a sequence of individual activities in which the only operator used is the prefix. As each activity α in the sequence is exponentially distributed with rate r_α, these rates constitute the rates of the stages of an hypoexponential distribution. As the hypoexponential distribution is NBUE, according to Property 11, the completion time of the sequence of activities of the component is NBUE. Consequently, this sequence of activities can be aggregated and replaced by a single individual activity with the same mean. □

According to Theorem 2, we can replace a PEPA component with successive individual activities by a component with a single individual activity. In this context, the stochastic comparison allows a drastic reduction of the complexity. Moreover, it allows a new type of aggregation which is not exact, but which provides proved bounds.

Thus, in our precedence PEPA model, we can aggregate the sequence of individual activities $(\alpha_{k,1}, r_{k,1}).(\alpha_{k,2}, r_{k,2}) \ldots (\alpha_{k,m_k}, r_{k,m_k})$ of component $Comp_k$ into a single activity (α_k, r_k) where $r_k = (\frac{1}{r_{k,1}} + \frac{1}{r_{k,2}} + \ldots + \frac{1}{r_{k,m_k}})^{-1}$.

More generally we get the following characterisation:

Property 12. *Consider an arbitrary PH distribution. If for all state i and j we have*

$$\sum_{i=1}^{N-1} \frac{a_{i,j}}{\mu_i} \leq \sum_{i=1}^{N-1} \frac{a_{i,1}}{\mu_i}$$

then the PH distribution is NBUE.

Proof: Again $E(X_t)$ is a convex sum with coefficients $Pr(Y_t = j | Y_0 = 1)$ of the first quantities in the relation. Thus if the set of inequalities is satisfied for all j and i, we get $E(X_t) \leq E(X)$.

Let us now consider acyclic PH distributions. Assume that the states of Y are ordered according to the natural ordering associated to this directed acyclic graph.

Such a family of distributions have been shown to be very efficient when we have to fit a general distribution [6]. This family is quite large and it contains Coxian distribution. For an acyclic PH distribution using this numbering assumption, we clearly have $a_{i,j} = 0$ if $j < i$. As the graph of Y does not contain any directed cycle, any state will be visited zero or once. The expected number of visits is also the probability of visit. It is quite simple to compute $a_{i,1}$ and $a_{i,j}$ from the transition probability matrix embedded in matrix T.

Once we have computed $a_{i,j}$ for all i and j we can check the sufficient relations stated in Property 12. In general Coxian distribution are not NBUE but Property 12 gives a very simple way to check it. Note that Property 12 also applies when the PH is not acyclic. However, the complexity of computing $a_{i,j}$ is now much higher.

Finally one can bound an arbitrary acyclic PH distribution by an hypoexponential distribution.

Theorem 3. *Let X be an arbitrary acyclic PH distribution associated with transition rate matrix Q. Let Z be the hypoexponential associated with transition matrix R. Assume now that the states of the chains are ordered according to the DAG. If*

$$R(i, i+1) = \sum_{j \geq i+1} Q(i,j) \quad and \quad R(i,j) = 0 \; \forall j \neq i, i+1$$

then $X <_{st} Z$.

Proof: As X and Z are PH distributions, they are also absorption times of CTMC. Theorem 1 states that the comparison of CTMC can be easily checked. Property 5 shows that the comparison of CTMC implies the comparison of absorption times. So it is sufficient here to state that the chains associated with the distributions satisfy both conditions of Theorem 1.

- The first condition is trivial as the initial distribution is the same.
- Remember that the states of the chains are ordered according to the DAG. Thus matrix Q is upper triangular. The lower triangle of Q and R clearly satisfy the constraints of Theorem 1. Finally one can easily check the upper triangle part of the relation as $R(i, i+1) = \sum_{j \geq i+1} Q(i,j)$.

Thus one can transform any acyclic PH distribution into an hypoexponential one. The PEPA sub-models (components) are transformed as well. The numbering of activities defines the sequential ordering of the activities. The definition of matrix R gives the activity rates in this transformed PEPA sub-model.

Let us now turn to other techniques based on the precedence relation at the higher level, the model level.

5.2   Changing the Precedence Model to Obtain Bounds

Such transformations of the model are strongly related to the rules proposed by Bacelli and Liu [2] for queueing networks with synchronisations and by Vincent and Pekergin for tasks graph [13]. Even if the problems are not the same, they all share this property of linear evolution equation with max-plus operators (see also [3] for Petri nets). The main transformations which have been proposed consist of the addition or the deletion of a node, an edge, a place or a transition. However these modifications of the graph do not always help for the resolution of the model.

To compute an upper bound for our system, we propose to add a new component in the precedence model. The main idea is to make the model separable. Then we divide the model into two sub-models which are analysed in isolation.

Assume that the precedence model has n components. Let us assume that the components of the model are ordered according to a topological ordering consistent with the precedence relation: if there exists a directed edge from $Comp_i$ to $Comp_j$ then $i < j$. We first add a new component (say $Comp_{n+1}$). Then we modify the directed edges of the precedence model. Let m be an arbitrary integer between 1 and n. We add directed edges in the precedence model from any component $Comp_i$ in $1..m$ to $n+1$ and from component $Comp_{n+1}$ to any component in $m+1..n$. Such a component is denoted as a *star*.

Note that now the model is not correctly ordered: the star component $(Comp_{n+1})$ does not have a correct index according to the precedence relation. However the new model is still a precedence model.

Let us now prove that this transformation provides an upper bound. First we reorder the state according to the new precedence model. The component we have added receives number $m+1$. Without loss of generality we assume that the components between 1 and m keep the same numbers they had before the insertion while the components numbers previously between $m+1$ and n increase by 1.

Considering equation 5.1, we just derive the new sets P_i as a function of the sets before the insertion. We have:

$$\begin{cases} P_i & \leftarrow P_i & \forall i = 1..m \\ P_{m+1} & \leftarrow \{1..m\} \\ P_i & \leftarrow P_{i-1} \bigcup \{m+1\} \; \forall i = m+2..n \end{cases}$$

Let us denote by t'_i the new values of the completion time. Clearly we have $t'_i = t_i$ for all $i \leq m$. As sets P_i are now larger, we also have: $t'_i \geq t_{i-1} + d_{m+1}$.

Theorem 4. *Let m be an arbitrary integer in 2..n-1, the absorption time is upper bounded in the strong stochastic sense by the absorption time of the same model with a star component added with label $m + 1$.*

Adding a *star* has also an effect on the resolution algorithm. The model is now separable into two sub-models containing $Comp_1$ to $Comp_m$ for the first one and $Comp_{m+1}$ to $Comp_{n+1}$ for the second one. Indeed, to be absorbed in $Comp_{n+1}$, one must visit first $Comp_{m+1}$ and then travel from $Comp_{m+1}$ to $Comp_{n+1}$. We compute the time to be absorbed in $Comp_{m+1}$ in a sub-model and then we compute the time to be absorbed in $Comp_{n+1}$ knowing that the initial component is $Comp_{m+1}$ at time 0. These two random variables are independent

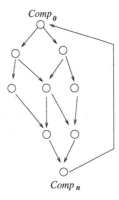
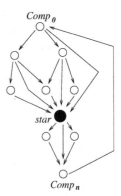

Fig. 2. Adding a star

and the distribution of the global absorption time is the convolution of the two distributions obtained from the sub-models. If we assume that the components set is equally divided by the insertion of the *star*, the stochastic comparison allows a drastic reduction of the complexity of the analysis.

6   Conclusion

The approach we have presented here constitutes a first step towards a new hierarchical resolution of hierarchical models. Indeed, we must improve our resolution techniques which are now far away from our modelling skills. Stochastic comparison is a very efficient approach to simplify models and obtain bounds. We can apply bounds on the transition times like in this paper or on the states. Both approaches rely on a monotonicity property which is implicit on transition instants associated with a precedence model. Precedence PEPA models are quite general but a natural extension to this work will be the generalisation of this type of method for an even larger set of models. It must be clear that this approach requires hierarchical models where the high level exhibits some monotonicity property which must be consistent with the comparison we made for sub-models absorption times. These are the key properties of the approach. However they are limited neither to precedence PEPA models nor to (max,+) semi-ring (again see [1]). For instance, PEPA nets, a new hierarchical modelling technique [9], are based on a high level model which is mainly a Finite State Machine (a simplified Petri Net with a limited interconnection between places and transitions) and on sub-models associated with the places of the net. The sub-models are PEPA models. It is worthy to remark that when the vertex cut of the directed cycles of the FSM has size one then we can derive the same linear equations on (max,+) semi-ring, from the PEPA net model, as the ones we have obtained here. Indeed when we remove this directed arc, the graph of the FSM becomes a DAG and it shows the relation with a precedence PEPA model. Thus all the techniques presented here can be applied to this new modelling technique as well.

References

1. F. Baccelli, G. Cohen, G.J. Olsder, J.P. Quadrat, "Synchronization and Linearity, an algebra for Discrete Event Systems", Wiley & Sons, 1992.
2. F. Baccelli, Z. Liu, "On the executions of parallel programs on multiprocessor systems - a queueing theory approach", JACM, V 37, N2, pp:373–414, 1990.
3. F. Baccelli, Z. Liu, "Comparison properties of stochastic decision free Petri nets", Inria Report 1433, 1991.
4. R. E. Barlow, F. Proschan, "Statistical Theory of Reliability and Life Testing", 1981.
5. M. Ben Mamoun, A. Busic, J.M. Fourneau, N. Pekergin, "Increasing Convex Monotone Markov Chains: Theory, Algorithm and Applications", Submitted.
6. A. Bobbio, A. Horvath, M. Scarpa, M. Telek, "Acyclic Discrete Phase type distributions; properties and a parameter estimation algorithm", Performance evaluation Vol.54, pp:1–32, 2003.
7. J. T. Bradley, N. Dingle, S.T. Gilmore, W.J. Knottenbelt "Extracting Passage Time form PEPA models with the Hydra tool: a case study", UKPEW 2003.
8. J.M. Fourneau, N. Pekergin. "An algorithmic approach to stochastic bounds", LNCS 2459, Performance evaluation of complex systems: Techniques and Tools, pp:64–88.
9. S. Gilmore and J. Hillston and L. Kloul and M. Ribaudo, "PEPA nets: A structured performance modelling formalism", Performance Evaluation, vol.54, pp:79–104, Elsevier Science, 2003.
10. J. Hillston, *A compositional Approach to Performance Modelling*, PhD Thesis, The University of Edinburgh, 1994.
11. J. Hillston, L. Kloul, "An Efficient Kronecker Representation for PEPA Models", LNCS, N.2165, pp:120-135, Springer Verlag, Proceedings of the Joint International Workshop, PAPM-PROBMIV 2001, Aachen, Germany, September 2001.
12. N. Pekergin, "Stochastic delay bounds on fair queueing algorithms", Proceedings of INFOCOM'99, pp:1212–1220, New York, 1999.
13. N. Pekergin, J.M. Vincent, "Stochastic Bounds on Execution Times of Parallel Programs", IEEE Transactions on Software Engineering, Vol. 17, No. 17, October 1991.
14. D. Stoyan, "Comparison Methods for Queues and Other Stochastic Models", Wiley & Sons, New York, 1983.

A Function-Equivalent Components Based Simplification Technique for PEPA Models*

Jane Hillston and Leïla Kloul

[1] LFCS, The University of Edinburgh, Edinburgh EH9 3JZ, Scotland
jeh@inf.ed.ac.uk
[2] PRiSM, Université de Versailles, 45, Av. des Etats-Unis, 78000 Versailles
kle@prism.uvsq.fr

Abstract. PEPA has recently been extended with functional rates [1][2]. These functions allow the specification of indirect interaction between components in such a way that the rate of an activity may be made dependent on the local state currently exhibited by one or more components. In this paper we demonstrate that these rates allow a systematic simplification of models in which there is appropriate indirect interaction between components. We investigate the interplay between this style of simplification and aggregation based on bisimulation, and establish a heuristic for applying both techniques in a complementary fashion.

1 Introduction

State space explosion remains the prevailing problem of most state-based modelling techniques. In general we focus on the impact of this problem on model solution when the size of the matrix representing the model becomes so large that the solution is intractable. However the largeness of models has other implications for the modelling process. During model construction the complexity of the system being represented may make it difficult for the modeller to keep track of all necessary aspects in the model. Compositional modelling techniques, such as stochastic process algebras, go some way towards alleviating this problem by supporting a *divide-and-conquer* approach to system representation. Nevertheless the number of components involved may still become large, representing a cognitive burden on the modeller.

In this paper we present a technique which aims to identify cases where components may be eliminated from a model description. In the simplest such cases the component may be eliminated without significant change to the remaining components. However, in general, these components may be playing a vital role within the model which must still be captured. In this case we achieve the same behaviour by the use of functional rates within the remaining components. Eliminating components in this way addresses the two issues of complexity

---

* This work was partially supported by the DEGAS IST-2001-32072, SENSORIA IST-3-016004-IP-09 funded by the FET Proactive Initiative on Global Computing and by EPSRC Advanced Research Fellowship EP/c543696/01.

A. Horváth and M. Telek (Eds.): EPEW 2006, LNCS 4054, pp. 16–30, 2006.

discussed above. The model construction complexity is reduced, as the expression of the model is now made in terms of a fewer number of components. Moreover, the internal representation of the model is also, in general, more compact, as the functional rates allow a reduction in the size of the corresponding matrix. For a formalism like PEPA, for which a Kronecker representation has been developed [1], the reduction of the number of components in a model implies also the reduction of the number of matrices required for the tensorial representation of the corresponding Markov chain.

Since we aim to preserve the same behaviour the underlying Markov process remains unchanged and so the reachable state space is not reduced. Nevertheless we feel that this approach can be regarded as a model simplification technique since it has the effect of extending the class of tractable models.

The rest of this paper is structured as follows. In the following section, we give a brief overview of PEPA. We then go on to explain the version of PEPA extended with functional rates that we will use in this paper. In Section 3 we give a definition of the notion of *function-equivalent components* and show how functional rates may be used to eliminate these components from a model. In Section 5 we investigate the interplay between the model-level simplification approach based on function-equivalent components and the state-level aggregation technique based on the bisimulation relation, *strong equivalence*. This is illustrated by a small example. We present the algorithm for the automatic removal of function-equivalent components and demonstrate its application to a larger example in Section 6. We discuss related work in Section 7. Finally, we conclude in Section 8 with a summary of the results and a discussion of future work.

2   PEPA

In PEPA a system is described as an interaction of *components* which engage, either singly or multiply, in *activities*. These basic elements of PEPA, components and activities, correspond to *states* and *transitions* in the underlying Markov process. Each activity has an *action type*. Activities which are private to the component in which they occur are represented by the distinguished action type, τ. The duration of each activity is represented by the parameter of the associated exponential distribution: the *activity rate*. This parameter may be any positive real number, or the distinguished symbol $\top$ (read as *unspecified*). Thus each activity, a, is a pair (α, r) consisting of the action type and the activity rate respectively. We assume a countable set of components, denoted $\mathcal{C}$, and a countable set, $\mathcal{A}$, of all possible action types. We denote by $\mathcal{A}ct \subseteq \mathcal{A} \times \mathbb{R}^+$, the set of activities, where $\mathbb{R}^+$ is the set of positive real numbers together with the symbol $\top$.

PEPA provides a small set of combinators which allow expressions to be constructed defining the behaviour of components, via the activities they undertake and the interactions between them.

Prefix $(\alpha, r).P$: This is the basic mechanism for constructing component behaviours. The component carries out activity (α, r) and subsequently behaves as component P.

Choice $P + Q$: This component may behave either as P or as Q: all the current activities of both components are enabled. The first activity to complete, determined by a *race condition*, distinguishes one component, the other is discarded.

Cooperation $P \bowtie_L Q$: Components proceed independently with any activities whose types do not occur in the *cooperation set L* (*individual activities*). However, activities with action types in the set L require the simultaneous involvement of both components (*shared activities*). When the set L is empty, we use the more concise notation $P \parallel Q$ to represent $P \bowtie_\emptyset Q$.

The published stochastic process algebras differ on how the rate of shared activities are defined [4]. In PEPA the shared activity occurs at the rate of the slowest participant. If an activity has an unspecified rate, denoted $\top$, the component is *passive* with respect to that action type. This means that the component does not influence the rate at which any shared activity occurs.

Hiding P/L: This behaves as P except that any activities of types within the set L are *hidden*, i.e. they exhibit the unknown type τ and can be regarded as an internal delay by the component. These activities cannot be carried out in cooperation with another component.

Constant $A \stackrel{def}{=} P$: Constants are components whose meaning is given by a defining equation. $A \stackrel{def}{=} P$ gives the constant A the behaviour of the component P. This is how we assign names to components (behaviours).

The evolution of a model is governed by the structured operational semantics rules of the language. These define the admissible transitions or state changes associated with each combinator. A race condition governs the dynamic behaviour of a model whenever more than one activity is enabled.

The action types which the component P may next engage in are the *current action types* of P, a set denoted $\mathcal{A}(P)$. This set is defined inductively over the syntactic constructs of the language [3]. For example, $\mathcal{A}(P + Q) = \mathcal{A}(P) \cup \mathcal{A}(Q)$.

The activities which the component P may next engage in are the *current activities* of P, a multiset denoted $Act(P)$. When the system is behaving as component P these are the activities which are enabled. Note that the dynamic behaviour of a component depends on the number of instances of each enabled activity and therefore we consider *multisets* of activities as opposed to *sets* of action types. $Act(P)$ is defined inductively over the structure of P.

The "states" of a PEPA model as it evolves are the syntactic terms, or *derivatives*, which the model will go through. The *derivative set* of a PEPA component C is denoted $ds(C)$ and is the set of components which capture all the reachable states of the system. It is also necessary to refer to the complete set of action types which are used within the behaviour of a component C, i.e. all the possible action types which may be witnessed as a component evolves. This set will be denoted $\boldsymbol{\mathcal{A}}(C)$. The *complete action type set* of a component C is:

$$\boldsymbol{\mathcal{A}}(C) = \bigcup_{C' \in ds(C)} \mathcal{A}(C').$$

Since we aim to undertake numerical solution it is important that we ensure that the components within the model, as well as the model itself, are finite and ergodic. Necessary (but not sufficient) conditions for the ergodicity of the Markov process in terms of the structure of the PEPA model have been identified and can be readily checked [3]. These conditions imply that the model must be a *cyclic* PEPA component.

A cyclic component is one in which behaviour may always be repeated, however the model evolves from this component it will always eventually return to this component and this set of behaviours. This leads us to define the syntax of PEPA expressions in terms of *sequential components* S and *model components* P:

$$P ::= P \bowtie_L P \mid P/L \mid A \qquad S ::= (\alpha, r).S \mid S + S \mid A_S$$

where A denotes a constant which is either a sequential or a model component and A_S denotes a constant which is a sequential component.

When a model component is defined it consists of one or more cooperating components, and these cooperating components remain apparent in every derivative of the model. Thus the sequential components involved in a model, and the cooperation sets in operation between them, will remain static throughout its evolution. Only the particular derivatives exhibited by each of the sequential components may change.

2.1 PEPA with Functional Rates

A functional dependency may involve one or several components. In a functional dependency involving a single component, the rate value of an activity of the component depends on the current state of the component itself. This is equivalent to the presence of several apparent rates for the activity in the component. Since each activity is represented explicitly in each local state it has always been possible to capture this form of dependency in PEPA. When this is expressed as a functional dependency, the rate value expressed as a function of the current component state is still a positive real number and can never be zero. This adds nothing new to the expressiveness of the language.

In contrast the ability to have an activity rate which is dependent on the local state of another component has not been possible previously (except in the special circumstance of shared activities). The introduction of this form of functional dependency into PEPA allows the dependent rate to include the value zero, indicating that an activity is blocked by the local state of another component. When the dependency is between two or more components it implies that either the activity to be performed by the first component and/or its rate value will be determined by the current state of the other component(s). The rate value may then be any non-negative real number $\mathbb{R}^+$ including zero, particularly when the choice of the activity to be performed is done according to the state of another component.

The introduction of functional dependencies in PEPA therefore requires us to relax the constraint on the definition domain of an activity rate. Thus, the set of activities $\mathcal{A}ct$ is now defined as $\mathcal{A}ct \subseteq \mathcal{A} \times \mathbb{R}^*$ where $\mathbb{R}^*$ is the set of non-negative real numbers together with symbol $\top$. The syntax of sequential components is modified to allow an activity to be defined in terms of an action type and an *expression e*, which can be either a rate, or a function, or a product of a rate and a function [1, 2].

$$S ::= (\alpha, e).S \mid S + S \mid A \qquad\qquad e ::= r \mid f \mid r \times f \mid \top$$

where $f : 2^{\mathcal{C}} \longrightarrow \mathbb{R}^*$ is a function from one or more components to the non-negative reals.

3   Function-Equivalent Components in PEPA

In this section we give a formal definition of the notion of *function-equivalent components* and show that PEPA models can be reduced by eliminating this type of component. This definition is the basis for automatically detecting suitable components within a model.

A sequential component S_k is a *function-equivalent* component in a model component C if S_k is a sequential component of C and for all derivatives $C_i \in ds(C)$ given the current derivatives of the other sequential components $S_{j_i}, j \neq k$ of the model, the current derivative of S_k, S_{k_i}, can be inferred. This definition implies that the function-equivalent component interacts with other components of the model in such a way that its states can always be inferred from the states of these components. For this to be the case it follows that the component never acts independently and all its activities are carried out in cooperation with the other components. As we will show later in the paper, if a sequential component is shown to be a function-equivalent component, then this component can be eliminated and replaced by appropriate functions in the other components of the model.

In order to formalise the definition of a function-equivalent component we consider first when a component can be identified as having no independent activities. Within a model component, each sequential component may be within the scope of several cooperation sets. For example, in the component

$$X \stackrel{def}{=} (P \underset{L}{\bowtie} R) \underset{K}{\bowtie} (S \underset{N}{\bowtie} T)$$

the subcomponent R can act independently on any action types in the set N which do not occur in K or L, but must have the cooperation of other subcomponents to achieve actions in the set $L \cup K$, whereas the subcomponent S can act independently on any action types in the set $L \setminus (K \cup N)$, but must have the cooperation of other subcomponents to achieve actions in the set $K \cup N$. Thus we can identify the *interface* of a component i.e. those activities on which it must interact. In the following we formalise this idea. First, we define a partial order, $\prec$, over components, which captures the notion of *being a subcomponent*:

Definition 1 (Subcomponents)

1. $R \prec P$ *if* $R \in ds(P)$
2. $R \prec P + Q$ *if* $(R \prec P) \vee (R \prec Q)$

3. $R \prec P \bowtie_L Q$ if $(R \prec P) \vee (R \prec Q)$
4. $R \prec P/\check{L}$ if $R \prec P$
5. $R \prec A$ if $(A \stackrel{\text{def}}{=} P) \wedge (R \prec P)$

The interface of a sequential component within a component model is defined to be the union of all the cooperation sets whose scope includes the component R.

Definition 2 (Interface). *For any sequential component R within a model component C (i.e. $R \prec C$) the interface of R within C, denoted $\mathcal{I}(C :: R)$, is the set of action types on which R is required to cooperate. It is defined in terms of the subsidiary function $\mathcal{J}$; $\mathcal{I}(P :: R) = \mathcal{J}(P :: R, \emptyset)$, where $\mathcal{J}$ is defined as follows*

1. $\mathcal{J}(R :: R, K) = K$
2. $\mathcal{J}(P \bowtie_L Q :: R, K) = K' \cup K''$ if $\mathcal{J}(P :: R, K \cup L) = K'$
   and $\mathcal{J}(Q :: R, K \cup L) = K''$
3. $\mathcal{J}(P/L :: R, K) = \mathcal{J}(P :: R, K \setminus L)$
4. $\mathcal{J}(A :: R, K) = \mathcal{J}(P :: R, K)$ if $A \stackrel{\text{def}}{=} P$
5. $\mathcal{J}(R' :: R, K) = \emptyset$ if $R \not\prec R'$.

When all the possible actions of a sequential component are constrained by its interface the component is never free to act independently; it must cooperate with other components to complete *any* action. Such a component can be viewed as being subservient to the rest of the model, and is called a *resource component*.

Definition 3 (Resource Components). *A sequential component R in a model C is a resource component if there is only one instance of R within C and the complete action type set of R is a subset of its interface within C, i.e.*

$$\mathcal{A}(R) \subseteq \mathcal{I}(C :: R)$$

or if each instance of R is a resource component within a submodel C' of C and the submodels are independent of each other (i.e. composed using $\|$).

Example 1: A distributed memory system. Consider a system in which two processors act independently using two different memory elements. Each processor accesses to the data in its memory element, does computations and finally stores the results in its memory. As the access to the memory elements to get or save the data is defined by the processors, both memory elements can be modelled using the same component *Memory*.

$Proc_1 \stackrel{\text{def}}{=} (get, p_1).(compute, p_2).Proc'_1$ $Proc_2 \stackrel{\text{def}}{=} (get, q_1).(compute, q_2).Proc'_2$
$Proc'_1 \stackrel{\text{def}}{=} (save, p_3).Proc_1$ $Proc'_2 \stackrel{\text{def}}{=} (save, q_3).Proc_2$

$Memory \stackrel{\text{def}}{=} (get, \top).(save, \top).Memory$
$$\textbf{System}_1 \stackrel{\text{def}}{=} (Memory \bowtie_{\{get, save\}} Proc_1) \| (Memory \bowtie_{\{get, save\}} Proc_2)$$

In this model defined by **System**$_1$, *Memory* is a resource component because each of its instances in the model must synchronise on both activities *get* and *save*.

Example 2: Consider the following model components

$$R \stackrel{\text{def}}{=} (\alpha, r_\alpha).(\beta, r_\beta).R \qquad P \stackrel{\text{def}}{=} (\alpha, r_1).P \qquad Q \stackrel{\text{def}}{=} (\beta, r_2).Q$$

$$\textbf{System}_2 \stackrel{\text{def}}{=} (R \underset{\{\alpha\}}{\bowtie} P) \parallel (R \underset{\{\beta\}}{\bowtie} Q)$$

In contrast, in this model, R is not a resource component since it can behave independently: one instance can act independently on α and the other can act independently on β.

In the following, we will focus on a particular class of resource components termed *simple resource components*. A sequential component R is a *simple component* if

$$R \equiv S_1 + S_2 + \cdots + S_n$$

for some distinct cyclic components $S_1, S_2, \ldots S_n$ constructed using only prefix, with no repeated activities within a cycle and such that the last action of each cycle returns to R.

If a resource component is simple it implies that it offers alternative behaviours through its interface but once one of those behaviours is chosen (on the first action) the pattern of behaviour is set until the chosen cycle is completed and the choice is offered again. This type of repeated cyclic behaviour is, for example, exhibited by web services.

Definition 4 (Arbiter). *A simple resource component $R \equiv S_1 + S_2 + \cdots + S_n$, in a model $C \equiv (P_1 \parallel P_2 \parallel \cdots \parallel P_k) \bowtie R$ is an* arbiter *between $P_1, P_2, \ldots, P_k$ if for all $i \in 1, \ldots, k$ and $j \in 1, \ldots, n$, if $\mathbf{A}(P_i) \cap \mathbf{A}(S_j) \neq \emptyset$ then $\mathbf{A}(S_j) \subseteq \mathbf{A}(P_i)$.*

Example 3: A simple web service. Consider a system in which two clients interact with a web service *WS*. *Client$_1$* repeatedly generates tasks of type 1 which it submits to the web service and waits for a response before displaying the results. *Client$_2$* generates tasks of type 2 or type 3. Type 2 tasks require interaction with the web service, analogously to type 1 tasks, whereas type 3 tasks are processed locally before display. The PEPA model is the following.

$Client_1 \stackrel{\text{def}}{=} (task_1, t_1).(request_1, \rho_1).Client_1'$
$Client_1' \stackrel{\text{def}}{=} (response_1, \top).(display, d).Client_1$

$Client_2 \stackrel{\text{def}}{=} (task_2, t_2).(request_2, \rho_2).Client_2'$
$\qquad\quad + (task_3, t_3).(process, p).(display, d).Client_2$
$Client_2' \stackrel{\text{def}}{=} (response_2, \top).(display, d).Client_2$

$WS \quad\;\; \stackrel{\text{def}}{=} (request_1, \top).(response_1, r_1).WS + (request_2, \top).(response_2, r_2).WS$
$\qquad\qquad \textbf{Web\_Service} \stackrel{\text{def}}{=} (Client_1 \parallel Client_2) \underset{L}{\bowtie} WS$

where $L = \{request_1, response_1, request_2, response_2\}$. In this model, component *WS* is an arbiter between components *Client$_1$* and *Client$_2$*.

Proposition 1. *If a simple resource component R is an arbiter within a PEPA model C, then R is a function-equivalent component and thus can be removed from the model, the Markov process generated by the resulting model C' being isomorphic to the Markov process underlying C.*

Proof: As all activities of an arbiter component are shared activities, each step of the evolution of this component coincide with one step of evolution of one of the other components of the model. The structure of the arbiter, and the form of its interaction with the other components of the model ensure that even if it changes state during the evolution of the model, all its states can be inferred from the other components of the model.   □

Such a component allows two or more other components of the model to indirectly influence one another. This kind of interaction between the components can be managed using functions in the rates of their shared activities. The definition of these functions takes into account the states of the components involved in the cooperation. This allows the model to keep the form of scheduling initially imposed by R.

The introduction of appropriate functional rates instead of an arbiter component will not have any impact on the correctness of the model and thus the Markov process underlying the reduced model is guaranteed to be isomorphic to the one generated by the initial model.

Corollary 1. *If a simple resource component R is a single state arbiter within a PEPA model C, then R is an identity function-equivalent component and thus can be removed from the model, the Markov process generated by the resulting model C' being isomorphic to the Markov process underlying C (subject to some transfer of rates when C is passive with respect to an activity).*

This corresponds to the case of an arbiter in which the cycle of each component S_i in R has only one activity:

$$R \stackrel{def}{=} (\alpha_1, r_1).R + (\alpha_2, r_2).R + \ldots + (\alpha_n, r_n).R$$

As R always exhibits the same state and all its activities are shared activities, R can be removed from the model. This type of component does not enforce any scheduling between the other components of the model as the cycle defining the use of R by any component P_i is limited to one activity. For this reason its removal is not conditioned by the use of functional rates. Therefore, when removed, R can be replaced by an identity function in the other components which share R's activities.

However we should consider carefully the activity rates of R. If all activities have unspecified rates ($\top$), then the rate of these activities are already defined by the other components of the model. So R can be eliminated without any impact on the other components of the model. If at least one of its activities α has a specified rate, then we need to compute the rate of each instance of α in each component P_i which shares this activity with R. As explained in Section 6 this computation takes place during the generation of the derivation graph.

In the following section, we show how an arbiter component can be eliminated from the model using functional rates.

4   A Function Based Simplification Approach

In PEPA components are able to influence one another in two ways, both related to activities. The first one is a direct interaction between the components and is modelled using shared activities (cooperation). The other form of interaction is less direct as the activity rate within a component can be influenced by the local states of one or more other components in the model. This implies that the activity may or may not be performed by the component according to a rate value determined by the current state of the other component(s). Indeed, this rate may have any non-negative value, including zero which aborts the activity.

In general, the use of functional rates can lead to a reduction in the model expression because they avoid explicitly modelling all parts of a system's behaviour. This is the case for PEPA models with arbiter resource components.

We have seen so far an arbiter component may be necessary to ensure the correct behaviour of a model; they enforce the necessary scheduling between the model's components. Thus, an arbiter component may be seen as another indirect means for the components of a model to influence one another. But, as stated previously, this is exactly what the functional rates allow us to do in PEPA. Therefore, we propose to replace arbiter components using functional rates in the other components of the model with which they share their activities. For example, consider again the web service model (**Example 3**). In this model, component *WS* is an arbiter component and therefore can be removed from the model and replaced with appropriate functions as follows:

$$Client_1 \stackrel{\text{def}}{=} (task_1, t_1).(request_1, f \times \rho_1).Client_1'$$
$$Client_1' \stackrel{\text{def}}{=} (response_1, r_1).(display, d).Client_1$$

$$Client_2 \stackrel{\text{def}}{=} (task_2, t_2).(request_2, g \times \rho_2).Client_2'$$
$$+ \ (task_3, t_3).(process, p).(display, d).Client_2$$
$$Client_2' \stackrel{\text{def}}{=} (response_2, r_2).(display, d).Client_2$$

$$\textbf{Web\_Service2} \stackrel{\text{def}}{=} Client_1 \parallel Client_2$$

where f and g are defined as follows:

$$f(x) = \begin{cases} 0 \ \textit{if} \ x \equiv Client_2' \\ 1 \ \textit{otherwise} \end{cases} \qquad g(y) = \begin{cases} 0 \ \textit{if} \ y \equiv Client_1' \\ 1 \ \textit{otherwise} \end{cases}$$

y and x being the state of component $Client_1$ and $Client_2$ respectively.

Example 4: A multiprocessor shared memory. Consider a system in which two processors compete for access to a shared memory via a bus. The processors are independent and both follow the same pattern of behaviour: each does computations, acquires the bus, sends the message and then releases the bus.

$$Proc \stackrel{def}{=} (compute, r_1).(acquire, r_2).Proc'$$
$$Proc' \stackrel{def}{=} (transmit, r_3).(release, r_4).Proc$$

$$Bus \stackrel{def}{=} (acquire, \top).Bus'$$
$$Bus' \stackrel{def}{=} (release, \top).Bus$$

$$Memory \stackrel{def}{=} (transmit, \top).Memory$$

$$\mathbf{Machine} \stackrel{def}{=} ((Proc \parallel Proc) \underset{L_1}{\bowtie} Bus) \underset{L_2}{\bowtie} Memory$$

where $L_1 = \{acquire, release\}$ and $L_2 = \{transmit\}$. In this model, components *Memory* and *Bus* are arbiter components and therefore can be removed from the model. The elimination of *Memory* is straightforward and does not require the modification of the other components because the rate of the shared activity *transmit* is unspecified in *Memory*. In contrast, in order to remove component *Bus*, we need to introduce appropriate functional rates in the other components where the cooperation activities *acquire* and *release* appear. By doing so, we obtain the following model:

$$Proc_{10} \stackrel{def}{=} (compute, r_1).Proc_{11}$$
$$Proc_{11} \stackrel{def}{=} (acquire, f_1 \times r_2).Proc_{12}$$
$$Proc_{12} \stackrel{def}{=} (transmit, r_3).Proc_{13}$$
$$Proc_{13} \stackrel{def}{=} (release, g_1 \times r_4).Proc_{10}$$

$$Proc_{20} \stackrel{def}{=} (compute, r_1).Proc_{21}$$
$$Proc_{21} \stackrel{def}{=} (acquire, f_2 \times r_2).Proc_{22}$$
$$Proc_{22} \stackrel{def}{=} (transmit, r_3).Proc_{23}$$
$$Proc_{23} \stackrel{def}{=} (release, g_2 \times r_4).Proc_{20}$$

$$\mathbf{Machine}' \stackrel{def}{=} Proc_{10} \parallel Proc_{20}$$

where f_j and g_j, $j = 1, 2$, are functions defined, when $k = 1, 2\ k \neq j$, as

$$f_j(y) = \begin{cases} 1 \ if \ y \equiv Proc_{k0} \\ 0 \ otherwise \end{cases} \qquad g_j(x) = \begin{cases} 1 \ if \ x \equiv Proc_{k0} \\ 0 \ otherwise \end{cases}$$

x and y being the state of $Proc_k$ appropriately. Note that the functions g_j are not essential for the correct behaviour of the model and may be omitted. The functions f_j are sufficient to guarantee the correct behaviour of the model.

Both previous examples show that the functions are only necessary in the first activity that a component P shares with the resource component. For P, the function associated with the rate of the first activity can be regarded as the *access ticket* to the resource component and this ticket must be validated to make the access possible. Once P is using the resource component, the other components of the model cannot use it.

5   Interplay Between the Function-Based Simplification Approach and the Aggregation Technique

There is an established aggregation technique for PEPA models based on the notion of *strong equivalence* between states. The aggregation may result in a single component being substituted for a number of components. Thus, like the function-based simplification technique, it can result in a reduction in the model expression. However, in the case of aggregation, this usually had the consequence that the underlying state space is also reduced. This suggests that the best results may be obtained if the two techniques are applied in conjunction. In this section we make some observations about how this can be achieved and the interplay between the two techniques.

Recall that if $\mathcal{C}$ is the set of all PEPA components, and $q[P, S, \alpha]$ is the total conditional transition rate from component P to the set of components S, then strong equivalence is defined as follows:

Definition 5 (Strong equivalence). *An equivalence relation* $\mathcal{R} \subseteq \mathcal{C} \times \mathcal{C}$ *is a strong equivalence if whenever* $(P, Q) \in \mathcal{R}$ *then for all* $\alpha \in \mathcal{A}$ *and for all* $S \in \mathcal{C}/\mathcal{R}$

$$q[P, S, \alpha] = q[Q, S, \alpha]$$

In many cases strong equivalence exists between the derivatives of a model because there is strong equivalence between components of the model and their interleaving can be eliminated.

Let us consider the original model of the multiprocessor system as given in **Example 4** and apply the aggregation technique on component $Proc \parallel Proc$ of the system equation. The model resulting from such an operation is the following, where a single derivative represents each equivalence class.

$Procs_{00} \stackrel{def}{=} (compute, 2r_1).Procs_{01}$ $\quad\quad [(Proc_{10}, Proc_{20})]_{00}$

$Procs_{01} \stackrel{def}{=} (compute, r_1).Procs_{11}$
$\quad\quad + (acquire, r_2).Procs_{02}$ $\quad [(Proc_{10}, Proc_{21}), (Proc_{11}, Proc_{20})]_{01}$

$Procs_{02} \stackrel{def}{=} (transmit, r_3).Procs_{03}$
$\quad\quad + (compute, r_1).Procs_{12}$ $\quad [(Proc_{10}, Proc_{22}), (Proc_{12}, Proc_{20})]_{02}$

$Procs_{03} \stackrel{def}{=} (compute, r_1).Procs_{13}$
$\quad\quad + (release, r_4).Procs_{00}$ $\quad [(Proc_{10}, Proc_{23}), (Proc_{13}, Proc_{20})]_{03}$

$Procs_{11} \stackrel{def}{=} (acquire, 2r_2).Procs_{12}$ $\quad [(Proc_{11}, Proc_{21})]_{11}$

$Procs_{12} \stackrel{def}{=} (transmit, r_3).Procs_{13}$ $\quad [(Proc_{11}, Proc_{22}), (Proc_{12}, Proc_{21})]_{12}$

$Procs_{13} \stackrel{def}{=} (release, r_4).Procs_{01}$ $\quad [(Proc_{11}, Proc_{23}), (Proc_{13}, Proc_{21})]_{13}$

$Bus \stackrel{def}{=} (acquire, \top).(release, \top).Bus$ $\quad\quad Memory \stackrel{def}{=} (transmit, \top).Memory$

$$\textbf{Machine}_\textbf{a} \stackrel{def}{=} (Procs_{00} \bowtie_{L_1} Bus) \bowtie_{L_2} Memory$$

where $L_1 = \{acquire, release\}$ and $L_2 = \{transmit\}$. In the new model, *Memory* is a single state arbiter component as before, and its removal is straightforward. Similarly, *Bus* is also an arbiter component as before. However, we would like to highlight that in the aggregated model, its removal is no longer conditioned by the use of functional rates in the other components of the model. Indeed, the aggregation has reduced the number of components that have to cooperate with *Bus* to one component. Moreover, the scheduling imposed previously by *Bus* between the two model components *Proc* is already taken into account in the resulting component $Procs_{00}$. Therefore the removal of *Bus* becomes straightforward and the new system equation is $\mathbf{Machine'_a} \stackrel{def}{=} Procs_{00}$.

In contrast, if we first apply the function-based simplification technique we obtain the model $\mathbf{Machine'} \stackrel{def}{=} Proc_{10} \parallel Proc_{20}$ defined earlier in which $Proc_1$ and $Proc_2$ involve functional rates. In order to apply aggregation to this model we must first define strong equivalence for components which contain functional rates. The original definition of strong equivalence suggests that this will be achieved by extending the definition of conditional transition rate to include the possibility that the transition rate concerned may be a function.

Definition 6 (Conditional transition rate). *The conditional transition rate between two derivatives C_i and C_j, via a given action type α, denoted $q(C_i, C_j, \alpha)$, is defined to be the sum of the constant and the functional activity rates associated with transitions between C_i and C_j in the derivation graph which are labelled by α.*

Note that the evaluation of a function is unequivocal because we are considering the transition rates from a particular derivative. Each derivative corresponds to a particular set of local states for each component, thus determining the appropriate value of the function.

The total conditional transition rate to a set is defined, as previously, as the sum of conditional transition rates from the component to elements of the set. Thus it follows that two derivatives with functional rates for an action type α will be strongly equivalent if the functions in each derivative will give the same transition rate to each strong equivalence class. For the example above this is readily shown to be the case. In the cases where the equivalence class has more than one element it is clear that $Proc_{10} \parallel Proc_{2k} \cong Proc_{1k} \parallel Proc_{20}$ for all $k = 0, 1, 2, 3$ and f_1 and f_2 (g_1 and g_2) will have the same evaluation.

If the techniques are considered as alternative means of model simplification there is a clear preference for strong equivalence based aggregation since this can reduce the size of the underlying state space. But when both techniques are applicable, it seems that it is possible to apply the techniques in either order. However, in general, establishing strong equivalence without functional rates will be less involved and therefore to be preferred computationally. Moreover, as we have seen, first carrying out the aggregation to remove interleavings may simplify the function-based reduction because the need for functions to control scheduling may have been eliminated.

In the following we describe the algorithm that allows the simplification of a PEPA model by removing the arbiter components.

6 An Algorithm for Eliminating Arbiter Components

Assume that R is an arbiter in model C, i.e. R is a simple resource component $R \equiv S_1 + S_2 + \cdots + S_n$, in a model $C \equiv (P_1 \parallel P_2 \parallel \cdots \parallel P_k) \bowtie_L R$. Then for each component P_i we can partition the derivative set of P_i into two disjoint subsets

$ds_R(P_i)$, corresponding to states where P_i is "using" R and $ds_{free}(P_i)$ where it is not. A component is "using" the resource when it has cooperated on the first activity of one of the cycles S_i in R, but not yet cooperated on the last activity of the cycle.

$$ds(P_i) = ds_R(P_i) \cup ds_{free}(P_i) \qquad\qquad ds_R(P_i) \cap ds_{free}(P_i) = \emptyset$$

Moreover, we denote by $C\_state(P_i)$ the current state of component P_i and define the two sets $\mathcal{B}(\alpha)$ and $\mathcal{I}nput(R)$. The former contains the components which have α in their action type set and the latter the action types that component R may engage in, in its initial state.

Single state arbiter components. This type of component has only one derivative but may have the choice between several activities to engage in.

$$R \stackrel{def}{=} (\alpha_1, r_1).R + (\alpha_2, r_2).R + \ldots + (\alpha_n, r_n).R$$

As stated before, when such a component is removed, logically it can be replaced by an identity function because it does not enforce any scheduling between the other components of the model. In practical terms the introduction of such a function can be omitted as it has no impact on the behaviour but overloads the notation and introduces an unnecessary extra computation time.

However, when removing such a component from a model, we should pay attention to the rates of the activities in this component. These rates may be real values or unspecified rates and according to this the elimination of this component may or may not bring changes to the other components of the model.

1. If all the activities enabled by the arbiter component have unspecified rates, then the component can be removed automatically from the model without any changes in the other components of the model.
2. If the rate of an action type $\alpha_i \in \mathcal{A}(R)$ is specified, then for each component P_j in the model and each instance α_i^* of α_i in $\mathbf{Act}(P_j)$, a new rate should be computed. For that we need to know the current state of each component in $\mathcal{B}(\alpha)$. To define this within a function would necessitate a complete derivation of the state space of the remainder of the model. Thus we leave this to be done during the usual generation of the derivation graph of the model. For each arc of the graph to generate with label α, we consider the components in competition for this action type and compute the associated rate for α considering the rates of these components at this stage of the graph. The functions instead are used to control whether an activity of this type should be allowed or not, without complete specification of the rate. Thus our functions always have the value 1 or 0 which can be regarded as switching an activity *on* or *off* respectively.

Note that from the point of view of the state space, the removal of a single state arbiter component does not bring any benefit.

Multi-states arbiter components. Unlike single state arbiter components, the removal of these components from the model allows us to reduce the size of the model, its representation and its state space when the Kronecker form is the internal representation used.

The general algorithm consists mainly in defining, for each component P_i and action type α shared between this component and an arbiter component, a function $g_i(\alpha)$. This function allows P_i to *know* when the arbiter component is free and thus usable. Application of the algorithm takes place at the model (syntactic) level and results in the removal of all arbiter components.

//**Algorithm**

for each component P_i
　// define a function f_i over $ds(P_i)$
　for each $P_i' \in ds(P_i)$

$$f_i = \begin{cases} 1 \ if \ P_i' \in ds_{free}(P_i) \\ 0 \ if \ P_i' \in ds_R(P_i) \end{cases}$$

　end for
end for

for each $\alpha \in \mathcal{I}nput(R)$
　for each $P_j \in \mathcal{B}(\alpha)$

$$g_j(\alpha) = \prod_{\substack{i=1, i \neq j \\ P_i' = C\_State(P_i)}}^{n} f_i(P_i')$$

　　replace (α, r) in P_j by $(\alpha, g_j(\alpha) \times r)$
　end for
end for

7 Related Work

Current research addresses the definition of efficient techniques for constructing and analysing large models. These techniques fall into two categories: "largeness avoidance" and "largeness tolerance" [9]. While the former refers to approaches that aim to keep the size of the model representation as small as possible at every stage of the modelling and analysis process, the latter category focusses on sparse storage techniques and memory-efficient numerical methods.

Like decomposition techniques, the Kronecker approach, and techniques which exploit model symmetries, the function-equivalent components based simplification technique belongs to the first category. However, unlike these techniques which have been widely reported in the literature, the possibility of using functional rates to eliminate components has not really been investigated. This technique has been identified for SAN for some time [5]. However, to the best of our knowledge, there has not been any work on a systematic way to identify suitable components and automatically eliminate them. Instead the previous approach relies on the expertise/skill of the modeller. Here we can envisage the elimination being carried out transparently to the user since the identification of suitable components is based on readily checked syntactic conditions, and the algorithm of the previous section provides an automatic means of carrying out the reduction.

Process algebras which encompass functions have previously appeared in the literature (see for example μCRL [6][7]). However the role of the functions here is somewhat different. Moreover this is the first stochastic process algebra to incorporate them.

8   Conclusions

In this paper, we have identified a class of *function-equivalent* PEPA components and we have shown, using functional rates, that any component of this class can be eliminated from a model. An algorithm allowing the automatic removal of these components has been developed.

This new simplification technique allows the reduction of the number of components in a model and thus the number of matrices required for a Kronecker representation of the underlying Markov process, when this internal representation is used. Furthermore the model expression is simplified although the state space remains the same and subsequent solution is exact.

Moreover, we have investigated the interplay between this simplification approach and the aggregation technique characterised by strong equivalence in PEPA. Combining these techniques, when possible, may allow the modeller to push the current limits of PEPA in terms of tractable systems. Our goal in the future is to extend the class of function-equivalent components and to integrate this new simplification approach into the PEPA Workbench [8].

References

1. J. Hillston and L. Kloul, An Efficient Kronecker Representation for PEPA Models, LNCS, N.2165, pp.120-135, Proc. of the Joint International Workshop, PAPM-PROBMIV 2001, Aachen
2. J. Hillston and L. Kloul, Formal Techniques for Performance Analysis: blending SAN and PEPA, Submitted
3. J. Hillston, A compositional approach to performance modelling, PhD. The University of Edinburgh, 1994
4. J. Hillston The Nature of Synchronisation Proc. of 2nd Process Algebra and Performance Modelling Workshop, U. Herzog and M. Rettelbach (Editors), 1994
5. P. Fernandes, B. Plateau and W.J. Stewart Optimizing Tensor Product Computations in Stochastic Automata Networks, RAIRO - Operations Research, vol. 32, no. 3, pp:325-351, July, 1998
6. J.F. Groote and A. Ponse, Proof Theory for μCRL: A Languages for Processes with Data, Semantics of Specification Languages 1993, pp.232-251
7. J.F. Groote and A. Ponse, The Syntax and Semantics of μCRL, In A.Ponse,C. Verhoef & S.F.M. van Vlijmen, eds, Algebra of Communicating Processes, Workshops in Computing, pp.26-62,1994
8. S. Gilmore and J. Hillston, The PEPA Workbench: A Tool to Support a Process Algebra-based Approach to Performance Modelling, Proc. of the 7th Int. Conf. on Modelling Techniques and Tools for Computer Performance Evaluation, LNCS, Vol.794, pp:353-368, Vienna 1994
9. K.S. Trivedi and M. Malhotra, Reliability and Performability Techniques and Tools: A Survey, In B. Walke and O. Spaniol, editors, Messung, Modellierung und Bewertung von Rechen- und Kommunikationssystemen, pages 27–48, Springer, Aachen, September 1993

Functional Performance Specification
with Stochastic Probes

Ashok Argent-Katwala and Jeremy T. Bradley

Department of Computing, Imperial College London
180 Queen's Gate, London SW7 2BZ, United Kingdom
{ashok, jb}@doc.ic.ac.uk

Abstract. In this paper, we introduce FPS, a mechanism to define performance measures for stochastic process algebra models. FPS is a functional performance specification language which describes passage-time, transient, steady-state and continuous state space performance questions. We present a generalisation of stochastic probes, a formalism-independent specification of behaviour in stochastic process algebra models. Stochastic probes select the performance-critical paths for which the measures are required; increasing their expressiveness in turn gives us greater expressive power to represent performance questions. We end by demonstrating these tools on an RSS syndication architecture of up to 1.5×10^{51} states.

1 Introduction

In this paper, we introduce functional performance specification (FPS) over stochastic probes: a mechanism to define performance measures for stochastic process algebra models, with a unified description to capture passage-time, transient, steady-state and continuous state space quantities.

These four kinds of soft performance bounds are an integral part of system performance validation. For example, we might have a service-level agreement (SLA) that a particular type of SQL query must return a result within 0.35 seconds 99% of the time; this would be derived from a passage-time quantile, based on an underlying stochastic model. Alternatively, we might need to assure ourselves that the probability that a just-in-time compiler is running native code exactly 5 seconds after loading a Java applet is at least 0.8; this would be a transient constraint. Finally, we might have to demonstrate that the long-term probability that our software is in a particular failure mode is less than 0.002; this is a steady-state measure. Continuous state space analysis is used to quantify massively parallel agent-based architectures, by providing counts of agent states at particular time points, e.g. there are 5,221 copies of a web client component in a queue for the web server at time 150 seconds.

When measuring the performance of a system, we see a need to separate the logic that specifies the performance query from the logic that defines the model; a modelling requirement described in [1]. Without such separation, it is

A. Horváth and M. Telek (Eds.): EPEW 2006, LNCS 4054, pp. 31–46, 2006.

common to see many distinct versions of the same system being created explicitly to capture distinct measurement-centred behaviour. Stochastic probes are one method of making this separation of model and query. A stochastic probe [2] is a measurement device that defines arbitrary start and end events for a performance measure over a stochastic process algebra model.

We base the stochastic probe specification on an action-based regular expression syntax. We provide a further separation between the behavioural properties that make up our performance measure (as described by the stochastic probe) and the quantitative questions that we typically need to ask, using the functional performance specification framework.

This work builds on many performance specification methodologies: the NICE performance measurement system [3] of Woodside *et al.*; the regular expression style behavioural specification of asCSL [4] and TIPPtool [5]; the path-based reward structures described by Obal and Sanders [1]. FPS and stochastic probes are, however, unique in offering the combination of functional-style performance questions and a simple regular-expression based behavioural specification.

In this paper, we show how stochastic probes can be used to specify expressive behavioural constraints (Section 2.1), while the functional performance specification layer uses the stochastic probes to define passage-time, transient, steady-state or continuous state-based measures (Section 4). We significantly augment the expressiveness of the stochastic probe language from the introduction presented in [2] and present a new formal semantic translation of probe operators to underlying stochastic process algebra components (Section 6). We conclude by demonstrating the use of functional performance specification and stochastic probes over a PEPA model of the publish–subscribe mechanism, *Really Simple Syndication* or RSS (Section 7).

2   Stochastic Probes

We use a regular expression [6] specification to describe the start and end points of a performance measurement. The atoms of the regular expression are action names in the target system, drawn from the alphabet of the underlying process algebra model. This specification is turned into a fragment of stochastic process algebra, for our purposes PEPA [7], but we could equally apply probes to other stochastic process algebras such as EMPA [8] or SFSP [9] according to our modelling requirements. These probe fragments are composed with the original model to produce a model–probe system from which the performance measure can be easily extracted using tools native to the formalism.

The precise meaning of the probe will depend on the semantics of the underlying process algebra, in particular how choice works. In principle the translation offered in Section 6 will apply for any stochastic process algebra which has choice, a passive cooperation and supports CSP-style multiway synchronisation.

2.1 Stochastic Probe Definition

In this enhanced version of stochastic probes, we add the *without* operator, R/L. This specifies that, for a given path, a set of behaviours R should be observed without seeing any of the actions in the set, L. This is a significant generalisation over [10], where the modeller is only allowed to specify start and stop actions actions with no additional constraints on intermediate behaviour. It also generalises [2] where the modeller is only allowed to specify behaviour that should be seen along a particular path. A stochastic probe definition, R, has the following syntax:

$$
\begin{aligned}
R &::= A \mid T, T \mid S \\
S &::= T|S \mid T \\
T &::= R \mid R\{n\} \mid R\{m,n\} \mid R^+ \mid R^\star \mid R? \mid R/act \\
A &::= act \mid act : \mathsf{start} \mid act : \mathsf{stop}
\end{aligned}
\tag{1}
$$

act is an action label that matches a label in the system being measured. Any action specified in the probe has to be observed in the model before the probe can advance a state. An action, *act*, can also be distinguished or tagged as a *start* or *stop* action in a probe and signifies an action which will start or stop a measurement, respectively.

R_1, R_2 is the **sequential** operation. R_1 is matched against the system's operation, then R_2 is matched.

$R_1 \mid R_2$ is the **choice** operation. Either R_1 or R_2 is matched against the system being probed.

$R^\star$ is the **closure** operation, where zero or more copies of R are matched against the system.

$R?$ is the **optional** operation, matching zero or one copy of R against the system.

$R\{n\}$ is the **iterative** operation. A fixed number of sequential copies of R are matched against the system e.g. $R\{3\}$ is simply shorthand for R, R, R.

$R\{m,n\}$ is the **range** operation. Between m and n copies of R are matched against the system's operation. $R\{m,n\}$ is equivalent to $R\{n,m\}$, and we consider the canonical form to have the smaller index first.

R^+ is the **positive closure** operation, where one or more copies of R are matched against the system. It is syntactic sugar for $R, R^\star$.

R/act is the **without** operation. R must begin again whenever the probe sees an *act* action that is not matched by R.

3   PEPA Stochastic Process Algebra

PEPA is used as the stochastic process algebra of choice for defining the probe semantics of Section 6 and the modelling example of Section 7. PEPA is a parsimonious stochastic process algebra that can describe compositional stochastic models and has been used for many performance modelling case studies. These models consist of components whose actions incorporate random exponential delays. Full details of the PEPA process algebra can be found in [7]. In brief, the syntax of a PEPA component, P, is represented by:

$$P ::= (a, \lambda).P \mid P + P \mid P \underset{s}{\bowtie} P \mid P/L \mid A$$

$(a, \lambda).P$ is an action prefix operation. It represents a process which does an action, a, and then becomes a new process, P. The time taken to perform a is described by an exponentially distributed random variable with parameter λ. The rate parameter may also take a $\top$-value, which makes the action passive in a cooperation (see below).

$P_1 + P_2$ is a choice operation between two components. A race is entered into between components P_1 and P_2. If P_1 evolves first then any behaviour of P_2 is discarded and vice-versa.

$P_1 \underset{s}{\bowtie} P_2$ is the cooperation operator between two components which synchronise over a set of actions, S. P_1 and P_2 run in parallel and synchronise over the set of actions in the set S. If P_1 is to evolve with an action $a \in S$, then it must first wait for P_2 to reach a point where it is also capable of producing an a-action, and vice-versa. In an active cooperation, the two components then jointly produce an a-action with a rate that reflects the slower of the two components (usually the minimum of the two individual a-rates). In a passive cooperation, where P_1, say, can evolve with an $(a, \top)$-transition, the joint a-action inherits its rate from the P_2 component alone.

P/L is a hiding operator of a set of actions, L. where actions in the set L that emanate from the component P are rewritten as silent τ actions (with the same appropriate delays). The actions in L can no longer be used in cooperation with other components.

A is a constant label. and allows, amongst other things, recursive definitions to be constructed.

Regarding related performance specification in PEPA, itself, Gilmore and Hillston [11] have developed their own *feature interaction* logic which explores a PEPA model, assigning rewards to component states for use in steady-state and transient-state analysis. This is an alternative technique to the one we are trying to achieve here. Instead of using a logic to interrogate a model, we use the language's own cooperation operator to observe the key events that we wish to measure. By selectively sampling a model's behaviour in this way, we can simplify the task of picking the states that are relevant to our measure.

Our method has the benefit of not requiring the user to learn an entirely different paradigm, being based on the process algebra in which the model is described. At the moment, it has the downside that, being observationally-based, it cannot distinguish actions that are generated by different copies of the same component. This is possible in a logic setting such as that set up by Gilmore *et al.* [12] for steady-state measure specification.

4   FPS: Functional Performance Specification

A functional performance specification is presented here as a contrast to well-established logical performance specification formalisms that have some from CSL [13]. Logical formalisms reduce all performance questions to a truth value, for instance in a later version of CSL [14], the expression $s \models \mathcal{S}_{<0.3}(\psi)$ means:

> Is the state s the initial state of a path that ends in the set of states defined by ψ where the total steady-state probability of being in those ψ states is less than 0.3?

This is how a performance modeller might phrase the same question:

> Is the steady-state probability of the states defined by ψ less than 0.3?

If we were to require the precise value of the steady-state probability in CSL, we would have to ask the more general question $s \models \mathcal{S}_{<p}(\psi)$ and observe the value of p at which the formula moves from being true to false. Of late, this situation has been in part remedied by the support of tools such as PRISM [15], which allow questions such as:

> Find p such that, given a start state s, $s \models \mathcal{S}_{<p}(\psi)$ is true.

However, we still feel that the question is not as directly or succinctly stated as it might be. Despite this, logical performance specification offers a very expressive and very powerful environment, especially in being able to construct compositional performance queries, due in a large part to its well-explored CTL pedigree. In developing a functional performance paradigm, we seek to be able to ask the quantitative performance question more directly, as in:

> What is the steady-state probability of being in a set of states, ψ?

while maintaining the compositional power of logical performance specification. However in this paper, since we favour a process framework for our underlying model, we use stochastic probes rather than logical atomic propositions of CSL to specify our state sets.

4.1   Performance Specification Syntax

With this motivation, we present a functional specification, which takes an input native to a stochastic process algebra model – i.e. a stochastic probe or component label – and generates a performance function, e.g. a passage time CDF, which can itself be sampled or composed into higher-order performance queries. A functional performance specification, $\mathcal{M}$, over a stochastic probe, R, has the following grammar:

$$\mathcal{M} \quad ::= \quad \mathcal{S}teady(R) \mid \mathcal{P}assage(R) \mid \mathcal{T}ransient(R) \mid \mathcal{N}umber(C)$$

and $\mathcal{S}teady(R)$ represents a steady-state measure; $\mathcal{P}assage(R)$ represents a passage-time cumulative distribution function; $\mathcal{T}ransient(R)$ represents a transient-state distribution function; and $\mathcal{N}umber(R)$ represents a deterministic component counting function. C is a component type from the process model.

4.2   Definitions

Let the joint probe–model system, $R \bowtie_L M$, be a Markov process, $\{Z(t) : t \geq 0\}$, where $Z(t)$ is the state of the system at time t. We can define the counting process, $N(t) = |\{Z(u) : 0 \leq u \leq t\}| - 1$, to be the number of state transitions that have occurred by time t.

In order to define the performance measure operators, $\mathcal{Passage}$ and $\mathcal{Transient}$, we will need to specify sets of source states, F, and target states, G, based on the instants after probe start and probe stop actions have occurred respectively. So we define:

$$F(R) = \{R'' \bowtie_L M'' \ : \ R' \bowtie_L M' \xrightarrow{(a:\text{start},\cdot)} R'' \bowtie_L M''\} \tag{2}$$

$$G(R) = \{R'' \bowtie_L M'' \ : \ R' \bowtie_L M' \xrightarrow{(a:\text{stop},\cdot)} R'' \bowtie_L M''\} \tag{3}$$

where R' and R'' are derivative or successor states of the probe, R. M represents the model being measured and M' and M'' are derivative states of M. It is worth noting, that although we have used PEPA notation to highlight the joint probe–model process, these definitions could easily be expressed in other process algebras.

In the following descriptions prob $\equiv [0, 1]$, the set of probability values and C is a component type from the process model.

Steady-state, $\mathcal{Steady}(R)$ **: prob.** Applying the steady-state operator to a probe, R, generates the steady-state probability for being in one of the states reachable by a probe stop action. For irreducible state spaces, this can be expressed as:

$$\mathcal{Steady}(R) = \sum_{x \in G(R)} \pi(x) \tag{4}$$

where $\pi(x)$ is the steady-state probability of being in the state x in the process $Z(t)$.

Passage-time CDF, $\mathcal{Passage}(R) : \mathbb{R}^+ \to$ **prob.** A passage-time measure over a probe R returns a cumulative distribution function for the passage-time that starts from a state reachable by a probe start action and finishes at a state reachable by a probe stop action. More precisely, using λ-notation to define the cumulative distribution function, we can say:

$$\mathcal{Passage}(R) = \lambda t \ . \ \sum_{x \in F(R)} \pi(x) \, \mathbb{P}(P_{xG(R)} \leq t) \tag{5}$$

where $P_{i\mathcal{J}}$ is the random variable representing the passage-time starting from a state i and terminating in one of the states in $\mathcal{J}$, as given by:

$$P_{i\mathcal{J}} = \inf\{u > 0 \ : \ Z(u) \in \mathcal{J}, N(u) > 0, Z(0) = i\} \tag{6}$$

In Eq. (5), we weight the passage with the steady-state probabilities of starting in any of the start states, as defined by the start actions in the probe. It is our intention to generalise this in future versions, so that we can specify a time-point from which we can generate a transient distribution to weight the passage with.

Clearly, the associated density function, $f(t)$, for this passage-time measurement can be obtained by differentiating the CDF, $f(t) = \mathcal{P}assage(R)'(t)$.

Transient-state function, $\mathcal{T}ransient(R) : \mathbb{R}^+ \to$ prob. A transient-state measure over a probe R returns the transient-state distribution function for having just completed the probe stop action at time t, having completed a probe start action at time, $t = 0$. It is defined as follows, again using the steady-state vector to weight the multiple start states that might arise from the stochastic probe:

$$\mathcal{T}ransient(R) = \lambda t \; . \sum_{x \in F(R)} \pi(x)\, \mathbb{P}(Z(t) \in G(R) \mid Z(0) = x) \qquad (7)$$

Component count function, $\mathcal{N}umber(C) : \mathbb{R}^+ \to \mathbb{R}^+$. Applying the component count function to a component C in the model yields a function which counts the number of that components in the system in the state C at time t. It relates to the recent innovations in continuous state space approximation of stochastic process algebra models [16], which solve systems of coupled of ODEs for systems with huge and otherwise computationally infeasible state spaces.

The model M is regarded as consisting of a cooperation of n classes of component, C_i, $1 \leq i \leq n$ and with each component class having m_i derivative states. At any time, there may be many components of the same class, but in a different state in the system. We let $v_{ij}(t)$ represent the number of components of type C_i in state j at time t for $1 \leq j \leq m_i$. This is found by solving a set of coupled ODEs of the form $v'_{ij}(t) = g(v_{11}(t), \ldots, v_{nm_n}(t))$. In effect:

$$\mathcal{N}umber(C_{ij}) = \lambda t \; . \; v_{ij}(t) \qquad (8)$$

5   Stochastic Probe Examples

We give a few examples of stochastic probes as specified by regular expressions over a simple PEPA model. Consider a Bartender and a few customers, specified in PEPA:

$$\text{Bartender} \stackrel{\text{def}}{=} (serve, r_s).\text{Bartender} + (restock, \mathrm{r_r}).\text{Bartender}$$

$$\text{Person} \stackrel{\text{def}}{=} (life, r).\text{Person} + (thirst, \mathrm{s}).\text{Thirsty}$$

$$\text{Thirsty} \stackrel{\text{def}}{=} (serve, \top).\text{Drinking}$$

$$\text{Drinking} \stackrel{\text{def}}{=} (drink, r_0).(resume, r_1).\text{Person} + (drink, \mathrm{r_0}).\text{Thirsty}$$

$$\text{Sys} \stackrel{\text{def}}{=} \text{Bartender} \underset{\{serve\}}{\bowtie} (\text{Person} \parallel \text{Person} \parallel \text{Person})$$

Let us ask a few simple questions of this model:

- How long between the first drink is served and the tenth?

$$serve: \mathsf{start}, serve\{8\}, serve: \mathsf{stop}$$

- Measure the time from the tenth serving till any of the drinkers returns to their normal life.

$$serve\{9\}, serve: \mathsf{start}, resume: \mathsf{stop}$$

- If the bar holds stocks for 100 drinks, and is restocked to back to 100 drinks every time the Bartender performs *restock* action, how long till the bar runs dry?

$$serve: \mathsf{start}, serve\{99\}/restock, serve: \mathsf{stop}$$

It is important to realise that the probe will never block the behaviour of the model it is synchronising with. As described in the next section, the probe will absorb behaviour (without altering state) which it sees that is not part of its next specified action. A probe that does not use the *without* construct asks the question "will I ever see this behaviour?". Using *without*, a modeller may also ask "will I see exactly this behaviour next?", if not then skip back to a particular point in the measure.

6   Stochastic Probe Translation

Fig. 1 depicts the conversion of the individual regular expression elements to process algebra components pictorially. The without operator acts at a different level to the other operators, and is concerned with the actions within a particular sub-expression, and not with composing expressions together. Dotted arrows denote that there is an immediate choice (with no prefix action) to continue in the successor state.

Note that the representation for $R\{m, n\}$ is not the same as $(R\{m\}|R\{m + 1\}|\ldots|R\{n\})$. That would be one way to translate it, but would mean committing, through random choice to matching a particular number of repetitions of R. This could be surprising to a modeller who has asked the probe to match any of the range of repetitions. Instead we treat $R\{m, n\}$ as $R\{m\}, R?\{n - m\}$ (or $R?\{n\}$ where $m = 0$).

Before translating the probe at all, we first build a parse tree, during which all the syntactic sugar is removed. We convert: R^+ to $R, R^\star$; $R\{n\}$ to $R, \ldots, R$ to give n explicit copies of R; and $R\{m, n\}$ to $R\{m\}, R?\{n-m\}$ or $R?\{n\}$ where $m = 0$. Now, we are left with probes which fit a smaller syntactic form, which we need to convert to our target process algebra. In particular, the syntax of the T component of the regular expression definition from Eq. (1) is reduced to:

$$T \quad ::= \quad R \mid R^\star \mid R? \mid R/act$$

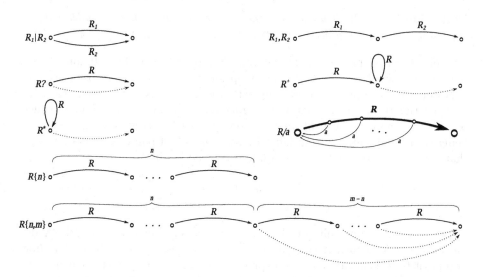

Fig. 1. The representation of the distinct regular expression terms as state-transitions in the underlying process algebra

6.1 Mapping Probes to PEPA

In the definitions below, we take as input the component name, P, we are to define, the component name, Q, we are to end at and a reset-list of action names and the component-label to which we return when we absorb that action. The reset-list is initially empty. We introduce new, intermediate component labels N_i, as required.

Throughout the conversion, only the topmost operator in the tree is considered, and the subtrees are handled recursively. First, a few definitions:

Definition 1. $\mathcal{F}(R)$ *denotes the first names of the probe expression R. These are the action names that are explicitly used at the beginning of R. It is defined over the terms for regular expressions.*

The sequence operator needs careful handling; where the first term is optional ($R^\star$ or $R?$ or $R\{0,n\}$) then the first actions of the second term are also immediately available. We take the first (which is also the most specific) definition below that matches the current situation:

$$\mathcal{F}(a{:}\mathsf{start}) = a$$
$$\mathcal{F}(a{:}\mathsf{stop}) = a$$
$$\mathcal{F}(a) = a$$
$$\mathcal{F}(R_1^\star, R_2) = \mathcal{F}(R_1) \cup \mathcal{F}(R_2)$$
$$\mathcal{F}(R_1?, R_2) = \mathcal{F}(R_1) \cup \mathcal{F}(R_2)$$
$$\mathcal{F}(R_1, R_2) = \mathcal{F}(R_1)$$

$$\mathcal{F}(R_1 \mid R_2) = \mathcal{F}(R_1) \cup \mathcal{F}(R_2)$$
$$\mathcal{F}(R?) = \mathcal{F}(R)$$
$$\mathcal{F}(R^+) = \mathcal{F}(R)$$
$$\mathcal{F}(R^\star) = \mathcal{F}(R)$$
$$\mathcal{F}(R/a) = \mathcal{F}(R)$$

Definition 2. $\mathcal{N}(R)$ *denotes the names that are not explicitly enabled at the beginning of R. For a probe that acts over the alphabet A,* $\mathcal{N}(R) = A - \mathcal{F}(R)$.

At every state, the probe will offer every action to lead somewhere. If not to move the probe forward, or to reset it to some prior state due to an enclosing *without* operator, then the probe absorbs the action and remains in the same state. To abstract this from the translation that follows, we define the function $\mathcal{S}$, which provides the sum (choice) of all the reset and self-loops for an expression R, being translated running from label P, with the set of pairs for resets X. Note that this procedure adds a transition for every action in $\mathcal{N}(R)$:

$$\mathcal{S}(R,P,X) \;=\; \sum_{(b,E)\in X \,:\, b\in \mathcal{N}(R)} (b,\top).\text{E} \;+\; \sum_{c\in\mathcal{N}(R)\,:\,\nexists x\,:\,(c,x)\in X} (c,\top).\text{P}$$

We now define the full translation, $\mathcal{T}$, which produces a set of PEPA definitions, and is a formal version of the English descriptions above. The first argument to $\mathcal{T}$ is always a probe expression, which is underlined, to avoid confusing the expression's sequence operator for the argument separator. The N_i are new process names for each recursive call.

The initial call to translate a probe is to $\mathcal{T}(\underline{R}, Probe, Probe, \emptyset)$. This creates a cyclic PEPA component, Probe, so when composed with an irreducible system, that may be preserved.

Action	$\mathcal{T}(\underline{a},P,Q,X)$	$=$	$\text{P} \stackrel{\text{def}}{=} (a,\top).\text{Q} + \mathcal{S}(\underline{a},\text{P},\text{X})$
Grouping	$\mathcal{T}((\underline{R}),P,Q,X)$	$=$	$\mathcal{T}(\underline{R},P,Q,X)$
Choice	$\mathcal{T}(\underline{R_1|R_2},P,Q,X)$	$=$	$\text{P} \stackrel{\text{def}}{=} N_1 + N_2 + \mathcal{S}(R_1|R_2,\text{P},\text{X});$
			$\mathcal{T}(\underline{R_1},N_1,Q,X); \mathcal{T}(\underline{R_2},N_2,Q,X)$
Sequence	$\mathcal{T}(\underline{R_1,R_2},P,Q,X)$	$=$	$\mathcal{T}(\underline{R_1},P,N_1,X); \mathcal{T}(\underline{R_2},N_1,Q,X)$
Closure	$\mathcal{T}(\underline{R^\star},P,Q,X)$	$=$	$\text{P} \stackrel{\text{def}}{=} N_1 + Q$
			$\quad + \mathcal{S}(\underline{R^\star},P,X); \mathcal{T}(\underline{R},N_1,P,X)$
Optional	$\mathcal{T}(\underline{R?},P,Q,X)$	$=$	$\text{P} \stackrel{\text{def}}{=} N_1 + Q$
			$\quad + \mathcal{S}(\underline{R?},P,X); \mathcal{T}(\underline{R},N_1,Q,X)$
Without	$\mathcal{T}(\underline{R/a},P,Q,X)$	$=$	$\mathcal{T}(\underline{R},P,Q,X')$
			where $X'=\{(c,x)\in X \mid c\neq a\} \cup (a,P)$

Note that the intention of the ";" operator here is as a separator between definitions. $\mathcal{T}(\ldots); \mathcal{T}(\ldots)$ means the PEPA system contains all the definitions from both calls.

Or in words (omitting the passive loops and resets):

Action a: is always a leaf node and translates to:

$$\text{P} \stackrel{\text{def}}{=} (a,\top).\text{Q}$$

Choice $R_1 \mid R_2$: translates to $\text{P} \stackrel{\text{def}}{=} N_1 + N_2$ and the algorithm is repeated for the sub-trees with R_1 running from N_1 to Q and R_2 running from N_2 to Q.

Sequence R_1, R_2: translates to R_1 running from P to N_1 and R_2 from N_1 to Q.

Closure $R^\star$: becomes $P \stackrel{\text{def}}{=} N_1 + Q$, where R is translated running from N_1 to P.

Optional $R?$: becomes $P \stackrel{\text{def}}{=} N_1 + Q$, where R is translated running from N_1 to Q.

Without R/a: R is translated running from P to Q and at every stage between, offers a choice of $(a, \top).P$ wherever R does not explicitly offer one. We do this by adding the pair (a,P) to the reset-list and removing any other a-reset pair. This ensures we use the most specific reset action that the modeller has chosen, should they choose to exclude the same action more than once.

The procedure above gives us a valid PEPA fragment which will behave properly as a probe. However, for our analysis with ipc/DNAmaca [10] we also need to be able to tell, purely from the state of the probe, whether it is running or stopped. To achieve this, we create an observationally equivalent probe which has a partition in its state space to enable ipc to specify the start and stop states for DNA-maca. The details of this procedure can be found in Argent-Katwala *et al.* [2].

7   Worked Example: An RSS Publish–Subscribe System

To demonstrate our functional performance specification framework, we introduce a simplified PEPA model of an RSS publish–subscribe system.

The RSS system under consideration consists of N_C RSS clients and a single RSS server comprising N_S virtual servers running in parallel. The clients and server are connected by a network capable of sustaining N_N concurrent network connections. This is described by the top-level system equation below:

$$RSS\_System \stackrel{\text{def}}{=} (RSS\_Client[N_C] \underset{L}{\bowtie} RSS\_Server[N_S, M])$$
$$\underset{L}{\bowtie} RSS\_Network[N_N]$$

where:

$$L = \{subscribe, unsubscribe, rss\_poll, rss\_update, rss\_cache\_hit\}$$
$$M = \{new\_feed, rss\_refresh\}$$

describes the set of actions that the RSS client and server cooperate over via the network. Note that in the above description, the $A[N]$ construction is shorthand for $A[N, \emptyset]$ and $A[N, M]$ represents N components of type A cooperating over the set of actions M, as in:

$$A[N, M] \equiv \underbrace{A \underset{M}{\bowtie} A \underset{M}{\bowtie} \cdots \underset{M}{\bowtie} A}_{N}$$

The RSS client can subscribe to a server feed, after which it can poll the RSS server for the current feed information. With some rate, λ_2, a client can withdraw from the system by unsubscribing. After polling, the client is given a newer version of the RSS feed or told that the cached version that the client has is current and no update is necessary (achieved through a choice between *rss_update* and *rss_cache_hit* actions in component RSS_Client_1). At this stage, the client will poll at different rates according to whether it has just been handed a new version of the feed or not. If an older cached version exists, it will poll more frequently, with $\lambda_4 > \lambda_3$.

$$RSS\_Client \stackrel{\text{def}}{=} (subscribe, \lambda_1).RSS\_Client_n$$

$$RSS\_Client_n \stackrel{\text{def}}{=} (rss\_poll, \lambda_3).RSS\_Client_1 + (unsubscribe, \lambda_2).RSS\_Client$$

$$RSS\_Client_c \stackrel{\text{def}}{=} (rss\_poll, \lambda_4).RSS\_Client_1 + (unsubscribe, \lambda_2).RSS\_Client$$

$$RSS\_Client_1 \stackrel{\text{def}}{=} (rss\_update, \top).RSS\_Client_n + (rss\_cache\_hit, \top).RSS\_Client_c$$
$$+ (unsubscribe, \lambda_2).RSS\_Client$$

The RSS virtual servers, of which there will be several working in parallel to update the feed information, keep track of the subscription list (not explicitly represented in this model). A current feed has a lifetime determined by the *new_feed* action at rate μ_1, which, together with the *rss_refresh* action, represent a feed content change on a shared disk, say. A client polling one of the servers receives either an *rss_update* or an *rss_cache_hit* with probabilities $\frac{\mu_u}{\mu_u+\mu_c}$ and $\frac{\mu_c}{\mu_u+\mu_c}$ respectively, where $\mu_c > \mu_u$ representing that sending a message that the feed has not modified is quicker than sending the whole body of the feed. This represents a type of HTTP conditional request, without greatly increasing the size of the model.

$$RSS\_Server \stackrel{\text{def}}{=} (subscribe, \top).RSS\_Server + (unsubscribe, \top).RSS\_Server$$
$$+ (rss\_poll, \top).RSS\_Server_2 + (new\_feed, \mu_1).RSS\_Server_1$$

$$RSS\_Server_1 \stackrel{\text{def}}{=} (rss\_refresh, \mu_2).RSS\_Server$$

$$RSS\_Server_2 \stackrel{\text{def}}{=} (rss\_update, \mu_u).RSS\_Server + (rss\_cache\_hit, \mu_c).RSS\_Server$$

Finally, a simple network model keeps track of limited bandwidth by capping the total number of connections within a given network window to N_N. The duration of the network window is governed by the *net_recover* action and the γ parameter.

$$RSS\_Network \stackrel{\text{def}}{=} (subscribe, \top).RSS\_Network_1$$
$$+ (unsubscribe.\top).RSS\_Network_1$$
$$+ (rss\_poll, \top).RSS\_Network_1$$
$$+ (rss\_update, \top).RSS\_Network_1$$
$$+ (rss\_cache\_hit, \top).RSS\_Network_1$$
$$RSS\_Network_1 \stackrel{\text{def}}{=} (net\_recover, \gamma).RSS\_Network$$

7.1   Functional Performance Queries

We present some questions and analysis of the RSS model in the functional performance specification style:

Steady-state query. What is the steady-state probability of seeing 4 consecutive *rss_poll* actions in the RSS model without having an *rss_update* action? This is translates into the formal functional performance query:

$$\mathcal{S}teady(\,(rss\_poll\!:\mathsf{start},\, rss\_poll\{2\},\, rss\_poll\!:\mathsf{stop})/rss\_update) \qquad (9)$$

We solved this query for a 1,494,288 state system of 7 clients, 3 servers and 2 network connections. $\mathcal{S}teady(R_1) = 0.19273$, for R_1 taken to be the probe of Eq. (9).

Passage-time query. What is the probability that the time between consecutive *rss_update* actions is between 2 and 4 time units? This translates into the formal functional performance query on the cumulative distribution function of the equivalent passage time, $\mathcal{P}assage(R_2)(4) - \mathcal{P}assage(R_2)(2)$ where $R_2 = rss\_update\!:\mathsf{start},\, rss\_update\!:\mathsf{stop}$.

We solved this for a 11,232 state system of 4 clients, 2 servers and 2 network connections. Fig. 2 shows a probability density function of the appropriate passage $f_p(t) = \mathcal{P}assage(R_2)'(t)$. Fig. 3 shows the cumulative distribution function for the appropriate passage $F_P(t) = \mathcal{P}assage(R_2)(t)$. From this second plot we can calculate the required probability $F_P(4) - F_P(2) = 0.1072793$.

Component counting. How many *RSS_Client* components are there at time 60, for a system with $N_C = 100$, $N_S = 3$, $N_N = 2$? This translates into the formal functional performance query on the component counting function $\mathcal{N}umber(RSS\_Client)(60)$. Although this query is not based on a stochastic probe, it is of fundamental interest as a quantitative measure to a performance modeller.

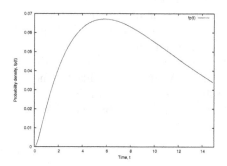 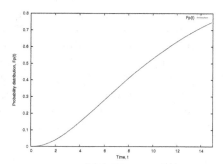

Fig. 2. The PDF for the passage time, $f_p(t) = \mathcal{P}assage(R_2)'(t)$, with $N_C = 4, N_S = 2, N_N = 2$

Fig. 3. The CDF for the passage time, $F_P(t) = \mathcal{P}assage(R_2)(t)$, with $N_C = 4, N_S = 2, N_N = 2$

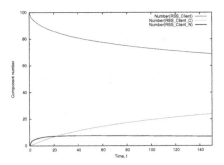

Fig. 4. The component counting functions, (top) $\mathcal{N}umber(RSS\_Client)(t)$, (middle) $\mathcal{N}umber(RSS\_Client_C)(t)$ and (bottom) $\mathcal{N}umber(RSS\_Client_N)(t)$, for RSS model $N_C = 100, N_S = 3, N_N = 2$

For parameters $N_C = 100$, $N_S = 3$, $N_N = 2$, the RSS model has approximately 1.5×10^{51} states. For this magnitude of calculation, the only practical option is to resort to the continuous state space techniques of Hillston [16]. The result of $\mathcal{N}umber(RSS\_Client)(60) = 77.4$ is derived from the appropriate counting function in Fig. 4

8   Conclusion

In this paper, we have developed FPS, a functional performance specification language which allows the modeller to derive quantitative performance functions using stochastic probes. We have also extended stochastic probes as a means of measuring soft performance characteristics of systems. We demonstrated a regular expression language which specifies the stochastic probe and is itself converted into a stochastic process algebra component. The probe is composed with the target system for the purposes of extracting the performance measurement.

We showed how this joint FPS/stochastic probe environment could be used to specify quantitative performance and reliability bounds on stochastic process algebra based systems. Finally, we applied these techniques to a model of an RSS system where we analysed PEPA models of 11 thousand, 1.5 million and 1.5×10^{51} states in size for quantitative performance measures.

Future improvements include allowing the specification of initial state distributions for passage-time and transient measures. We would also like to find an intuitive but unrestrictive way of using probes to define the continuous state space measure, in addition to or maybe as an alternative to using the SPA component type.

Acknowledgements

The authors would like to thank anonymous referees for their insightful comments and suggestions. AAK is supported by EPSRC under the PerformDB grant EP/D054087/1. JB is supported in part by EPSRC under the GRAIL grant EP/D505933/1 and the PerformDB grant EP/D054087/1.

References

1. W. D. Obal and W. H. Sanders, "State-space support for path-based reward variables," *Performance Evaluation*, vol. 35, pp. 233–251, May 1999.
2. A. Argent-Katwala, J. T. Bradley, and N. J. Dingle, "Expressing performance requirements using regular expressions to specify stochastic probes over process algebra models," in *WOSP 2004, Proceedings of the 4th International Workshop on Software and Performance* (V. Almeida and D. Lea, eds.), (Redwood City, California), pp. 49–58, ACM, January 2004.
3. C. M. Woodside and C. Shramm, "Complex performance measurements with NICE (notation for interval combinations and events)," *Software—Practice and Experience*, vol. 24, pp. 1121–1144, December 1994.
4. C. Baier, L. Cloth, B. R. Haverkort, M. Kuntz, and M. Siegle, "Model checking action- and state-labelled Markov chains," *DSN'04, Proceedings of International Conference on Dependable Systems and Networks*, pp. 701–710, June 2004.
5. H. Hermanns, U. Herzog, U. Klehmet, V. Mertsiotakis, and M. Siegle, "Compositional performance modelling with the TIPPtool," *Performance Evaluation*, vol. 39, no. 1–4, pp. 5–35, 2000.
6. S. C. Kleene, "Representation of events in nerve nets and finite automata," in *Automata Studies* (C. E. Shannon and J. McCarthy, eds.), pp. 3–41, Princeton, New Jersey: Princeton University Press, 1956.
7. J. Hillston, *A Compositional Approach to Performance Modelling*, vol. 12 of *Distinguished Dissertations in Computer Science*. Cambridge University Press, 1996.
8. M. Bernardo and R. Gorrieri, "Extended Markovian Process Algebra," in *CONCUR'96, Proceedings of the 7th International Conference on Concurrency Theory* (U. Montanari and V. Sassone, eds.), vol. 1119 of *Lecture Notes in Computer Science*, pp. 315–330, Springer-Verlag, Pisa, August 1996.
9. T. Ayles, A. J. Field, and J. N. Magee, "Adding performance evaluation to the LTSA tool," in *Proceedings of 13th International Conference on Computer Performance Evaluation: Modelling Techniques and Tools*, 2003.
10. J. T. Bradley, N. J. Dingle, S. T. Gilmore, and W. J. Knottenbelt, "Derivation of passage-time densities in PEPA models using ipc: the Imperial PEPA Compiler," in *MASCOTS'03, Proceedings of the 11th IEEE/ACM International Symposium on Modeling, Analysis and Simulation of Computer and Telecommunications Systems* (G. Kotsis, ed.), (University of Central Florida), pp. 344–351, IEEE Computer Society Press, October 2003.
11. S. Gilmore and J. Hillston, "Feature interaction in PEPA," in *Process Algebra and Performance Modelling Workshop* (C. Priami, ed.), pp. 17–26, Università Degli Studi di Verona, Nice, September 1998.
12. S. Gilmore, J. Hillston, and G. Clark, "Specifying performance measures for PEPA," in *Proceedings of the 5th International AMAST Workshop on Real-Time and Probabilistic Systems*, vol. 1601 of *Lecture Notes in Computer Science*, (Bamberg), pp. 211–227, Springer-Verlag, 1999.
13. A. Aziz, K. Sanwal, V. Singhal, and R. Brayton, "Verifying continuous-time Markov chains," in *Computer-Aided Verification*, vol. 1102 of *Lecture Notes in Computer Science*, pp. 269–276, Springer-Verlag, 1996.

14. C. Baier, J.-P. Katoen, and H. Hermanns, "Approximate symbolic model checking of continuous-time Markov chains," in *CONCUR'99, Proceedings of the 10th International Conference on Concurrency Theory*, vol. 1664 of *Lecture Notes in Computer Science*, pp. 146–162, Springer-Verlag, 1999.
15. M. Kwiatkowska, G. Norman, and D. Parker, "PRISM: Probabilistic symbolic model checker," in *TOOLS'02, Proceedings of the 12th International Conference on Modelling Techniques and Tools for Computer Performance Evaluation* (A. J. Field et al., ed.), vol. 2324 of *Lecture Notes in Computer Science*, (London), pp. 200–204, Springer-Verlag, 2002.
16. J. Hillston, "Fluid flow approximation of PEPA models," in *QEST'05, Proceedings of the 2nd International Conference on Quantitative Evaluation of Systems*, (Torino), pp. 33–42, IEEE Computer Society Press, September 2005.

Embedding Real Time
in Stochastic Process Algebras

Jasen Markovski* and Erik P. de Vink

Technische Universiteit Eindhoven, Formal Methods Group
Den Dolech 2, 5612 AZ, Eindhoven, The Netherlands
j.markovski@tue.nl

Abstract. We present a stochastic process algebra including immediate actions, deadlock and termination, and explicit stochastic delays, in the setting of weak choice between immediate actions and passage of time. The operational semantics is a spent time semantics, avoiding explicit clocks. We discuss the embedding of weak-choice real-time process theories and analyze the behavior of parallel composition in the weak choice framework.

Keywords: Stochastic delay, weak choice, race condition, real-time and stochastic process algebra.

1 Introduction

Traditionally, *process algebras* (PAs) like ACP, CCS and CSP are used for qualitative description and verification of processes. In this setting, process behaviour is reflected by the order of actions. However, untimed description of processes is frequently not sufficiently expressive. (See, e.g., [1].) Thus, several timed extensions of traditional PAs emerged. (A detailed overview can be found in [2].) Also, probabilistic behavior of processes was included in PAs supporting probabilistic analysis. (Cf. [3], for example.) Combined efforts, like [4], considering timing aspects and probability, are reported as well.

Often, real-world processes require stochastic behaviour to be incorporated in their description. Early PAs doing so, employed exponentially distributed stochastic delays. Modeling with exponential distributions greatly simplifies the treatment of parallel composition, because of the memoryless property. Prominent Markovian PAs include EMPA, PEPA and Algebra of IMC [5, 6, 7]. The first two associate exponential rates with actions, whereas the latter clearly distinguishes between actions and rates.

Although much success has been reported, an abundance of processes cannot be dealt with exponentially. Consequently, several stochastic PAs with general distributions are proposed like SPADES, IGSMP and NMSPA [8, 9, 10]. SPADES introduces clocks to record the residual lifetime of stochastic delays. Each clock

---

* Corresponding author. Supported by Bsik-project BRICKS AFM 3.2.

initialization is governed by a general distribution. Actions are only enabled after all clocks from a particular set have expired. Semantics for SPADES is given in terms of stochastic automata [11]. IGSMP uses clocks to record spent lifetimes. The clocks have an associated expiration time distribution. When a clock expires other clocks are redistributed according to the time that has passed. IGSMP semantics is given using generalized semi-Markov processes extended with actions. An interesting feature is the definition of the alternative composition modeled as a probabilistic choice between differently distributed clocks. NMSPA exploits random variables for the distribution of stochastic delays of actions. Also here, expiration of a stochastic delay induces redistribution of other variables according to the time that has passed. The semantics is given in terms of transition systems. The alternative composition is defined over an arbitrary number of summands in order to achieve maximal progress for internal actions. In NMSPA alternative composition of discrete stochastic delays followed by an internal action represents an inherent probabilistic choice. Other stochastic PAs that we mention here are the extension of LOTOS for performance analysis of distributed systems, the stochastic π-calculus and TIPP [12, 13, 14]. More details can be found in the overview papers [15, 16].

The main goal of our paper is to deal with standard real-time in stochastic PAs with an semantics that exploits spent-time and avoids explicit clocks. Our aims is to report on preliminary research on the conservative extension of real-time process algebra where delays are governed by probabilistic distributions. To this end, we consider a stochastic PA with immediate actions, deadlock and termination. We model stochastic delays as timed delays guided by discrete random variables, as we wish to distinguish between actions and stochastic delays, similar to IMC [7]. The alternative composition implements weak choice between immediate actions and passage of time similar to real-time PAs in the style of [1]. Here, we give the semantics in terms of stochastic transition systems. In comparison to other stochastic PA our approach is closest to NMSPA. Unlike NMSPA, we define alternative composition on two processes rather than on arbitrary sums and, in our setting, the alternative composition makes no choice in case both summands can delay together as in the real-time PAs. We propose an appropriate version of stochastic bisimulation for our setting, which is a congruence. α-conversion is introduced to pave the way for a treatment of the parallel operator. However, as we show, no expansion law is available in this set-up. We justify, via an embedding of transition systems, the proposed stochastic process algebra being called an extension of real-time process algebra. In our present work, we consider only discrete stochastic delays, mainly because they almost effortlessly model real-time delays as degenerated discrete random variables. Also, as a technical convenience, they allow two different delays to have the same duration, a property not shared by continuous distributions.

Related work. Surprisingly, there is not much work on embedding real-time into stochastic time PAs. Markovian PAs cannot embed real-time because they employ exponential distributions only. The extension of LOTOS for performance analysis is an extension of timed LOTOS with stochastic timers, but there are strong syntax restrictions and no embedding is given. We remind the reader that the semantics of SPADES [8] is given in terms of stochastic automata [11]. A structural translation from stochastic automata to timed automata with deadlines is given in [17]. The translation is shown to preserve timed traces, so SPADES can imitate real-time behaviour. There is a translation from IGSMP into pure real-time models termed Interactive Timed Automata (ITA) [9].

The rest of this paper is organized as follows. Section 2 gives the mathematical background for the stochastic delays. Section 3 introduces a basic stochastic PA with alternative composition and stochastic delay prefix. Section 4 provides the transition system and a notion of stochastic bisimulation, for which congruence properties are given. We define in Section 5 a variant of α-conversion to support the operational semantics. Sections 6 and 7 discuss the parallel operator and the embedding of real-time process theories. Section 8 wraps up with concluding remarks. For the complete proofs we refer to the full version of the paper [19].

2   Preliminaries

We denote the set of discrete random variables by $\mathcal{V}$. For $S \subseteq \mathcal{V}$, $y \in \mathbb{R}$ and $\diamond$ either $<, >, =$, we write $S \diamond y$ for $X \diamond y$, $X \in S$. We use X, Y and Z for random variables and $F_X(t)$, $F_Y(t)$ and $F_Z(t)$, for $t \geq 0$, for their distribution functions, unless stated otherwise. For durations of a stochastic delay we have $F_X(t) = 0$ for $t < 0$ and we denote the set of such discrete distribution functions by $\mathcal{F}_d$. The support set of random variable X, denoted by $\mathrm{supp}(X)$ contains the values for which $P(X = t) > 0$. By $\overline{F}_X(t)$ we denote the residual distribution function $1 - F_X(t)$. We extend the notion of support set to a set S of random variables by $\mathrm{supp}(S) = \bigcap_{X \in S} \mathrm{supp}(X)$.

A *stochastic delay* is a time delay which duration is guided by a random variable. It is discrete if the random variable is discrete. The notions of stochastic delay and random variable are used interchangeably depending on the context. We observe simultaneous passage of time for a number of stochastic delays until at least one of their duration passes. This phenomenon is referred to as the *race condition*. In general, simultaneous multiple stochastic delays can be observed as being the shortest; the shortest duration itself can be different and provided by different delays in different observations. Observing several stochastic delays we call a *race*. The stochastic delay or delays that have the shortest duration are called 'winners'. The other ones are called 'losers' of the race.

In general, if one observes a race of a set of random variables $V \subseteq \mathcal{V}$, the resulting delay of the race will be distributed as the minimum $\min(V)$ of these random variables with a distribution function $F_{\min(V)}(t) = 1 - \prod_{X \in V} \overline{F}_X(t)$. The probability that the winners are in the set $W \subseteq V$ is

$$P(W = \min(V)) = \sum_{t \in \mathrm{supp}(W)} P(W = t, (V \setminus W) > t).$$

The stochastic delay performed by the winners, is distributed as

$$P(\langle\, X \mid W = \min(V)\,\rangle = t) = \frac{P(W = t, (V \setminus W) > t)}{P(W = \min(V))},$$

for any $X \in W$. We use angle brackets to denote conditional random variables.

Because of associativity and commutativity of the minimum of random variables, it holds that simultaneous observation of all delays amounts to the same as iterated observation of disjoint sets.

3   Basic Processes with Discrete Stochastic Time

In this section we introduce $\mathrm{BSP}^{\mathrm{dst}}(\mathcal{A}, \mathcal{V})$, a stochastic PA with immediate actions, termination and deadlock, that implements weak choice between actions and time. We refer to $\mathrm{BSP}^{\mathrm{dst}}$ as Basic Process Theory with Discrete Stochastic Time. The terminology is adopted from [18] and we build on the untimed version $\mathrm{BSP}(\mathcal{A})$. Here, $\mathcal{A}$ is the set of actions and $\mathcal{V}$ is the set of random variables. A new unary operator scheme $\sigma_X._{-}$ for $X \in \mathcal{V}$ represents stochastic delays.

The process $\sigma_X.p$ executes a stochastic delay guided by the random variable X and continues behaving as p. Because of the race condition, one cannot observe the execution of a stochastic delay in isolation. Informally, an example of a transition system that corresponds to a race between two discrete stochastic delays is depicted in Fig. 1.

Fig. 1. Race condition   **Fig. 2.** Weak choice

The relations in the brackets give the condition that enables the transition. Each $\mapsto$ transition represents a stochastic delay. The label shows the winners of the race and their observed duration. The duration is determined by the support set of the winning delay. For clarity, we represent all the transitions by a single transition scheme. For example, the transitions of the stochastic delay guided by X in Fig. 1 are represented by one transition scheme labeled by X and d_X. The observed winning duration d_X takes its values from $\mathrm{supp}(\langle\, X \mid X < Y\,\rangle)$. Thus, the transition scheme replaces $|\mathrm{supp}(\langle\, X \mid X < Y\,\rangle)|$ different transitions, each executed with its own probability.

When considering the interaction of action transitions and termination versus stochastic delay, we employ weak choice, i.e. a non-deterministic choice between immediate actions, termination and passage of time. The alternative composition depicted in Fig. 2 allows execution of the stochastic delay in the rightmost transition even though the choice is made between an immediate action and passage of time. As a consequence, the losers of the race become dependent on the amount of time that has passed for the winners as in Fig. 1. Thus, the random variables of the remaining stochastic delays do not retain their initial distributions. Another issue we consider is the interaction between immediate actions and zero duration delays. Similar to the timed process theories [1, 2] we take zero duration not to disable immediate actions, as depicted by the middle transition in Fig. 2. Note that the immediate action is enabled only if $F_Y(0) \neq 1$. In order to distinguish between zero and non-zero transitions, we use the notation d_X^+ to denote only positive durations.

In an alternative composition of two stochastic delays, we obtain three transitions. In case the winner is the first summand, one obtains the leftmost transition. The rightmost transition is obtained when the winner is the second summand. The middle transition shows that both delays win the race together with non-zero probability. In this case, the race cannot determine one winner and passage of time does not determine a choice similar as for the real-time setting.

In Fig. 1, the altered probability distributions of X and Y are denoted by X' and Y', respectively. They are termed 'aged' probability distributions of X and Y by the duration d_Y and d_X, respectively. The probability distribution of X' is the aged probability distribution of X by d_Y given by

$$F_{X'}(t) = P(X \leq t \mid X > Y, Y = d_Y) = \frac{F_X(t + d_Y) - F_X(d_Y)}{1 - F_X(d_Y)}.$$

In order to calculate the actual distribution functions in each state, we require the original distribution function and its age. In order to keep track of the ages of the stochastic delays we introduce an environment to the transition system. The basic idea underlying the environments is that they store the actual distribution function of the random variables. The following definition and property of aging justify the use of environments.

Definition 1. *A distribution function F can be 'aged' by a time duration $d \geq 0$ if $F(d) < 1$. The resulting distribution $F|d$ is $(F|d)(t) = \frac{F(t+d) - F(d)}{1 - F(d)}$.*

If the conditions of Definition 1 are fulfilled, then $F|d$ is again a distribution function. We have that iterative application of the aging function is the same as aging the function once by the sum of the time durations (for proof see [19]), i.e.

$$(\ldots (F|d_1) \ldots)|d_n = F|\left(\sum_{i=1}^n d_i\right).$$

Using this property one easily calculates the age of the losers after each stochastic delay transition by adding the duration for the winners to the existing ages.

The environment is implemented using two injective functions: $\Phi \colon \mathcal{V} \to \mathcal{F}_d$ for the distribution functions and $\Delta \colon \mathcal{V} \to \mathbb{R}_0^+ \cup \{\bot\}$ for the age of the stochastic delays. We add the special symbol $\bot$ to denote that no time has passed for the stochastic delay, i.e. the delay has not participated in a race yet. Note that this is not the same as saying that the delay is of age zero. Having age zero means that the variable has lost a race with a zero duration and, ultimately, that disabled its possible zero duration transitions. Thus, we have to extend the domain of $|$ to $|: \mathcal{F}_d \times (\mathbb{R}_0^+ \cup \{\bot\}) \to \mathcal{F}_d$. We put $F|\bot = F$, $x + \bot = x$, for $x \in \mathbb{R}_0^+$, and we write $\mathbb{R}_\bot^+$ instead of $\mathbb{R}_0^+ \cup \{\bot\}$. We consider a well-defined environment to be a pair of two injective functions $(\Phi, \Delta) \in \mathcal{F}_d^{\mathcal{V}} \times \mathbb{R}_\bot^{+\mathcal{V}}$ such that for all $X \in \mathcal{V}$ the probability distribution function $\Phi(X) \mid \Delta(X)$ is defined. The set of well-defined environments is denoted by Env. Next, we introduce the signature of $\mathrm{BSP}^{\mathrm{dst}}$ and describe its constants and operators.

Definition 2. *The signature of* $\mathrm{BSP}^{\mathrm{dst}}$ *contains the two constants* δ *and* ϵ, *the two unary operator schemes* $a._-$, *for* $a \in A$ *and* $\sigma_X._-$, *for* $X \in \mathcal{V}$ *and the binary operator* $_- + _-$. *The syntax of* $\mathrm{BSP}^{\mathrm{dst}}$ *is given by*

$$P ::= \delta \mid \epsilon \mid a.P \mid \sigma_X.P \mid P + P,$$

with $a \in A$ *and* $X \in \mathcal{V}$. *The set of closed terms over the signature of* $\mathrm{BSP}^{\mathrm{dst}}$ *is denoted by* $\mathcal{C}(\mathrm{BSP}^{\mathrm{dst}})$ *and it is ranged over by* p, q *and* r.

We adopt the signature from $\mathrm{BSP}(\mathcal{A})$ [18] where immediate constants and actions are denoted by $\tilde{\tilde{\delta}}$, $\tilde{\tilde{\epsilon}}$ and $\tilde{\tilde{a}}$. However, here, we do not use the $\approx$-notation. The constant δ represents an immediate deadlock which does not allow passage of time. Immediate termination ϵ terminates without allowing any time to pass. The unary operator scheme $a.p$, for $a \in A$, comprises processes that execute the action a without consuming any time and continue behaving as p. The unary operator scheme $\sigma_X.p$ provides processes that execute a stochastic delay guided by the random variable X and afterwards continue behaving as p. The alternative composition behaves differently depending on three different contexts. It makes a non-deterministic choice between actions, a weak choice between actions, successful termination and stochastic delays, and imposes a race condition on stochastic delays.

4   Structural Operational Semantics

First, we define a *stochastic transition system* (STS) that deals with aging of distributions as informally discussed in the example of Fig. 1. The transitions of the STS are performed in an environment that keeps track of the up-to-date distribution functions of the racing stochastic delays. It contains the distribution functions for the random variables and the age of the delays.

Definition 3. *STS is a structure* $STS = (\mathcal{S}, (\Phi, \Delta), \to, \mapsto, \downarrow)$ *where*

- $\mathcal{S}$ *is a set of states labeled by closed* $\mathrm{BSP}^{\mathrm{dst}}$-*terms;*
- $(\Phi, \Delta) \in$ Env *is a well-defined environment;*
- $\to \subseteq \mathcal{S} \times$ Env $\times A \times \mathcal{S} \times$ Env *is a labeled transition relation;*
- $\mapsto \subseteq \mathcal{S} \times$ Env $\times 2^{\mathcal{V}} \times \mathbb{R}_0^+ \times \mathcal{S} \times$ Env *is a stochastic delay (probabilistic) transition relation;*
- $\downarrow \subseteq \mathcal{S}$ *is an immediate termination predicate.*

For $\to$ and $\mapsto$ we will use infix notation. By $\langle p, (\Phi, \Delta) \rangle \xrightarrow{a} \langle p', (\Phi, \Delta') \rangle$ we denote that a process term p in the environment (Φ, Δ) does an action transition with the label a to the term p' and changes the environment to (Φ, Δ'). By $\langle p, (\Phi, \Delta) \rangle \xmapsto{S}_{d_S} \langle p', (\Phi, \Delta') \rangle$ we denote that a term p in the environment (Φ, Δ) exhibits a passage of time of duration d_S, transforms to p' and changes the environment to (Φ, Δ'). The observed time is a result of a race won by the set of stochastic delays that are guided by the set of random variables S. The possible durations of the winners are determined by $d_S \in \text{supp}(\langle\, X \mid S = \min(\text{rd}(p))\,\rangle)$, where $\text{rd}(p)$ (we define this function later) is the set of racing delays of p and $X \in S$. In case there is a separation between zero duration and non-zero duration, we denote the non-zero durations by $d_S^+ > 0$. The random variables $X \in \mathcal{V}$ obtain their probability distributions as $F_X = \Phi(X) \mid \Delta(X)$. The race changes the age binding function Δ by setting age $\perp$ to every winning stochastic delay and increasing the ages of the losing delays by d_S.

Since all transitions only change the 'age parameter' Δ that assigns the ages, we suppress Φ and use the shorthand Δ for the environment (Φ, Δ). The STS represents a scheme because we leave implicit the conditions that enable the transitions and we parameterize multiple delay transitions by their support set. Also, we write X for $\{X\}$ and d_X for $d_{\{X\}}$ in the transition labels.

We introduce the the set of all age parameters as $\text{Del} = \mathbb{R}_\perp^{+\mathcal{V}}$. In case we wish to give a transition system for a specific term $p \in \mathcal{C}(\text{BSP}^{\text{dst}})$ we write $STS(p, (\Phi, \Delta_0))$, where (Φ, Δ_0) is the initial environment. We denote the set of STS's as $\mathcal{STS}$.

The sets of winning stochastic delays are given as labels of the probabilistic transitions. However, not all stochastic delays participate in a race at the same time. So, we have to identify only the racing stochastic delays, i.e. the ones that participate in the race. A function named $\text{rd} \colon \mathcal{C}(\text{BSP}^{\text{dst}}) \to 2^{\mathcal{V}}$ extracts the random variables that guide the racing delays of a process term. They are identified as all stochastic delays that are directly connected by alternative composition.

$$\text{rd}(\epsilon) = \emptyset \quad \text{rd}(a.p) = \emptyset \quad \text{rd}(\delta) = \emptyset \quad \text{rd}(\sigma_X.p) = \{X\} \quad \text{rd}(p + q) = \text{rd}(p) \cup \text{rd}(q)$$

In order to provide a concise presentation of the operational semantics, we define two functions res and age which alter the age parameter Δ of the environment. The function res resets the images of the winners to $\perp$, whereas age ages the losers by the duration observed for the winners.

Definition 4. *For an environment Δ, a set of winners $W \subseteq \mathcal{V}$ and a set of losers $L \subseteq \mathcal{V}$ of a race of duration d, the functions* $\text{res} \colon \text{Del} \times 2^{\mathcal{V}} \to \text{Del}$ *and* $\text{age} \colon \text{Del} \times 2^{\mathcal{V}} \times \mathbb{R}_0^+ \to \text{Del}$ *are defined as*

$$\text{res}(\Delta, W) = \begin{cases} \Delta(X) & \text{if } X \notin W \\ \perp & \text{if } X \in W \end{cases} \qquad \text{age}(\Delta, L, d) = \begin{cases} \Delta(X) & \text{if } X \notin L \\ \Delta(X) + d & \text{if } X \in L. \end{cases}$$

Next, we give the structural operational semantics for $\mathrm{BSP}^{\mathrm{dst}}$.

$$1\ \langle \epsilon, \Delta \rangle \downarrow \quad 2\ \frac{\langle p, \Delta \rangle \downarrow}{\langle p+q, \Delta \rangle \downarrow} \quad 4\ \langle a.p, \Delta \rangle \xrightarrow{a} \langle p, \Delta \rangle \quad 5\ \langle \sigma_X.p, \Delta \rangle \xmapsto{X}_{d_X} \langle p, \mathrm{res}(\Delta, \{X\}) \rangle$$

$$6\ \frac{\langle p, \Delta \rangle \xrightarrow{a} \langle p', \Delta' \rangle,\ \langle q, \Delta \rangle \not\mapsto}{\langle p+q, \Delta \rangle \xrightarrow{a} \langle p', \Delta' \rangle} \qquad 7\ \frac{\langle p, \Delta \rangle \xrightarrow{a} \langle p', \Delta' \rangle,\ \langle q, \Delta \rangle \xmapsto{T}_{d_T^+} \langle q', \Delta'' \rangle}{\langle p+q, \Delta \rangle \xrightarrow{a} \langle p', \mathrm{res}(\Delta', \mathrm{rd}(q)) \rangle}$$

$$10\ \frac{\langle p, \Delta \rangle \xmapsto{S}_0 \langle p', \Delta' \rangle,\ \langle q, \Delta \rangle \not\mapsto}{\langle p+q, \Delta \rangle \xmapsto{S}_0 \langle p'+q, \Delta' \rangle} \qquad 11\ \frac{\langle p, \Delta \rangle \xmapsto{S}_{d_S^+} \langle p', \Delta' \rangle,\ \langle q, \Delta \rangle \not\mapsto}{\langle p+q, \Delta \rangle \xmapsto{S}_{d_S^+} \langle p', \Delta' \rangle}$$

$$14\ \frac{\langle p, \Delta \rangle \xmapsto{S}_{d_S} \langle p', \Delta' \rangle,\ \langle q, \Delta \rangle \xmapsto{T}_{d_T} \langle q', \Delta'' \rangle,\ d_S < d_T}{\langle p+q, \Delta \rangle \xmapsto{S}_{d_S} \langle p'+q, \Delta''' \rangle},$$
$$\text{where } \Delta''' = \mathrm{age}(\Delta', \mathrm{rd}(q), d_S)$$

$$16\ \frac{\langle p, \Delta \rangle \xmapsto{S}_{d_S} \langle p', \Delta' \rangle,\ \langle q, \Delta \rangle \xmapsto{T}_{d_T} \langle q', \Delta'' \rangle,\ d_S = d_T}{\langle p+q, \Delta \rangle \xmapsto{S \cup T}_{d_{S \cup T}} \langle p'+q', \Delta''' \rangle},$$
$$\text{where } \Delta''' = \mathrm{res}(\mathrm{age}(\Delta, \mathrm{rd}(p+q), d_{S \cup T}), S \cup T)$$

Rules 1, 2, and 4 are the standard rules for termination and action prefix. Rule 5 states that stochastic delays $\sigma_X.p$ allow passage of time sampling from $\Phi(X)|\Delta(X)$. The non-deterministic choice made by action transitions from the first summand is shown by Rule 6 when the second summand cannot do a stochastic delay and by Rule 7 when it can do a stochastic delay with non-zero duration. Rule 10 states that zero delay of p does not enforce a choice, still allowing action transitions from q. In case p does perform a non-zero delay as in Rule 11 weak choice is enabled between action transitions and passage of time, where passage of time disables the action transitions of q. Rule 14 describes the race in case when the first summand wins the race. The winners given by the set S perform a stochastic delay transition with duration d_S. The racing delays of the losing summand ($\mathrm{rd}(q)$) are aged by d_S using the function age and the environment of the winner Δ' (in which the losers of the first summand are already aged). Note that since the second summand can perform a stochastic delay $d_T > d_S$, the aging of its racing delays is allowed. Rule 16 states that if both summands have stochastic delays that can win with the same duration, the joint race enabled by the alternative composition can be won by the union of the winners of the both summands. The new environment is obtained by aging all racing delays of both summands in the original environment and resetting the winners. (Because of lack of space we omit the symmetric rules 3, 8, 9, 12, 13 and 15, analogous to 2, 6, 7, 10, 11 and 14.)

Next, we define when two STS's are bisimilar. Intuitively, two STS should be bisimilar if related states (1) do the same action transitions, (2) have the same termination options and (3) go to another class of states with the same accumulative probability of performing a stochastic delay with the same duration. The following definition defines the accumulative probability of (3).

Definition 5. *Let R be an equivalence relation on $S \times \mathrm{Env}$, $C \in (S \times \mathrm{Env})/R$ an arbitrary class and $(\Phi, \Delta) \in \mathrm{Env}$, where $S \subseteq C(\mathrm{BSP}^{\mathrm{dst}})$. By $\mathrm{ws}(p, \Delta, C, d)$ we define the set of sets of winning stochastic delays that p can do in time d and afterwards transform into a process that belongs to the class C, i.e.*

$$\mathrm{ws}(p, \Delta, C, d) = \bigcup\nolimits_{\langle p', \Delta' \rangle \in C} \{ \, S \subseteq \mathrm{rd}(p) \mid \langle p, \Delta \rangle \stackrel{S}{\mapsto}_d \langle p', \Delta' \rangle \, \}.$$

The accumulative probability of doing a transition from a term to an equivalence class in time d is given as

$$\mathrm{ap}(p, \Delta, C, d) = \begin{cases} 0 & \mathrm{ws}(p, \Delta, C, d) = \emptyset \\ \sum_{S \in \mathrm{ws}(p, \Delta, C, d)} P(S = \min(\mathrm{rd}(p)), S = d) & \mathrm{ws}(p, \Delta, C, d) \neq \emptyset. \end{cases}$$

Next, we define strong bisimulation on STS's.

Definition 6. *A strong bisimulation on $STS = (S, (\Phi, \Delta), \rightarrow, \mapsto, \downarrow)$ is an equivalence relation R on $S \times \mathrm{Env}$ such that the following conditions hold:*

1. *if $\langle p, \Delta \rangle \stackrel{a}{\rightarrow} \langle p', \Delta' \rangle$, then $\langle q, \Delta \rangle \stackrel{a}{\rightarrow} \langle q', \Delta' \rangle$, such that $(\langle p', \Delta' \rangle, \langle q', \Delta' \rangle) \in R$,*
2. *for all $d \geq 0$, it holds that $\mathrm{ap}(p, \Delta, C, d) = \mathrm{ap}(q, \Delta, C, d)$,*
3. *if $\langle p, \Delta \rangle \downarrow$ then $\langle q, \Delta \rangle \downarrow$,*

for all $p, p', q, q' \in S$ and all $C \in (S \times \mathrm{Env})/R$ such that $(\langle p, \Delta \rangle, \langle q, \Delta \rangle) \in R$.

Note that the second transfer condition implies that after doing a stochastic delay, both terms must result again in bisimilar terms. If $\langle p, \Delta \rangle$ and $\langle q, \Delta \rangle$ are related by a strong bisimulation we write $\langle p, \Delta \rangle \leftrightarrow \langle q, \Delta \rangle$. We also note, that if we consider the time duration as a constant in the transition system, we obtain the probabilistic bisimulation given in [20].

Theorem 7. *The bisimulation relation $\leftrightarrow$ is a congruence [19].*

5 α-Conversion

We proceed by analyzing a conflicting behaviour of the STSs defined so far that occurs when two racing delays are guided by the same random variable. Consider the following example.

Example 8. Suppose $p \equiv \sigma_X . \epsilon$. We observe $STS(p + p, (\Phi, \Delta))$. Consider the transition $\langle \sigma_X . \epsilon + \sigma_X . \epsilon, \Delta \rangle \stackrel{X}{\mapsto}_{d_X} \langle \epsilon + \sigma_X . \epsilon, \mathrm{res}(\mathrm{age}(\Delta, \{X\}, d_X), X) \rangle$. In the resulting environment, X is a random variable that guides both the winning and the losing stochastic delay. Such behavior leads to conflict because $\Delta(X)$ should contain both, $\perp$, because X won the race and d_X, because X lost the race. On the other hand, the term $p + p$ is not bisimilar to $\sigma_X . (\epsilon + \epsilon)$ because, in general, the distribution functions of X and $\min(X, X)$ are not equal. Therefore, we wish to express that the left and the right summand have equally distributed stochastic delays and the distribution function is provided by the random variable X.

We resolve the conflict by renaming one of the variables and ensuring that the original and the replacement have the same distribution. So, $\sigma_X.\epsilon + \sigma_X.\epsilon$ and $\sigma_X.\epsilon + \sigma_Y.\epsilon$ behave the same under the assumption that $F_X = F_Y$, because the behavior of the STS does not depend on the name of the variable, but on its distribution function. However, the second term has proper semantics, since there is no conflicting behavior in its STS. For an technical underpinning of this, we define the relation $\simeq_\alpha$ on $\mathcal{C}(\mathrm{BSP}^{\mathrm{dst}}) \times \mathrm{Env}$ as the least relation such that

$$\langle \delta, \Delta \rangle \simeq_\alpha \langle \delta, \Delta \rangle \qquad \langle \epsilon, \Delta \rangle \simeq_\alpha \langle \epsilon, \Delta \rangle \qquad \frac{\langle p, \Delta \rangle \simeq_\alpha \langle q, \Delta \rangle}{\langle a.p, \Delta \rangle \simeq_\alpha \langle a.q, \Delta \rangle}$$

$$\frac{\langle p, \Delta \rangle \simeq_\alpha \langle q, \Delta \rangle, \Phi(X) = \Phi(Y), \Delta(X) = \Delta(Y)}{\langle \sigma_X.p, \Delta \rangle \simeq_\alpha \langle \sigma_Y.q, \Delta \rangle} \qquad \frac{\langle p, \Delta \rangle \simeq_\alpha \langle q, \Delta \rangle, \langle p', \Delta \rangle \simeq_\alpha \langle q', \Delta \rangle}{\langle p + p', \Delta \rangle \simeq_\alpha \langle q + q', \Delta \rangle}$$

Clearly, $\simeq_\alpha$ is a congruence. In the literature, a relation as $\simeq_\alpha$ is referred to as α-congruence or α-conversion [13, 8].

We define a function $\mathrm{cv} \colon \mathcal{C}(\mathrm{BSP}^{\mathrm{dst}}) \to 2^{\mathcal{V}}$ to identify conflicting random variables that guide multiple stochastic delays in the same race. The function cv is defined using structural induction.

$$\mathrm{cv}(\epsilon) = \emptyset \qquad \mathrm{cv}(\delta) = \emptyset \qquad \mathrm{cv}(a.p) = \emptyset \qquad \mathrm{cv}(\sigma_X.p) = \emptyset$$
$$\mathrm{cv}(p + q) = \mathrm{cv}(p) \cup (\mathrm{rd}(p) \cap \mathrm{rd}(q)) \cup \mathrm{cv}(q).$$

If a term does not contain conflicting variables, we say that it is conflict-free. We characterize such terms using a predicate cf that checks whether the set of conflict variables in the current step is empty. Given a process term p, $\mathrm{cf}(p)$ is true if and only if $\mathrm{cv}(p) = \emptyset$.

We add an α-conversion rule to the structural operational semantics, viz.

$$(\alpha) \quad \frac{\langle q, \Delta \rangle \overset{S}{\mapsto}_{ds} \langle p', \Delta' \rangle, \ \mathrm{cf}(q), \ \mathrm{cf}(p'), \ p \simeq_\alpha q}{\langle p, \Delta \rangle \overset{S}{\mapsto}_{ds} \langle p', \mathrm{res}(\Delta', \mathrm{rd}(p') \setminus \mathrm{rd}(q)) \rangle}.$$

This rule guarantees that the stochastic delay transitions are performed as a result of a race which does not lead to conflicting behavior. This is achieved by finding an α-converted term that is conflict-free and performing the race with it. Note that the non-racing terms of p' can get an age in the process of α-converting p to q, so we have to reset them in the resulting environment. For example, α-converting $\sigma_Y.\sigma_X.\epsilon + \sigma_X.\epsilon$ to $\sigma_Y.\sigma_U.\epsilon + \sigma_X.\epsilon$, where $\Delta(X) \neq \bot$ results in $\Delta(U) \neq \bot$, but U has not participated in any race. In order to exclude conflicting behavior, we use the predicate cf.

This means that we have to adapt the operational semantics by adding an extra conflict-freeness condition for every state that has the option to perform a stochastic delay. For example, the adapted version of Rule 11 is:

$$11\alpha \quad \frac{\langle p, \Delta \rangle \overset{S}{\mapsto}_{d_S^+} \langle p', \Delta' \rangle, \ \langle q, \Delta \rangle \not\mapsto, \ \mathrm{cf}(p + q)}{\langle p + q, \Delta \rangle \overset{S}{\mapsto}_{ds} \langle p', \Delta' \rangle}.$$

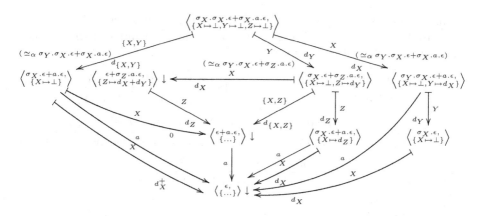

Fig. 3. Stochastic transition system of $\sigma_X.\sigma_X.\epsilon + \sigma_X.a.\epsilon$

The obtained theory is denoted as $\mathrm{BSP}^{\mathrm{dst}}_\alpha$. In the following we give an example of a STS in order to illustrate the operational semantics rules.

Example 9. In Fig. 3 we give the $STS(\sigma_X.\sigma_X.\epsilon + \sigma_X.a.\epsilon, (\Phi, \Delta_0))$, where initially $\Phi = \{X \mapsto F, Y \mapsto F, Z \mapsto F\}$ and $\Delta_0 = \{X \mapsto \bot, Y \mapsto \bot, Z \mapsto \bot\}$. Note that we give possible α-conversions in brackets for clarification, but it is not a part of the transition system.

Because of lack of space we do not present the equational theory of $\mathrm{BSP}^{\mathrm{dst}}_\alpha$, for which the reader is referred to [19]. Next, we investigate the behaviour of the parallel composition in the current setting.

6   Parallel Composition

We add an ACP-style parallel composition to the theory $\mathrm{BSP}^{\mathrm{dst}}_\alpha$ and obtain the theory of Basic Communication Processes with Discrete Stochastic Time and α-conversion $\mathrm{BCP}^{\mathrm{dst}}_\alpha(\mathcal{A}, \mathcal{V}, \gamma)$, where γ is the ACP-style communication function. As the parallel composition allows both interleaving and communication of immediate actions, in the present setting it should also cater for interleaving and synchronization of stochastic delays. Similarly to real-time PA's, we merge the delays in case the processes perform stochastic delays of different duration. We synchronize the processes in case their delays are of the same duration. Immediate actions always take precedence over time in the parallel composition, except when performing zero duration delays. It is important to perform all possible zero delays and afterwards the immediate actions because otherwise we may lose communication options. For example, $\sigma_X.a.\epsilon \parallel b.\epsilon$ should allow a and b to communicate if $F_X(0) \neq 0$.

The definitions of rd, cv and $\simeq_\alpha$ are extended straightforwardly to apply to a parallel process $p \parallel q$. We give the operational semantics of the parallel composition in the following table:

$$17\ \frac{\langle p, \Delta \rangle \downarrow, \langle q, \Delta \rangle \downarrow}{\langle p \parallel q, \Delta \rangle \downarrow}$$

$$18\ \frac{\langle p, \Delta \rangle \overset{S}{\mapsto}_0 \langle p', \Delta' \rangle, \ \langle q, \Delta \rangle \not\mapsto}{\langle p \parallel q, \Delta \rangle \overset{S}{\mapsto}_0 \langle p' \parallel q, \Delta' \rangle}$$

$$20\ \frac{\langle p, \Delta \rangle \overset{a}{\rightarrow} \langle p', \Delta' \rangle, \ \langle q, \Delta \rangle \not\mapsto}{\langle p \parallel q, \Delta \rangle \overset{a}{\rightarrow} \langle p' \parallel q, \Delta' \rangle}$$

$$22\ \frac{\langle p, \Delta \rangle \overset{a}{\rightarrow} \langle p', \Delta' \rangle, \ \langle q, \Delta \rangle \overset{T}{\mapsto}_{d_T^+} \langle q', \Delta'' \rangle}{\langle p \parallel q, \Delta \rangle \overset{a}{\rightarrow} \langle p' \parallel q, \mathrm{age}(\Delta', \mathrm{rd}(q), 0) \rangle}$$

$$24\ \frac{\langle p, \Delta \rangle \overset{a}{\rightarrow} \langle p', \Delta' \rangle, \ \langle q, \Delta \rangle \overset{b}{\rightarrow} \langle q', \Delta' \rangle, \ \gamma(a, b) = c}{\langle p \parallel q, \Delta \rangle \overset{c}{\rightarrow} \langle p' \parallel q', \Delta' \rangle}$$

$$25\ \frac{\langle p, \Delta \rangle \overset{S}{\mapsto}_{d_S} \langle p', \Delta' \rangle, \ \langle q, \Delta \rangle \overset{T}{\mapsto}_{d_T} \langle q', \Delta'' \rangle, \ d_S < d_T}{\langle p \parallel q, \Delta \rangle \overset{S}{\mapsto}_{d_S} \langle p' \parallel q, \Delta''' \rangle},$$
where $\Delta''' = \mathrm{age}(\Delta', \mathrm{rd}(q), d_S)$

$$27\ \frac{\langle p, \Delta \rangle \overset{S}{\mapsto}_{d_S} \langle p', \Delta' \rangle, \ \langle q, \Delta \rangle \overset{T}{\mapsto}_{d_T} \langle q', \Delta'' \rangle, \ d_S = d_T}{\langle p \parallel q, \Delta \rangle \overset{S \cup T}{\mapsto}_{d_{S \cup T}} \langle p' \parallel q', \Delta''' \rangle},$$
where $\Delta''' = \mathrm{res}(\mathrm{age}(\Delta, \mathrm{rd}(p \parallel q), d_{S \cup T}), S \cup T)$.

We briefly discuss the new rules. Rule 17 states when the parallel composition has the termination option. Rule 18 enables zero delays before immediate actions similar to the alternative composition. Rules 20 and 22 enable interleaving of actions, by allowing the left operand to perform an immediate action if the right one cannot delay or it can delay with positive duration, in which case the zero durations are disabled by aging of 0 in Rule 22. Rule 24 states that synchronization of actions can occur, only if their communication is defined by the communication function γ. Rule 25 enables the race condition, similar to the Rule 14 for the alternative composition. Rule 27 enables simultaneous passage of time for the left and right operand which allows synchronization of stochastic delays that exhibit the same duration. (Rules 19, 21, 23 and 26 are omitted as analogous to the rules 18, 20, 22 and 25.)

It is easily observed that the parallel operator is both commutative and associative. The proof for the action transitions is standard. Regarding stochastic delays, the properties follow immediately from the structural operational semantics. Note that the race imposed by the parallel operator is the same as for the alternative composition. In the following example we illustrate some problems introduced by the weak choice and the α-conversion for the parallel operator, ultimately leading to absence of a standard expansion law.

Example 10 (No expansion law for $\mathrm{BCP}_\alpha^{\mathrm{dst}}$). Let $p \equiv \sigma_X.\epsilon$ and $q \equiv \sigma_Y.\epsilon$. We observe their parallel composition $p \parallel q$ and $p \parallel q + q \parallel p + p \mid q$ as its standard expansion. Note that $p \parallel q$ can perform a delay guided by X if $P(X < Y) > 0$. Same holds for $q \parallel p$, whereas $p \mid q$ performs a delay if $P(X = Y) > 0$. Suppose (Φ, Δ) is the environment. Then $\langle \sigma_X.\epsilon, \Delta \rangle \overset{X}{\mapsto}_{d_X} \langle \epsilon, \Delta' \rangle$

and $\langle \sigma_Y.\epsilon, \Delta \rangle \overset{Y}{\mapsto}_{d_Y} \langle \epsilon, \Delta' \rangle$. Let us assume that $d_X < d_Y$. Then one obtains the transition $\langle \sigma_X.\epsilon \parallel \sigma_Y.\epsilon, \Delta \rangle \overset{X}{\mapsto}_{d_X} \langle \epsilon \parallel \sigma_Y.\epsilon, \Delta'' \rangle$, where $\Delta''(Y) = d_X$ and the transition system deadlocks.

Next, let us observe the process term obtained by the standard expansion law $\sigma_X.\epsilon \parallel \sigma_Y.\epsilon + \sigma_Y.\epsilon \parallel \sigma_X.\epsilon + \sigma_X.\epsilon \mid \sigma_Y.\epsilon$. This term has semantics only if it is first α-converted to $\sigma_X.\epsilon \parallel \sigma_Y.\epsilon + \sigma_{Y'}.\epsilon \parallel \sigma_{X'}.\epsilon + \sigma_{X''}.\epsilon \mid \sigma_{Y''}.\epsilon$, where $F_X = F_{X'} = F_{X''}$ and $F_Y = F_{Y'} = F_{Y''}$. Now, it is straightforward to observe that the parallel composition and its standard expansion do not have the same transition systems. For example, due to the weak choice the standard expansion term can do a stochastic delay guided by X, followed by a stochastic delay guided by Y' and aged by d_X and afterwards it finally deadlocks.

Based on the previous observations we conclude that the lack of total order on the durations of the stochastic delays and the presence of weak choice and α-conversion made it difficult to obtain a standard expansion law. However, because we retained the weak choice we are able to embed real-time in the STS's, which is presented in the following section.

7   Embedding Real Time in Stochastic Time

We consider the embedding of BCP^{srt} into $\text{BCP}^{\text{dst}}_\alpha$. $\text{BCP}^{\text{srt}}(\mathcal{A}, \gamma)$ is a real-time extension of $\text{BSP}(\mathcal{A})$ with parallel composition that allows synchronization of time delays with the same duration. It is a variant of the process algebra $\text{TCP}_{\text{srt}}(\mathcal{A}, \gamma)$ of [18] without sequential composition. Its semantics is given in terms of *timed transition systems* (TTS's).

Definition 11. *TTS is a structure* $TTS = (\mathcal{S}, \rightarrow, \mapsto, \downarrow)$ *where*

- $\mathcal{S}$ *is a set of states labeled by closed* BCP^{srt}*-terms;*
- $\rightarrow \subseteq \mathcal{S} \times \mathcal{A} \times \mathcal{S}$ *is a labeled transition relation;*
- $\mapsto \subseteq \mathcal{S} \times \mathbb{R}_0^+ \times \mathcal{S}$ *is a timed transition relation;*
- $\downarrow \subseteq \mathcal{S}$ *is an immediate termination predicate.*

Similarly to STSs, we use infix notation for $\rightarrow$ and $\mapsto$. By $\overset{t}{\mapsto}$ we denote that time $t \geq 0$ has passed. The TTS of a term p is denoted by $TTS(p)$. We denote the set of TTSs by $\mathcal{TTS}$.

The embedding of TTSs into STSs is given by an embedding of BCP^{srt}-terms in $\text{BCP}^{\text{dst}}_\alpha$-terms that will effectively replace each timed delay of duration d by a stochastic delay guided by a degenerated random variable X_{d}, such that $P(X_{\text{d}} = d) = 1$. The restrictions to degenerated random variables are denoted by a subscript deg. The embedding is given by the mapping $\xi \colon \mathcal{TTS} \rightarrow \mathcal{STS}$:

$$\xi(TTS(p)) = STS(\varepsilon(p), (\Phi_{\text{deg}}, \Delta_\perp)),$$

where Φ_{deg} is restricted to degenerated distributions, $\Delta_\perp(X) = \perp$, for all $X \in \mathcal{V}_{\text{deg}}$ and the mapping $\varepsilon \colon \mathcal{C}(\text{BCP}^{\text{srt}}) \rightarrow \mathcal{C}(\text{BCP}^{\text{dst}}_\alpha)$ is given by:

$$\varepsilon(\epsilon) = \epsilon \qquad \varepsilon(\delta) = \delta \qquad \varepsilon(a.p) = a.\varepsilon(p)$$
$$\varepsilon(\sigma^t.p) = \sigma_{X_t}.\varepsilon(p) \qquad \varepsilon(p+q) = \varepsilon(p) + \varepsilon(q) \qquad \varepsilon(p \parallel q) = \varepsilon(p) \parallel \varepsilon(q).$$

Note that because of the degenerated distributions the stochastic transition system only deals with the probabilities 0 and 1. Therefore, in that setting our bisimulation coincides with strong timed bisimulation of [18], were only the durations of delays are required to match. We observe that only one of the operational rules 12, 13 and 14 is applicable at the same time and the stochastic delay with the shortest duration wins. Moreover, we realize that in this setting there is no need for α-conversion, since all stochastic delays guided by the same random variable either win the race together or age the same duration of time together. The behavior of the zero delay is captured by the rules 8 and 10 and the weak choice by the rules 9 and 11. The time interpolation of the real-time PA's is embedded by aging the racing delays by the interpolation time.

Taking all together we have the following theorem.

Theorem 12. *The mapping $\xi \colon TTS \to STS$ is an embedding.*

The proof of the theorem can be found in [19]. Next we give an example to illustrate the embedding.

Example 13. In Fig. 4, we have for the term $p \equiv \sigma^{t+s}.a.\epsilon \parallel \sigma^t.(\sigma^s.b.\epsilon + a.\epsilon)$, for $s, t > 0$ and $\gamma(a, b) = c$ the original $TTS(p)$ on the left, and its embedding, the $STS(\varepsilon(p), (\Phi_{\mathrm{deg}}, \Delta_\perp))$ on the right, where $\varepsilon(p) = \sigma_{X_{t+s}}.a.\epsilon \parallel \sigma_{X_t}.(\sigma_{X_s}.b.\epsilon + a.\epsilon)$. We represent only the important part of the environment.

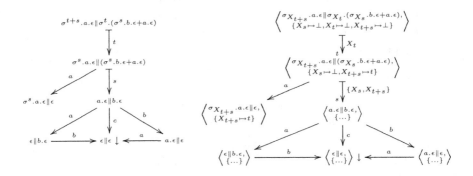

Fig. 4. Example embedding

8   Conclusion and Future Work

We have proposed a stochastic process algebra with immediate actions, termination and deadlock, and discrete distributions as an extension of un-timed process algebra. We introduced a notion of a stochastic transition system and gave a definition of strong bisimulation in that setting that conforms to the probabilistic bisimulation when considering the time as a constant and it corresponds to strong timed bisimulation when only considering probabilities of 0 and 1. We have argued that the bisimulation is a congruence. We showed conflicting behavior of the STS's and introduced α-conversion in order to deal with stochastic delays that are guided by conflicting variables.

We considered extending the algebra with parallel composition. However, expansion of the parallel operator using the alternative composition with weak choice turned out to be problematic. We identified the lack of total ordering on the durations observed by the stochastic delays as the main reason for failure of the standard expansion law when considering alternative composition with weak choice and α-conversion. However, because we retained the weak choice, we were able to propose an intuitive embedding of TTS into stochastic ones by restricting to discrete degenerated stochastic delays.

As future work we schedule an alternative way to obtain an expansion law for the parallel composition, as part of the identification of an axiomatic theory that conservatively extends the underlying real-time theory. Because of the semantical basis, we do not expect major difficulties when incorporating recursion. Also, we plan to extend the current setting with continuous stochastic time. Afterwards, we will consider case studies, especially in protocol verification (e.g. sliding window protocols), since successful modeling of real-time delays paves the way for an easy specification of time-outs.

Acknowledgment. We are grateful to Jos Baeten for his support, reviews and comments and for the many fruitful discussions on the topic.

References

1. Baeten, J., Middelburg, C.: Process Algebra with Timing. Monographs in Theoretical Computer Science. Springer (2002)
2. Nicollin, X., Sifakis, J.: An overview and synthesis of timed process algebras. In de Bakker, J., et al, eds.: Real-Time: Theory in Practice. Volume 600 of LNCS. Springer (1992) 526–548
3. Jonsson, B., Larsen, K.G.: Probabilistic extensions of process algebras. In Bergstra, J.A., Ponse, A., Smolka, S.A., eds.: Handbook of Process Algebras. Elsevier (2001)
4. Andova, S.: Time and probability in process algebra. In: AMAST '00, Springer (2000) 323–338
5. Bernardo, M., Gorrieri, R.: A tutorial on EMPA: A theory of concurrent processes with nondeterminism, priorities, probabilities and time. Theoretical Computer Science **202**(1–2) (1998) 1–54
6. Hillston, J.: A compositional approach to performance modelling. Cambridge University Press (1996)
7. Hermanns, H.: Interactive Markov Chains And the Quest For Quantified Quantity. Volume 2428 of LNCS. Springer (2002)
8. D'Argenio, P., Katoen, J.P.: A theory of stochastic systems, part II: Process algebra. Information and Computation **203**(1) (2005) 39–74
9. Bravetti, M.: Specification and Analysis of Stochastic Real-time Systems. PhD thesis, Universita di Bologna (2002)
10. Lopez, N., Nunez, M.: NMSPA: A non-markovian model for stochastic processes. In: DSVV'2000, IEEE Computer Society Press (2000)

11. D'Argenio, P., Katoen, J.P.: A theory of stochastic systems, part I: Stochastic automata. Information and Computation **203**(1) (2005) 1–38
12. Marsan, M.A., Bianco, A., Ciminiera, L., Sisto, R., Valenzano, A.: A LOTOS extension for the performance analysis of distributed systems. IEEE/ACM Trans. Netw. **2**(2) (1994) 151–165
13. Priami, C.: Stochastic π-calculus with general distributions. In Ribaudo, M., ed.: 4th Workshop on PAPM, Torino, Italy (1996) 41–57
14. Hermanns, H., Mertsiotakis, V., Rettelbach, M.: Performance analysis of distributed systems using TIPP. In Pooley, Hillston, King, eds.: UKPEW'94, University of Edinburgh (1994) 131–144
15. Katoen, J.P., D'Argenio, P.R.: General distributions in process algebra. In Brinksma, H., et al., eds.: Lectures on formal methods and performance analysis. Volume 2090 of LNCS. Springer (2001) 375–429
16. Bravetti, M., D'Argenio, P.: Tutte le algebre insieme. In Baier, C., et al, eds.: Validation of Stochastic Systems. Volume 2925 of LNCS. Springer (2004) 44–88
17. D'Argenio, P.: From stochastic automata to timed automata: Abstracting probability in a compositional manner. In Fiore, M., Fridlender, D., eds.: Proceedings of WAIT 2003. Associated to the 32 JAIIO., Buenos Aires, Argentina (2003)
18. Baeten, J.C.M., Reniers, M.A.: Timed process algebra (with a focus on explicit termination and relative-timing). In Bernardo, M., Corradini, F., eds.: Formal Methods for the Design of Real-Time Systems. Volume 3185 of LNCS. Springer (2004) 59–97
19. Markovski, J., de Vink, E.P.: Embedding real time in stochastic time process algebras. Technical Report CS 06/15, Technische Universiteit Eindhoven (2006)
20. Larsen, K.G., Skou, A.: Bisimulation through probabilistic testing. Information and Computation **94**(1) (1991) 1–28

Precise Regression Benchmarking with Random Effects: Improving Mono Benchmark Results

Tomas Kalibera and Petr Tuma

Distributed Systems Research Group, Department of Software Engineering
Faculty of Mathematics and Physics, Charles University
Malostranske nam. 25, 118 00 Prague, Czech Republic
Tel.: +420-221914232; Fax: +420-221914323
{kalibera, tuma}@nenya.ms.mff.cuni.cz

Abstract. Benchmarking as a method of assessing software performance is known to suffer from random fluctuations that distort the observed performance. In this paper, we focus on the fluctuations caused by compilation. We show that the design of a benchmarking experiment must reflect the existence of the fluctuations if the performance observed during the experiment is to be representative of reality.

We present a new statistical model of a benchmark experiment that reflects the presence of the fluctuations in compilation, execution and measurement. The model describes the observed performance and makes it possible to calculate the optimum dimensions of the experiment that yield the best precision within a given amount of time.

Using a variety of benchmarks, we evaluate the model within the context of regression benchmarking. We show that the model significantly decreases the number of erroneously detected performance changes in regression benchmarking. .

Keywords: performance evaluation, benchmark precision, random effects, regression benchmarking.

1 Introduction

Software performance engineering is generally understood as a systematic process of planning and evaluating software performance [1]. One of the principal approaches to evaluating performance is benchmarking, where the system under test executes a model task, called benchmark, and the observed performance is used for the evaluation. An important feature of benchmarking is that a choice of a realistic benchmark and a realistic configuration of the benchmarking experiment makes the observed performance representative of the performance of a real system. This makes benchmarking an indispensable complement of other approaches to evaluating performance based on modeling and simulation.

Both the performance of a benchmarking experiment and the performance of a real system are subject to random fluctuations. Well known causes of these fluctuations include for example the asynchronous device interrupts, whose often unpredictable occurrence can add the device interrupt service time to the observed

A. Horváth and M. Telek (Eds.): EPEW 2006, LNCS 4054, pp. 63–77, 2006.

performance. To keep the observed performance representative, benchmarking experiments typically measure the benchmark multiple times. Averaging over the multiple measurements is then used to filter out the random fluctuations. In [2], however, we show that this practice suffers from a lack of understanding of the causes of random fluctuations. Consequently, even after averaging, the performance of a benchmarking experiment is not necessarily representative of the performance of a real system.

In order to correctly understand the causes of random fluctuations in observed performance, a benchmarking experiment must be viewed as a sequence of steps. This sequence begins with the compilation of the benchmark and proceeds through booting of the system under test to the execution of the process implementing the benchmark and the measurement of the benchmark itself as the final steps. Importantly, each of the steps has the potential to influence the observed performance, and each of the steps can be subject to nondeterminism that makes the influence assume the form of random fluctuations. In [2], we illustrate this influence by showing how the choice of physical memory pages used to store the benchmark impacts the observed performance. This choice cannot be practically influenced and as such is one of the sources of nondeterminism in the execution of a benchmark.

The common practice of averaging can still be made to cover all the causes of random fluctuations. To achieve this, all the steps of the benchmarking experiment would have to be done once for each measurement, rather than just once for all the measurements. Unfortunately, some of the steps of the benchmarking experiment can take a long time and repeating them enough times to obtain enough measurements for a representative average would take a prohibitively long time. To avoid this problem, we propose a novel statistical model that reflects the understanding of the benchmarking experiment as a sequence of steps that can be repeated starting with any step of the experiment and finishing with the measurement step (e.g. compiling multiple times, executing each compiled binary multiple times, collecting multiple measurements for each execution).

The model makes it possible to derive the asymptotic distribution of the average of the observed performance, and use this distribution to create the asymptotic confidence interval for the mean observable performance, as well as determine the optimal ratio of the repetitions of the individual benchmark experiment steps. The model can describe benchmark experiments where at most three of the steps influence the observed performance, and is an extension of the model from [3] that could describe benchmark experiments where at most two of the steps influenced the observed performance.

As a proof of concept, we apply the statistical model in regression benchmarking. Regression benchmarking [4] is a new methodology for automated tracking of performance during software development. In our evaluation, we apply the methodology on omniORB [5] and Mono [6] as large open source projects with frequent changes. The omniORB platform is an open source implementation of the CORBA standard, consisting of an IDL compiler, an object request broker and object services, totaling almost 200k lines of code. The Mono platform is an open source implementation of the Common Language Infrastructure [7], also known as Microsoft .NET, consisting of a C# compiler, a virtual machine and application libraries, totaling almost 3M lines of code. Our evaluation relies on the Mono Regression Benchmarking Project [8], which tracks performance of daily Mono versions on several different benchmarks since August 2004, with the results continuously available on the web [8].

In the proof of concept, we focus on the nondeterminism in the compilation step of a benchmark experiment, thus complementing [3], where only the nondeterminism in the execution and measurement steps of a benchmark experiment is tackled. The quantification of the benefits is based on the percentage of "false alarms" in the form of spurious reports of performance changes by the regression benchmarking methodology, which can be reduced from as high as 50% when using the model from [3] to as low as 4% when using the proposed model.

The paper follows by analysis and quantification of the random effects of compilation in Section 2. A new statistical model that describes benchmarking experiments with random effects of compilation is described in Section 3. The model is evaluated in the context of the regression benchmarking methodology in Section 4. The paper is concluded in Section 5.

2   Problem of Random Effects of Compilation

The compilation of benchmarks for complex software is necessarily a complex task in itself. Using the example of the omniORB platform, compiling a typical benchmark includes compiling the core libraries, compiling and linking the IDL compiler, using this IDL compiler to generate stubs and skeletons, compiling the benchmark itself and linking the benchmark with the core libraries. Similarly, using the example of the Mono platform, compiling a typical benchmark includes compiling and linking the virtual machine, compiling the C# compiler using another bootstrap compiler and using this compiler to compile the core libraries and the benchmark itself. It is important to note that the process of compilation is not always entirely reproducible.

In [2], we have identified one particular source of nondeterminism in compilation of C++ code by the GNU C++ compiler [9]. The compiler generates random names for symbols defined in anonymous namespaces. As a consequence, the linker places these symbols in different locations within the binary for each compilation. During execution, a difference in the location of the symbols is reflected as a difference in the number of cache misses. This source of nondeterminism can influence the compilation of the omniORB platform, other sources of nondeterminism exist that can influence the compilation of the Mono platform.

It should be emphasized that various sources of nondeterminism exist in various processes of compilation [10]. These are frequently associated with the internal workings of a particular compiler on a particular platform. An exhaustive search for all sources of nondeterminism in compilation with the goal of eliminating them from benchmarking experiments is therefore not a feasible approach. To characterize how much the random effects of compilation impact the observed performance in a way that is independent of the particular sources of nondeterminism in compilation, we have introduced a metric called "impact factor of random effects of compilation" [2]. The metric is defined as a ratio of the standard deviation of the mean response times from different binaries to the standard deviation of the mean response times from the same binary. An impact factor of 1 indicates no impact of random effects on the response time, values larger than 1 indicate an impact of the random effects. The value of the impact factor is estimated by simulation (bootstrap). More details can be found in [2].

In Figure 1, we show the impact factors for selected benchmarks that cover a range of software applications. The Ping and Marshal benchmarks are omniORB benchmarks that assess remote method invocation, the other benchmarks are Mono benchmarks that assess remote method invocation, numerical computation and cryptography, see Appendix C and [8]. The figure also lists the variation of the results attributed to the random effects in compilation, related to the mean. Figure 1 shows that random effects of compilation influence results of almost all of the selected benchmarks. For these benchmarks, ignoring these effects can therefore mean that the performance of a benchmarking experiment will not be representative of the performance of a real system. The practical impact of relying on such benchmarking experiments depends on the particular use of the experiment. An evaluation in the context of regression benchmarking follows in Section 4.

Benchmark	Impact Factor	Relative (%) Variation
FFT	1.18	4.1
FFT (NA)	1.08	3.35
FFT (NA,OPT)	1.08	3.42
FFT (OPT)	1.13	4.41
HTTP	1.03	0.19
HTTP (OPT)	1.03	0.23

Benchmark	Impact Factor	Relative (%) Variation
Rijndael	1.01	0.38
Rijndael (OPT)	1.	0.38
TCP	1.05	0.56
TCP (OPT)	1.04	0.56
Marshal	1.05	2.
Ping	1.12	0.81

Fig. 1. Impact factor of random effects in compilation and relative variation caused by these effects for selected benchmarks

3   Benchmarking with Random Effects of Compilation

As suggested in Section 1, a simplistic solution to the problem of random effects of compilation is to repeat all the steps of the benchmarking experiment that preceed the measurement once for each measurement rather than just once for all the measurements, and to estimate the response time of the benchmark from the individual response times collected one in each measurement. Formally, the mean response time can be estimated by average and the precision of the estimate by an asymptotic confidence interval. Increasing the number of repetitions improves the precision, with an obvious drawback – the repetition of the compilation step takes too long.

In this section, we provide a statistical model of a benchmark experiment, that covers random effects at all three levels – compilation, execution and measurement. The model allows both to estimate the result precision and to choose the optimal number of measurements per execution and the optimal number of executions per binary. These numbers are optimal in respect that they minimize the time needed for the benchmarking experiment. The model is designed to be as generic as possible, so that it covers the widest possible range of benchmarks. In particular, the model works both for benchmarks where repeating measurements or executions helps as well as for benchmarks where it does not help. As a consequence, the model requires to always repeat the executions and measurements several times to adapt to a particular benchmark. This is not a problem, since compilation of large projects takes several orders of magnitude longer than execution or measurement.

3.1   Statistical Model of Benchmark with Random Effects

The intuitive idea behind the model is that the mean of measured response times in each execution is in fact a realization of a random variable, which is characteristic for the respective binary (the response times in an execution are prone to random effects). Similarly, the mean of this random variable is also in fact a realization of another random variable, which is characteristic for the respective software version (the execution means are prone to random effects).

We will now formalize the intuitive idea. Let $Y \sim F_Y\left(\mu_Y, \sigma_Y^2\right)$ denote a random operation response time in a given software version. The distribution F_Y of Y is unknown; we assume that it has finite mean μ_Y and finite variance σ_Y^2. The parameter of interest is the mean response time μ_Y.

We assume that response times in each benchmark execution are independent identically distributed (i.i.d.), with a finite variance σ_E^2 that is fixed for all executions in a given software version, and with a finite mean μ_E that differs for each execution. The parameter μ_E is in fact a sample from a random variable M_E. For better readability, we will write "μ_E" and "$Y|\mu_E$" instead of "M_E" and "$Y\,|\,[M_E = \mu_E]$":

$$E\left(Y|\mu_E\right) = \mu_E, \quad var\left(Y|\mu_E\right) = \sigma_E^2. \tag{1}$$

We assume that the execution mean times μ_E for each binary are random i.i.d., with a finite variance σ_B^2 that is fixed for all binaries in a given software version, and with a finite mean μ_B that differs for each binary:

$$E\left(\mu_E|\mu_B\right) = \mu_B, \quad var\left(\mu_E|\mu_B\right) = \sigma_B^2. \tag{2}$$

We assume that binary mean times μ_B for each software version are random i.i.d., with a finite mean μ_V and a finite variance σ_V^2, which are fixed for a given software version:

$$E\left(\mu_B\right) = \mu_V, \quad var\left(\mu_B\right) = \sigma_V^2. \tag{3}$$

In this model, $\mu_Y = \mu_V$. This can be easily shown using The Rule Of Iterated Expectations [11], which says that for random variables X and Y, assuming the expectations exist,

$$E\left[E(Y|X)\right] = E(Y): \tag{4}$$

$$\mu_Y = E(Y) =^{(4)} E\left[E(Y|\mu_E)\right] =^{(1)} E(\mu_E) =^{(4)}$$
$$= E\left[E(\mu_E|\mu_B)\right] =^{(2)} E(\mu_B) =^{(3)} \mu_V.$$

It can also be shown, that $\sigma_Y^2 = \sigma_E^2 + \sigma_B^2 + \sigma_V^2$, using The Rule Of Iterated Expectations and a known property of conditional variance [11], which says that for random variables X and Y,

$$var(Y) = E\left[var(Y|X)\right] + var\left[E(Y|X)\right]: \tag{5}$$

$$\sigma_Y^2 = var(Y) =^{(5)} E\left[var(Y|\mu_E)\right] + var\left[E(Y|\mu_E)\right] =^{(4),(1)}$$
$$= \sigma_E^2 + var(\mu_E) =^{(5)} \sigma_E^2 + E\left[var(\mu_E|\mu_B)\right] + var\left[E(\mu_E|\mu_B)\right] =^{(4),(2)}$$
$$= \sigma_E^2 + \sigma_B^2 + var(\mu_B) =^{(3)} \sigma_E^2 + \sigma_B^2 + \sigma_V^2.$$

The parameter of interest μ_Y is unknown, we will estimate it from the data: let us assume that we have compiled a given software version l times creating l binaries, and that we have executed each benchmark binary m times, getting n post–warmup measurements in each execution. In the rest of this section, we will show that μ_Y can be estimated by average of all the measurements

$$\overline{Y}_{\bullet\bullet\bullet} \overset{def}{=} \frac{1}{lmn} \sum_{k=1}^{l}\sum_{j=1}^{m}\sum_{i=1}^{n} Y_{ijk},$$

and that this estimate is asymptotically normal:

$$\overline{Y}_{\bullet\bullet\bullet} \approx N\left(\mu_Y, \frac{\sigma_E^2}{lmn} + \frac{\sigma_B^2}{lm} + \frac{\sigma_V^2}{l}\right). \tag{6}$$

Lemma 3.1. Let $X_1, ..., X_n$ be i.i.d. with mean μ and finite positive variance σ^2. Then, $\overline{X}_{\bullet}$ has asymptotically normal distribution: $\overline{X}_{\bullet} \approx N\left(\mu, \frac{\sigma^2}{n}\right)$. Lindeberg–Levy Central Limit Theorem.

Lemma 3.2. Let $X_1, ..., X_n$ be independent, $X_i \sim N\left(\mu_i, \sigma_i^2\right)$. From the properties of normal distribution [11], it follows that: $\overline{X}_{\bullet} \sim N\left(\overline{\mu}_{\bullet}, \overline{\sigma^2}_{\bullet}\right)$.

Lemma 3.3. Let $X \sim N\left(\mu_X, \sigma_X^2\right)$ and $Y|\left[X = x\right] \sim N\left(x, \sigma^2\right)$. Then, $Y \sim N\left(\mu_X, \sigma_X^2 + \sigma^2\right)$. The proof is outlined in Appendix A.

By Lemma 3.1 we have, from (1),(2),(3):

$$\overline{Y}_{kj\bullet}|\mu_{Ekj} \approx N\left(\mu_{Ekj}, \frac{\sigma_E^2}{n}\right), \tag{7}$$

$$\overline{\mu_E}_{k\bullet}|\mu_{Bk} \approx N\left(\mu_{Bk}, \frac{\sigma_B^2}{m}\right), \tag{8}$$

$$\overline{\mu_B}_{\bullet} \approx N\left(\mu_V, \frac{\sigma_V^2}{l}\right). \tag{9}$$

By applying Lemma 3.2 on (7),(8), we get by turns (10),(11). Then, by applying the same lemma again on (10), we get (12):

$$\overline{Y}_{k\bullet\bullet}|\overline{\mu_E}_{k\bullet} \approx N\left(\overline{\mu_E}_{k\bullet}, \frac{\sigma_E^2}{mn}\right) \tag{10}$$

$$\overline{\mu_E}_{\bullet\bullet}|\overline{\mu_B}_{\bullet} \approx N\left(\overline{\mu_B}_{\bullet}, \frac{\sigma_B^2}{lm}\right) \tag{11}$$

$$\overline{Y}_{\bullet\bullet\bullet}|\overline{\mu_E}_{\bullet\bullet} \approx N\left(\overline{\mu_E}_{\bullet\bullet}, \frac{\sigma_E^2}{lmn}\right) \tag{12}$$

By applying Lemma 3.3 on (9) and (11), we get

$$\overline{\mu_E}_{\bullet\bullet} \approx N\left(\mu_V, \frac{\sigma_B^2}{lm} + \frac{\sigma_V^2}{l}\right). \tag{13}$$

Finally, by applying Lemma 3.3 on (13) and (12), we get (6)   □

3.2   Change Detection

In regression benchmarking, we need to detect a performance change between two consecutive versions of selected software. Currently, we focus only on mean response time. In terms of the model described above, we want to detect a change, whenever μ_Y changes between two consecutive versions. Because we cannot assume to have a long period of versions without a change, we cannot directly use methods of change–point detection or quality control. The option of modifying some of these methods for regression benchmarking is left for future work.

Currently, we use a simple comparison method based on confidence intervals: we detect a change whenever confidence intervals for the mean from two consecutive versions do not overlap. The method is similar to the Approximate Visual Test described by Jain [12], where t–test is used to detect changes in case the center of one confidence interval falls into the other confidence interval.

The asymptotic confidence interval for μ_Y can be constructed using (6). We can estimate the unknown variances σ_E^2, σ_B^2 and σ_E^2 by S_E^2, S_B^2 and S_V^2 as follows:

$$S_E^2 = \frac{1}{lm(n-1)} \sum_{k=1}^{l} \sum_{j=1}^{m} \sum_{i=1}^{n} \left(Y_{kji} - \overline{Y}_{kj\bullet}\right)^2 \tag{14}$$

$$S_B^2 = \frac{1}{l(m-1)} \sum_{k=1}^{l} \sum_{j=1}^{m} \left(\overline{Y}_{kj\bullet} - \overline{Y}_{k\bullet\bullet} \right)^2 \tag{15}$$

$$S_V^2 = \frac{1}{l-1} \sum_{k=1}^{l} \left(\overline{Y}_{k\bullet\bullet} - \overline{Y}_{\bullet\bullet\bullet} \right)^2 \tag{16}$$

Since we do not assume normal distributions of μ_B, $\mu_E|\mu_B$ and $Y|\mu_E$, we cannot assume $\overline{Y}_{\bullet\bullet\bullet}$ to follow the t–distribution. We therefore have to rely on the asymptotic normality of $\overline{Y}_{\bullet\bullet\bullet}$, even after the estimates of the variances are used instead of the unknown variances. The asymptotic $(1 - \alpha)$ confidence interval for μ_Y used for change detection therefore is

$$\overline{Y}_{\bullet\bullet\bullet} \pm u_{1-\frac{\alpha}{2}} \sqrt{\frac{S_E^2}{lmn} + \frac{S_B^2}{lm} + \frac{S_V^2}{l}}, \tag{17}$$

where $u_\bullet$ is the quantile function of the standard normal distribution. Thus, the probability that μ_Y lies within this interval is asymptotically $(1 - \alpha)$.

3.3   Determining Optimum Number of Executions and Measurements

When detecting changes using confidence intervals as described above, the shorter the interval is, the higher is the chance of discovering a performance change. The width of the confidence interval (17) can be reduced only by proper selection of the numbers of measurements, executions and binaries – n, m, l, because the confidence level $(1 - \alpha)$ is fixed and the variance estimates S_E^2, S_B^2 and S_V^2 are properties of the given software version.

From (17), it is clear that increasing the number of binaries l always reduces the interval width. Increasing the number of executions m reduces the width only partially, because it does not reduce the impact of S_V^2 (random effects in compilation). Similarly, increasing the number of measurements n does not reduce the impact of S_B^2 (random effects in execution) and S_V^2 . On the other hand, increasing the number of measurements n is usually less expensive than increasing the number of executions m, which is in turn less expensive than increasing the number of compilations l. Therefore, optimum values of n and m should exist, that guarantee the shortest confidence interval given a fixed time for the benchmarking experiment. The optimum values would depend on S_E^2, S_B^2 and S_V^2. This intuitive idea will be formalized further in this section.

We define the cost c of a benchmarking experiment:

$$c = (b + (w + n) \cdot m) \cdot l, \tag{18}$$

where w is the number of measurements in the warm–up stage of each benchmark execution (price for a new execution) and b is the number of measurements that could be taken in the time needed for compilation (price for a new binary). The values of w and b have to be estimated or determined by experience, as discussed below. Our objective is to find m,n such that for the fixed cost c, $f(m,n,l)$ is minimal:

$$f(m,n,l) = \frac{S_E^2}{lmn} + \frac{S_B^2}{lm} + \frac{S_V^2}{l}. \tag{19}$$

After eliminating l using (18), $f(m,n)$ is

$$f(m,n) = \frac{mw + mn + b}{c} \cdot \left(\frac{S_E^2}{mn} + \frac{S_B^2}{m} + S_V^2 \right). \tag{20}$$

It is shown in Appendix B that the minimum is reached in

$$m_0 = \sqrt{\frac{b}{w} \cdot \frac{S_B^2}{S_V^2}}, \quad n_0 = \sqrt{w \cdot \frac{S_E^2}{S_B^2}}. \tag{21}$$

In practice, the length of the warm–up stage w depends on the benchmark platform and benchmark application and can be set by experience. It is important not to understate w in order to get relevant results [13]. The value of b can be estimated by experiments, it depends on the used compiler, the build scripts and the code size. From our experience, neither b nor w vary significantly between software versions. Still, the variances σ_E^2, σ_B^2 and σ_V^2 do vary between versions, and we have to collect enough measurements in enough executions for enough binaries to get variance estimates S_E^2, S_B^2, S_V^2. How much is enough depends on each benchmark and platform. With these estimates, we can calculate the confidence interval width (17), and if the width is too large, we can run an additional experiment with the optimum values of m and n using (21).

Some benchmarks measure only the response time of a part of a larger operation, where the whole operation is repeatedly invoked. An example of such a benchmark is the Marshal benchmark, which in fact repeatedly runs a remote procedure call, but measures only the marshaling part of the call. Let us assume that the measured operation takes q times less time than the repeated operation. The cost of the experiment is then still expressed in the number of measurements of the measured operation:

$$c = (b + (w + n) \cdot m \cdot q) \cdot l. \tag{22}$$

It is shown in Appendix B that the optimum numbers of measurements and executions are:

$$m_0 = \frac{1}{\sqrt{q}} \cdot \sqrt{\frac{b}{w} \cdot \frac{S_B^2}{S_V^2}}, \quad n_0 = \sqrt{w \cdot \frac{S_E^2}{S_B^2}}. \tag{23}$$

The optimum number of executions m_0 is smaller than in (21), because the cost of the execution has been understated compared to the cost of the compilation. The optimum number of measurements n is the same, because the cost of the measurement compared to the cost of the execution did not change: both in warm–up phase and non warm–up phase, the whole operation is repeated. The value of q can be estimated by experiments. By our experience, it does not vary significantly between software versions.

4   Evaluation

The evaluation of the proposed statistical model is done in the context of regression benchmarking [4]. The essential part of regression benchmarking is an automated comparison of observed performance between different software versions, with the goal of identifying instances of performance changes from version

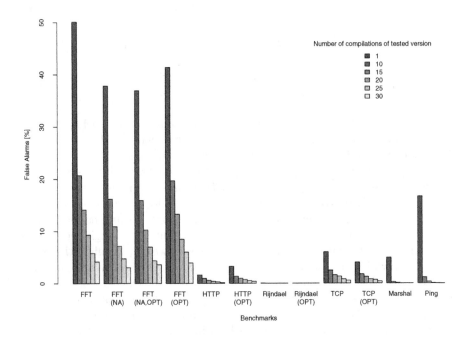

Benchmark	False Alarms (%) for Different Numbers of Compilations					
	1	10	15	20	25	30
FFT	50.09	20.69	14.09	9.29	5.79	4.15
FFT (NA)	37.80	16.16	10.88	7.13	4.74	3.04
FFT (NA,OPT)	36.88	15.87	10.22	6.96	4.36	3.61
FFT (OPT)	41.35	19.66	13.25	8.46	6.01	3.95
HTTP	1.64	0.95	0.59	0.40	0.27	0.13
HTTP (OPT)	3.29	1.38	0.96	0.72	0.51	0.37
Rijndael	0.03	0.01	0.02	0.02	0.00	0.01
Rijndael (OPT)	0.00	0.00	0.00	0.01	0.01	0.00
TCP	6.01	2.50	1.63	1.36	0.82	0.55
TCP (OPT)	4.03	1.77	1.29	0.84	0.70	0.41
Marshal	4.97	0.29	0.10	0.01	0.02	0.00
Ping	16.68	1.16	0.35	0.08	0.03	0.00

Fig. 2. Reduction of false alarms in regression benchmarking for different numbers of compilations. The same values are presented both in the graph and in the table.

to version. Regression benchmarking is therefore sensitive to random fluctuations in the observed performance, which exhibit themselves as "false alarms" – spurious reports of performance changes that are caused by the random fluctuations rather than differences between software versions.

The evaluation is made difficult by the fact that deciding whether a change in observed performance corresponds to a change between software versions requires manual analysis of the software versions in question. Such an analysis becomes prohibitively expensive when enough data for a statistically significant evaluation needs to be collected. We overcome this obstacle by comparing multiple benchmarking experiments on the same software version in place of multiple benchmarking experiments on multiple software versions. Then, all the detected changes are necessarily false alarms.

In more detail, the evaluation begins with compiling the same software version many times into a number of binaries, executing each binary a number of times and collecting a number of measurements from each execution. The exact numbers of compilations, executions and measurements are chosen to maximize the reliability of the evaluation. The evaluation proceeds with simulation (bootstrap). For each benchmark, the simulation is repeated a number of times, each time two groups of binaries are chosen by random and compared using the proposed statistical model. The results are shown in Figure 2, contrasted against the results obtained using the model from [3] with only a single binary per group.

The evaluation suggests that different benchmarks suffer from false alarms to different degrees. The FFT benchmarks suffer most – this can be explained by the fact that they use a lot of memory and are therefore sensitive to the performance of the memory cache. On the other hand, the Rijndael benchmark does not suffer from false alarms at all – the encryption and decryption is computationally intensive, but does not need much memory. It is also interesting that in omniORB benchmarks, the decrease in the number of false alarms with the growing number of binaries is much faster than in Mono benchmarks. We attribute this to the fact that the random effects of compilation in Mono benchmarks are more complex than in omniORB benchmarks.

5 Conclusion

The compilation of large applications is often a non–repeatable process. Compiling the same sources with the same compiler under the same settings can and often does result in different binaries that deliver different performance. As a result and contrary to the common practice, multiple binaries should be used for benchmarking. We show on a diverse set of benchmarks how using only a single binary for benchmarking can lead to severe distortion of the benchmark results.

We introduce a new statistical model of a benchmark experiment, one which allows to estimate the precision of benchmark results, taking into account the random effects in compilation, but also the random effects in benchmark execution described in [2] and the widely known random effects in individual measurements.

In addition to this, the model makes it possible to determine the optimum number of measurements within each benchmark execution and the optimum number of executions for each benchmark binary, which allows us to achieve the best possible precision for a given time limit on the benchmark experiment.

As an application of the model, we demonstrate a significant reduction of the number of erroneously detected performance changes between different versions of the same software in the context of regression benchmarking [4]. As a striking example, with 25 Mono binaries, the number of erroneous detections using a standard numerical benchmark falls down from 50% to 6%, as illustrated in Figure 2. This improvement is achieved by incorporating the random effects of compilation into the precision estimates of the results.

There are numerous related projects that track performance changes during software development, such as [14, 15]. Although these projects do not attempt to detect the changes in performance automatically, their results would benefit from using the proposed statistical model. At the time of this writing, we are not aware of any other project that would attempt to handle the problems associated with random effects of compilation in performance.

Acknowledgement. This work was partially supported by the Grant Agency of the Czech Republic project GD201/05/H014 and the Czech Academy of Sciences project 1ET400300504.

References

1. Smith, C.U., Williams, L.G.: Performance Solutions: A Practical Guide to Creating Responsive, Scalable Software. Addison–Wesley, Reading, MA, USA (2001)
2. Kalibera, T., Bulej, L., Tuma, P.: Benchmark precision and random initial state. In: Proceedings of SPECTS 2005, SCS (2005) 853–862
3. Kalibera, T., Bulej, L., Tuma, P.: Automated detection of performance regressions: The Mono experience. In: MASCOTS, IEEE Computer Society (2005) 183–190
4. Bulej, L., Kalibera, T., Tuma, P.: Repeated results analysis for middleware regression benchmarking. Performance Evaluation **60** (2005) 345–358
5. Lo, S.L., Grisby, D., Riddoch, D., Weatherall, J., Scott, D., Richardson, T., Carroll, E., Evers, D., , Meerwald, C.:   Free high performance orb. http://omniorb.sourceforge.net (2006)
6. Novell, Inc.: The Mono Project. http://www.mono-project.com (2006)
7. ECMA: ECMA-335: Common Language Infrastructure (CLI). ECMA (2002)
8. Distributed Systems Research Group: Mono regression benchmarking. http://nenya.ms.mff.cuni.cz/projects/mono (2005)
9. Free Software Foundation: The gnu compiler collection. http://gcc.gnu.org (2006)
10. Gu, D., Verbrugge, C., Gagnon, E.: Code layout as a source of noise in JVM performance. In: Component And Middleware Performance Workshop, OOPSLA 2004. (2004)
11. Wasserman, L.:   All of Statistics: A Concise Course in Statistical Inference. Springer, New York, NY, USA (2004)
12. Jain, R.: The Art of Computer Systems Performance Analysis: Techniques for Experimental Design, Measurement, Simulation, and Modeling. Wiley–Interscience, New York, NY, USA (1991)

13. Buble, A., Bulej, L., Tuma, P.: CORBA benchmarking: A course with hidden obstacles. In: IPDPS, IEEE Computer Society (2003) 279
14. DOC Group: TAO performance scoreboard. http://www.dre.vanderbilt.edu/stats/performance.shtml (2006)
15. Prochazka, M., Madan, A., Vitek, J., Liu, W.: RTJBench: A Real-Time Java Benchmarking Framework. In: Component And Middleware Performance Workshop, OOPSLA 2004. (2004)
16. Weisstein, E.W.: Mathworld–a wolfram web resource. http://mathworld.wolfram.com (2006)

A   Proof of Lemma 3.3

Let f be the probability density function of the normal distribution with mean μ and variance σ^2:

$$f(x; \mu, \sigma) = \frac{1}{\sigma\sqrt{2\pi}} exp\left(-\frac{(x-\mu)^2}{2\sigma^2}\right), \quad exp(z) = e^z.$$

The density functions of X and $Y|X$ from Lemma 3.3 are:

$$f_X(x) = f(x; \mu_X, \sigma_X), \quad f_{Y|X}(y|x) = f_{Y|x}(y) = f(y; x, \sigma).$$

By the definition of conditional density:

$$f_{Y,X}(y, x) = f_{Y|X}(y|x) \cdot f_X(x).$$

It follows, that:

$$f_Y(y) = \int f_{Y,X}(y, x)\, dx = \int f_{Y|X}(y|x) f_X(x) dx =$$

$$= \int \frac{1}{\sigma\sqrt{2\pi}} exp\left(-\frac{(y-x)^2}{2\sigma^2}\right) \cdot \frac{1}{\sigma_X\sqrt{2\pi}} exp\left(-\frac{(x-\mu_X)^2}{2\sigma_X^2}\right) dx =$$

$$= \int \frac{1}{\sigma\sqrt{2\pi}} exp\left(-\frac{(y-\mu_X-u)^2}{2\sigma^2}\right) \cdot \frac{1}{\sigma_X\sqrt{2\pi}} exp\left(-\frac{u^2}{2\sigma_X^2}\right) du =$$

$$= \int f(y-u; \mu_X, \sigma) f(u; 0, \sigma_X) du. \qquad |u = x - \mu_X$$

Lemma A.1. *Let $f(t; \mu_1, \sigma_1), f(t; \mu_2, \sigma_2)$ be density functions of normal variates. Then,*

$$\int f(\tau; \mu_1, \sigma_1) f(t - \tau; \mu_2, \sigma_2)) d\tau = f\left(t; \mu_1 + \mu_2, \sqrt{\sigma_1^2 + \sigma_2^2}\right).$$

In other words, convolution of Gaussians is also a Gaussian (Convolution, [16]).

By Lemma A.1:

$$f_Y(y) = \int f(y-u; \mu_X, \sigma) f(u; 0, \sigma_X) du = f\left(y; \mu_X, \sqrt{\sigma^2 + \sigma_X^2}\right),$$

and thus

$$Y \sim N(\mu_X, \sigma_X^2 + \sigma^2). \qquad \Box$$

B   Proof of (21) and (23)

We will show only (23), because (21) is a special case of (23), where $q = 1$. Let f, g be defined as follows:

$$g(l, m, n) = (b + (w + n) \cdot mq) \cdot l - c,$$

$$f(l, m, n) = \frac{S_E^2}{lmn} + \frac{S_B^2}{lm} + \frac{S_V^2}{l}.$$

Our objective is to find a minimum of $f(l, m, n)$, subject to the constraint $g(l, m, n) = 0$. Using Lagrange Multiplier Theorem [16], we can find l, m, n where the minimum must be, provided that the minimum exists. The partial derivatives are:

$$\left(\frac{\partial g}{\partial l}, \frac{\partial g}{\partial m}, \frac{\partial g}{\partial n} \right)(l, m, n) = ((w + n) \cdot mq + b, (w + n) \cdot ql, mql),$$

$$\left(\frac{\partial f}{\partial l}, \frac{\partial f}{\partial m}, \frac{\partial f}{\partial n} \right)(l, m, n) = \left(-\frac{S_E^2}{l^2 mn} - \frac{S_B^2}{l^2 m} - \frac{S_V^2}{l^2}, -\frac{S_E^2}{lm^2 n} - \frac{S_B^2}{lm^2}, -\frac{S_E^2}{lmn^2} \right).$$

By Lagrange Multiplier Theorem, the local extremum can only be in l, m, n, that solve the following system of equations:

$$\frac{\partial f}{\partial l}(l, m, n) + \lambda \frac{\partial g}{\partial l}(l, m, n) = 0 \tag{24}$$

$$\frac{\partial f}{\partial m}(l, m, n) + \lambda \frac{\partial g}{\partial m}(l, m, n) = 0 \tag{25}$$

$$\frac{\partial f}{\partial n}(l, m, n) + \lambda \frac{\partial g}{\partial n}(l, m, n) = 0 \tag{26}$$

$$g(l, m, n) = 0 \tag{27}$$

We can express m^2 and l^2 from (26), for $\lambda > 0, q > 0$:

$$m^2 = \frac{S_E^2}{\lambda q l^2 n^2}, \quad l^2 = \frac{S_E^2}{\lambda q m^2 n^2}. \tag{28}$$

By substituting m^2 from (28) into (25), we get for $n > 0$:

$$n_0 = n = \sqrt{\frac{w S_E^2}{S_B^2}}.$$

By substituting l^2 from (28) into (24), we get for $m > 0, w > 0$:

$$m_0 = m = \sqrt{\frac{b S_B^2}{q w S_V^2}}.$$

We are not interested in the values of l and λ solving the system of equations. Still, it remains to be shown that there really is a local minimum of $f(l, m, n)$ in

$m = m_0, n = n_0$. This can be done directly by checking the first and the second partial derivatives of $f(m, n)$,

$$f(m, n) = \frac{mqw + mqn + b}{c} \cdot \left(\frac{S_E^2}{mn} + \frac{S_B^2}{m} + S_V^2 \right),$$

as described in Second Derivative Test [16]. The procedure is quite straightforward, but involves some labor algebra. We do not include the details here.

C   Description of Used Benchmarks

All benchmarks were run on a single machine, Dell Precision 340, with a single Pentium 4 processor, 512M RAM. The CORBA benchmarks were run on Fedora 2 operating system, the Mono benchmarks were run on Fedora 4. All benchmarks were run with a disconnected network interface and with all unnecessary system services shut down.

The Ping benchmark measures the response time of a simple CORBA remote procedure call, the Marshal benchmark measures only marshaling part of the remote call. Both benchmarks comprise of a client and a server process, both of which are restarted in each execution. The evaluation was done with 100 CORBA/benchmark binaries, each benchmark binary was executed 25 times. The Ping and Marshal benchmarks are described in [2] in more detail, including the platform information.

The other benchmarks are from the Mono Regression Benchmarking Project [8]. The TCP Ping and HTTP Ping benchmarks measure response time of a single remote procedure call using TCP and HTTP channels, both benchmarks comprise of two processes. The Rijndael benchmark measures the aggregated time for encryption and decryption of a constant short text in memory. The FFT benchmark measures the aggregated time for forward and inverse Fast Fourier Transformation of a constant vector. There are two versions of the FFT benchmark: the original version allocates the memory for computation repeatedly at the beginning of each measurement, the NA ("no allocation") version allocates the memory once at the benchmark process start–up. Each benchmark was run both with the default virtual machine optimizations turned on, and with all the implemented virtual machine optimizations turned on (OPT). The evaluation was carried out with 150 binaries, each benchmark binary was executed 100 times. Detailed description of the benchmarks and platform information are available on the web [8].

Working Set Characterization of Applications with an Efficient LRU Algorithm[*]

Lodewijk Bonebakker[1], Andrew Over[2], and Ilya Sharapov[1]

[1] Sun Microsystems Laboratories
[2] Australian National University[**]

Abstract. This paper describes a methodology for a very efficient characterization of a workload's memory access properties using the least recently used (LRU) replacement policy. The resulting access reuse profile captures working set sizes of a workload and can be used to characterize the amount of locality of data references and predict its general caching behavior.

The approach discussed in this paper is flexible and can be used in conjunction with tracing or execution-driven techniques. Because of the efficiency of the proposed algorithm - processing over one million memory accesses per second - the LRU profiles can be collected for a large number of workloads and the resulting data can be used in early stages of computer system design.

We illustrate the method with data collected for NAS Parallel Benchmarks. For selected benchmarks we compare the miss rate profiles for various sizes of the workload. We also compare the resulting LRU profiles with point predictions of miss rates generated with conventional cache simulations and observe a good match. In the concluding part of the paper we report the performance results for the proposed method.

Keywords: workload characterization, cache, LRU, working sets, NAS benchmarks.

1 Introduction

Workload characterization is an essential part of performance analysis and computer system design. Properties that are typically analyzed include resource utilization and the types of operations the workload performs. The characterization of memory utilization becomes particularly important because of the increasing impact of the memory system on application performance.

Characterizations of applications that are independent of underlying architectures are valuable in early stages of computer system or component design because they can guide design decisions that can be subsequently refined by modeling specific architectural features, for example the size or associativity of

[*] This material is based upon work supported by DARPA under Contract No. NBCH3039002 and by the Australian Research Council Linkage Grant LP0347178.
[**] This work was completed wile interning at Sun Labs.

A. Horváth and M. Telek (Eds.): EPEW 2006, LNCS 4054, pp. 78–92, 2006.

caches in the system. Efficient characterization algorithms allow one to build a repository of workload properties of representative applications.

In this paper we focus on the analysis of memory reuse for a range of workloads and continuous profiles that can be used for cache miss rate estimation and for capturing the working set sizes of applications. We propose an efficient algorithm based on the least recently used (LRU) stack model, which makes it feasible to quickly generate a large collection of memory reuse profiles.

The next section of this paper discusses common memory characterization methodologies. The fast LRU algorithm is presented in Section 3. Section 4 shows the results of the algorithm applied to the NAS Parallel Benchmarks and is followed by the analysis of the results. We conclude the paper with a discussion of the performance of the proposed algorithm.

2 Background

There are a number of established methodologies for the analysis of the memory access properties of a workload. Regularity of computational applications can be analyzed based on striding properties [1]. This methodology can be combined with APEX map [2] characterization to analyze the spatial and temporal locality of memory accesses of an application in an architecture-independent way [3].

Another approach for the memory access characterization is the dynamic characterization of the working set size of an application [4,5]. This approach can be applied to both cache utilization analysis and memory paging algorithms.

A thriving area of research is the cache miss rate analysis [6]. Cache simulators based on instructions traces and on execution-driven techniques are common in the industry. In addition, there are a number of analytical techniques, such as Cache Miss Equations [7], that are applicable for compile-time cache analysis.

In this work we base our characterizations on the LRU [8] stack histogram, which accurately models fully associative LRU caches. We generate continuous profiles of miss ratios that capture working set sizes of an application. This temporal locality characterization is similar to the approach applied to compiler loop analysis in [9] for memory ranges up to 2^{11} bytes. We propose a highly efficient algorithm that allowed us to capture application-wide memory reuse profiles for memory sizes of up to 2^{26} bytes.

We perform workload characterization using the traditional LRU stack method. A stack of a fixed length N keeps an ordered list of N most recently accessed elements. Each access moves an element, which may or may not be already in the stack to the top. If the element was taken from the stack its previous position is recorded in the histogram. Aggegated histogram values are scaled to generate a workload profile that shows the reuse ratios for a range of stack or cache sizes up to the size actually used in the analysis.

Specific examples and results will be discussed in Section 4. Here we will refer to Figure 5 to illustrate this characterization. The miss rate of 0.03 for a 4 MB (2^{14} bytes) cache for all three problem sizes means that 97% of newly considered entries were already present in the top 4 MB part of the stack. Vertical drops at the tail ends of the curves correspond to different amounts of memory used by the three versions of the benchmark. This particular application performs a computation on a fixed three-dimensional grid. Intermediate vertical drops in the profiles illustrate intermediate working set sizes corresponding to the amount of data required to perform the computation in two dimensional planes.

3   Fast LRU Stack Algorithm

The proposed algorithm efficiently provides the rank for any element in the LRU stack, even when the LRU stack is large. The algorithm addresses some of the common obstacles that make traditional implementations of LRU stack algorithms inefficient. First, while maintaining an LRU stack in memory is simple using a double linked list, finding the rank of an element in the list would require counting from the beginning of the list until the element is found. Second, addressing the first point by attributing a static rank to the elements in an LRU will not work because that rank will change as soon as an element is added to the top of the list. These problems limit the usability of conventional implementations to short LRU stacks. With the new algorithm we demonstrate that with sufficient memory we can use LRU stacks very effectively.

We base our algorithm on two observations. First, many distributions common to computer science have uneven reuse of stack elements where most activity is in the top of the stack. Such behavior is true for Pareto and exponential distributions [10, 11]. Second, when an element is moved to the top of the stack, the order of the other elements is not changed, rather all elements after the removed element remain unchanged while the lower ranking elements shift down one step. Based on these observations we optimize the algorithm for the cases where the distribution of reused values is biased towards the top of the stack. Here we assume that we are performing cache analysis and the elements we are storing in the stack are memory references with values between 0 and $2^{64} - 1$. This type of stack analysis is relevant for any analysis where LRU is appropriate, like memory or web server caches [10].

3.1   Rank Ordering

Throughout the algorithm we maintain a linked list of stack entries. Checking whether a newly issued address is on the stack is implemented via hashing. For performance reasons, we pick the size of the hash table comparable with size of the LRU stack. Our experiments have shown that the table lookup does not amount to an appreciable cost. When we have found an element using the hashtable, we want to determine its rank in the stack before we move it to the top of the stack. In order to do this we maintain a rank record for every element in the LRU stack. This rank record is an *estimation* of its rank. These rankings in the LRU stack are re-initialized to true values at certain intervals discussed later. This re-initialization or *reranking* means that we assign every element the value of the counter as we count down from the top to the bottom of the LRU stack, starting with the number one. Reranking is very expensive and we aim

```
// return rank of element value
getactualrank(value) {
   stack_t stack;          // stacktype
   element_t element;      // stack element type
   // find the element in the hash-code
   element=findelement(value);
   if(element==NULL) {    //value is not on the stack
      deletelast(stack); //remove last entry
      element=newelement(value); // create new
      actualRank=0;
   } else {               // value found on the stack
      if (element.rank==0) {    // previously moved
         actualRank=findrank(stack,element)
      } else {            // unmoved
         actualRank=changelist(stack,element.rank)
      }
   }
   element.rank=0;        // set rank zero and place
   placeontop(stack,element); // on top of stack
   if (stack.findcount>stack.rerankcount) {
      rerank(stack);      // reinitialize the rankings
      stack.rerankcount+=stack.size;
   }
   return actualRank;
}
```

```
// find element from top of stack
findrank(stack,element) {
   element_t current;
   current=stack.head->next; // first data element
   rank=1;
   while (current.value!=element.value) {
      current=current.next;
      rank++;
   }
   stack.findcount+=rank;
   return(rank);
}

// correct estimated rank with changelist
changelist(stack,element.rank) {
   deltarank=0;
   for(i=0; i<sizeof(rank.changelist);i++) {
      if(rank.changelist[i]>element.rank)
         deltarank++;
   }
   stack.findcount+=sizeof(rank.changelist);
   addtochangelist(element.rank,rank.changelist);
   return(element.rank+deltarank);
}
```

Fig. 1. LRU stack algorithm pseudo code

to minimize its use. Between rerankings we maintain a *change list,* an array containing the estimated ranks of previous elements removed from the stack and placed on top. Elements moved to the top of the stack since the last reranking are assigned an estimated rank zero.

When we move an element to the top of the stack the algorithm performs a number of steps (illustrated in Figure 2 with pseudo-code in Figure 1). If the element is not in the stack, it is moved to the top of the stack and assigned an estimated rank zero. In this case the last entry of the stack is removed. If the element is found in the stack we need to determine its real rank to update the histogram. If the estimated rank of the current element is greater than zero we know that we have found an element that has not been accessed since the last reranking. We calculate the real rank from the estimated rank by finding how many places the element was moved down the stack since the last reranking. We start by assigning the real rank the value of the estimated rank. We then traverse the change list and for every entry whose rank is greater than the estimated rank of our element, we increment the real rank by one, since every element removed from below the current element would have moved the element one rank down. If an element was moved to the top from above our current element, then the position of our current element would not have changed. Once the change list is traversed, we add the original estimated rank to the change list. Finally we add the number of unique new elements added since the last reranking to the real rank.

If the estimated rank of the element is zero, we determine the real rank by counting from the top of the stack until we have found the correct element. Since the estimated rank is zero it does not need to be added to the change list.

As more and more elements are moved to the top of the stack, the number of elements with estimated rank zero increases. As a result of this increase, the amount of work the algorithm has to perform to determine the correct rank quickly increases with any top-biased distribution. This is caused by the increasing number of hits on elements with estimated rank zero, forcing a count from

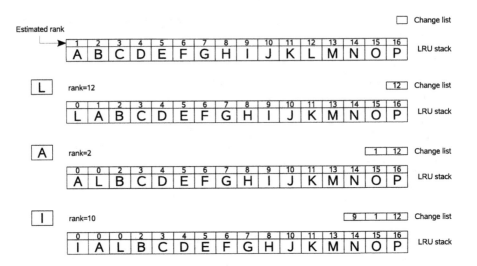

Fig. 2. Rank algorithm using L,A,I as values

the top of the stack until the element is found. By keeping track of the balance of work done between reranking the entire stack and counting from the top, we rerank the stack when the total amount of work done based on counting (*findcount*) exceeds the total amount of work done based on reranking (*rerankcount*).

3.2 Stack Buckets

We can improve the performance of the algorithm by partitioning the stack into contiguous regions or *buckets*. This optimization is based on an observation that under an exponential distribution of element reuse (ie cache locality), the distribution of reuse within each bucket will be exponential as well.

We split the stack into buckets of exponentially increasing size and make the algorithm work identically for each bucket. Each bucket is considered to have a fixed length. If a new element is added to the top of a bucket and the bucket overflows, the last element of that bucket is moved to the next bucket. If the last element is the last element of the stack, it is destroyed and removed from the stack as well as from the hash-table. When we take an element from the stack, the rank can then be calculated by finding the rank in its bucket and then adding the bucket offset to that rank. Each bucket independently manages its counting versus reranking balance.

The efficiency of the algorithm is significantly improved by partitioning. Assuming any reference locality, reused elements will be found towards the front of the list. The closer an element is to the front of the list, the shorter the bucket containing it, and therefore the cheaper the bucket is to maintain. Each bucket effectively acts as a filter reducing the amount of work which needs to be performed on more expensive buckets. By covering the most volatile areas of the LRU stack with smaller buckets (see Figure 3) we ensure that the cost of

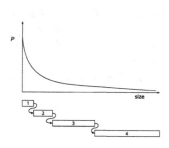

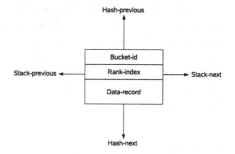

Fig. 3. The relationship between hitrate and bucket size

Fig. 4. An LRU bucket element with pointers

reranking each region is approximately equal (larger and therefore more expensive buckets require reranking far less frequently).

3.3 Implementation

We have implemented this algorithm in the C programming language making extensive use of pointer based lists and structures. Each element structure in a bucket has two pairs of pointers, for the hash table as well as the bucket (see figure 4). In addition, each element structure contains the bucket counter and the estimated rank. It is therefore clear that the price of the efficiency of this algorithm is in its extensive use of memory. Our 64-bit implementation requires 360 bits in order to store all the information pertaining to a single 64 bit value. The memory requirements are further increased by the hash-table and stack histogram size.

In order to achieve a high level of efficiency inside the algorithm and make trade-off decisions between either reranking the bucket or just counting, we track two values. The first value, *rerankcount*, is the total number of reranking operations performed while the second value, *findcount*, is the total number of counts we have performed. The *findcount* is incremented whenever the algorithm iterates from the top of the bucket (to calculate the rank of a recently inserted element), and also when iterating through the change list (to calculate the true rank from the estimated rank). Whenever *findcount* exceeds *rerankcount* (providing some indication that it is becoming costly to calculate rank), we rerank the bucket and add the current size of the bucket to the *rerankcount*. We have found through experimentation that this delivers a good results. Finding an optimal heuristic for reranking is a subject for further research.

4 Results and Analysis

In order to evaluate the LRU stack as described in Section 3 we applied it to a series of well known applications. The serial versions of the NAS Parallel Benchmarks [12, 13] were chosen for their ready availability, well understood behavior, and demonstration of regimes common to scientific applications. These benchmarks include a variety of problem sizes, making them particularly well suited for working-set analysis. A variety of problem sizes is included, from smallest to largest, S and W for testing and debugging, A, B and C for benchmarking. Larger problem sizes scale the working set, the number of iterations, or both. These applications are considered representative of a number of common scientific workloads.

4.1   Methodology

As the algorithm is based on a stream of memory references, address traces are a necessary prerequisite. Due to the scale of some problem sizes (several billion data references in a single iteration of the compute phase), dynamic trace generation was considered preferable to using stored traces.

Trace generation was handled using valgrind[14, 15], a dynamic binary translation (DBT) framework allowing run-time instrumentation of existing, compiled binaries. A native binary is translated by valgrind into an intermediate representation (IR), which may be modified, before being translated back into native code and executed. The design of the framework makes it comparatively simple to implement different "skins" which modify the IR in different ways; the default skin validates memory references, but the tool is in no way constrained by this. As the tool executes generated code, rather than simulating an application, the performance overhead is quite low. Currently valgrind runs on Linux under the x86 (32/64 bit) and PowerPC (32-bit) instruction sets.

A new skin was written to collect address references and submit them to an integrated implementation of the algorithm. Prior to each atomic, load or store (a complicated process given the x86 instruction set), the referenced address was submitted to the LRU stack.

The bt, ft, is, lu, lu-hp, mg, sp and ua benchmarks were tested in each of the S, W and A problem sizes. Benchmarks were compiled in 64-bit mode using gcc version 3.3, and run on an AMD64-based linux system. All benchmarks were optimized (using -O2). The benchmarks were modified slightly to evaluate a single iteration (after application setup and two iterations of warming) rather than a complete run.

A second valgrind skin was written to act as a trivial cache simulation. It employed the same IR modifications as mentioned above, however, the address trace was passed to a simple cache model which allowed variation of associativity, size and replacement policy (either LRU, round-robin or pseudo-random). Multiple cache models were employed simultaneously to reduce the number of required simulation runs.

Both skins were written to support a warming mode in which addresses were used to initialize the data structures, but no results were collected.

A necessary element of the algorithm is the assumed size of a cache line, which is used to map an address to a cacheline, and to convert between number of stack elements and working set size. All simulations described employed an LRU stack with one million entries and a cache line size of 64 bytes, allowing working set characterization of up to 2^{26} bytes (64 MB).

Problem set sizes were constrained by the amount of memory available in the test machines. Due to the use of `valgrind`, sufficient memory for both the application and the LRU stack was required simultaneously. To expand on Section 3.3, memory requirements are strictly determined by the maximum size of the LRU. Each entry requires 360 bits (in practice 48 bytes), with additional (but smaller) overhead due to the use of a hash table and the histogram. If sufficient storage is available, tracing and trace processing could be performed independently to reduce the memory overhead. Another alternative is to increase the underlying cacheline size (causing a corresponding reduction in the number of entries required to cover a given working set). This can produce slightly misleading results for small number of entries (due to striding touching differing combinations of cache lines).

4.2   Results

In order to calculate the projected miss rates, a histogram is maintained recording the depth at which a given entry was found before moving it to the top of the stack. For notational purposes, a new entry is considered to have a rank of 0. An entry with a given rank could be found only in a cache with at least that number of cachelines. If the cache contained fewer lines, the entry in question would already have been victimized subject to the LRU policy and should therefore be considered a miss.

Miss rates are therefore given by:

$$m_n = 1 - \frac{\sum_{i=1}^{n} h_i}{\sum_{j=0}^{max} h_j}$$

where m_n is the miss rate for n cachelines, and h_i is the number of elements with rank i (with h_0 the number of elements not found in the stack).

Based upon this equation, miss rates were calculated for the family of `bt` (Figure 5) and `sp` (Figure 6) benchmarks. These benchmarks were chosen as they provide an illustration of properties discussed below. As mentioned in Section 4.1, these results arise from a single iteration of the respective benchmark.

With a single simulation run, it is immediately possible to gain some insight into the expected miss rate for any cache size within the range of analysis. The ability to generate a continuous curve rather than a number of discrete points provides an enormous amount of information in a single run, rather than requiring numerous cache simulations. In particular, the effects of algorithmic blocking are clearly visible, particularly in Figure 5. Due to the continuous nature of the generated miss rates, the presence of loop constructs (and their respective working set size) may immediately be seen. This behavior may not be nearly so obvious given only a series of points.

In order to validate the simulation results generated by this technique, address traces were also run through a traditional cache simulation model, employing a range of replacement policies.

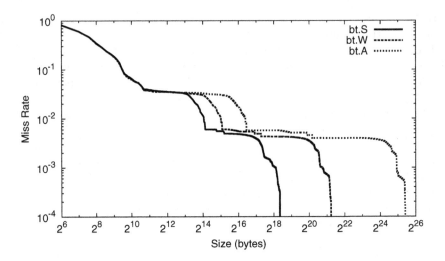

Fig. 5. Cache behavior of `bt`

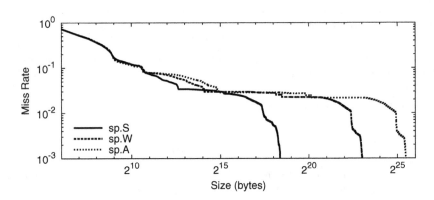

Fig. 6. Cache behavior of `sp`

Figure 7 shows the comparison for `bt.A` while Figure 8 shows the comparison for `lu-hp.A`. In both cases, the LRU stack results were compared against a simple 4-way set associative cache of a variety of sizes using either an LRU, a round-robin or a pseudo-random replacement policy.

The results predicted by both conventional techniques and LRU stack based analysis correspond quite well although with some discrepancy around sudden changes in miss-rate (see Figure 8). This discrepancy is attributed to the pathological case of an LRU replacement policy and a working set which slightly exceeds the length of the LRU. A conventional cache design (and therefore simulator) is protected from this effect to some extent by the partitioning provided by indexing. A large fully-associative design has no such protection.

In spite of this mild discrepancy, the LRU stack algorithm quickly identifies the region in question as one subject to changing miss rate behavior and an ideal

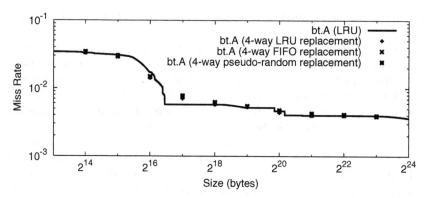

Fig. 7. Cache analysis comparison of `bt.A`

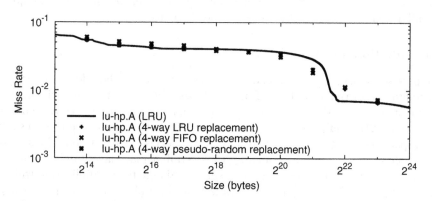

Fig. 8. Cache analysis comparison of `lu-hp.A`

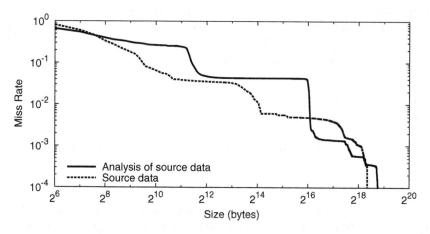

Fig. 9. Cache Behavior of LRU Stack Algorithm

candidate for further examination if this were a workload of importance to the designer.

As a point of curiosity, a standalone version of this algorithm was examined while processing a 64-bit version of a `bt.S` trace (including startup), and the result is illustrated in Figure 9. Both the cache behavior of the analysis tool and the behavior of the source trace are shown. The source trace is a set of 256 million address references taken from the start of `bt.S`, while the analysis trace is from a complete analysis of the source trace (without warming).

Notice the clear demonstration of blocking behavior at several points; this is to be expected given the use of buckets to model the LRU, and the size (and location) of the drop offs in miss rates will be partially contingent on the data supplied to the algorithm. If a working set strongly exercises only the top few buckets, the LRU stack working set will be composed principally of those buckets. On the other hand, an application with a larger working set will require a similar increase in the working set of the simulator.

4.3   Additional Considerations

Some final consideration should be given to the methodology employed. Although `valgrind` is a DBT framework, as both the host and the target are identical, word sizes, data segment positioning, and addresses are largely preserved. `valgrind`'s source code is resident within the traced application's address space (due to the need to translate and supervise its execution). This presence within the address space can alter the overall memory layout of application. For example, the overall size of address space available to the application will be reduced by `valgrind`'s requirements (a potential problem on 32-bit platforms), and this reduction may result in `mmap` calls mapping to different addresses. Given the use of scientific workloads, these effects are presumed to be minimal and the resulting address traces are assumed to be representative.

Furthermore, only data references are captured and used within this simulation, while a real system would observe fetch traffic at the L2 cache. For the purposes of our analysis this is considered a low order effect.

5   Performance

The performance of the algorithm described in Section 3 has been characterized in several ways, both on its own, and in comparison to a set of alternatives.

5.1   Raw Performance

Table 1 illustrates the raw performance of the algorithm itself when isolated from tracing infrastructure and most other sources of overhead. The values in this table were obtained by supplying a pre-captured trace of the first 2^{28} (256 million) data references in the compute phase of the benchmark in question to a standalone implementation of the algorithm.

Table 1. LRU simulation benchmarks

	bt.A (2^{28} records)		mg.A (2^{28} records)		lu.A (2^{28} records)	
	time (s)	addr/s	time (s)	addr/s	time (s)	addr/s
1.4 GHz Opteron 240 (64-bit)	160.24	1.675 M	234.90	1.142 M	179.34	1.497 M
2.2 GHz Opteron 848 (64-bit)	144.92	1.852 M	235.51	1.140 M	172.69	1.155 M
1.86 GHz Pentium M (32-bit)	102.09	2.629 M	112.22	2.392 M	70.83	3.790 M

Three different systems were employed for testing:

- 1.4 GHz Opteron 240, 1 MB L2, 2 GB RAM, Linux 2.4.21
- Quad 2.2 GHz Opteron 848, 1 MB L2, 8 GB RAM, Linux 2.6.7
- 1.87 GHz Pentium M, 2 MB L2, 1 GB RAM, Linux 2.6.13

Native word sizes were used on each platform; 32-bit traces on the Pentium M, and 64-bit traces on the two AMD64 systems. Timings are not directly comparable between systems of differing word sizes, due to the difference in the size of trace data and algorithm memory footprint.

The run times vary somewhat for the various benchmarks tested. This is a consequence of the relationship between bucket usage and cache hit rate illustrated in Figure 3. Benchmarks which demonstrate greater locality will find their accesses confined to the top-most buckets, which incur substantially lower costs for both lookup and rank maintenance due to their smaller size. This overhead will increase with the working set (and thus bucket) size, and thus algorithmic efficiency is expected to decrease with larger problem sizes.

Regardless of the problem size, however, within the examined benchmarks, performance exceeds one million processed records per second. The Pentium M based system appears to hold a substantial advantage, presumably due to the smaller size of each record (32-bit pointers) and the larger L2.

5.2 Algorithmic Variation

To examine the performance gains made possible by book keeping and the use of buckets, three different versions of the algorithm were compared on the same traces as above.

The *efficient* algorithm is as described in Section 3. The *nobuckets* algorithm is a degraded version of *efficient*. The details of the algorithm remain largely the same (including hash table and book-keeping), however, the list is not partitioned into multiple buckets.

The *naive* algorithm is a simple linked-list based implementation of a stack. On each lookup, the list is scanned, and the matching entry is shifted to the front. Some improvement could be gained by using a hash table to track elements in the list. This would avoid an unsuccessful scan on new elements (quite significant when the working set exceeds the number of entries in the stack), and reduce the number of comparisons needed to find an element. As this case is intended to provide a performance baseline, this optimization has not been made.

Table 2. Algorithmic performance comparison

Algorithm		bt.A	mg.A	lu.A
naive	time (s)	16336.28	> 25200	2966.50
	slowdown	160.02	> 224.56	41.90
nobuckets	time (s)	1369.32	1552.75	708.30
	slowdown	14.40	13.83	10.00
efficient	time (s)	102.09	112.22	70.83

All benchmarks were run on the Pentium M system described above, and timing information is shown in Table 2. The times result from runs over traces of the first 2^{28} instructions of the compute phase of each benchmark, as used in Table 1. All runs were made with a stack size of one million (2^{20}) entries, modeling working sets of up to 64 MB (2^{26} bytes). In the case of mg, the *naive* algorithm proved too slow, and the simulation run was terminated.

While the use of careful bookkeeping (the primary difference between the *naive* and the *nobuckets* approach) does significantly improve performance, the addition of buckets yields an order of magnitude performance improvement. The variation in degree of slowdown is largely attributable to the source data. The manipulation of small buckets is much faster than that of larger buckets, and an application with highly localized accesses would be largely confined to the top few (small and therefore cheap) buckets. Such an application would thus experience a large slowdown without the use of buckets (see Figure 3).

As noted above, the naive algorithm experienced severe slowdowns when the size of the working set exceeded the LRU stack size (as is the case with mg.A).

5.3 Tracing Overhead

Although all runtimes discussed thus far have referred purely to trace processing, it is also instructive to consider the performance of run-time trace generation (i.e. the use of valgrind). While in some instances it may be practical to store complete traces for billions of instructions, storage constraints may make this undesirable in many environments, particularly if tracing overhead is low.

Table 3 compares the time taken to examine a single iteration of the compute phase for several benchmarks under a variety of conditions. The time taken to complete an iteration on the host is given by *native*. valgrind records the time taken using the "none" skin. This translates from native code to the intermediate representation and back again without performing any transformations on the IR, and gives a baseline indicator of valgrind's overhead. The skin used to generate address traces is shown by *tracing*. Finally the runtime when performing the LRU stack simulation is given by *simulation*. These performance numbers are taken from the quad Opteron 848 system mentioned earlier.

From this table it may be seen that the combination of valgrind and the stack algorithm incurs roughly a 500 fold slowdown, while valgrind itself incurs a 5–10 fold slowdown. Interestingly, the record processing rates quoted are roughly

Table 3. Overall run-time (one compute iteration)

		bt.A	mg.A	lu.A
records	(million)	1040	1208	440
simulation	time (s)	369.72	964.41	301.81
	slowdown	513	771	419
	million rec/s	2.81	1.12	1.45
tracing	time (s)	19.59	25.08	9.03
	slowdown	27	20.06	12.54
valgrind	time (s)	6.84	11.97	4.05
	slowdown	9.50	9.57	5.62
native	time (s)	0.72	1.25	0.72

comparable to those in Table 1, suggesting that the simulation itself swamps the overhead of trace generation when applied in this manner.

Owing to the use of a dynamic translation framework, it is possible to run a given application uninstrumented (incurring a 5 to 10 fold slowdown) until an area of interest is reached. At this point instrumentation could be enabled (imposing a 500 fold slowdown). These numbers are sufficiently low to make instrumentation of large applications quite practical.

6   Conclusions

In this work we have demonstrated the ability to generate very efficiently continuous curves outlining the working set behavior of an application in a single pass. These graphs very quickly pinpoint important working set regions, and blocking behavior within the target application.

Using a dynamic binary translation framework, this algorithm is capable of modeling working set behavior with only a 500-fold slowdown. The same framework imposes only a five to ten-fold slowdown when not instrumenting, making the examination of large applications practical.

Comparison against a traditional cache simulator has shown that while quite close, the miss rates do not always match precisely in the vicinity of sudden changes due to structural differences between an LRU stack and a real cache. In spite of these differences, the curves generated by the LRU stack closely approximate the miss rates projected by a cache simulator, and provide a useful baseline for targeting more detailed analysis.

References

1. Carrington, L., Snavely, A., Gao, X., Wolter, N.: Performance prediction framework for scientic applications. In: Lecture Notes in Computer Science, 2659. Springer (2003) 926–935
2. Strohmaier, E., Shan, H.: Architecture independent performance characterization and benchmarking for scientific applications. In: 12th IEEE International Symposium on Modeling, Analysis, and Simulation of Computer and Telecommunications Systems (MASCOTS'04). (2004) 467–474

3. Weinberg, J., Snavely, A., McCracken, M.O., Strohmaier, E.: Quantifying locality in the memory access patterns of hpc applications. In: SC2005: High Performance Networking and Computing. (2005)

4. Denning, P.J.: The working set model for program behavior. Commun. ACM **11**(5) (1968) 323–333

5. Denning, P.J., Schwartz, S.C.: Properties of the working-set model. Commun. ACM **15**(3) (1972) 191–198

6. Smith, A.J.: Cache memories. ACM Comput. Surv. **14**(3) (1982) 473–530

7. Ghosh, S., Martonosi, M., Malik, S.: Cache miss equations: a compiler framework for analyzing and tuning memory behavior. ACM Transactions on Programming Languages and Systems **21**(4) (1999) 703–746

8. Rau, B.R.: Properties and applications of the least-recently-used stack model. Technical report, Stanford, CA, USA (1977)

9. Cascaval, C., Padua, D.A.: Estimating cache misses and locality using stack distances. In: ICS '03: Proceedings of the 17th annual international conference on Supercomputing, New York, NY, USA, ACM Press (2003) 150–159

10. Arlitt, M.F., Williamson, C.L.: Internet web servers: workload characterization and performance implications. IEEE/ACM Trans. Netw. **5**(5) (1997) 631–645

11. Paxson, V., Floyd, S.: Wide area traffic: the failure of poisson modeling. IEEE/ACM Trans. Netw. **3**(3) (1995) 226–244

12. NASA Advanced Supercomputing: NAS Parallel Benchmarks. http://www.nas.nasa.gov/Software/NPB/ (2005) Version 3.1 Serial.

13. Bailey, D.H., Barszcz, E., Barton, J.T., Browning, D.S., Carter, R.L., Dagum, D., Fatoohi, R.A., Frederickson, P.O., Lasinski, T.A., Schreiber, R.S., Simon, H.D., Venkatakrishnan, V., Weeratunga, S.K.: The NAS Parallel Benchmarks. The International Journal of Supercomputer Applications **5**(3) (1991) 63–73

14. : Valgrind. http://www.valgrind.org/ (2005) Version 3.0.1.

15. Nethercote, N.: Dynamic Binary Analysis and Instrumentation. PhD thesis, University of Cambridge (2004)

Model Checking for a Class of Performance Properties of Fluid Stochastic Models

Manuela L. Bujorianu[1] and Marius C. Bujorianu[2]

[1]Faculty of Computer Science
University of Twente
L.M.Bujorianu@cs.utwente.nl
[2]Computing Laboratory
University of Kent
Canterbury CT2 7NF, UK
mcb8@kent.ac.uk

Abstract. Recently, there is an explosive development of fluid approaches to computer and distributed systems. These approaches are inherently stochastic and generate continuous state space models. Usually, the performance measures for these systems are defined using probabilities of reaching certain sets of the state space. These measures are well understood in the discrete context and many efficient model checking procedures have been developed for specifications involving them. The continuous case is far more complicated and new methods are necessary. In this paper we propose a general model checking strategy founded on advanced concepts and results of stochastic analysis. Due to the problem complexity, in this paper, we achieve the first necessary step of characterizing mathematically the problem. We construct upper bounds for the performance measures using Martin capacities. We introduce a concept of bisimulation that preserves the performance measures and a metric that characterizes the bisimulation.

Keywords: Fluid models, performance measure, bisimulation, modelchecking, computer networks, Markov processes, capacity.

1 Introduction

Performance analysis is an important activity for systems having continuous state components and / or continuous time transitions. Such systems include fluid models of communicating and computer networks [22], [20], stochastic fluid Petri nets [18], [12], stochastic hybrid systems and their applications (air traffic control systems, chemical engineering, automated highway systems, power systems, nuclear plants, wireless gadgets). In most cases performance analysis is carried out probabilistically. The most used (engineering) measure for system performance is also a measure in the mathematical sense, i.e. a probability. We follow the probabilistic model checking approach [25] that defines the performance measure as a probability of a specific set of events, each event being defined as a system path with some properties. The probability is counted for

A. Horváth and M. Telek (Eds.): EPEW 2006, LNCS 4054, pp. 93–107, 2006.

those sets of paths that start from a given state and pass through a target set in the state space. We extend this definition from the discrete case to the fluid case (continuous and / or transitions). The countable system paths are replaced by dense (i.e. contiguous) system trajectories. The working mathematicians will remark that trajectories can be discontinuous, but they have the cadlag property (right continuous with left limits). Of course, the way we specify the trajectories differs largely from the manner to specifying discrete paths. The situation becomes more complicated when estimations of the probabilities are constructed. If, in probabilistic model checking [26], combinatorics and discrete mathematics are used, for contiguous trajectories we have to use advanced stochastic analysis concepts. In probabilistic model checking both maximal and minimal reachability probabilities are estimated. In this paper, we construct upper bounds estimation only.

Most of the fluid models for performance analysis of distributed systems adopts the Petri nets model of concurrency. In this paper, we adhere to the process algebra philosophy. A process algebra fluid has been introduced and investigated in [8]. We have shown that the study of performance analysis of these systems is equivalent to the performance analysis of strong Markov processes with cadlag property, which we investigate in this paper.

In this paper, we consider those performability properties that specify upper bounds for performance measures. In order to make formal these properties we need a suitable continuous stochastic logic. In [9], we have defined approximate abstractions for some classes of fluid models for which there exists available a version of the continuous stochastic logic. This logic may be used to specify the performability properties of interest to us. The full formality of the approach we propose can not be achieved because of the limited room of this paper. Therefore, we present only a strategy based on semantic arguments. Even the properties would be formally fully specified, their semantics would be a mathematical statement about upper bounds of the performance measure. Every model checking procedure for performability properties needs mathematical solutions for inequality problems involving the performance measure. This absolutely necessary first step for performability properties model checking is achieved in this paper.

In application domains like air traffic control there are often sudden physical changes that requires modifications in the mathematical model and consequently the probabilities change. A similar case appears in practical situations when approximations of probabilities are used in decision making and because of changes in the environment require the recalculation of the approximations. Our approach covers these kind of situations in a dynamic, configurable change prone environment. Moreover, we consider a version of stochastic model checking, meaning that one could get a system abstraction (hopefully simpler or even finite state) that preserves the probabilities of critical situations. This technique requires a suitable concept of bisimulation. In this paper, we present a bisimulation concept and prove that two bisimilar processes have the same probabilities of reach a safety critical (hazardous) situation - called reach set probabilities.

The bisimulation concept is very robust because it does not involve the stochastic equivalence of the Markov processes considered. In practice probabilities are approximated by various statistical methods and therefore it is difficult to check the equality of transition probabilities (in order to prove the stochastic equivalence of processes).

The basic ingredients we use are Markov processes, capacities, belief functions, and semigroups. Advanced concepts of stochastic analysis have been used for a long time in modelling computer networks and the Internet, for example by Kelly and co-workers [22], [23], Hespanha [21], Katoen, Baier and co-workers [20] etc.

The paper is structured as follows. The next section provides the paper motivation. The basic background in Markov processes and capacities is given in section 3. The section 4 contains the problem formulation and characterization. In section 5 a new concept of stochastic bisimulation is introduced and investigated. The paper ends with some final remarks.

2   Motivation

Nowadays, there is a proliferation of models for very large communicating (computer) networks that consider the overall network behaviour as being continuous. These models are called generically 'fluid'. The interested reader can easily find nice tutorial on this issue like [23, 22]. As the world, we live in, is getting more and more interconnected, these fluid models become more efficient for studying the congestion control, the quality of services and various performance measures. These methods are analytical and the only verification methodologies available are based on stochastic (Monte Carlo) simulations. Other analytical verification methods use some tricky discretisations by employing queue systems.

The focus of the 'fluid' approach on modelling is natural, but the approach suffers because of the ad-hoc verification methods. In particular, model checking, the mostly used verification technique in performability analysis, is not available. This is because of the lack of sound, adequate analytical techniques. When probabilities and continuous aspects are considered altogether, the mathematical problems get a formidable complexity. In this paper, we address the mathematical foundations for the stochastic model checking of performability properties in the 'fluid' approach.

The corner stones of the model checking strategy, which we propose here, are given by a mathematically sound upper estimations of the performance measure and a bisimulation relation that preserve it. The class of systems that can be checked has behaviour as strong Markov processes with the cadlag property. This class is very large and it includes, for example, continuous Petri nets, fluid stochastic Petri nets (FSPNs), continuous places and / or fluid flow arcs FSPNs, and stochastic hybrid systems (SHS). Of course, each subclass of systems add specific properties to the class Markov processes representing their behaviour. Our strategy will be refined for subclasses of systems, in particular, for stochastic hybrid systems in a forthcoming paper. Actually, a research project [27] has been undertaken at the University of Twente to explore these issues.

FSPNs [24] extend stochastic Petri Nets (SPNs) by introducing positive real tokens to special continuous places. The set of places is partitioned as follows: (i) a set of discrete places, characterised by an integer number of tokens; (ii) a set of fluid (or continuous) places containing a real fluid level.

Stochastic fluid flow models [33] have been used extensively to evaluate the performance of high-speed networks, for which the underlying stochastic processes can be viewed as continuous state whilst the network speed increases (for example, the ATM networks where the cell transmission delay is 3 microseconds in 155 Mb/s). Moreover, the fluid models can be employed to deal with the problem of largeness.

Stochastic hybrid systems are 'traditional' hybrid systems with some stochastic features [5, 28]. These systems typically contain variables or signals that take values from a continuous set and also variables that take values from a discrete (finite or countable) set. Differential equations or stochastic differential equations generally give the continuous dynamics of such systems. A Markov chain generally governs the discrete-variable dynamics of stochastic hybrid systems. The stochastic features might be present in the continuous dynamics or in the discrete dynamics, or in both. The continuous and discrete dynamics coexist and interact with each other and because of this it is important to use models that accurately describe the dynamic behaviour of such hybrid systems. The realizations of the different models of stochastic hybrid systems (see [28] for an overview) can be thought of as particular classes of strong Markov processes with the continuous evolution disturbed by forced or spontaneous transitions.

3   Background

In this section we present the necessary results and concepts about Markov processes and capacities to make this paper self-contained.

3.1   Stochastic Analysis of Markov Processes

We fix $(\Omega, \mathcal{F})$ a measurable space. Let $\mathcal{M}_t$, $t \in [0, \infty]$ be a *filtration* on $(\Omega, \mathcal{F})$ (i.e. a non-decreasing family of sub-σ-algebras of $\mathcal{F}$). Denote $\mathcal{M}_\infty = \bigvee_{t \in [0, \infty)} \mathcal{M}_t$, i.e. $\mathcal{M}_\infty$ is the smallest σ-algebra containing all $\mathcal{M}_t$, $t \in [0, \infty)$. A filtration $\{\mathcal{M}_t\}$ is *right continuous* if $\mathcal{M}_t = \mathcal{M}_{t+} = \cap\{\mathcal{M}_{t'} | t' > t\}$. A filtration is a way of representing our information about a system growing over time. To see what right-continuity is about, suppose it failed, i.e. $\mathcal{M}_t \subset \cap\{\mathcal{M}_{t'} | t' > t\}$. Then there would have to be events which were detectable at all times after t, but not at time t itself. This means we have some sudden jump in our information right after t. A stochastic process (x_t) is *adapted* to a filtration $(\mathcal{M}_t)$ if x_t is $\mathcal{M}_t$-measurable for all $t \geq 0$ (or $(\mathcal{M}_t)$ is an *admissible filtration*). Any process is adapted to the filtration it induces $\mathcal{F}_t^0 = \sigma\{x_s, s \leq t\}$ for $t \in [0, \infty)$ and $\mathcal{F}^0 = \vee_t \mathcal{F}_t^0$. $(\mathcal{F}_t^0)$ is called the *minimum admissible filtration* or the *natural filtration*. A process being adapted to a filtration just means, for each time, the filtration gives us enough information to find the value of the process.

Let X be a topological Hausdorff space and assume that $\mathcal{B}$ is the Borel σ-algebra of X. We adjoin an extra point Δ (the cemetery) to X as an isolated point, $X_\Delta = X \cup \{\Delta\}$. Let $\mathcal{B}(X_\Delta)$ be the Borel σ-algebra of X_Δ.

Let $M = (\Omega, \mathcal{F}, (x_t)_{t \geq 0}, (P_x)_{x \in X_\Delta})$ be a Markov process with the state space $(X, \mathcal{B})$, life time $\zeta(\omega)$ (when the process M escapes to and is trapped at Δ) and corresponding filtration $(\mathcal{M}_t)$. The elements $\mathcal{F}_t$, P_x are defined as follows.

- $P_x : (\Omega, \mathcal{F}) \to [0, 1]$ is a probability measure (called *Wiener probability*) such that $P_x(x_t \in E)$ is $\mathcal{B}$-measurable in $x \in X$ for each $t \geq 0$ and $E \in \mathcal{B}$.
- If $\mu \in \mathcal{P}(X_\Delta)$, i.e. μ is a probability measure on $(X_\Delta, \mathcal{B}(X_\Delta))$ then we can define $P_\mu(\Lambda) = \int_{X_\Delta} P_x(\Lambda) \mu(dx)$, $\Lambda \in \mathcal{F}$. The completion of $\mathcal{F}_t^0$, for $t \in [0, \infty]$, w.r.t. all P_μ, $\mu \in \mathcal{P}(X_\Delta)$, is denoted by $\mathcal{F}_t$.

Given an admissible filtration $\{\mathcal{M}_t\}$, a $[0, \infty)$-valued function T on Ω is called an $\{\mathcal{M}_t\}$-*stopping time or optional time* if $\{T \leq t\} \in \mathcal{M}_t$, $\forall t \geq 0$.

For an admissible filtration $\{\mathcal{M}_t\}$, we say that M is *strong Markov* w.r.t. $\{\mathcal{M}_t\}$ if $\{\mathcal{M}_t\}$ is right continuous and for any $\{\mathcal{M}_t\}$-stopping time T

$$P_\mu(x_{T+t} \in E | \mathcal{M}_T) = P_{x_T}(x_t \in E); \ P_\mu - a.s.$$

$\mu \in \mathcal{P}(X_\Delta)$, $E \in \mathcal{B}$, $t \geq 0$.

M has the *càdlàg property* if for each $\omega \in \Omega$, the sample path $t \mapsto x_t(\omega)$ is right continuous on $[0, \infty)$ and has left limits on $(0, \infty)$ (inside X_Δ).

Let (P_t) denote the operator semigroup associated to M defined by

$$P_t f(x) = E_x f(x_t), \ f \in \mathcal{B}^b(X)$$

where $\mathcal{B}^b(X)$ is the set of all bounded measurable real valued functions on X and E_x is the expectation w.r.t. P_x.

3.2 Capacities

The information input into different real-world models may be imprecise for several reasons. For example, for computer models, imprecision is often a consequence of measurement processes (e.g. using digital sensors). Prior information is sometime recorded as intervals without any information about probability distributions [15].

The extension of probabilistic analysis to include imprecise information is now well established in the theory of imprecise probabilities [32], robust Bayesian analysis [19] and fuzzy statistics [31].

The imprecise probabilities are modelled by sets of probability measures which might generate upper/lower probabilities [15], Choquet capacities [10], etc.

In the following, first, we shortly present the concept of Choquet capacity and then we give the construction of the capacity associated to a Borel right Markov process. This later concept is used in the next section to give a new definition for stochastic bisimulation.

Intuitively, a capacity is a set function which extend the concept of measure. The additivity property is not longer true for a capacity.

For every space X and algebra $\mathcal{A}$ of subsets of X a set-function $c : \mathcal{A} \to [0, 1]$ is called a *normalized capacity* if it satisfies the following:

(i) $c(\emptyset) = 0$, $c(X) = 1$, (ii) $\forall A, B \in \mathcal{A}$: $A \subset B \Rightarrow c(A) \leq c(B)$.

A capacity is called *convex (or supermodular)* if in addition to (i)-(ii) it satisfies the additional property:

(iii) $\forall A, B \in \mathcal{A}$: $c(A \cup B) \geq c(A) + c(B) - c(A \cap B)$.

A special type of convex capacities are the *belief functions* presented and discussed by Dempster [15] and Shafer [29]. A capacity is called a probability if (iii) holds everywhere with equality, i.e. it is additive. If a capacity satisfies the inverse inequality in (iii) then it is called *submodular or strongly subadditive*.

Let Λ be a set and $\mathcal{C}$ a σ-algebra of subsets of Λ. Given a measurable function $F : \Lambda \times \Lambda \to [0, \infty]$ and a finite measure μ on $(\Lambda, \mathcal{C})$, the *F-energy* of μ is

$$F(\mu) = F(\mu, \mu) = \int_\Lambda \int_\Lambda F(\alpha, \beta) d\mu(\alpha) d\mu(\beta).$$

The *capacity with respect to F* is

$$Cap_F(\Lambda) = [\inf F(\mu)]^{-1} \tag{1}$$

where the infimum is over probability measures μ on $(\Lambda, \mathcal{C})$ and by the convention, $\infty^{-1} = 0$.

Since we allow the possibility that c is not additive, we can not use the integral in the Lebesgue sense to integrate w.r.t. c. The notion of integral we use is due originally to Choquet [10] and it was independently rediscovered and extended by Schmeidler [30]. If $f : X \to \mathbb{R}$ is bounded $\mathcal{A}$-measurable function and c is any capacity on X we define the Choquet integral of f w.r.t. c to be the number

$$\int_X f(x) dc(x) = \int_0^\infty c(\{x \in X | f(x) \geq \alpha\}) d\alpha +$$
$$+ \int_{-\infty}^0 [c(\{x \in X | f(x) \geq \alpha\}) - 1] d\alpha$$

where the integrals are taken in the sense of Riemann.

3.3   Markov Process Capacity

Throughout this paper $M = (\Omega, \mathcal{F}, \mathcal{F}_t, x_t, P_x)$ will be a Borel right Markov process on $(X, \mathcal{B})$. This means that (see, for example, [13] and the references therein):

- Its state space $(X, \mathcal{B})$ is a Lusin state space (i.e. X is a separable metric space homeomorphic to a Borel subset of some compact metric space, with Borel σ-algebra $\mathcal{B}(X)$ or shortly $\mathcal{B}$). It will be equipped with a σ-finite measure m.
- M is a strong Markov process and the sample paths $t \to x_t(\omega)$ are almost surely right continuous.
- the transition operator semigroup $(P_t)_{t \geq 0}$ of M maps $\mathcal{B}^b$ (the lattice of bounded real measurable functions defined on X) into itself.

In addition, in this paper we suppose that M has the cadlag property and that M is *transient*. This means that there exists a strictly positive Borel function q such that Uq is bounded (where $Uf = \int_0^\infty P_t f \, dt$ is the *kernel operator*).

One can take the sample space Ω for M to be the set of all paths $(0, \infty) \ni t \mapsto \omega(t) \in X_\Delta$ such that (i) $t \mapsto \omega(t)$ is X-valued and cadlag on $(0, \zeta(\omega))$ where $\zeta(\omega) := \inf\{s > 0 | \omega(s) = \Delta\}$, (ii) $\omega(t) = \Delta$ for all $t \geq \zeta(\omega)$, and (iii) $\zeta(\omega) < \infty$. In this way, M is realized as the coordinate process on Ω: $x_t(\omega) = \omega(t)$, $t > 0$. We complete the definition of M by declaring $x_0(\omega) = \lim_{t \searrow 0} \omega(t)$, $t > 0$.

Because of transience condition, it is possible to construct a probability measure $\mathbb{P}$ on $(\Omega, \mathcal{F}_t^0)$ under which the coordinate process $(x_t)_{t>0}$ is Markovian with transition semigroup $(P_t)_{t \geq 0}$ and one-dimensional distributions $\mathbb{P}(x_t \in A) = \mu_t(A)$, $\forall A \in \mathcal{B}$, $t > 0$, where $(\mu_t)_{t>0}$ is an appropriate entrance law (see [17] and the references therein).

The *capacity* associated to M is defined as follows (see [7] and the references therein): for all $B \in \mathcal{B}$

$$Cap_M(B) = \mathbb{P}(T_B < \infty) = \mathbb{P}(T_B < \zeta), \qquad (2)$$

where T_B is the first hitting time of B, i.e. $T_B = \inf\{t > 0 | x_t \in B\}$.
This capacity can be written as a non-additive set function $Cap_M : (X, \mathcal{B}) \to [0, 1]$, which is finer than a measure. The capacity of a measurable set B can be thought of as a 'measure' of all process trajectories that ever visit B over an infinite horizon time. It can be shown that Cap_M is monotone increasing, submodular, and countably subadditive [17]. The initial definition (see the references therein [17]) of this notion gives the capacity Cap_M as an upper envelope of a non-empty class of probability measures on $\mathcal{B}$.

4   Problem Formulation and Characterization

Randomness or uncertainty is ubiquitous in scientific and engineering systems. Stochastic effects are not just introduced to compensate for defects in deterministic models, but are often rather intrinsic phenomena. In this section, we consider a performance measure for stochastic fluid systems defined as a probability for a stochastic reachability problem. We show that this problem is well defined and construct an upper bound for reach set probabilities based on capacities.

4.1   Performance Measure

Let us consider $M = (\Omega, \mathcal{F}, \mathcal{F}_t, x_t, P_x)$, as in subsection 3.3, the realization of a stochastic fluid system. We use the definition from [25] of *the performance measure as a reachability probability*. To address the reachability problem assume that we have a given set $E \in \mathcal{B}(X)$ and a horizon time $T > 0$. Let us define

$$Reach_T(E) = \{\omega \in \Omega \mid \exists t \in [0, T] : x_t(\omega) \in E\}$$
$$Reach_\infty(E) = \{\omega \in \Omega \mid \exists t \geq 0 : x_t(\omega) \in E\}. \qquad (3)$$

These two sets are the sets of trajectories of M, which reach the set E (the flow that enters E) in the interval of time $[0, T]$ or $[0, \infty)$. The reachability problem consists of determining the probabilities of such sets. The reachability problem should be well-defined, i.e. $Reach_T(A)$, $Reach_\infty(A)$ are indeed measurable sets. Then *the performance measures are the probabilities of reach events are*

$$P(T_A < T) \text{ or } P(T_A < \infty) \tag{4}$$

where $T_A = \inf\{t > 0 | x_t \in A\}$ and P is a probability on the measurable space $(\Omega, \mathcal{F})$ of the elementary events associated to M. P can be chosen to be P_x (if we want to consider the trajectories, which start in x) or P_μ (if we want to consider the trajectories, which start in x_0 given by the distribution μ). Recall that $P_\mu(A) = \int P_x(A)d\mu$, $A \in \mathcal{F}$. In this way, the reachability problem is related with the computation of the capacities associated to the processes M_T and M, where M_T is the process M "killed" after the time T (see [13] for the details about the killed process).

In the case of stochastic reachability the types of properties which can expressed can be classified as follows [25]:

- *Reachability:* The system can reach a certain set of states with a given probability.
- *Invariance:* The system does not leave a certain set of states with a given probability (viability problem). In this context, the reachability problem can be formulated as [5]: given a system and a set of initial conditions S_0, determine the set of states that can be reached by the system starting from S_0. Reachability analysis can be used for safety verification, that means one has to check that the trajectories starting in S_0 remains in a safe set F, i.e. $Reach_{S_0} \subset safe\ set\ F$. This implies that the system is operating in safe conditions. Contrary, if $Reach_{S_0} \not\subset safe\ set\ F$ then the system is operating in unsafe conditions.
- *Time bounded reachability:* The system can reach a certain set of states within a certain time deadline (horizon time) and probability threshold. In safety-critical system, some region of the state space is "unsafe". One has to verify that the system operates in safe conditions, i.e. it keeps staying inside the safe set. If that is not the case the system has to be modified so as to guarantee safety. For example, this is the case for the mathematical models for the *safety critical air traffic management situations* [5, 28]. A central problem in air traffic control is determining the *conflict probability*, i.e. the probability two aircraft come closer than a minimum allowed distance within a certain time deadline. If this probability can be computed, an alert can be issued when it exceeds a certain threshold.
- *Bounded response:* The system inevitably reaches a certain set of states within a certain time deadline with a given probability. Critical issue for systems operating in a highly dynamic uncertain environment: safety has to be repeatedly verified on-line based on updated information, so as timely take appropriate corrective actions for steering the system trajectory outside of the unsafe set. This reachability analysis can provide useful information for diagnosis purposes and corrective action design like controller design based on reachability analysis.

4.2   Measurability of Reach Events

In this subsection, we show that the performance measures defined in the previous subsection are well defined, i.e. the reach events (3) are, indeed, measurable sets in the underlying probability space. The proof (see the Appendix) argument is based on analytic set properties.

Analytic Sets. Let F be a set. A *paving* on F is any family of subsets of F which contains the empty set. The pair $(F, \mathcal{E})$ consisting of a set F and a paving $\mathcal{E}$ is called *paved set*.

   The closure of a family of subsets $\mathcal{E}$ under countable unions (resp. intersections) is denoted by $\mathcal{E}_\sigma$ (resp. $\mathcal{E}_\delta$). We shall write $\mathcal{E}_{\sigma\delta} = (\mathcal{E}_\sigma)_\delta$.
Let $(F, \mathcal{E})$ be a paved set. A subset $A \in \mathcal{E}$ is called $\mathcal{E}$-*analytic* if there exists an auxiliary compact metrizable space $\mathbf{K}$ and a subset $B \subseteq K \times F$ belonging to $(\mathcal{K}(\mathbf{K}) \times \mathcal{E})_{\sigma\delta}$, such that A is the projection of B onto F. The paving of F consisting of all $\mathcal{E}$-analytic sets is denoted by $\mathcal{A}(\mathcal{E})$.

Remark 1. $\mathcal{E} \subset \mathcal{A}(\mathcal{E})$; and the paving $\mathcal{A}(\mathcal{E})$ is closed under countable unions and intersections.

Let $\mathcal{B}(\mathbb{R})$ be the Borel sets in $\mathbb{R}$, $\mathcal{K}(\mathbb{R})$ the paving of all compact sets in $\mathbb{R}$ and $(\Omega, \mathcal{E})$ be a measurable space.

Theorem 1. *[2] (1)* $\mathcal{B}(\mathbb{R}) \subset \mathcal{A}(\mathcal{K})$, $\mathcal{A}(\mathcal{B}(\mathbb{R})) = \mathcal{A}(\mathcal{K})$. *(2) The product* $\sigma-$*field* $\mathcal{G} = \mathcal{B}(\mathbb{R}) \times \mathcal{E}$ *on* $\mathbb{R} \times \Omega$ *is contained in* $\mathcal{A}(\mathcal{K}(\mathbb{R}) \times \mathcal{E})$. *(3) The projection onto* Ω *of an element of* $\mathcal{G}$ *(or, more generally, of* $\mathcal{A}(\mathcal{G})$*) is* $\mathcal{E}$-*analytic.*

Recall that a Borel space is a topological space which is homeomorphic to a Borel subset of a complete separable metric space. Every Borel subset of a Borel space is analytic [2].

   We denote the set of all probability measures on Ω by $\mathcal{P}(\Omega)$. If Ω is a Borel space and P is a probability measure on $(\Omega, \mathcal{B}(\Omega))$ we define $\mathcal{B}_\Omega(P)$ the completion of $\mathcal{B}(\Omega)$ under P. The *universal* σ-*algebra* $\mathcal{U}_\Omega$ is defined as the intersection of $\{\mathcal{B}_\Omega(P), P \in \mathcal{P}(\Omega)\}$.

Proposition 1. *[2] Every analytic subset of a Borel space is universally measurable.*

Measurability. Using the canonical representation of a Markov process, we can choose Ω as $\overline{D}_X[0, \infty)$ the set of right continuous functions with left limits with values in X. $D_X[0, \infty)$ is a Borel space [4].

Theorem 2. *Let* $E \in \mathcal{B}(X)$ *be a given Borel set. Then* $Reach_T(E)$ *and* $Reach_\infty(E)$ *are universally measurable sets in* Ω.

The proof of theorem 2 is based only on two properties of the Markov process in cause: (i) the process is measurable; (ii) its probability space is Borel space.

4.3   Upper Bounds

Let $p_t(x, B) = P_x(x_t \in B) = P_t 1_B(x)$, $t > 0$, $x \in X$, $B \in \mathcal{B}(X)$ the transition function associated to the given Markov process.

Assumption 1. *All the measures $p_t(x, \cdot)$ are absolutely continuous with respect to a σ-finite measure m on $(X, \mathcal{B}(X))$.*

We denote the Radon-Nycodim derivative of $p_t(x, \cdot)$ by $\rho_t(x, \cdot)$, i.e. $\rho_t(x, y) = p_t(x, dy)/m(dy)$. This can be chosen to be measurable in x, y and to satisfy $\int_X \rho_s(x, y) m(dy) \rho_t(y, z) = \rho_{t+s}(x, z)$.
A σ-finite measure m on $(X, \mathcal{B}(X))$ is called *reference measure* if $m(B) = 0$ if and only if $p_t(x, B) = 0$ for all t and x. Throughout this paper we suppose that m, in the absolutely continuity assumption, is a reference measure.
We define the *Green kernel* as $u(x, y) = \int_0^\infty \rho_t(x, y) dt$.

Assumption 2. *i) $y \to u(x, y)^{-1}$ is finite continuous, for $y \in X$; ii) $u(x, y) = +\infty$ if and only if $x = y$.*

For a target set E we define a random variable $\gamma_E < \infty$ (M is transient), called the *last exit time* from E as follows:

$$\gamma_E(\omega) = \begin{cases} \sup\{t > 0 | x_t(\omega) \in E\} & \text{if } \omega \in Reach_\infty(E) \\ 0 & \text{if } \omega \in \Omega \backslash Reach_\infty(E) \end{cases}$$

Then, the *distribution of the last exit position* x_{γ_E-} is given by

$$L^E(x, A) = P_x(\gamma_E > 0; \alpha_{\gamma_E-} \in A), \ x \in X, \ A \in \mathcal{B}(X).$$

Theorem 3. *Suppose that M satisfies the Assumptions 1 and 2. Let $x_0 \in X$ be initial state. For any closed set E of X we have*

$$P_{x_0}(T_E < \infty) \leq Cap_K(E) \tag{5}$$

where Cap_K is the capacity[1] defined, using (1), w.r.t. the Martin kernel K

$$K(x, y) = \frac{u(x, y)}{u(x_0, y)}.$$

5   Stochastic Bisimulation

Let $(X, \mathcal{B}(X))$ and $(Y, \mathcal{B}(Y))$ be Lusin spaces[2] and let $\mathcal{R} \subset X \times Y$ be a relation such that $\Pi^1(\mathcal{R}) = X$ and $\Pi^2(\mathcal{R}) = Y$. We define the equivalence relation on X that is induced by the relation $\mathcal{R} \subset X \times Y$, as the transitive closure of $\{(x, x') | \exists y$ s.t. $(x, y) \in \mathcal{R}$ and $(x', y) \in \mathcal{R}\}$. Analogously, the induced (by $\mathcal{R}$) equivalence

---

[1] This capacity is called Martin capacity.
[2] The equivalence relation introduced in this section can be defined in a more general setting of the analytic spaces.

relation on Y is defined. We write $X/_{\mathcal{R}}$ and $Y/_{\mathcal{R}}$ for the sets of equivalence classes of X and Y induced by $\mathcal{R}$. We denote the equivalence class of $x \in X$ by $[x]$. We define now the notion of *measurable relation*. Let $\mathcal{B}^*(X) = \mathcal{B}(X) \cap \{A \subset X | $ if $x \in A$ and $[x] = [x']$ then $x' \in A\}$ be the collection of all Borel sets in which any equivalence class of X is either totally contained or totally not contained. It can be checked that $\mathcal{B}^*(X)$ is a σ-algebra. Let $\pi_X : X \to X/_{\mathcal{R}}$ be the mapping that maps each $x \in X$ to its equivalence class and let

$$\mathcal{B}(X/_{\mathcal{R}}) = \{A \subset X/_{\mathcal{R}} | \pi_X^{-1}(A) \in \mathcal{B}^*(X)\}.$$

Then $(X/_{\mathcal{R}}, \mathcal{B}(X/_{\mathcal{R}}))$, which is a measurable space, is called the quotient space of X w.r.t. $\mathcal{R}$. The quotient space of Y w.r.t. $\mathcal{R}$ is defined in a similar way. We define a bijective mapping $\psi : X/_{\mathcal{R}} \to Y/_{\mathcal{R}}$ as $\psi([x]) = [y]$ if $(x, y) \in \mathcal{R}$ for some $x \in [x]$ and some $y \in [y]$. We say that the relation $\mathcal{R}$ is *measurable* if X and Y if for all $A \in \mathcal{B}(X/_{\mathcal{R}})$ we have $\psi(A) \in \mathcal{B}(Y/_{\mathcal{R}})$ and vice versa, i.e. ψ is a homeomorphism. Then the real measurable functions defined on $X/_{\mathcal{R}}$ can be identified with those defined on $Y/_{\mathcal{R}}$ through the homeomorphism ψ. We can write $\mathcal{B}^b(X/_{\mathcal{R}}) \overset{\psi}{\cong} \mathcal{B}^b(Y/_{\mathcal{R}})$. Moreover, these functions can be thought of as real functions defined on X or Y measurable w.r.t. $\mathcal{B}^*(X)$ or $\mathcal{B}^*(Y)$.

In the following we introduce a new concept of equivalence between two capacities w.r.t. a measurable relation defined on the product of their underlying spaces.

Definition 1. *Suppose we have the capacities c_X and c_Y on the Lusin spaces $(X, \mathcal{B}(X))$ and $(Y, \mathcal{B}(Y))$ respectively and a measurable relation $\mathcal{R} \subset X \times Y$. The capacities c_X and c_Y are called equivalent w.r.t. $\mathcal{R}$ if they define the same capacity on the quotient space of X and Y, i.e. if we have $c_X(\pi_X^{-1}(A)) = c_Y(\pi_Y^{-1}[\psi(A)])$ for all $A \in \mathcal{B}(X/_{\mathcal{R}})$.*

Suppose we have two Borel right Markov processes M and W with the state spaces X and Y. The equivalence between capacities will be employed in defining a new 'equivalence' between Markov processes, as follows.

Definition 2. *A measurable relation $\mathcal{R} \subset X \times Y$ is a bisimulation between M and W if their associated capacities Cap_M and Cap_W are equivalent w.r.t. $\mathcal{R}$.*

It is known that for symmetric processes (equal with their time reversed processes) defined on the same state space, the equality of their capacities implies that they are time changes of one another [17].

We can define now a *pseudometric w.r.t. a measurable relation $\mathcal{R} \subset X \times Y$* between the processes M and W as follows:

$$d_{\mathcal{R}}(M, W) = \sup_{f \in \mathcal{B}^{*b}(X)} | \int f dCap_M - \int f \circ \psi dCap_W|$$

where $\mathcal{B}^{*b}(X)$ is the set of bounded real $\mathcal{B}^*(X)$-measurable functions on X.

Proposition 2. *A measurable relation* $\mathcal{R} \subset X \times Y$ *is a bisimulation between* M *and* W *if and only if* $d_{\mathcal{R}}(M, W) = 0$.

In the classical theory of stochastic processes, one process is a modification of another iff their transition probabilities differ on set of times of measure zero.

Proposition 3. *A Borel right Markov process is bisimilar with any of its modifications.*

We can refine further this result by considering another way to define equivalence between stochastic processes. Two Markov processes are equivalent if they possess a common exceptional set (a set with zero capacity) outside which their transition functions coincide. This constitues now a classical concept in the theory of Markov processes [4].

Proposition 4. *Two equivalent Markov processes are bisimilar.*

The way to define bisimulation between two Markov processes is, in fact, a new approach to define coarser versions of the concept of equivalence between stochastic processes. In this approach, two processes are bisimilar (weak equivalent) if one can define an equivalence relation on the product of their state spaces such that the quotient processes have associated equal capacities (i.e. this weak equivalence preserves the probability to 'reach' certain state spaces over infinite horizon time).

Proposition 5. $\mathcal{R} \subset X \times Y$ *is a bisimulation relation between* M *and* W *if and only if the probabilities of reachable events (3) associated to "saturated" (w.r.t.* $\mathcal{R}$*) Borel sets are equal, i.e.* $\mathbb{P}_M(T_E < \infty) = \mathbb{P}_W(T_{\psi(E)} < \infty)$, $\forall E \in \mathcal{B}^*(X)$.

The proof is a clear consequence of definition of a bisimulation relation between two Markov processes.

6   Final Remarks

In this paper, we have defined a new model checking strategy and a stochastic bisimulation concept for a class of Markov processes (Borel right Markov processes) based on the notions of capacity and measurable relation. These processes can be understood as behaviours of fluid stochastic system models comprising stochastic hybrid systems, FSPNs and process algebra fluid models.

A bisimulation relation is defined as a measurable relation between two processes (i.e. a relation on the product of their state spaces, which induces two homeomorphic quotient measurable spaces) which preserves the capacities (i.e. the reach set probabilities). A capacity is non-additive set-function used to represent uncertainty. The mathematical theory of non-additive set-functions got its first contribution with Gustave Choquet's "Theory of Capacities" [10] in 1953. Choquet's interest was applications to potential theory. For continuous dynamical systems, the classical concept of measure is too rough to provide the negligible sets. Two dynamical (deterministic or random) systems that differ only on a negligible set are considered to be the same. The capacity has higher discrimination power and a negligible set is defined as a zero capacity set. This short definition was the solution for more than a century of mathematical research. A bisimulation defined using this interpretation of capacity would be too strong: bisimilar processes would be equivalent in a classical sense. In this paper, we have used modern, probabilistic interpretations of capacity as non-linear generalisations of probabilities. The modern capacity theory has found applications in decision theory [15, 30], robust Bayesian inference [19], automated reasoning [16], etc. Capacities have been recently used in computer science, notably in the context of linear logic and in the study of labelled Markov processes (see, for example, [14] and the references therein).

Moreover, using the concept of integral associated to a capacity we have introduced a pseudometric between processes. The distance between two processes is measured in terms of probabilities of the set of trajectories which ever visit the sets that can be "identified" through the homeomorphism induced by a measurable relation.

Examples of fluid models can be found in the references on FSPNs and stochastic hybrid systems. The general approach followed in this paper served to identify the fundamental principles and to distinguish generally applicable techniques from ad-hoc methods.

The natural step to be developed further is to employ the extensions of the continuous stochastic logic for formal specification of performability properties. The semantics of this logic is fully compatible with the semantic framework we have proposed in this paper. Then a complete numerical case study could be developed. The present paper is the (necessary) first step in creating the sound mathematical foundations of a model checking strategy. In a further paper, we apply this model checking strategy to a fluid model of TCP/IP in a form of a stochastic hybrid system.

There are various approaches to the formal specifications and / or model checking probabilistic properties of systems with continuous state space components. The references list some of these approaches, but, of course, the list could have been continued. However, to the authors' knowledge, the approach presented in this paper is new and it does not relate easily with the existing ones.

Acknowledgements. The first author thanks Prof. Holger Hermanns, principal investigator of the AiSHA project [27].

References

1. Alur, R., Pappas, G. Eds., *Hybrid Systems: Computation and Control* 7th International Workshop, HSCC04, Springer LNCS 2993 (2004).
2. Bertsekas, D.P., Shreve, S.E.: *"Stochastic Optimal Control: The Discrete-Time Case"*. Athena Scientific (1996).
3. Bohacek S., Hespanha J., Lee J., Obraczka K., *Modeling Data Communication Networks Using Hybrid Systems*. IEEE/ACM Trans. on Networking, (2006).

4. Borkar, V.S.: *"Probability Theory"*. An Advance Course. Springer (1995).
5. Bujorianu, M.L : *Extended Stochastic Hybrid Systems and their Reachability Problem*. In [1], (2004), 234-249.
6. Bujorianu, M.L., Lygeros, J., Bujorianu, M.C.: *Bisimulation for General Stochastic Hybrid Systems*. In M. Morari, L. Thiele Eds., *Hybrid Systems: Computation and Control* 8th Int. Workshop, HSCC04, Springer LNCS **3414** (2005), 198-214.
7. Bujorianu. M.L: *Capacities and Markov Processes*, Lib. Math. **24** (2004), 201-210.
8. Bujorianu, M.L., Bujorianu, M.C.: *Distributed Stochastic Hybrid Systems*. In A. Kucera Ed., *Proceedings of IFAC 2005*, Elsevier Press.
9. Bujorianu, M.L, Bujorianu, M.C., Blom, H.A.P.: *Towards Model Checking Stochastic Hybrid Systems by Approximate Abstractions*. Submitted.
10. Choquet, G.: *Theory of Capacities*. Annales de l'Institut Fourier, Grenoble, **5** (1953), 131-291.
11. Chung, K.L.: *Probabilistic Approach in Potential Theory to the Equilibrium Problem*. Annales de L'Institut Fourier,Grenoble, **23** (1973), 313-322.
12. Ciardo G., Nicol D., Trivedi K.S., *Discrete-Event Simulation of Fluid Stochastic Petri Nets* Proc 7th Int. Workshop on Petri Nets and Performance Models (1997) 217-225.
13. Davis, M.H.A.: *"Markov Models and Optimization"*, Chapman & Hall, London (1993).
14. Desharnais, J., Gupta, V., Jagadeesan, Panangaden, P.: *Weak Bisimulation is Sound and Complete for PCTL*. Proc.13th Int. Conference on Concurrency Theory. Springer LNCS **2421** (2002), 355-370.
15. Dempster, D.: *Upper and Lower Probabilities Induced by a Multi-valued Mapping*. Ann. Math. Statist. **38** (1967), 325-339.
16. Dubois, D., Prade, H.: *Modelling Uncertainty and Inductive Inference: A Survey of Recent Non-Additive Probability Systems*. Acta Psychologica **68** (1988), 53-78.
17. Fitzsimmons, P.J.: *Markov Processes with Equal Capacities*. J. Theor. Prob. **12** (1999), 271-292.
18. Horton G., Kulkarni V., Nicol D., Trivedi K.S.: *Fluid Stochastic Petri Nets: Theory, Applications, and Solution*. Eur. J. Oper. Res.**105**(1) (1998), 184-201.
19. Huber, P.J.: *"Robust Statistics"*. Willey, New York, 1980.
20. Hermanns, H., Katoen, J-P: *Automated Compositional Markov Chain Generation for a Plain-old Telephone System*. Science of Computer Programming, **36(1)**, (2000), 97 - 127.
21. Hespanha, J.P.: *Stochastic Hybrid Systems: Application to Communication Networks*. In [1] (2004) 387-401.
22. Kang W., Kelly F. P., Lee, N. H., Williams, R. J.: *Fluid and Brownian Approximations for an Internet congestion control model*. Proceedings of the 43rd IEEE Conference on Decision and Control (2004).
23. Kelly F. P.: *Mathematical Modelling of the Internet*. In B. Engquist, W. Schmid eds. "Mathematics Unlimited - 2001 and Beyond" Springer-Verlag (2001), 685-70.
24. Kulkarni V., Trivedi K.S., *FSPNs: Fluid Stochastic Petri Nets* In Proc. 14th Int. Conf. On the Application and Theory of Petri Nets (1993) 24-31.
25. Kwiatkowska, Norman, G., Parker, D., Sproston, J.: *Performance Analysis of Probabilistic Timed Automata using Digital Clocks*. Formal Methods in System Design. Springer. To appear (2006).
26. Kwiatkowska, M., Norman, G., Segal R., Sproston, J.: *Automatic Verification of Real Time Systems with Discrete Probability Distribution* Theoretical Computer Science 282, (2002), 101-150.

27. NWO Project Description AiSHA: "Abstraction in Stochastic and Hybrid process Algebra" www.onderzoekinformatie.nl/en/oi/nod/onderzoek/OND1303139
28. Pola G., Bujorianu, M.L., Lygeros, J., Di Benedetto, M. D.: *Stochastic Hybrid Models: An Overview with applications to Air Traffic Management*. Proccedings Analysis and Design of Hybrid Systems IFAC ADHS03, (2003), 45-50.
29. Shafer G.: *"A Mathematical Theory of Evidence"*. Princeton Univ. Press (1976).
30. Schmeidler D.: *Subjective Probability and Expected Utility Without Additivity*. Econometrica **57** (1989), 571-587.
31. Viertl R.: *"Statistical Methods for Non-Precise Data"*. CRC Press (1996).
32. WalleyP.: *Statistical Reasoning with Imprecise Probabilities*.Chapman&Hall (1991).
33. Wolter K. *Second Order Fluid Stochastic Petri Nets: an Extension of GSPNs for Approximate and Continuous Modeling*. World Congress on System Simulation (1997), 328-332.

Appendix

Proof. of Th.2. Since the process has cadlag property then $x : \mathbb{R}_+ \times \Omega \to X$ is a measurable function w.r.t. $\mathcal{B}(\mathbb{R}_+) \times \mathcal{F}^0$ and $\mathcal{B}(X)$. Since $E \in \mathcal{B}(X)$, then clearly $x^{-1}(E) \in \mathcal{B}(\mathbb{R}_+) \times \mathcal{F}^0$. For $T > 0$, we set $A_T(E) = x^{-1}(E) \cap [0, T] \times \Omega$. Since $[0, T] \times \Omega \in \mathcal{B}(\mathbb{R}_+) \times \mathcal{F}^0$ then $A_T(E) \in \mathcal{B}(\mathbb{R}_+) \times \mathcal{F}^0$. Now, using the theorem 1 we obtain that $Reach_T(E) = Proj_\Omega A_T(E)$ is an $\mathcal{F}^0$-analytic set. Therefore, because Ω is a Borel space, this implies (cf. to prop 1) that $Reach_T(E)$ is an universally measurable set. Obviously, $Reach_\infty(E)$ is, also, an universally measurable set. Since $\mathcal{U}_\Omega$ the $\sigma-$algebra of universally measurable sets is included in $\mathcal{F}$ (which is the completion of $\mathcal{F}^0$ w.r.t. all probabilities P_μ, where μ runs in the set $\mathcal{P}(X)$.

Proof. of Th.3. To bound from above the probability of ever hitting E, consider the hitting time T_E and the last exit time γ_E of E, and the distribution

$$\nu_{x_0}(\Lambda) = L^E(x_0, \Lambda) = P_{x_0}(t < \gamma_E | \alpha_{\gamma_E-} \in \Lambda); \ \Lambda \in \mathcal{B}(X)$$

The Kai Lai Chung's [11] result says that $L^E(\rho, \Lambda) = \int_\Lambda u(x, y)\mu_E(d\beta); \ \Lambda \in \mathcal{B}(X)$, where μ_E is the equilibrium measure of E is given by

$$\mu_E(dy) = L^E(x, dy)u(x, y)^{-1} = \nu_x(dy)u(x, y)^{-1}, \forall x \in X$$

in particular, for the initial state $x_0 \in X$

$$\mu_E(dy) = L^E(x_0, dy)u(x_0, y)^{-1} = \nu_{x_0}(dy)u(x_0, y)^{-1}.$$

It follows that $\int_E K(x, y)\nu_{x_0}(d\beta y) = \int_E K(x, y)u(x_0, y)\mu_E(dy) = \int_E u(x, y)\mu_E(dy) = P_x(T_E < \infty) \leq 1$. Therefore $K(\nu_{x_0}, \nu_{x_0}) \leq \nu_{x_0}(E)$ and thus $Cap_K(E) \geq [K(\nu_{x_0}/\nu_{x_0}(E))]^{-1} \geq \nu_{x_0}(E)$, which yields the upper bound on the probability of hitting E.

Explicit Inverse Characterizations of Acyclic MAPs of Second Order

Armin Heindl[1], Gábor Horváth[2], and Karsten Gross[1]

[1] Universität Erlangen-Nürnberg
Computer Networks and Communication Systems
91058 Erlangen, Germany
[2] Technical University of Budapest
Dept. of Telecommunications
1521 Budapest, Hungary

Abstract. This paper shows how to construct a Markovian arrival process of second order from information on the marginal distribution and on its autocorrelation function. More precisely, closed-form explicit expressions for the MAP(2) rate matrices are given in terms of the first three marginal moments and one parameter that characterizes the behavior of the autocorrelation function. Besides the permissible moment ranges, which were known before, also the necessary and sufficient bounds for the correlation parameter are computed and shown to depend on a free parameter related to equivalent acyclic PH(2) representations of the marginal distribution. We identify the choices for the free parameter that maximize the correlation range for both negative and positive correlation parameters.

Keywords: Acyclic Markovian arrival processes of second order, inverse characterization, moment and correlation bounds.

1 Introduction

Matrix-analytic methods ([1, 2, 3], also see the journal on *Stochastic Models* for recent advances) provide a wide range of efficient algorithms to evaluate diverse queueing systems. Especially for application studies, it is also important to provide convenient ways to inversely characterize (correlated) arrival and service processes, which are represented by the matrices of Markovian arrival processes (MAPs)[1]. In the wide sense, inverse characterization refers to constructing the MAP matrices from observations (e.g., data traces) or other information, like performance metrics, of the considered process. In the narrow sense, which we adopt here, inverse characterization means to find analytic expressions for the MAP matrices in terms of their marginal distribution and their autocorrelation behavior – along with bounds for the permissible ranges of the involved input parameters in order to ensure valid MAP representations. It is clear that both rate expressions and bounds will depend on the order of the MAPs to be characterized.

Recent years have seen significant advances in the field of inverse characterization of MAPs both in the wide and narrow sense. Regarding the former case, quite general

---

[1] MAPs can be generalized to processes with batch arrivals, so-called batch Markovian arrival processes. We will not consider batches in this paper.

A. Horváth and M. Telek (Eds.): EPEW 2006, LNCS 4054, pp. 108–122, 2006.

fitting techniques for MAPs of arbitrary (preferably small) orders have been proposed. Usually, these algorithms are based on some optimization [4, 5], which may be computationally expensive and/or which may result in models, which differ significantly from identified key characteristics like the marginal moments. Also, approximately capturing non-Markovian behavior (e.g., self-similarity) by Markovian models such as MAPs has received a lot of attention (see [6] for an introduction to the topic).

Exact and inexpensive moment/correlation fitting, as it ensues from an inverse characterization in the narrow sense, has obvious advantages. Especially, explicit closed-form expressions for the MAP representations are desired, but have only been found for special cases.

Without correlations, i.e., when phase-type (PH) distributions need to be fitted to moments, analytical results are now available to map an arbitrary number of moments to acyclic PH distributions of minimal order [7]. Explicit expressions for the moment bounds of the first three moments for acyclic PH distributions may be found in [8] for order 2 and in [9] for arbitrary order n. Including correlations into distributional models has not yet led to complete inverse characterizations. For correlated matrix-exponential processes, which are algebraic generalizations of MAPs, a general order-n representation has been developed based on the first $2n - 1$ marginal moments and $2n - 3$ correlation parameters, but lacks the corresponding bounds to decide when this representation is valid [10]. In [11], a representation of order n with a single correlation parameter is proposed that guarantees validity, however, at the expense of reduced flexibility in capturing correlations.

In the Markovian domain, attention has so far focused on correlated MAP representations of order 2. The inverse problem for general MAP(2)s has already been studied in [12], but neither the MAP(2) representation nor the related correlation bounds were given explicitly therein. For an important special case, namely MAP(2)s with the marginal distribution being a mixture of two exponentials, this was achieved in [13]. Beyond the more compact and closed forms, these results generalize the applicability as compared with analytical techniques of moment/correlation fitting for Markov-modulated Poisson processes (MMPPs) of order 2 [14, 15]. However, both the MMPP structure and the mixtures of exponentials as marginals limited the mapping to MAP(2)s with squared coefficients of variations greater than (or equal to) one.

In this paper, we finally provide a complete and explicit characterization of acyclic MAP(2)s with hyperexponential and hypoexponential marginals. For both cases, dedicated closed-form representations as well as correlation bounds are given, where a new approach to the symbolic solution allows to yet extend the known results even for hyperexponential MAP(2)s. The provided MAP(2) representation and its bounds fully exploit the capabilities of these processes to capture correlations. Thus, a very simple and easy-to-implement correlated traffic/service model is at hand, which may not only be used efficiently in matrix-analytic methods, but also in discrete-event simulation. Despite its limitations due to the minimal order, it is ideally suited to study the impact of short- and long-term correlation on systems, the importance of which has already been highlighted in [16, 17].

The paper is organized as follows: In Section 2, we first review the existing explicit representation for MAP(2)s with mixtures of exponentials as their marginal, which is extended to general acyclic MAP(2)s – both with hyper- and hypoexponential marginals – in Section 4. In between, Section 3 outlines how the latter representation and the necessary and sufficient bounds were derived. Section 5 translates the inverse characterization of MAP(2)s into a practical fitting algorithm that fully exploits the moment and correlation ranges of MAP(2)s. Section 6 concludes the paper.

2   Second-Order Markovian Arrival Processes with Two-Branch Marginal Distributions

In general, Markovian Arrival Processes (MAPs) are ergodic Continuous-Time Markov Chains (CTMCs), in which transitions are distinguished by whether they cause an event or not. The rates are grouped into two matrices $\mathbf{D}_1$ and $\mathbf{D}_0$, such that

$\mathbf{D}_1$ is a nonnegative $(m_{\text{MAP}} \times m_{\text{MAP}})$-rate matrix, where m_{MAP} is the order of the MAP.
$\mathbf{D}_0$ is a matrix of the same dimension as $\mathbf{D}_1$, with negative diagonal and nonnegative off-diagonal elements.

The matrix $\mathbf{Q}_{\text{MAP}} = \mathbf{D}_0 + \mathbf{D}_1$ is the irreducible infinitesimal generator of the CTMC, where $\mathbf{D}_0$ governs transitions that do not correspond to events, while $\mathbf{D}_1$ governs those transitions that do correspond to events. Special cases of MAPs include Markov-modulated Poisson processes (MMPPs) and PH-type renewal processes.

2.1   Analytic Construction

In this paper, we focus on MAPs of order 2, i.e., $m_{\text{MAP}} = 2$, and even more specifically in this section, on MAP(2)s, whose marginal distribution is a mixture of two exponentials. For such MAP(2)s, a closed-form representation for the two-dimensional matrices $\mathbf{D}_0$ and $\mathbf{D}_1$ was given explicitly in terms of the first three moments and a correlation parameter [13]. The solution of this inverse problem leads to the CTMC in Figure 1 (left-hand side), where each transition causes an event and the corresponding rates λ_{ij} $(i, j = 1, 2)$ thus appear matrix $\mathbf{D}_1$. Since associated events and interevent times between them are considered for MAPs (and not only state probabilities), it is important to preserve event-related self-loops in the CTMC. For MAP(2)s, whose marginal distribution is a mixture of two exponentials (see right-hand side of Figure 1 with an additional absorbing state besides the two now transient states of the CTMC), $\mathbf{D}_0$ will be a diagonal matrix. Thus, $\mathbf{D}_0$ and $\mathbf{D}_1$ take the form

$$\mathbf{D}_0 = \begin{bmatrix} -\lambda_1 & 0 \\ 0 & -\lambda_2 \end{bmatrix}, \mathbf{D}_1 = \begin{bmatrix} \lambda_{11} & \lambda_{12} \\ \lambda_{21} & \lambda_{22} \end{bmatrix} \quad ,$$

where $\lambda_i = \lambda_{i1} + \lambda_{i2}$ for $i = 1, 2$. Rates related to the leftmost state in Figure 1 appear in row 1 of matrices $\mathbf{D}_0$ and $\mathbf{D}_1$.

Before we give the functions, which explicitly compute the rate parameters λ_{ij} from the first three moments of the marginal distribution and a correlation parameter, we introduce some auxiliary notation and explain the meaning of the correlation parameter. Let us denote the four input parameters by $r_i = \frac{E[X^i]}{i!}$, $i = 1, 2, 3$, the first three (reduced) moments of the marginal distribution, and γ, the correlation parameter. Random

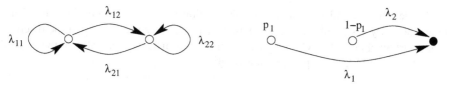

Fig. 1. Markov chain for the MAP(2), where each transition causes an event (left), and its hyper-exponential two-branch marginal PH distribution (right): $\lambda_i = \lambda_{i1} + \lambda_{i2}$ for $i = 1, 2$

variable X (also used with a subscript, as in X_k, to indicate the interevent times in a sequence) stands for a generic interevent time of the MAP point process. For MAPs of second order, the lag-k covariances of interevent times can be characterized by [12]

$$\text{cov}[X_0, X_k] = E[(X_0 - r_1)(X_k - r_1)] = \gamma^k(r_2 - r_1^2) \quad k \in \mathbb{N} \quad . \tag{1}$$

Here, X_0 and X_k denote two interevent times k lags apart. Therefore, the decay of the correlation structure of a MAP(2) is determined by the parameter γ (where the first two marginal moments serve to scale the correlation function). The correlation function decays geometrically in absolute terms.

Now, with the auxiliary variables

$$h_2 \equiv \frac{r_2 - r_1^2}{r_1^2} \qquad h_3 \equiv \frac{r_3 r_1 - r_2^2}{r_1^4} \tag{2}$$

$$b \equiv h_3 + h_2^2 - h_2 \qquad c \equiv \sqrt{b^2 + 4h_2^3} \quad , \tag{3}$$

the MAP(2) matrices $\mathbf{D}_0$ and $\mathbf{D}_1$ are explicitly constructed as

$$\mathbf{D}_0 = \frac{1}{2r_1 h_3} \begin{bmatrix} -(2h_2 + b - c) & 0 \\ 0 & -(2h_2 + b + c) \end{bmatrix} \tag{4}$$

$$\mathbf{D}_1 = \frac{1}{4r_1 h_3} \begin{bmatrix} (2h_2 + b - c)(1 - \frac{b}{c} + \gamma(1 + \frac{b}{c})) & (2h_2 + b - c)(1 + \frac{b}{c})(1 - \gamma) \\ (2h_2 + b + c)(1 - \frac{b}{c})(1 - \gamma) & (2h_2 + b + c)(1 + \frac{b}{c} + \gamma(1 - \frac{b}{c})) \end{bmatrix} \tag{5}$$

where, of course, $\lambda_1 = \frac{2h_2 + b - c}{2r_1 h_3}$ for instance.

2.2   Performance Measures

Generally for arbitrary MAPs, a variety of performance measures can be computed from $\mathbf{D}_0$ and $\mathbf{D}_1$. Here, we specialize the general formulas to verify the above MAP(2) representation. The stationary probability vector of the CTMC generator is defined by $\boldsymbol{\pi}_{\text{MAP}} \mathbf{Q}_{\text{MAP}} = \mathbf{0}$ with normalization $\boldsymbol{\pi}_{\text{MAP}} \mathbf{e} = 1$, where $\mathbf{0}$ and $\mathbf{e}$ denote the row/column vectors of zeros or ones of the appropriate dimension. In two dimensions with representation (4) and (5), we obtain

$$\boldsymbol{\pi}_{\text{MAP2}} = \frac{1}{2c} \begin{bmatrix} c + 2h_2^2 - b & c - 2h_2^2 + b \end{bmatrix} \quad . \tag{6}$$

Besides the general-time stationary distribution π_{MAP}, we also consider the event-time stationary distribution, i.e., the stationary probability vector $\mathbf{p}_{\text{MAP}}$ of the discrete-time Markov chain (DTMC) embedded at the event instants. Specializing the general formula for the MAP(2) representation yields:

$$\mathbf{p}_{\text{MAP}} = \frac{\pi_{\text{MAP}}\mathbf{D}_1}{\pi_{\text{MAP}}\mathbf{D}_1\mathbf{e}} = \frac{1}{2c}\begin{bmatrix} c - b & c + b \end{bmatrix} = \begin{bmatrix} p_1 & 1 - p_1 \end{bmatrix} = \mathbf{p}_{\text{MAP2}} \quad . \tag{7}$$

Note that the tuple $(\mathbf{p}_{\text{MAP}}, \mathbf{D}_0)$ specifies the marginal PH distribution of a MAP. The right-hand side of Figure 1 depicts this distribution in our special case with the two-dimensional initial probability vector $\mathbf{p}_{\text{MAP2}}$.

Of course, with representation (4) and (5), we should be able to reproduce the marginal moments and the correlation structure as specified by the input parameters. And indeed, the arrival rate, the squared coefficient of variation (of the PH-type marginal distribution) and the autocorrelation function of the MAP reduce to

$$\lambda_{\text{MAP}} = \pi_{\text{MAP}}\mathbf{D}_1\mathbf{e} = \frac{1}{r_1} \tag{8}$$

$$c_{\text{MAP}}^2 = \frac{E[X^2]}{(E[X])^2} - 1 = 2\lambda_{\text{MAP}}\pi_{\text{MAP}}(-\mathbf{D}_0)^{-1}\mathbf{e} - 1 = 2h_2 + 1 = \frac{2r_2}{r_1^2} - 1 \tag{9}$$

$$\begin{aligned}
\text{corr}[X_0, X_k] &= \frac{E[(X_0 - E[X])(X_k - E[X])]}{\text{Var}[X]} \\
&= \frac{\lambda_{\text{MAP}}\pi_{\text{MAP}}((-\mathbf{D}_0)^{-1}\mathbf{D}_1)^k(-\mathbf{D}_0)^{-1}\mathbf{e} - 1}{2\lambda_{\text{MAP}}\pi_{\text{MAP}}(-\mathbf{D}_0)^{-1}\mathbf{e} - 1} \\
&= \gamma^k\frac{h_2}{2h_2 + 1} = \gamma^k\frac{r_2 - r_1^2}{2r_2 - r_1^2} \quad .
\end{aligned} \tag{10}$$

As opposed to the covariances in (1), we gave here the lag-k coefficients of correlation ($k > 0$) [18].

2.3   Limitations

While the usefulness of the MAP(2) with a mixture of two exponentials as its marginal has been demonstrated in [5], it is of course subject to a number of limitations. These stem primarily from the low order of the MAP(2), but also from the additional constraint that the marginal distribution is a mixture of two exponentials.

For second-order PH distributions, moment bounds for the first three (reduced) moments have been established in [8] and remain invariant when these distributions are embedded into MAP(2)s as marginals. Table 1 summarizes the moment bounds, which differ for the hypo- ($c_{\text{MAP2}}^2 < 1$ or $h_2 < 0$) and hyperexponential ($c_{\text{MAP2}}^2 > 1$ or $h_2 > 0$) setting. For simplicity, these bounds are encoded in terms of the auxiliary variables h_2 and h_3. Variables h_2 and h_3 are related to Hankel determinants and their values can be interpreted as the (normalized) additional information carried by the respective moment that cannot be implied from the lower moments [19].

The case $h_2 = 0$ (i.e., $c_{\text{MAP2}}^2 = 1$) has been excluded, because then a PH(2) representation must be stochastically equivalent to an exponential distribution (and a MAP(2) with such a marginal distribution cannot capture any correlations [12]).

Table 1. Bounds for the first three moments of PH(2) distributions in terms of r_1, h_2, h_3

$r_1 > 0$	hypoexponential	hyperexponential
h_2	$-\frac{1}{4} \leq h_2 < 0$	$0 < h_2$
h_3	$h_2(1 - h_2 - 2\sqrt{-h_2}) \leq h_3 \leq -h_2{}^2$	$0 < h_3$

Since mixtures of exponentials will always result in distributions with a squared coefficient of variation greater than 1, the marginal distribution of the MAP(2) representation (4) and (5) implies $h_2, h_3 > 0$, thus excluding the hypoexponential setting. As we will see in Section 4, the diagonal structure of $\mathbf{D}_0$, as it ensues from a mixture of two exponentials, additionally restricts the capabilities by which correlations can be introduced into a MAP(2) with hyperexponential marginals.

In [13], the bounds on the correlation parameter γ for representations (4) and (5) were shown to depend on the sign of parameter b:

$$\text{if } b > 0: \qquad \text{if } b = 0: \qquad \text{if } b < 0: \qquad (11)$$
$$\gamma \geq \gamma_{\min} = \frac{b-c}{b+c} \qquad \gamma \geq \gamma_{\min} = -1 \qquad \gamma \geq \gamma_{\min} = \frac{b+c}{b-c}$$

where $1 > \gamma$ always holds. Furthermore, the lower bound $\gamma_{\min}$ is negative in all cases, but never below -1.

From the moment and correlation bounds for MAP(2) representation (4) and (5), we see that such hyperexponential MAPs can only have completely nonnegative correlation structures or alternating correlation structures starting with a negative first coefficient of correlation (see (10) or (1)). In contrast, MAP(2)s with hypoexponential marginals might also exhibit a completely negative correlation structure or alternating correlation structures starting with a positive first coefficient of correlation. This paper will provide an acyclic MAP(2) representation that fully exploits the possibilities to jointly capture marginal moments and correlations for two-dimensional MAPs.

3   Outline of Derivations for Acyclic MAP(2)s

The inverse problem for general MAP(2)s has been studied in [12]. While the permissibility of the first three moments can be confirmed by means of Table 1, the general bounds for the correlation parameter γ could only be obtained numerically in [12]. The approach followed in this reference exploited a moment/correlation-fitting canonical form of second-order matrix-exponential processes, which was converted to MAP(2) representations. Success and failure of this algorithmic conversion – dependent on the moment/correlation input parameters – allowed to locate bounds of the correlation parameter.

In [5], a rather direct non-linear optimization approach for fitting MAPs of arbitrary order was proposed. However, it turns out that the equations involved in the optimization can be manipulated to yield a closed-form representation of acyclic MAP(2)s as well as an explicit formulation of the correlation bounds. In this section, we will not give the full and cumbersome derivation details, but rather outline the steps from the initial set of equations to the final results presented in Section 4.

Fig. 2. The canonical representation of second-order PH distributions (left) and its transformation (right)

The left-hand side of Figure 2 shows a commonly used canonical form of acyclic PH distributions of second order. For order 2, the class of acyclic PH distributions is equivalent to that of cyclic PH distributions (which may contain loops). Thus, all PH(2) distributions – be they hyper- or hypoexponential – may be represented in the given acyclic canonical form. However, when using this form as a basis to construct MAP(2)s, no correlation may be introduced into these MAPs. Obviously, with only a single transition to generate events (namely, that from the central to the absorbing state), this canonical form is not flexible enough to accommodate correlations. However, the desired flexibility (with two event-generating transitions) may be achieved by transforming the canonical form into the representation on the right-hand side of Figure 2. This transformation for better correlation fitting was already proposed in [5] and – in our case – can be performed by solving two linear equations symbolically. In PH notation, the transformed distribution is written as

$$\mathbf{p}_{\text{MAP2}} = \begin{bmatrix} p_1 & 1 - p_1 \end{bmatrix} = \frac{1}{\lambda_2 - a\lambda_1} \begin{bmatrix} \lambda_2 p_1' & \lambda_2(1 - p_1') - a\lambda_1 \end{bmatrix} \quad , \tag{12}$$

$$\mathbf{D}_0 = \begin{bmatrix} -\lambda_1 & \lambda_1(1 - a) \\ 0 & -\lambda_2 \end{bmatrix} \quad , \tag{13}$$

where parameter a may be chosen arbitrarily in $[0, 1]$. Note that $a = 0$ yields the original canonical form and that, in the canonical form, the rate parameters are usually chosen such that $\lambda_1 \leq \lambda_2$.

The parameters p_1', λ_1 and λ_2 can be determined from the first three moments r_1, r_2, r_2, or equivalently from r_1, h_2, h_3. Corresponding analytic three-moment fitting techniques are found in [8, 9].

In going from a PH(2) distribution to a MAP(2) with a prescribed correlation parameter γ (i.e., with a correlation structure $\text{corr}[X_0, X_k] = \gamma^k \frac{h_2}{2h_2+1}$), we have to find a suitable matrix $\mathbf{D}_1$ with nonnegative entries. Let

$$\mathbf{D}_1 = \begin{bmatrix} x_{11} & x_{12} \\ x_{21} & x_{22} \end{bmatrix} \quad .$$

The four unknowns x_{ij} can be determined from the following equations:

$$(\mathbf{D}_0 + \mathbf{D}_1)\,\mathbf{e} = \mathbf{e} \tag{14}$$

$$\mathbf{p}_{\text{MAP2}}\,(-\mathbf{D}_0)^{-1}\,\mathbf{D}_1 = \mathbf{p}_{\text{MAP2}} \tag{15}$$

$$\frac{\lambda_{\text{MAP2}}\boldsymbol{\pi}_{\text{MAP2}}(-\mathbf{D}_0)^{-1}\mathbf{D}_1(-\mathbf{D}_0)^{-1}\mathbf{e} - 1}{2\lambda_{\text{MAP2}}\boldsymbol{\pi}_{\text{MAP2}}(-\mathbf{D}_0)^{-1}\mathbf{e} - 1} = \gamma\frac{h_2}{2h_2 + 1} \tag{16}$$

Equation (14), which contributes two scalar equations, ensures that the CTMC generator of the constructed MAP(2) has zero row sums. Equation (15) guarantees that $\mathbf{D}_1$ is built in such a way that the event-stationary distribution of the MAP(2), i.e., the stationary distribution of the DTMC embedded at the event instants, equals $\mathbf{p}_{\text{MAP2}}$ obtained from (12) via moment matching. Only one of the two linearly dependent equations of (15) will be considered. Finally, scalar equation (16) sets the result of the general formula for the first coefficient of correlation equal to the value specified in terms of the given correlation parameter γ (also see (10) for $k = 1$). Using (9) and the relationship $\pi_{\text{MAP2}} = \frac{\mathbf{p}_{\text{MAP2}}(-\mathbf{D}_0)^{-1}}{r_1}$, equation (16) may also be simplified to

$$\mathbf{p}_{\text{MAP2}}(-\mathbf{D}_0)^{-2}\mathbf{D}_1(-\mathbf{D}_0)^{-1}\mathbf{e} - 1 = \gamma h_2 r_1^2 \quad . \tag{17}$$

In total, we thus have four equations, which are linear in the four unknowns x_{ij} ($i, j = 1, 2$).

Overall, the analytic MAP fitting now comprises the following steps:

- Perform a symbolic three-moment fitting to the PH(2) canonical form (lhs of Figure 2) in order to obtain the parameters p_1', λ_1 and λ_2 as functions of r_1, h_2 and h_3.
- Using representation (12) and (13) for the marginal distribution, solve equations (14), (15) and (17) to obtain the entries of matrix $\mathbf{D}_1$.

Explicit closed-form bounds for the permissible range of correlation parameter γ are found by checking the requirements $x_{ij} \geq 0$ ($i, j = 1, 2$) for a MAP(2) proper. These bounds are then sufficient and necessary, but will depend on the specific choice of the free parameter a in representation (13). In other words, the amount of correlation that can be introduced into an acyclic MAP(2) generally depends on the specific representation selected for its marginal distribution.

4   The Characterization of Acyclic MAP(2)s

Following the outline in Section 3, a compact MAP(2) representation based on the first three moments, the correlation parameter and the free parameter a may be derived. We spare the reader the details of these algebraic manipulations and directly provide the explicit closed-form expressions for the matrices $\mathbf{D}_0$ and $\mathbf{D}_1$. Regarding the correlation bounds, we identify the choices for the free parameter a that maximize the upper bound for γ or minimize the lower bound, respectively. The coordinates for these extremal values turn out to be surprisingly simple so that very efficient moment/correlation-fitting rules can be designed for MAP(2)s.

Both these rules and the actual representations differ for MAP(2)s with hyperexponential and hypoexponential marginal distributions. We first treat the hyperexponential setting, where the MAP(2) discussed in Section 2 is identified as a special case for $a = 1$. In fact, for both cases, we use the notation introduced in Section 2, namely the normalized moment parameters h_2 and h_3 and the auxiliary variables b and c (see (2) and (3), respectively).

4.1 MAP(2)s with Hyperexponential Marginals

MAPs of order 2 may be constructed from the first three moments of the marginal distribution (e.g., given by r_1, r_2, r_3 or equivalently by r_1, h_2, h_3) and the correlation parameter γ. For the hyperexponential case (i.e., $h_2, h_3 > 0$), the derivations outlined in Section 3 lead to the following acyclic MAP(2) representation:

$$\mathbf{D}_0 = \frac{1}{2r_1 h_3} \begin{bmatrix} -(2h_2 + b - c) & +(2h_2 + b - c)(1 - a) \\ 0 & -(2h_2 + b + c) \end{bmatrix} \tag{18}$$

$$\mathbf{D}_1 = \frac{1}{2r_1 h_3} \begin{bmatrix} (2h_2 + b - c)d_1 & (2h_2 + b - c)(a - d_1) \\ (2h_2 + b + c)d_2 & (2h_2 + b + c)(1 - d_2) \end{bmatrix} \tag{19}$$

$$d_1 = \frac{(1 - a)(2h_2\gamma + b - c) + \gamma(b + c) - (b - c)}{(1 - a)(2h_2 + b - c) + 2c} \tag{20}$$

$$d_2 = \frac{(\gamma - 1)(b - c)}{(1 - a)(2h_2 + b - c) + 2c} \tag{21}$$

First of all, we recognize the structure of the transformed canonical form (13) in (18) with free parameter $a \in [0, 1]$. In fact, for $a = 1$, representation (18)/19) reduces to the one presented in Section 2 for MAP(2)s with a mixture of two exponentials as their marginal distribution. The definition of the rate parameters λ_1 and λ_2 remained invariant. Both matrices $\mathbf{D}_0$ and $\mathbf{D}_1$ are again scaled by the mean r_1 (which leaves the normalized moments unchanged). The parameter h_3 in the denominator indicates that the lower bound $h_3 = 0$ is excluded in the parameter range.

For $a = 1$, the permissible range of the correlation parameter was given in Section 2. For $a = 0$ (i.e., $\mathbf{D}_0$ takes the canonical form), one can easily verify that γ must be zero for the entries of $\mathbf{D}_1$ to be nonnegative. Thus, the permissible correlation range depends on parameter a. Does the choice of $a = 1$ maximize the range of γ both in the positive and negative domain? As indicated in Figure 3 (for specific choices of h_2 and h_3), this is only true, if auxiliary parameter $b = h_3 + h_2^2 - h_2$ is greater than or equal to 0. In the complementary case $b < 0$ (left-hand side of Figure 3), an additional (linear) lower γ-bound becomes relevant causing the absolute minimum of γ to be assumed for a value $a < 1$.

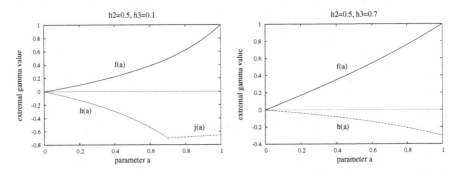

Fig. 3. Nature of bounds for maximal and minimal values of γ for hyperexponential MAP(2)s for $b < 0$ (left) and $b \geq 0$ (right)

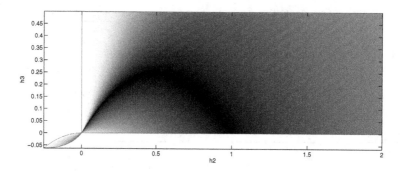

Fig. 4. Visualizing the moment pairs (h_2, h_3), for which γ assumes low values (by dark shading)

Let us first focus on the values of a, for which γ takes extreme values. In Section 5, we present an analytic fitting algorithm that exhausts the capabilities of MAP(2)s to match r_1, h_2, h_3 and γ exactly.

For any combination of hyperexponential moment values $h_2, h_3 > 0$ (and $r_1 > 0$), the upper (positive) bound of γ is maximized at $a = 1$. Then $\gamma < \gamma_{\max} = 1$.

In order to minimize the lower (negative) bound of γ, we have to distinguish two cases:

- If $b \geq 0$ (i.e., $h_3 \geq h_2 - h_2^2$): The lower (negative) bound of γ is also minimized at $a = 1$. Then $\gamma \geq \gamma_{\min} = \frac{b-c}{b+c}$.
- If $b < 0$ (i.e., $h_3 < h_2 - h_2^2$): The lower (negative) bound of γ is minimized at $a = \frac{h_3 + h_2^2}{h_2}$. Then $\gamma \geq \gamma_{\min} = -\frac{h_3 + h_2^2}{h_2}$.

For completeness sake, we also give the symbolic definitions of the a-dependent γ-bounds. The proofs of these linear and hyperbolic functions (called $f(a), h(a)$ and $j(a)$ in Figure 3) are found in [20].

$$f_{\text{hyper}}(a) = \frac{a\left[2(h_3 + h_2^2) - a(2h_2 + b - c)\right]}{(2h_2 + b + c) - 2h_2 a} \tag{22}$$

$$h_{\text{hyper}}(a) = \frac{a(b - c)}{(2h_2 + b + c) - 2h_2 a} \tag{23}$$

$$j_{\text{hyper}}(a) = \frac{2(h_3 + h_2^2) - a(2h_2 + b - c)}{b - c} \tag{24}$$

Finally, Figure 4 shows in the permissible moment ranges for h_2 and h_3, where γ assumes its lower values as depicted by darker shades. Absolute minima (i.e., $\gamma = -1$) are reached along the black arc in the hyperexponential domain ($h_2, h_3 > 0$).

4.2 MAP(2)s with Hypoexponential Marginals

The situation for MAP(2)s with hypoexponential marginals is slightly more involved. Recall that here $h_2, h_3 < 0$ (see Table 1 for the precise moment bounds).

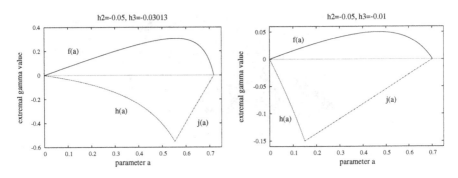

Fig. 5. Illustration of bounds for maximal and minimal values of γ for hypoexponential MAP(2)s

With respect to matrices $\mathbf{D}_0$ and $\mathbf{D}_1$ expressed in terms of the first three moments and the correlation parameter, the representation given in (18) through (21) for the hyperexponential setting only needs to be minutely modified: Simply change the sign before all occurrences of parameter c!

Regarding the bounds of correlation parameter γ, Figure 5 again illustrates representative dependencies of the permissible γ-ranges on parameter a (for specific values of h_2 and h_3). Several observations can be generalized:

- In the hypoexponential setting, the area of permissible tuples (a, γ) is always confined by the three (intersecting) boundary functions $f_{\text{hypo}}(a)$, $h_{\text{hypo}}(a)$ and $j_{\text{hypo}}(a)$ defined at the end of this subsection.
- There exist a unique maximum and a unique minimum for γ at usually different locations of a.
- In order to capture non-zero correlations, parameter a can no longer be chosen arbitrarily in $[0, 1]$, but is restricted to the interval $[0, \frac{(h_3 + h_2{}^2)(2h_2 + b - c)}{2h_2 h_3}$. In the end points of this interval, boundary functions intersect in their zero values (enforcing $\gamma = 0$).
- We observe the following trends: With decreasing h_2 (and h_3 fixed) or increasing h_3 (and h_2 fixed), the permissible range for parameter a decreases. At the same time, maximum and minimum of γ draw nearer to the zero.
- Finally, and not shown in Figure 5, the boundary equations additionally admit a singular solution at $a = 1$, where $\gamma = 1$. However, this corresponds to a *reducible* MAP(2) with diagonal matrices $\mathbf{D}_0$ and $\mathbf{D}_1$. Therefore, we exclude this case of two independent Poisson processes.

As in the hyperexponential setting, let us also provide the location of the maximal and minimal values of γ for the hypoexponential setting ($h_2, h_3 < 0$):

- The upper (positive) bound of γ is maximized at $a = \frac{(2h_2 + b - c)(h_2 + \sqrt{-h_3})}{2h_2 \sqrt{-h_3}}$. Then $\gamma \leq \gamma_{\max} = -\frac{(h_2 + \sqrt{-h_3})^2}{h_2}$.
- The lower (negative) bound of γ is minimized at $a = \frac{h_3 + h_2{}^2}{h_2}$. Then $\gamma \geq \gamma_{\min} = -\frac{h_3 + h_2{}^2}{h_2}$.

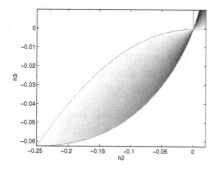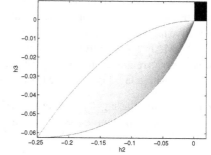

Fig. 6. Visualizing the moment pairs (h_2, h_3), for which γ assumes low negative (left) and large positive (right) values (by dark shading, respectively)

These expressions are easily obtained by discussion of the a-dependent γ-bounds below, which are formally identical to the corresponding ones in the hyperexponential case (see (22), (23), (24)) except for the changed signs before all occurrences of parameter c:

$$f_{\text{hypo}}(a) = \frac{a\left[2(h_3 + h_2{}^2) - a(2h_2 + b + c)\right]}{(2h_2 + b - c) - 2h_2 a}$$

$$h_{\text{hypo}}(a) = \frac{a(b + c)}{(2h_2 + b - c) - 2h_2 a}$$

$$j_{\text{hypo}}(a) = \frac{2(h_3 + h_2{}^2) - a(2h_2 + b + c)}{b + c}$$

Figure 6 visualizes – in particular for the hypoexponential domain – when γ takes lower negative (left) and larger positive values (right) in the permissible moment ranges. The darker the shading, the more extremal the minima and maxima, respectively. For example, in the hypoexponential domain, the largest flexibility in γ is achieved for h_2 near 0 and h_3 at its lower bound.

5   Moment and Correlation Mapping to MAP(2)s

In this section, we compile different results of the previous sections for an algorithm that decides whether given first three moments of a marginal distribution and a correlation parameter can be mapped to a valid acyclic MAP(2). If yes, the algorithm provides the corresponding two-dimensional matrices $\mathbf{D}_0$ and $\mathbf{D}_1$.

Let us assume that, besides the first three reduced moments $r_i = \frac{E[X^i]}{i!}$, $i = 1, 2, 3$, we only know the lag-1 covariance $\text{cov}[X_0, X_1] = E[(X_0 - r_1)(X_1 - r_1)]$ of the wide-sense stationary correlated process – either as sample values from measurements or as output from other algorithms. We explicitly state that knowledge of lag-k covariances for larger values of k or of the decay behavior of the correlation structure may affect how the correlation parameter γ is determined (as e.g., outlined in [13]). Note again that due to (1),

MAP(2)s with hyperexponential marginals can only capture either nonnegative autocorrelation functions or autocorrelations with alternating signs starting with a negative lag-1 covariance (or lag-1 correlation coefficient).

Inversely, MAP(2)s with hypoexponential marginals can only capture either nonpositive autocorrelation functions or autocorrelations with alternating signs starting with a positive lag-1 covariance (or lag-1 correlation coefficient).

By matching only the lag-1 covariance, we ignore the autocorrelation behavior of the considered process beyond lag 1, which may result in significant deviations in related parameters.

The Moment/Correlation Fitting Algorithm for MAP(2)s

1. Input parameters: $r_1, r_2, r_3, \text{cov}[X_0, X_1]$
2. Quit, if $r_1 \leq 0$.
3. Compute h_2, h_3 via (2).
4. Quit, if $h_2 = 0$: No correlated MAP(2) with $c_{\text{MAP}}^2 = 1$ can be fitted. All MAP(2)s with $h_2 = 0$ are stochastically equivalent to Poisson processes, for which also $\gamma = 0$ and $h_3 = 0$ hold.
5. Compute γ from $\gamma = \frac{\text{cov}[X_0, X_1]}{r_2 - r_1^2}$ (see (1) for $k = 1$).
6. Compute auxiliary variables b and c via (3).
7. Check moment bounds for h_2, h_3 according to Table 1:
   if $h_2 > 0$ **and** $h_3 > 0$: Goto step 8 (Hyperexponential case)
   else if $-\frac{1}{4} \leq h_2 < 0$ **and** $h_2(1 - h_2 - 2\sqrt{-h_2}) \leq h_3 \leq -h_2^2$: Goto step 9 (Hypoexponential case)
   else: Quit (moments out of bounds).
8. Hyperexponential case:
   if $b \geq 0$:
      if $\frac{b-c}{b+c} \leq \gamma < 1$: Choose MAP(2) representation (4)/(5)
      else: Quit (correlation parameter out of bounds).
   else if $b < 0$:
      if $0 \leq \gamma < 1$: Choose MAP(2) representation (4)/(5)
      else if $-\frac{h_3 + h_2^2}{h_2} \leq \gamma < 0$: Choose MAP(2) representation (18)/(19) with $a = \frac{h_3 + h_2^2}{h_2}$
      else: Quit (correlation parameter out of bounds).
9. Hypoexponential case:
   if $\gamma \geq 0$:
      if $\gamma \leq -\frac{(h_2 + \sqrt{-h_3})^2}{h_2}$: Choose MAP(2) representation (18)/(19) with changed signs before all occurrences of parameter c and with $a = \frac{(2h_2 + b - c)(h_2 + \sqrt{-h_3})}{2h_2\sqrt{-h_3}}$
      else: Quit (correlation parameter out of bounds).
   else if $\gamma < 0$:
      if $\gamma \geq -\frac{h_3 + h_2^2}{h_2}$: Choose MAP(2) representation (18)/(19) with changed signs before all occurrences of parameter c and with $a = \frac{h_3 + h_2^2}{h_2}$
      else: Quit (correlation parameter out of bounds).

Either the algorithm is aborted with an out-of-bounds message or the appropriate MAP(2) representation is chosen that matches r_1, r_2, r_3 and $\text{cov}[X_0, X_1]$ exactly. In the former case, one might want to step back in the algorithm, set the out-of-bounds parameter to the closest permissible boundary value and continue. The tradeoff in such an approximate moment/correlation fitting will be studied in future work.

6   Concluding Remarks

Inverse characterizations of MAPs are important to reflect commonly used traffic metrics in the matrix notation of matrix-analytic methods. In this paper, we showed how to construct analytically an acyclic MAP of order 2 from the first three marginal moments and a correlation parameter. These parameters were mapped exactly in three stages: first, the moments were fitted into a canonical PH representation. Second, this canonical form was transformed into an equivalent one, which permitted to introduce correlations in a process with this marginal distribution. Third, equations defining the MAP rates associated with events were solved symbolically.

Following this approach, an existing MAP(2) representation based on a mixture of two exponentials as the marginal representation could be extended. The enhanced hyperexponential representation now allows to capture stronger alternating correlations. Even more important, a symbolic inverse characterization for MAP(2)s with hypoexponential marginals is now available for the first time. Furthermore, the behavior of the correlation range and its dependence on the representation of the marginal acyclic PH(2) distribution are now understood. Exploiting the extrema of the correlation parameter, a moment/correlation fitting algorithm was given that fully exploits the capabilities of MAP(2)s to capture correlations dependent on the marginal moments. The relationship between acyclic and cyclic MAP(2)s yet has to be proven, but these classes are widely conjectured to be identical.

The provided characterization of second-order MAPs may be helpful on many occasions: It may be used as a correlated input model both in analysis and discrete-event simulation. As a building block for arrival or service significantly alleviate the state-space explosion problem. Its acyclic Markovian structure enables very efficient (correlated) random variate generation. Of course, the rather restrictive moment and correlation bounds, especially in the hypoexponential domain, limit the applicability of the MAP(2) traffic model in real-data fitting. But in the context of sensitivity analysis, the depoupling of moment and correlation fitting may prove invaluable: Thus, for instance, it can be qualitatively and quantitatively studied how systems react to correlated input as opposed to uncorrelated input (with invariant marginal distributions). Also, modifying the exact moment/correlation fitting algorithm of Section 5 into an approximate one will further widen the applicability of such a MAP(2) model.

References

1. Neuts, M.: Matrix-Geometric Solutions in Stochastic Models. John Hopkins University Press (1981)
2. Neuts, M.: Structured Stochastic Matrices of M/G/1-type and their Applications. Marcel Dekker, New York, NY (1989)

3. Latouche, G., Ramaswami, V.: Introduction to Matrix-Analytic Methods in Stochastic Modeling. Series on statistics and applied probability. ASA-SIAM (1999)
4. Buchholz, P.: An EM-algorithm for MAP fitting from real traffic data. In Kemper, P., Sanders, W., eds.: Proc. 13th Int. Conf. on Modelling Techniques and Tools for Computer Performance Evaluation. Volume 2794 of LNCS., Urbana, IL, USA (2003) 218–236
5. Horváth, G., Buchholz, P., Telek, M.: A MAP fitting approach with independent approximation of the inter-arrival time distribution and the lag correlation. In: Proc. 2nd Int. Conf. on Quantitative Evaluation of Systems, Torino, Italy (2005) 124–133
6. Horváth, A., Telek, M.: Markovian modeling of real data traffic: Heuristic phase-type and MAP fitting of heavy tailed and fractal-like samples. In: Tutorials of the IFIP WG7.3 Int. Symposium on Computer Performance Modeling, Measurement and Evaluation. LNCS 2459, Rome, Italy (2002)
7. Horváth, A., Telek, M.: Fitting more than three moments with acyclic phase-type distributions. submitted in (2006)
8. Telek, M., Heindl, A.: Matching moments for acyclic discrete and continuous phase-type distributions of second order. Intl. Journal of Simulation 3 (2003) 47–57
9. Bobbio, A., Horváth, A., Telek, M.: Matching three moments with minimal acyclic phase-type distributions. Stochastic Models 21 (2005) 303–323
10. Mitchell, K., van de Liefvoort, A.: Approximation models of feed-forward G/G/1/N queueing networks with correlated arrivals. Performance Evaluation 51 (2003) 137–152
11. Mitchell, K.: Constructing a correlated sequence of matrix exponentials with invariant first-order properties. Operations Research Letters 28 (2001) 27–34
12. Heindl, A., Mitchell, K., van de Liefvoort, A.: The correlation region of second-order MAPs with application to queueing network decomposition. In Kemper, P., Sanders, W., eds.: Proc. 13th Int. Conf. on Modelling Techniques and Tools for Computer Performance Evaluation. Volume 2794 of LNCS., Urbana, IL, USA (2003) 237–254
13. Heindl, A.: Inverse characterization of hyperexponential MAP(2)s. In: Proc. 11th Int. Conference on Analytical and Stochastic Modelling Techniques and Applications, Magdeburg, Germany (2004) 183–189
14. Heffes, H., Lucantoni, D.M.: A Markov-modulated characterization of packetized voice and data traffic and related statistical multiplexer performance. IEEE J. on Selected Areas in Commun. 4 (1986) 856–868
15. Ferng, H.W., Chang, J.F.: Connection-wise end-to-end performance analysis of queueing networks with MMPP inputs. Performance Evaluation 43 (2001) 39–62
16. Livny, M., Melamed, B., Tsiolis, A.K.: The impact of autocorrelation on queueing systems. Management Science 39 (1993) 322–339
17. Patuwo, B., Disney, R., McNickle, D.: The effect of correlated arrivals on queues. IIE Transactions 25 (1993) 105–110
18. Neuts, M.: Algorithmic Probability: A Collection of Problems. Chapman and Hall (1995)
19. van de Liefvoort, A.: The moment problem for continuous distributions. Technical Report WP-CM-1990-02, School of Computing and Engineering, University of Missouri – Kansas City, USA (1990)
20. Gross, K.: Analytische Konstruktion korrelierter Prozesse zur Lastmodellierung in Kommunikationssystemen. Master's thesis, Informatik 7, Universität Erlangen-Nürnberg, Germany (2006)

Implementation Relations for Stochastic Finite State Machines*

Mercedes G. Merayo, Manuel Núñez, and Ismael Rodríguez

Dept. Sistemas Informáticos y Programación
Universidad Complutense de Madrid, 28040 Madrid, Spain
mgmerayo@fdi.ucm.es,
{mn, isrodrig}@sip.ucm.es

Abstract. We present a timed extension of the classical finite state machines model where time is introduced in two ways. On the one hand, *timeouts* can be specified, that is, we can express that if an input action is not received before a fix amount of time then the machine will change its state. On the other hand, we can associate time with the performance of actions. In this case, time will be given by means of *random variables*. Intuitively, we will not have conditions such as "the action a takes t time units to be performed" but conditions such as "the action a will be completed before time t with probability p." In addition to introducing the new language, we present several conformance relations to relate implementations and specifications that are defined in terms of our new notion of stochastic finite state machine.

1 Introduction

Formal analysis techniques rely on the idea of constructing a *formal model* that represents the critical aspects of the system under study. These models, simpler and more handleable than the original system, allow to perform a systematic analysis that would be harder, or ever impossible, in the system. For example, the model can be formally manipulated to find out whether a given property holds (for instance, by using *model checking* [CGP00]). The model can be also used to define the specification of a system being constructed. Then, we can check its correctness with respect to the specification by comparing its empirical behavior with that of the model (for instance, by using *formal testing* techniques [BU91, LY96]). In order to use a formal technique, we need that the systems under study can be expressed in terms of a formal language. These languages became more sophisticated as they provided more expressivity capabilities. The first languages represented only the functional behavior of systems (i.e., what must or must not be done). Then, a new generation of languages allowed to explicitly represent non-functional aspects of systems (the probability of performing a certain task [GSS95, CDSY99, SV03, CCV+03, Núñ03, LNR06],

---

* Research partially supported by the Spanish MCYT project TIC2003-07848-C02-01, the Junta de Castilla-La Mancha project PAC-03-001, and the Marie Curie project MRTN-CT-2003-505121/TAROT.

A. Horváth and M. Telek (Eds.): EPEW 2006, LNCS 4054, pp. 123–137, 2006.

the time consumed by the system while performing tasks, being it either given by fix amounts of time [RR88, NS91, HR95] or defined in probabilistic/stochastic terms [Hil96, BG98, Her98, LN01, BG02], the dependence of the system on the available resources [BL97, NR01, CdAHS03], etc).

A suitable representation of the temporal behavior is critical for constructing useful models of real-time systems. A language to represent these systems should enable the definition of temporal conditions that may direct the system behavior, as well as the time consumed by the execution of tasks. Moreover, global temporal requirements should be easily extracted from the requirements of each activity in the system. We can split the time consumed during the execution of a system into the following categories:

(a) The system consumes time while it performs its tasks.
(b) The time passes while the system waits for a reaction from the environment. In particular, the system can change its internal state if an interaction is not received before a certain amount of time.

A language focusing on temporal issues should allow models to explicitly define how the time of type (a) is consumed. Besides, it should allow to define how the system behavior is affected by both types of temporal aspects (e.g., a task is performed if executing the previous task took too much time, if the environment did not react for a long time, if the addition of both times exceeded a given threshold, etc). Finally, the twofold relation between functional activities and temporal aspects should be defined so that they influence each other in an easy way.

In this paper we present a formalism, based on *finite state machines*, allowing to take into account the subtle temporal aspects considered before. Even though there exists a myriad of timed extensions of classical frameworks, this number is not so big in the framework of finite state machines. Moreover, when considering that time is stochastically defined, there are almost no proposals ([NR03] is an exception). Besides, most approaches specialize only in one of the previous variants: Time is either associated with actions or associated with delays/timeouts. Our formalism allows to specify in a natural way both time aspects. In our framework, timeouts are specified by using fix amounts of time. In contrast, the duration of actions will be given by *random variables*. That is, instead of having expressions such as "the action o takes t units of time to be performed" we will have expressions such as "with probability p the action o will be performed before t units of time". We will consider a suitable extension of finite state machines where (stochastic) time information is included. Intuitively, transitions in finite state machines indicate that if the machine is in a state s and receives and input i then it will produce and output o and it will change its state to s'. An appropriate notation for such a transition could be $s \xrightarrow{i/o} s'$. If we consider a timed extension of finite state machines, transitions as $s \xrightarrow{i/o}_t s'$ indicate that the time between receiving the input i and returning the output o is equal to t. In the new model that we introduce in this paper for stochastic transitions, we will consider that the time consumed between the input is applied and the output is received is given by a random variable ξ. Thus the interpretation of a transition $s \xrightarrow{\ i/o\ }_\xi s'$ is "if the machine is in state s and receives an input i then it will produce the output o before time t with probability $P(\xi \leq t)$ and it will change its state to s'". The definition of conformance testing relations is more difficult than usually. In particular, even in the absence of non-determinism, the same sequence of actions may take different time values to be performed in different runs of the system. While the definition of the new language is not difficult, mixing these temporal requirements strongly complicates the posterior theoretical analysis.

We propose several *stochastic-temporal conformance relations*: An implementation is correct with respect to a specification if it does not show any behavior that is forbidden by the specification, where both the functional behavior and the temporal behavior are considered (and, implicitly, how they affect each other). From the functional point of view, the idea underlying the definition of the conformance relations is that the implementation does not *invent* anything for those sequences of inputs that are *specified* in the specification. Moreover, regarding functional conformance we have to consider not only that the sequences of inputs/outpus produced by the implementation must be considered in the specification. We also have to take into account the possible timeouts. For example, a sequence of inputs/outputs could be accepted after different timeouts have been triggered, and not in the case of other combinations. Regarding stochastic-time, we might require that any trace of the specification that can be performed by the implementation must have the same associated delay, that is, an identically distributed random variable. Even though this is a very reasonable notion to define conformance, if we assume a black-box testing framework then we cannot check whether the corresponding random variables are identically distributed. In fact, we would need an infinite number of observations from a random variable of the implementation (with an unknown distribution) to assure that this random variable is distributed as another random variable from the specification (with a known distribution). Thus, we have to give more *realistic* implementation relations based on a finite set of observations. The idea will be to check that for any trace observed in the implementation that can be performed by the specification, the observed execution times *fit* the random variable indicated by the specification. This notion of *fitting* will be given by means of a hypothesis contrast.

In terms of related work, a lot of formalisms have been proposed to describe the temporal behavior of systems. If we restrict ourselves to time values given by fix amounts, instead of using random variables, our formalism is as expressive as the most popular one: *Timed automata* [AD94]. Thus, our formalism can compare in terms of expressivity with stochastic extensions of timed automata (e.g. [DK05]). However, our way to deal with time is different. As we said before, we can associate time with the performance of actions while timeouts can be easily represented as fix amounts of time. These features do not only improve the modularity of models, but they are also suitable for clearly identifying IUT requirements and responsibilities in a testing methodology. Besides, the formalism underlying our language is not based on automata but on *finite state machines* (i.e., Mealy machines), which have been extensively used by the formal testing community. Regarding testing of temporal requirements, there exist several proposals (e.g., [CL97, HNTC99, SVD01, NR03, ED03]) but most of them, with the exception of our previous work, are based on timed automata.

The rest of the paper is structured as follows. In the next section we introduce our notion of stochastic finite state machine. In Section 3 we introduce an implementation relation that takes into account only functional aspects, that is, which actions can be performed and how timeouts are specified. This notion is extended in Section 4 to cope with performance time of actions. In Section 5 we present our conclusions and some lines for future work. Finally, in the appendix of the paper, we show how hypothesis contrasts can be performed.

2 A Stochastic Extension of the EFSM Model

In this section we introduce our notion of finite state machines with stochastic time. We use random variables to model the (stochastic) time output actions take to be executed. Thus, we need to introduce some basic concepts on random variables. We will consider that the sample space, that is, the domain of random variables, is a set of numeric time values $\texttt{Time}$. Since this is a *generic* time domain, the specifier can choose whether the system will use a discrete/continuous time domain. We simply assume that $0 \in \texttt{Time}$. Regarding passing of time, we will also consider that machines can evolve by raising *timeouts*. Intuitively, if after a given time, depending on the current state, we do not receive any input action then the machine will change its current state.

During the rest of the paper we will use the following notation. Tuples of elements $(e_1, e_2 \ldots, e_n)$ will be denoted by $\bar{e}$. $\hat{a}$ denotes an interval of elements $[a_1, a_2]$, with $a_1, a_2 \in \texttt{Time}$ and $a_1 < a_2$. We will use the projection function π_i such that given a tuple $\bar{t} = (t_1, \ldots, t_n)$, for all $1 \le i \le n$ we have $\pi_i(\bar{t}) = t_i$. Let $\bar{t} = (t_1, \ldots, t_n)$ and $\bar{t}' = (t'_1, \ldots, t'_n)$. We write $\bar{t} = \bar{t}'$ if for all $1 \le j \le n$ we have $t_j = t'_j$. We write $\bar{t} \le \bar{t}'$ if for all $1 \le j \le n$ we have $t_j \le t'_j$. We denote by $\sum \bar{t}$ the addition of all the elements belonging to the tuple $\bar{t}$, that is, $\sum_{j=1}^n t_j$. The number of elements of the tuple will be represented by $|\bar{t}|$. Finally, if $\bar{t} = (t_1 \ldots t_n)$, $\bar{p} = (\hat{t}_1 \ldots \hat{t}_n)$ and for all $1 \le j \le n$ we have $t_j \in \hat{t}_j$, we write $\bar{t} \in \bar{p}$.

Definition 1. We denote by $\mathcal{V}$ the set of random variables ($\xi, \psi, \ldots$ range over $\mathcal{V}$). Let ξ be a random variable. We define its *probability distribution function* as the function $F_\xi : \texttt{Time} \longrightarrow [0,1]$ such that $F_\xi(x) = P(\xi \le x)$, where $P(\xi \le x)$ is the probability that ξ assumes values less than or equal to x.

Given two random variables ξ and ψ we consider that $\xi + \psi$ denotes a random variable distributed as the addition of the two random variables ξ and ψ. We will call *sample* to any multiset of elements belonging to $\texttt{Time}$. We denote the set of multisets in $\texttt{Time}$ by $\wp(\texttt{Time})$. Let ξ be a random variable and J be a sample. We denote by $\gamma(\xi, J)$ the *confidence* of ξ on J.   □

In the previous definition, a sample simply contains an observation of values. In our setting, samples will be associated with the time values that implementations take to perform sequences of actions. We have that $\gamma(\xi, J)$ takes values in the interval $[0, 1]$. Intuitively, bigger values of $\gamma(\xi, J)$ indicate that the observed sample J is more likely to be produced by the random variable ξ. That is, this function decides how *similar* the probability distribution function generated by J and the one corresponding to the random variable ξ are. In the appendix of this paper we show one of the possibilities to formally define the notion of confidence by means of a hypothesis contrast.

Definition 2. A *Stochastic Finite State Machine*, in short SFSM, is a tuple $M = (S, I, O, \delta, TO, s_{in})$ where S is the set of states, with $s_{in} \in S$ being the *initial state*, I and O denote the sets of input and output actions, respectively, δ is the set of transitions, and $TO : S \longrightarrow S \times (\text{Time} \cup \{\infty\})$ is the *timeout function*. Each transition belonging to δ is a tuple (s, i, o, ξ, s') where $s, s' \in S$ are the initial and final states, $i \in I$ and $o \in O$ are the input and output actions, and $\xi \in \mathcal{V}$ is the random variable defining the time associated with the transition.

Let $M = (S, I, O, \delta, TO, s_{in})$ be a SFSM. We say that M is *input-enabled* if for all state $s \in S$ and input $i \in I$ there exist s', o, ξ, such that $(s, i, o, \xi, s') \in \delta$. We say that M is *deterministically observable* if for all s, i, o there do not exist two different transitions $(s, i, o, \xi_1, s_1), (s, i, o, \xi_2, s_2) \in \delta$. □

Intuitively, a transition (s, i, o, ξ, s') indicates that if the machine is in state s and receives the input i then the machine emits the output o before time t with probability $F_\xi(t)$ and the machine changes its current state to s'. Let us remark that non-deterministic choices will be resolved before the timers indicated by random variables start counting, that is, we follow a *pre-selection* policy. Thus, if we have several transitions, outgoing from a state s, associated with the same input i, and the system receives this input, then the system *at time* 0 non-deterministically chooses which one of them to perform. So, we do not have a *race* between the different timers to decide which one is faster. In order to avoid side-effects, we will assume that all the random variables appearing in the definition of a SFSM are independent. Let us note that this condition does not restrict the distributions to be used. In particular, there can be random variables identically distributed even though they are independent.

For each state $s \in S$, the application of the timeout function $TO(s)$ returns a pair (s', t) indicating the time that the machine can remain at the state s waiting for an input action and the state to which the machine evolves if no input is received on time. We indicate the absence of a timeout in a given state by setting the corresponding time value to ∞. In addition, we assume that $TO(s) = (s', t)$ implies $s \neq s'$, that is, timeouts always produce a change of the state. In fact, let us note that a definition such as $TO(s) = (s, t)$ is equivalent to set the timeout for the state s to infinite.

Regarding the notion of deterministically observable, it is worth to point out that it is different from the more restricted notion of deterministic finite state machine. In particular, we allow transitions from the same state labelled by the same input action, as far as the outputs are different. Let us remark that both

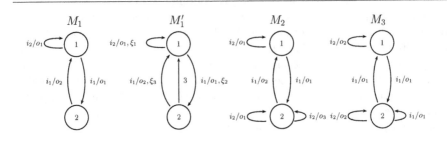

Fig. 1. Examples of (Stochastic) Finite State Machines

the concept of deterministically observable and input-enabled are independent of the stochastic information appearing in SFSMs.

Example 1. Let us consider the finite state machines M_1, M_2, and M_3 depicted in Figure 1. In order to *transform* these machines into stochastic finite state machines, we simply need to add random variables to all the transitions and timeouts to all the states. We assume that absent timeouts correspond to timeouts having ∞ as parameter. For example, if we transform M_1 into a stochastic state machine we obtain M_1'. Then we have $M_1' = (\{1,2\}, \{i_1, i_2\}, \{o_1, o_2\}, \delta, TO, 1)$ where the set of transitions δ is given by:

$$\delta = \{(1, i_2, o_1, \xi_1, 1), (1, i_1, o_1, \xi_2, 2), (2, i_1, o_2, \xi_3, 1)\}$$

In order to complete our specification of M_1' we need to say how random variables are distributed. Let us suppose the following distributions:

$$F_{\xi_1}(x) = \begin{cases} 0 & \text{if } x \leq 0 \\ \frac{x}{3} & \text{if } 0 < x < 3 \\ 1 & \text{if } x \geq 3 \end{cases}$$

$$F_{\xi_2}(x) = \begin{cases} 0 & \text{if } x < 4 \\ 1 & \text{if } x \geq 4 \end{cases}$$

$$F_{\xi_3}(x) = \begin{cases} 1 - e^{-3 \cdot x} & \text{if } x \geq 0 \\ 0 & \text{if } x < 0 \end{cases}$$

We say that ξ_1 is uniformly distributed in the interval $[0,3]$. Uniform distributions allow us to keep compatibility with time intervals in (non-stochastic) timed models in the sense that the same *weight* is assigned to all the times in the interval. We say that ξ_2 is a Dirac distribution in 4. The idea is that the corresponding delay will be equal to 4 time units. Dirac distributions allow us to simulate deterministic delays appearing in timed models. We say that ξ_3 is exponentially distributed with parameter 3. Let us consider the transition $(1, i_2, o_1, \xi_1, 1)$. Intuitively, if M_1' is in state 1 and it receives the input i_2 then it will produce the output o_2 after a delay given by ξ_1. For example, we know that this delay will be less than 1 unit of time with probability $\frac{1}{3}$, it will be less than 1.5 units of time with probability $\frac{1}{2}$, and so on. Finally, once 3 units of time has passed we know that the output o_1 has been performed (that is, we have probability 1). Regarding the timeout function, we have $TO(1) = (2, \infty)$ and $TO(2) = (1, 3)$. In this case, if the machine is in state 2 and no input is received before 3 units of time then the state is changed to 1.

Regarding the notions of input-enabled and deterministically observable, the first property does not hold in M_1 (there is no outgoing transition labelled by i_2 from the state 2) while the second one does. We have that M_3 fulfills the first of the properties but not the second one (there are two transitions from the state 2 labelled by i_1/o_1). Finally, both properties hold for M_2.   □

Definition 3. Let $M = (S, I, O, \delta, TO, s_{in})$ be a SFSM. We say that a tuple $(s_0, s, i/o, \hat{t}, \xi)$ is a *step* for the state s_0 of M if there exist k states $s_1, \ldots, s_k \in S$, with $k \geq 0$, such that $\hat{t} = \left[\sum_{j=0}^{k-1} \pi_2(TO(s_j)), \sum_{j=0}^{k} \pi_2(TO(s_j)) \right)$ and there exists a transition $(s_k, i, o, \xi, s) \in \delta$.

We say that $(\hat{t}_1/i_1/\xi_1/o_1, \ldots, \hat{t}_r/i_r/\xi_r/o_r)$ is a *stochastic evolution* of M if there exist r steps of M $(s_{in}, s_1, i_1/o_1, \hat{t}_1, \xi_1), \ldots, (s_{r-1}, s_r, i_r/o_r, \hat{t}_r, \xi_r)$ for the states $s_{in} \ldots s_{r-1}$, respectively. We denote by $\mathtt{SEvol}(M)$ the set of stochastic evolutions of M. In addition, we say that $(\hat{t}_1/i_1/o_1, \ldots, \hat{t}_r/i_r/o_r)$ is a *functional evolution* of M. We denote by $\mathtt{FEvol}(M)$ the set of functional evolutions of M. We will use the shortenings $(\sigma, \bar{p})$ and $(\sigma, \bar{p}, \bar{\xi})$ to denote a functional and a stochastic evolution, respectively, where $\sigma = (i_1/o_1 \ldots i_r/o_r)$, $\bar{p} = (\hat{t}_1 \ldots \hat{t}_r)$ and $\bar{\xi} = (\xi_1 \ldots \xi_r)$.   □

Intuitively, a step is a sequence of transitions that contains an action transition preceded by zero or more timeouts. The interval $\hat{t}$ indicates the time values where the transition could be performed. In particular, if the sequence of timeouts is empty then we have the interval $\hat{t} = [0, TO(s_0))$. An evolution is a sequence of inputs/outputs corresponding to the transitions of a chain of steps, where the first one begins with the initial state of the machine. In addition, stochastic evolutions also include time information which inform us about possible timeouts (indicated by the intervals $\hat{t}_j$) and random variables associated to the execution of each output after receiving each input in each step of the evolution. In the following definition we introduce the concept of *instanced evolution*. Intuitively, instanced evolutions are constructed from evolutions by instantiating to a concrete value each timeout, given by an interval, of the evolution.

Definition 4. Let $M = (S, I, O, \delta, TO, s_{in})$ be a SFSM and let us consider a stochastic evolution $e = (\hat{t}_1/i_1/\xi_1/o_1, \ldots, \hat{t}_r/i_r/\xi_r/o_r)$. We say that the tuple $(t_1/i_1/\xi_1/o_1, \ldots, t_r/i_r/\xi_r/o_r)$ is an *instanced stochastic evolution of* e if for all $1 \leq j \leq r$ we have $t_j \in \hat{t}_j$. Besides, we say that the tuple $(t_1/i_1/o_1, \ldots, t_r/i_r/o_r)$ is an *instanced functional evolution* of e.

We denote by $\mathtt{InsSEvol}(M)$ the set of instanced stochastic evolutions of M and by $\mathtt{InsFEvol}(M)$ the set of instanced functional evolutions of M.   □

3   A First Implementation Relation

In this section we introduce an implementation relation to deal with functional aspects. It follows the pattern borrowed from $\mathtt{conf}_{nt}$ [NR02]: An implementation I *conforms* to a specification S if for all possible evolution of S the outputs that the implementation I may perform after a given input are a subset of those for the specification. In addition to the non-stochastic conformance of the implementation, we require other additional conditions, related to time, to hold. Specifically, we require that the implementation always complies with the timeouts established by the specification.

Next, we fix the sets of specifications and implementations. A specification is a stochastic finite state machine. Regarding implementations, we consider that they are also given by means of SFSMs. We will consider that both specifications and implementations are given by deterministically observable SFSMs. That is, we do not allow a machine to have two different transitions such as (s, i, o, ξ_1, s') and (s, i, o, ξ_2, s''). Let us note that we do not restrict observable non-determinism, that is, we may have the transitions (s, i, o_1, ξ_1, s_1) and $(s, i, o_2, \xi_2, s_2,)$ as far as $o_1 \neq o_2$. Besides, we assume that input actions are always enabled in any state of the implementation, that is, implementations are input-enabled according to Definition 2. This is a usual condition to assure that the implementation will react (somehow) to any input appearing in the specification.

First, we introduce the implementation relation $\mathtt{conf}_f$, where only functional aspects of the system (i.e., which outputs are allowed/forbidden and how timeouts are defined) are considered while the performance of the system (i.e., how fast outputs are executed) is ignored. Let us note that the time spent by a system waiting for the environment to react has the capability of affecting the set of available outputs of the system. This is because this time may trigger a change of the state. So, a relation focusing on functional aspects must explicitly take into account the maximal time the system may stay in each state. This time is given by the *timeout* of each state.

Definition 5. Let S and I be SFSMs. We say that I *functionally conforms* to S, denoted by $I \mathtt{conf}_f S$, if for each functional evolution $e \in \mathtt{FEvol}(S)$, with $e = (\hat{t}_1/i_1/o_1, \ldots, \hat{t}_r/i_r/o_r)$ and $r \geq 1$, we have that for all $t_1 \in \hat{t}_1, \ldots, t_r \in \hat{t}_r$ and o'_r

$$e' = (t_1/i_1/o_1, \ldots, t_r/i_r/o'_r) \in \mathtt{InsFEvol}(I) \text{ implies } e' \in \mathtt{InsFEvol}(S)$$

□

Intuitively, the idea underlying the definition of the functional conformance relation $I \mathtt{conf}_f S$ is that the implementation I does not *invent* anything for those sequences of inputs that are *specified* in the specification S. Let us note that if the specification has also the property of input-enabled then we may remove the condition "for each functional evolution $e \in \mathtt{FEvol}(S)$, with $e = (\hat{t}_{t1}/i_1/o_1, \ldots, \hat{t}_{tr}/i_r/o_r)$ and $r \geq 1$".

In addition to requiring this notion of *functional* conformance, we have to ask for some conditions on delays. As indicated in the introduction, a first approach would be to require that the random variables associated with evolutions of the implementation are identically distributed as the ones corresponding to the specification. However, the fact that we assume a black-box testing framework disallows us to check whether these random variables are indeed identically distributed. Thus, we have to give more *realistic* implementation relations based on finite sets of observations. Next, we present implementation relations that are less *accurate* but that are *checkable*.

4 Implementation Relations Based on Samples

In the previous section we discussed how an appropriate implementation relation can be defined. Unfortunately, this notion is useful only from a theoretical point of view. In this section we introduce implementation relations that take into account the observations that we may get from the implementation. We will collect a sample of time values and we will *compare* this sample with the random variables appearing in the specification. By comparison we mean that we will apply a contrast to decide, with a certain confidence, whether the sample could be generated by the corresponding random variable.

Definition 6. Let I be a SFSM. We say that $(\sigma, \bar{t}, \bar{t}')$, with $\sigma = i_1/o_1, \ldots, i_n/o_n$, $\bar{t} = (t_1 \ldots t_n)$, and $\bar{t}' = (t_1' \ldots t_n')$, is an *observed time execution* of I, or simply *time execution*, if the observation of I shows that for all $1 \leq j \leq n$ we have that the time elapsed between the acceptance of the input i_j and the observation of the output o_j is t_j' units of time, being the input i_j accepted t_j units of time after the last output was observed.

Let $\Phi = \{(\sigma_1, \bar{p}_1), \ldots, (\sigma_m, \bar{p}_m)\}$ where for all $1 \leq j \leq n$ we have $\bar{p}_j = (\hat{t}_1 \ldots \hat{t}_n)$, and let $H = \{(\sigma_1', \bar{t}_1, \bar{t}_1'), \ldots, (\sigma_n', \bar{t}_n, \bar{t}_n')\}$ be a multiset of timed executions. We say that $\texttt{Sampling}_{(H,\Phi)}^k : \Phi \longrightarrow \wp(\texttt{Time})$ is a *k-sampling application* of H for Φ if $\texttt{Sampling}_{(H,\Phi)}^k(\sigma, \bar{p}) = \{\!\!\{\pi_k(\bar{t}') \mid (\sigma, \bar{t}, \bar{t}') \in H \wedge |\sigma| \geq k \wedge \bar{t} \in \bar{p}\}\!\!\}$, for all $(\sigma, \bar{p}) \in \Phi$. We say that $\texttt{Sampling}_{(H,\Phi)} : \Phi \longrightarrow \wp(\texttt{Time})$ is a *sampling application* of H for Φ if $\texttt{Sampling}_{(H,\Phi)}(\sigma, \bar{p})) = \{\!\!\{\sum \bar{t}' \mid (\sigma, \bar{t}, \bar{t}') \in H \wedge \bar{t} \in \bar{p}\}\!\!\}$, for all $(\sigma, \bar{p}) \in \Phi$. $\qquad\square$

Regarding the definition of k-sampling applications, we just associate with each subtrace of length k the observed time of each transition of the execution at length k. In the definition of sampling applications, we assign to each trace the total observed time corresponding to the whole execution.

Definition 7. Let I and S be SFSMs, H be a multiset of timed executions of I, $0 \leq \alpha \leq 1$, $\Phi = \texttt{FEvol}(S)$, and let us consider $\texttt{Sampling}_{(H,\Phi)}$ and $\texttt{Sampling}_{(H,\Phi)}^k$, for all $1 \leq k \leq max\{|\sigma| \mid (\sigma, \bar{p}) \in \Phi\}$.

We say that I $(\alpha, H)-$*strong stochastically conforms* to S, and we denote it by $I \texttt{ confs}_s^{(\alpha,H)} S$, if $I \texttt{ conf}_f S$ and for all $(\sigma, \bar{t}, \bar{t}') \in H$ we have

$$\exists (\sigma, \bar{p}, \bar{\xi}) \in \texttt{SEvol}(S) : \bar{t} \in \bar{p}$$
$$\Downarrow$$
$$\forall 1 \leq j \leq |\sigma| : \gamma(\pi_j(\bar{\xi}), \texttt{Sampling}_{(H,\Phi)}^j(\sigma, \bar{p})) > \alpha$$

We say that I $(\alpha, H)-$*weak stochastically conforms* to S, and we denote it by $I \, \mathtt{confs}_w^{(\alpha,H)} \, S$, if $I \, \mathtt{conf}_f \, S$ and for all $(\sigma, \bar{t}, \bar{t}') \in H$ we have

$$\exists (\sigma, \bar{p}, \bar{\xi}) \in \mathtt{SEvol}(S) : \bar{t} \in \bar{p}$$
$$\Downarrow$$
$$\gamma \left(\sum_{j=1}^{|\sigma|} \pi_j(\bar{\xi}), \mathtt{Sampling}_{(H,\Phi)}(\sigma, \bar{p}) \right) > \alpha$$

$\square$

The idea underlying the new relations is that the implementation must conform to the specification in the usual way (that is, $I \, \mathtt{conf}_f \, S$). Besides, for all observation of the implementation that can be performed by the specification, the observed execution time values *fit* the random variable indicated by the specification. This notion of *fitting* is given by the function γ that it is formally defined in the appendix of this paper. While the *weak* notion only compares the total time, the *strong* notion checks that the time values are appropiate for each performed output. A first direct result says that if we decrease the confidence level then we keep conformance.

Lemma 1. Let I and S be SFSMs. If $I \, \mathtt{confs}_s^{(\alpha_1,H)} \, S$ and $\alpha_2 < \alpha_1$ then we have $I \, \mathtt{confs}_s^{(\alpha_2,H)} \, S$. If $I \, \mathtt{confs}_w^{(\alpha_1,H)} \, S$ and $\alpha_2 < \alpha_1$ then we have $I \, \mathtt{confs}_w^{(\alpha_2,H)} \, S$.

$\square$

The next result, whose proof is straightforward, states that if we have two samples sharing some properties then our conformance relations give the same result for both of them.

Lemma 2. Let I and S be SFSMs, H_1 and H_2 be multisets of timed executions for I, and let $b_i = \{(\sigma, \bar{t}, \bar{t}') \, | \, (\sigma, \bar{t}, \bar{t}') \in H_i \wedge (\sigma, \bar{t}) \in \mathtt{InsFEvol}(I) \cap \mathtt{InsFEvol}(S)\}$, for $i \in \{1, 2\}$. If $b_1 = b_2$ then we have $I \, \mathtt{confs}_s^{(\alpha,H_1)} \, S$ iff $I \, \mathtt{confs}_s^{(\alpha,H_2)} \, S$. Similarly, if $b_1 = b_2$ then we have $I \, \mathtt{confs}_w^{(\alpha,H_1)} \, S$ iff $I \, \mathtt{confs}_w^{(\alpha,H_2)} \, S$.

$\square$

Lemma 3. Let I and S be SFSMs. We have $I \, \mathtt{confs}_s^{(\alpha,H)} \, S$ implies $I \, \mathtt{confs}_w^{(\alpha,H)} \, S$.

$\square$

Next we present different variations of the previous implementation relation. First, we define the concept of *shifting* a random variable with respect to its mean. For example, let us consider a random variable ξ following a Dirac distribution in 4 (see Example 1 for the formal definition). If we consider a new random variable ξ' following a Dirac distribution in 3, we say that ξ' represents a shift of ξ. Moreover, we also say that ξ and ξ' belong to the same family.

Definition 8. We say that ξ' is a *mean shift* of ξ with mean M', and we denote it by $\xi' = \mathtt{MShift}(\xi, M')$, if ξ, ξ' belong to the same family and the mean of ξ', denoted by $\mu_{\xi'}$, is equal to M'.

Let I and S be SFSMs, H be a multiset of timed executions of I, $0 \leq \alpha \leq 1$, $\Phi = \mathtt{FEvol}(S)$, and let us consider $\mathtt{Sampling}_{(H,\Phi)}$ and $\mathtt{Sampling}^k_{(H,\Phi)}$ for all $1 \leq k \leq max\{|\sigma| \mid (\sigma,\bar{p}) \in \Phi\}$. We say that I $(\alpha, H)-strongly$ $stochastically$ $conforms$ to S $with$ $speed$ π, denoted by $I\mathtt{confm}^{(\alpha,H)}_{s\pi}S$, if $I\,\mathtt{conf}_f\,S$ and for all $(\sigma, \bar{t}, \bar{t}') \in H$ we have

$$\exists\,(\sigma, \bar{p}, \bar{\xi}) \in \mathtt{SEvol}(S) : \bar{t} \in \bar{p}$$
$$\Downarrow$$
$$\forall\,1 \leq j \leq |\sigma| : \gamma(\mathtt{MShift}(\pi_j(\xi), \mu_{\pi_j(\xi)} \cdot \pi), \mathtt{Sampling}^j_{(H,\Phi)}(\sigma, \bar{p})) > \alpha$$

We say that I $(\alpha, H)-weakly$ $stochastically$ $conforms$ to S $with$ $speed$ π, denoted by $I\mathtt{confm}^{(\alpha,H)}_{w\pi}S$, if $I\,\mathtt{conf}_f\,S$ and for all $(\sigma, \bar{t}, \bar{t}') \in H$ we have

$$\exists\,(\sigma, \bar{p}, \bar{\xi}) \in \mathtt{SEvol}(S) : \bar{t} \in \bar{p}$$
$$\Downarrow$$
$$\gamma(\mathtt{MShift}(\xi, \mu_\xi \cdot \pi), \mathtt{Sampling}_{(H,\Phi)}(\sigma, \bar{p})) > \alpha$$

where we have considered $\xi = \sum_{j=1}^{|\sigma|} \pi_j(\bar{\xi})$. $\qquad\square$

An interesting remark regarding these new relations is that when α is *small enough* and/or π is *close enough* to 1, then it may happen that we have both $I\mathtt{confs}^{(\alpha,H)}_s S$ and $I\mathtt{confm}^{(\alpha,H)}_{s\pi}S$, and similarly for the case of $I\mathtt{confs}^{(\alpha,H)}_w S$ and $I\mathtt{confm}^{(\alpha,H)}_{w\pi}S$. Nevertheless, it is enough to increase α, as far as $\pi \neq 1$, so that we do not have both results strong/weak conformance notions simultaneously. Let us note that in the previous definition, a value of π greater than 1 indicates that the new delay is *slower*. This observation induces the following relation.

Definition 9. Let I and S be SFSMs. Let H be a multiset of timed executions of I. We say that I is *strong-generally faster* (respectively *strong-generally slower*) than S for H if there exist $0 \leq \alpha \leq 1$ and $0 < \pi < 1$ (respectively $\pi > 1$) such that $I\mathtt{confm}^{(\alpha,H)}_{s\pi}S$ but $I\,\mathtt{confs}^{(\alpha,H)}_s S$ does not hold. We say that I is *weak-generally faster* (respectively *weak-generally slower*) than S for H if there exist $0 \leq \alpha \leq 1$ and $0 < \pi < 1$ (respectively $\pi > 1$) such that $I\mathtt{confm}^{(\alpha,H)}_{w\pi}S$ but $I\,\mathtt{confs}^{(\alpha,H)}_w S$ does not hold. $\qquad\square$

Given the fact that, in our framework, an implementation could *fit better* to a specification with higher or lower speed, it will be interesting to detect which variations of speed would make the implementation to fit better the specification. Intuitively, the best variation will be the one allowing the implementation to conform to the specification with a *higher* level of confidence α.

Definition 10. Let I and S be SFSMs. Let H be a multiset of timed executions of I. Let us consider $0 \leq \alpha \leq 1$ such that $I\mathtt{confm}^{(\alpha,H)}_{s\pi}S$, $I\mathtt{confm}^{(\alpha,H)}_{w\pi}S$, and there do not exist $\alpha' > \alpha$ and $\pi' \in \mathbb{R}^+$ with $I\mathtt{confm}^{(\alpha',H)}_{s\pi'}S$. Then, we say that π is a *relative speed* of I with respect to S for H. $\qquad\square$

The concept of relative speed allows us to define another implementation relation which is more restrictive than those presented so far. Basically, the implementation must both (α, H)−stochastically conform to the specification and have 1 as a relative speed. Let us note that the latter condition means that the implementation fits perfectly in its current speed.

Definition 11. Let I and S be SFSMs. Let H be a multiset of timed executions of I and let us consider $0 \leq \alpha \leq 1$. We say that I (α, H)−*stochastically and precisely strong conforms* to S, denoted by $I \, \mathtt{confp}_s^{(\alpha,H)} \, S$, if $I \, \mathtt{confs}_s^{(\alpha,H)} \, S$ and we have that 1 is a relative speed of I with respect to S for H. Similarly, we say that I (α, H)−*stochastically and precisely weak conforms* to S, denoted by $I \mathtt{confp}_S^{(\alpha,H)w}$, if $I \, \mathtt{confs}_w^{(\alpha,H)} \, S$ and we have that 1 is a relative speed of I with respect to S for H. $\qquad\square$

The following result relates some of the notions presented in this section.

Lemma 4. Let I and S be SFSMs. We have $I \, \mathtt{confp}_s^{(\alpha,H)} \, S$ iff $I \, \mathtt{confs}_s^{(\alpha,H)} \, S$ and neither I is strong-generally faster than S for H nor I is strong-generally slower than S for H.
  We have $I \, \mathtt{confp}_w^{(\alpha,H)} \, S$ iff $I \, \mathtt{confs}_w^{(\alpha,H)} \, S$ and neither I is weak-generally faster than S for H nor I is weak-generally slower than S for H. $\qquad\square$

5   Conclusions and Future Work

In this paper we have presented a new notion of finite state machine. In contrast with most timed extensions, our formalism allows to specify in an easy way both the passing of time due to timeouts and the time due to the performance of actions. In the first case, we consider that timeouts are given by fix amounts of time. For each state of the machine, if after a certain time no input action is received then the machine changes the state. In the second case, time is introduced by means of random variables. Thus, we are able to specify the time elapsed from the reception of an input until the observation of an output. These time values are specified by means of random variables. Finally, we have presented several implementation relations based on the notion of conformance. These relations share a common pattern: The implementation must conform to the specification regarding functional aspects. In addition to require that different sequences of actions are performed in the implementation as indicated by the specification, the timeouts of the implementation have also to be placed according to the ones of the specification. Our implementation relations also impose some conditions regarding the random variables appearing in both specifications and implementations.

As future work we plan to introduce an appropriate notion of test and to define how tests are applied to implementations. In this sense, we will give a notion of passing a test suite *up to a certain probability*. The final goal will be to relate our implementation relations with this notion of passing tests. This will be done by providing a test derivation algorithm to obtain sound and complete test suites with respect to some of the implementation relations given in this paper.

References

[AD94]   R. Alur and D. Dill. A theory of timed automata. *Theoretical Computer Science*, 126:183–235, 1994.

[BG98]   M. Bernardo and R. Gorrieri. A tutorial on EMPA: A theory of concurrent processes with nondeterminism, priorities, probabilities and time. *Theoretical Computer Science*, 202:1–54, 1998.

[BG02]   M. Bravetti and R. Gorrieri. The theory of interactive generalized semi-Markov processes. *Theoretical Computer Science*, 282(1):5–32, 2002.

[BL97]   P. Brémond-Grégoire and I. Lee. A process algebra of communicating shared resources with dense time and priorities. *Theoretical Computer Science*, 189(1-2):179–219, 1997.

[BU91]   B.S. Bosik and M.U. Uyar. Finite state machine based formal methods in protocol conformance testing. *Computer Networks & ISDN Systems*, 22:7–33, 1991.

[CCV+03]   D. Cazorla, F. Cuartero, V. Valero, F.L. Pelayo, and J.J. Pardo. Algebraic theory of probabilistic and non-deterministic processes. *Journal of Logic and Algebraic Programming*, 55(1–2):57–103, 2003.

[CdAHS03] A. Chakrabarti, L. de Alfaro, T.A. Henzinger, and M. Stoelinga. Resource interfaces. In *3rd Int. Conf. on Embedded Software, EMSOFT 2003, LNCS 2855*, pages 117–133. Springer, 2003.

[CDSY99]   R. Cleaveland, Z. Dayar, S.A. Smolka, and S. Yuen. Testing preorders for probabilistic processes. *Information and Computation*, 154(2):93–148, 1999.

[CGP00]   E.M. Clarke, O. Grumberg, and D. Peled. *Model Checking*. MIT Press, 2000.

[CL97]   D. Clarke and I. Lee. Automatic generation of tests for timing constraints from requirements. In *3rd Workshop on Object-Oriented Real-Time Dependable Systems*, 1997.

[DK05]   P.R. D'Argenio and J.-P. Katoen. A theory of stochastic systems part I: Stochastic automata. *Information and Computation*, 203(1):1–38, 2005.

[ED03]   A. En-Nouaary and R. Dssouli. A guided method for testing timed input output automata. In *TestCom 2003, LNCS 2644*, pages 211–225. Springer, 2003.

[GSS95]   R. van Glabbeek, S.A. Smolka, and B. Steffen. Reactive, generative and stratified models of probabilistic processes. *Information and Computation*, 121(1):59–80, 1995.

[Her98]   H. Hermanns. *Interactive Markov Chains*. PhD thesis, Universität Erlangen-Nürnberg, 1998.

[Hil96]   J. Hillston. *A Compositional Approach to Performance Modelling*. Cambridge University Press, 1996.

[HNTC99]   T. Higashino, A. Nakata, K. Taniguchi, and A. Cavalli. Generating test cases for a timed I/O automaton model. In *12th Workshop on Testing of Communicating Systems*, pages 197–214. Kluwer Academic Publishers, 1999.

[HR95]   M. Hennessy and T. Regan. A process algebra for timed systems. *Information and Computation*, 117(2):221–239, 1995.

[LN01]   N. López and M. Núñez. A testing theory for generally distributed stochastic processes. In *CONCUR 2001, LNCS 2154*, pages 321–335. Springer, 2001.

[LNR06]   N. López, M. Núñez, and I. Rodríguez. Specification, testing and implementation relations for symbolic-probabilistic systems. *Theoretical Computer Science*, 353(1–3):228–248, 2006.

[LY96]   D. Lee and M. Yannakakis. Principles and methods of testing finite state machines: A survey. *Proceedings of the IEEE*, 84(8):1090–1123, 1996.

[NR01]   M. Núñez and I. Rodríguez. PAMR: A process algebra for the management of resources in concurrent systems. In *FORTE 2001*, pages 169–185. Kluwer Academic Publishers, 2001.

[NR02]   M. Núñez and I. Rodríguez. Encoding PAMR into (timed) EFSMs. In *FORTE 2002, LNCS 2529*, pages 1–16. Springer, 2002.

[NR03]   M. Núñez and I. Rodríguez. Towards testing stochastic timed systems. In *FORTE 2003, LNCS 2767*, pages 335–350. Springer, 2003.

[NS91]   X. Nicollin and J. Sifakis. An overview and synthesis on timed process algebras. In *Computer Aided Verification'91, LNCS 575*, pages 376–398. Springer, 1991.

[Núñ03]   M. Núñez. Algebraic theory of probabilistic processes. *Journal of Logic and Algebraic Programming*, 56(1–2):117–177, 2003.

[RR88]   G.M. Reed and A.W. Roscoe. A timed model for communicating sequential processes. *Theoretical Computer Science*, 58:249–261, 1988.

[SV03]   M. Stoelinga and F. Vaandrager. A testing scenario for probabilistic automata. In *ICALP 2003, LNCS 2719*, pages 464–477. Springer, 2003.

[SVD01]   J. Springintveld, F. Vaandrager, and P.R. D'Argenio. Testing timed automata. *Theoretical Computer Science*, 254(1-2):225–257, 2001.

Appendix. Statistics Background: Hypothesis Contrasts

In this appendix we introduce one of the standard ways to measure the confidence degree that a random variable has on a sample. In order to do so, we will present a methodology to perform *hypothesis contrasts*. The underlying idea is that a sample will be *rejected* if the probability of observing that sample from a given random variable is low. In practice, we will check whether the probability to observe a *discrepancy* lower than or equal to the one we have observed is low enough. We will present *Pearson's χ^2* contrast. This contrast can be applied both to continuous and discrete random variables. The mechanism is the following. Once we have collected a sample of size n we perform the following steps:

- We split the sample into k classes which cover all the possible range of values. We denote by O_i the *observed frequency* at class i (i.e. the number of elements belonging to the class i).
- We calculate the probability p_i of each class, according to the proposed random variable. We denote by E_i the *expected frequency*, which is given by $E_i = np_i$.

- We calculate the *discrepancy* between observed frequencies and expected frequencies as $X^2 = \sum_{i=1}^{n} \frac{(O_i - E_i)^2}{E_i}$. When the model is correct, this discrepancy is approximately distributed as a random variable χ^2 .
- We estimate the number of freedom degrees of χ^2 as $k - r - 1$. In this case, r is the number of parameters of the model which have been estimated by maximal likelihood over the sample to estimate the values of p_i (i.e. $r = 0$ if the model completely specifies the values of p_i before the samples are observed).
- We will *accept* that the sample follows the proposed random variable if the probability to obtain a discrepancy greater or equal to the discrepancy observed is high enough, that is, if $X^2 < \chi_\alpha^2(k - r - 1)$ for some α low enough. Actually, as such margin to accept the sample decreases as α decreases, we can obtain a measure of the validity of the sample as $max\{\alpha \mid X^2 < \chi_\alpha^2(k - r - 1)\}$.

According to the previous steps, we can now present an operative definition of the function γ which is used in this paper to compute the confidence of a random variable on a sample.

Definition 12. Let ξ be a random variable and let J be a multiset of real numbers representing a sample. Let X^2 be the discrepancy level of J on ξ calculated as explained above by splitting the sampling space into the set of classes $C = \{[0, a_1), [a_1, a_2), \ldots, [a_{k-1}, a_k), [a_k, \infty)\}$, where k is a given constant and for all $1 \le i \le k$ we have $a_i = q$ where $P(\xi \le q) = \frac{i}{k+1}$. We define the confidence of ξ on J with classes S, denoted by $\gamma(\xi, J)$, as $max\{\alpha \mid X^2 < \chi_\alpha^2(k - 1)\}$.   □

Let us comment some important details. First, given the fact that the random variables that we use in our framework denote the passing of time, we do not need classes to cover negative values. Thus, we will suppose that the class containing 0 will also contain all the negative values. Second, let us remark that in order to apply this contrast it is strongly recommended that the sample has at least 30 elements while each class must contain at least 3 elements.

On the Convergence Rate of Quasi Lumpable Markov Chains

András Faragó

The University of Texas at Dallas
Richardson, Texas, USA
farago@utdallas.edu

Abstract. Our main result is a new bound on the rate at which the aggregated state distribution approaches its limit in *quasi-lumpable Markov chains*. We also demonstrate that in certain cases this can lead to a significantly accelerated way of estimating the measure of subsets in Markov chains with very large state space.

Keywords: Markov chain, convergence rate, lumpable and quasi-lumpable Markov chain.

1 Introduction

Markov chain based models in performance analysis often encounter the difficulty that the chain has a huge state space, which may significantly slow down any practical computation or convergence rate. In such cases it is very useful if the state space can be partitioned such that the states belonging to the same partition class "behave the same way", in the sense defined formally in the next section. This is the well known concept of *lumpability* [6]. Informally speaking, it means that some sets of states can be lumped together and replaced by a single state, thus obtaining a Markov chain which has a smaller state space, but its essential behavior is the same as the original.

In some cases the lumpability of the Markov chain can have a very significant effect on the efficiency of the model. A practical example is discussed in [8], where the authors present a fast algorithm to compute the PageRank vector, which is an important part of search engine algorithms in the World Wide Web. The PageRank vector can be interpreted as the stationary distribution of a Markov chain. This chain has a huge state space, yielding excessive computation times. This Markov chain, however, is lumpable. Making use of the lumpability, the computation time can be reduced to 20% of the original, according to the experiments presented in [8].

Unfortunately, it happens relatively rarely that the Markov chain satisfies the definition of lumpability *exactly*. This motivates the concept of *quasi-lumpability* [1, 2]. Informally, a Markov chain is quasi-lumpable if its transition matrix is obtainable by a small perturbation from a matrix that exactly satisfies the lumpability condition (see the formal definition in the next section).

A. Horváth and M. Telek (Eds.): EPEW 2006, LNCS 4054, pp. 138–147, 2006.

In this paper we are interested in the following problem, which is often encountered in applications: how long do we have to run the Markov chain if we want to get close to the stationary distribution within a prescribed error? While generally this question is widely discussed in the literature (see, e.g., [7, 10]), to the author's best knowledge no specific result exists that utilizes the special structure of quasi-lumpable Markov chains in the convergence rate analysis. Our goal is to (partially) fill this gap.

2   Lumpable and Quasi-lumpable Markov Chains

We assume the reader is familiar with the fundamental concepts of Markov chains. We adopt the notation that a Markov chain $\mathcal{M}$ is given by a set S of states and by a transition probability matrix P, so we write $\mathcal{M} = (S, P)$. We do not include the initial distribution in the notation, because it is assumed arbitrary.

First we define the *lumpability* of a Markov chain. Informally, as mentioned in the Introduction, a chain is lumpable if its states can be aggregated into larger subsets of S, such that the aggregated (lumped) chain remains a Markov chain with respect to the set-transition probabilities (i.e, it preserves the property that the future depends on the past only through the present). Let us introduce now the formal definition.

Definition 1 (Lumpability of Markov chain). *Let* $\mathcal{M} = (S, P)$ *be a Markov chain. Let* $\mathcal{Q} = \{A_1, \ldots, A_m\}$ *be a partition of* S. *The chain* $\mathcal{M}$ *is called* lumpable *with respect to* $\mathcal{Q}$ *if for any initial distribution the relationship*

$$\Pr(X_t \in A_j \mid X_{t-1} \in A_{i_1}, \ldots, X_{t-k} \in A_{i_k}) = \Pr(X_t \in A_j \mid X_{t-1} \in A_{i_1}) \quad (1)$$

holds for any $t, k, j, i_1, \ldots, i_k$, *whenever these conditional probabilities are defined (i.e., the conditions occur with positive probability).*

A fundamental result on the lumpability of Markov chains is the following theorem, see [6], Theorem 6.3.2. We use the notation that $p(x, A)$ denotes the probability that the chain moves into a set $A \subseteq S$, given that it is in the state $x \in S$. Note that x itself may or may not be in A.

Theorem 1 (Necessary and sufficient condition for lumpability). *A Markov chain* $\mathcal{M} = (S, P)$ *is lumpable with respect to a partition* $\mathcal{Q} = \{A_1, \ldots, A_m\}$ *of* S *if and only if for any* i, j *the value of* $p(x, A_j)$ *is the same for every* $x \in A_i$. *These common values define the transition probabilities* $\hat{p}(A_i, A_j)$ *for the* lumped *chain, which is a Markov chain with state set* $\mathcal{Q}$ *and state transition probabilites*

$$\hat{p}(A_i, A_j) = p(x, A_j) = \Pr(X_t \in A_j \mid X_{t-1} \in A_i)$$

where x *is any state in* A_i.

Whenever our Markov chain is lumpable, we can reduce the number of states by the above aggregation, and that is usually advantageous for faster convergence (a specific bound will be proven in Section 3).

Now let us relax the concept of lumpability to broaden the family of the considered Markov chains. Informally, a Markov chain is called *quasi-lumpable* or *ε-quasi-lumpable* or simply *ε-lumpable*, if it may not be perfectly lumpable, but it is "close" to that. This "ε-closeness" is defined in [1, 2] in a way that the transition matrix can be decomposed as $P = P^- + P^\epsilon$. Here P^- is a componentwise nonnegative lower bound for P, such that P^- satisfies the necessary and sufficient condition of Theorem 1. The other matrix, P^ϵ, is an arbitrary nonnegative matrix in which each entry is bounded by ϵ. In our discussion we prefer the following simpler but equivalent definition.

Definition 2 (ε-lumpability). *Let $\epsilon \geq 0$. A Markov chain $\mathcal{M} = (S, P)$ is called ε-lumpable with respect to a partition $\mathcal{Q} = \{A_1, \ldots, A_m\}$ of S if*

$$|p(x, A_j) - p(y, A_j)| \leq \epsilon$$

holds for any $x, y \in A_i$ and for any $i, j \in \{1, \ldots, m\}$.

Note that if we take $\epsilon = 0$, then we get back the ordinary concept of lumpability. Thus, quasi-lumpability is indeed a relaxation of the original concept. It can also be interpreted in the following way. If $\epsilon > 0$, then the original definition of lumpability may not hold. This means, the aggregated process may not remain Markov. i.e., it does not satisfy (1). On the other hand, if ϵ is small, then the aggregated process will be, in a sense, "close" to being Markov, that is, to satisfying (1).

What we are interested in is the convergence analysis of quasi lumpable Markov chains, typically for a small value of ϵ (but the result of the next section formally holds for any ϵ). For the analysis we need to introduce another definition.

Definition 3 (Lower and upper transition matrices). *Let $\mathcal{M} = (S, P)$ be a Markov chain which is ε-lumpable with respect to a partition $\mathcal{Q} = \{A_1, \ldots, A_m\}$. The lower and upper transition matrices $L = [l_{ij}]$ and $U = [u_{ij}]$ are defined as $m \times m$ matrices with entries*

$$l_{ij} = \min_{x \in A_i} p(x, A_j) \quad \text{and} \quad u_{ij} = \max_{x \in A_i} p(x, A_j),$$

respectively, for $i, j = 1, \ldots, m$.

Note that it always holds (componentwise) that $L \leq U$. If the chain is lumpable, then these matrices coincide, so then $L = U = \tilde{P}$, where $\tilde{P}$ is the transition matrix of the lumped chain. If the chain is ε-lumpable, then L and U differ at most by ϵ in each entry.

Generally, L and U are not necessarily stochastic matrices[1], as their rows may not to sum up to 1.

---

[1] A vector is called stochastic if each coordinate is nonnegative and their sum is 1. A matrix is called stochastic if each row vector of it is stochastic.

3 Convergence Analysis

An important concept in Markov chain convergence analysis is the *ergodic coefficient* or *coefficient of ergodicity*, see, e.g., [7].

Definition 4. *Let $P = [p_{ij}]$ be an $n \times n$ matrix. Its ergodic coefficient is defined as*

$$\rho(P) = \frac{1}{2} \max_{i,j} \sum_{k=1}^{n} |p_{ik} - p_{jk}|.$$

For stochastic matrices two well known properties of the ergodic coefficient are the following [7]:

(i) $0 \leq \rho(P) \leq 1$
(ii) $\rho(AB) \leq \rho(A)\rho(B)$

The importance of the ergodic coefficient lies in its relationship to the convergence rate of the (finite state) Markov chain. It is well known that the convergence rate is determined by the second largest eigenvalue of the transition matrix (that is, the eigenvalue which has the largest absolute value less than 1), see, e.g., [10]. If this eigenvalue is denoted by λ_1, then the convergence to stationarity happens at a rate of $O(\lambda_1^t)$, where t is the number of steps. It is also known [7] that the ergodic coefficient is always an upper bound on this eigenvalue, it satisfies $\lambda_1 \leq \rho(P) \leq 1$. Therefore, the distance to the stationary distribution is also bounded by $O(\rho(P)^t)$. Thus, the smaller is the ergodic coefficient, the faster convergence we can expect. Of course it only provides any useful bound if $\rho(P) < 1$. If $\rho(P) = 1$, then a way out is considering the k-step transition matrix P^k for some k. If k is large enough, then we can certainly achieve $\rho(P^k) < 1$, since it is known [7] that $\lim_{k \to \infty} \rho(P^k) = 0$.

Now we are ready to present the main result, which is a bound on how fast will an ϵ-lumpable Markov chain converge to its stationary distribution on the sets that are in the partition which is used in defining the ϵ-lumpability of the chain. We are going to discuss the applicability of the result in the next section.

Theorem 2. *Let $\epsilon \geq 0$ and $\mathcal{M} = (S, P)$ be an irreducible, aperiodic Markov chain that has a stationary distribution π. Assume the chain is ϵ-lumpable with respect to a partition $\mathcal{Q} = \{A_1, \ldots, A_m\}$ of S. Let ρ be any upper bound on the ergodic coefficient of the lower transition matrix L (Definition 3), that is, $\rho(L) \leq \rho$. Let π_0 be any initial probability distribution on S, such that $P(X_t \in A_i) > 0$ for any i and $t = 0, 1, 2, \ldots$ Then for every $t \geq 1$ the following estimation holds:*

$$\sum_{i=1}^{m} |\pi_t(A_i) - \pi(A_i)| \leq 2(\rho + \epsilon m/2)^t + \epsilon m \frac{1 - (\rho + \epsilon m/2)^t}{1 - \rho - \epsilon m/2}$$

assuming $\rho + \epsilon m/2 < 1$.

For the proof we need a lemma of D.J. Hartfiel about stochastic vectors and matrices (Lemma 3.4 on p. 70 in [3], see also [4]):

Lemma 1. (Hartfiel [3, 4]) *Let x, y be n-dimensional stochastic vectors. Further, let $B_1, \ldots, B_k$ and $C_1, \ldots, C_k$ be $n \times n$ stochastic matrices. If $\rho(B_i) \leq \rho_0$ and $\rho(C_i) \leq \rho_0$ for all i, $1 \leq i \leq k$, then*

$$\|xB_1 \ldots B_k - yC_1 \ldots C_k\| \leq \rho_0^k \|x - y\| + (\rho_0^{k-1} + \ldots + 1)\mathcal{E}$$

where $\mathcal{E} = \max_i \|B_i - C_i\|$. The vector norm used is the L_1-norm $\|x\| = \sum_{i=1}^n |x_i|$ and the matrix norm is

$$\|A\| = \sup_{z \neq 0} \frac{\|zA\|}{\|z\|} = \max_i \sum_{j=1}^n |a_{ij}|$$

for any $n \times n$ real matrix $A = [a_{ij}]$.

Lemma 1 can be proved via induction on k, see [3, 4]. Now, armed with the lemma, we can prove our theorem.

Proof of Theorem 2. Let π_0 be an initial state distribution of the Markov chain $\mathcal{M}$, let π_t be the corresponding distribution after t steps and $\pi = \lim_{t \to \infty} \pi_t$ be the (unique) stationary distribution of $\mathcal{M}$. For a set $A \subseteq S$ of states the usual notations $\pi_t(A) = \mathrm{P}(X_t \in A)$, $\pi(A) = \lim_{t \to \infty} \pi_t(A)$ are adopted.

Using the sets $A_1, \ldots, A_m$ of the partition $\mathcal{Q}$, let us define the stochastic vectors

$$\tilde{\pi}_t = \big(\pi_t(A_1), \ldots, \pi_t(A_m)\big) \tag{2}$$

for $t = 0, 1, 2, \ldots$ and the $m \times m$ stochastic matrices

$$\tilde{P}_t(\pi_0) = [p_t^{(\pi_0)}(i, j)] = \big[\mathrm{P}(X_{t+1} \in A_j \mid X_t \in A_i)\big] \tag{3}$$

for $t = 1, 2, \ldots$. Let us call them aggregated state distribution vectors and aggregated transition matrices, respectively. Note that although the entries in (3) involve only events of the form $\{X_t \in A_k\}$, they may also depend on the detailed state distribution within these sets, which is in turn determined by the initial distribution π_0. In other words, if two different initial distributions give rise to the same probabilities for the events $\{X_t \in A_k\}$ for some t, they may still result in different conditional probabilities of the form $\mathrm{P}(X_{t+1} \in A_j \mid X_t \in A_i)$, since the chain is not assumed lumpable in the ordinary sense. This is why the notations $\tilde{P}_t(\pi_0)$, $p_t^{(\pi_0)}(i, j)$ are used. Also note that the conditional probabilities are well defined for any initial distribution allowed by the assumptions of the lemma, since then $\mathrm{P}(X_t \in A_i) > 0$.

For any fixed t the events $\{X_t \in A_i\}$, $i = 1, \ldots, m$, are mutually exclusive with total probability 1, therefore, by the law of total probability,

$$\mathrm{P}(X_{t+1} \in A_j) = \sum_{i=1}^m \mathrm{P}(X_{t+1} \in A_j \mid X_t \in A_i)\mathrm{P}(X_t \in A_i), \qquad j = 1, \ldots, m$$

holds. This implies $\tilde{\pi}_{t+1} = \tilde{\pi}_t \tilde{P}_t(\pi_0)$, from which

$$\tilde{\pi}_t = \tilde{\pi}_0 \tilde{P}_1(\pi_0) \dots \tilde{P}_t(\pi_0) \tag{4}$$

follows.

We next show that for any $t = 1, 2, \dots$ the matrix $\tilde{P}_t(\pi_0)$ falls between the lower and upper transition matrices, i.e., $L \le \tilde{P}_t(\pi_0) \le M$ holds. Let us use short notations for certain events: for any $i = 1, \dots, m$ and for a fixed $t \ge 1$ set $H_i = \{X_t \in A_i\}$, $H_i' = \{X_{t+1} \in A_i\}$, and for $x \in S$ let $E_x = \{X_t = x\}$. Then $E_x \cap E_y = \emptyset$ holds for any $x \ne y$ and $\sum_{x \in S} E_x = 1$. Applying the definition of conditional probability and the law of total probability, noting that $P(H_i) > 0$ is provided by the assumptions of the lemma, we get

$$
\begin{aligned}
p_t^{(\pi_0)}(i,j) = P(H_j' \mid H_i) &= \frac{P(H_j' \cap H_i)}{P(H_i)} \\
&= \frac{\sum_{x \in S} P(H_j' \cap H_i \cap E_x)}{P(H_i)} \\
&= \frac{\sum_{x \in S} P(H_j' \mid H_i \cap E_x) P(H_i \cap E_x)}{P(H_i)} \\
&= \sum_{x \in S} P(H_j' \mid H_i \cap E_x) \frac{P(H_i \cap E_x)}{P(H_i)} \\
&= \sum_{x \in S} P(H_j' \mid H_i \cap E_x) P(E_x \mid H_i).
\end{aligned}
$$

Whenever $x \notin A_i$ we have $P(E_x \mid H_i) = P(X_t = x \mid X_t \in A_i) = 0$. Therefore, it is enough to take the summation over A_i, instead of the entire S. For $x \in A_i$, however, $H_i \cap E_x = \{X_t \in A_i\} \cap \{X_t = x\} = \{X_t = x\}$ holds, so we obtain

$$p_t^{(\pi_0)}(i,j) = \sum_{x \in A_i} P(X_{t+1} \in A_j \mid X_t = x) P(X_t = x \mid X_t \in A_i).$$

Thus, $p_t^{(\pi_0)}(i,j)$ is a weighted average of the $P(X_{t+1} \in A_j \mid X_t = x)$ probabilities. The weights are $P(X_t = x \mid X_t \in A_i)$, so they are nonnegative and sum up to 1. Further,

$$l_{ij} \le P(X_{t+1} \in A_j \mid X_t = x) \le u_{ij}$$

must hold, since l_{ij}, u_{ij} are defined as the minimum and maximum values, respectively, of

$$p(x, A_j) = P(X_{t+1} \in A_j \mid X_t = x)$$

over $x \in A_i$. Since the weighted average must fall between the minimum and the maximum, therefore, we have

$$l_{ij} \le p_t^{(\pi_0)}(i,j) \le u_{ij}, \tag{5}$$

that is,

$$L \le \tilde{P}_t(\pi_0) \le M \tag{6}$$

for any $t \geq 1$ and for any initial distribution π_0 allowed by the conditions of the Theorem.

Let us now start the chain from an initial distribution π_0 that satisfies the conditions of the Theorem. We are going to compare the arising aggregated state distribution vectors (2) with the ones resulting from starting the chain from the stationary distribution π. Note that, due to the assumed irreducibility of the original chain, $\pi(x) > 0$ for all $x \in S$, so π is also a possible initial distribution that satisfies the conditions $P(X_t \in A_i) > 0$.

When the chain is started from the stationary distribution π, then, according to (4), the aggregated state distribution vector at time t is $\tilde{\pi}\tilde{P}_1(\pi)\ldots\tilde{P}_t(\pi)$ where $\tilde{\pi} = (\pi(A_1), \ldots, \pi(A_m))$. On the other hand, $P(X_t \in A_i)$ remains the same for all $t \geq 0$ if the chain starts from the stationary distribution. Therefore, we have

$$\tilde{\pi}\tilde{P}_1(\pi)\ldots\tilde{P}_t(\pi) = \tilde{\pi} = (\pi(A_1), \ldots, \pi(A_m)). \tag{7}$$

When the chain starts from π_0, then we obtain the aggregated state distribution vector

$$\tilde{\pi}_t = \tilde{\pi}_0\tilde{P}_1(\pi_0)\ldots\tilde{P}_t(\pi_0) \tag{8}$$

after t steps. Now we can apply Lemma 1 for the comparison of (7) and (8). The roles for the quantities in Lemma 1 are assigned as $x = \tilde{\pi}_0$, $y = \tilde{\pi}$, $k = t$, $n = m$, and, for every $\tau = 1, \ldots, k$, $B_\tau = \tilde{P}_\tau(\pi_0)$, $C_\tau = \tilde{P}_\tau(\pi)$. To find the value of ρ_0 recall that by (6) we have $L \leq \tilde{P}_\tau(\pi_0) \leq M$ and $L \leq \tilde{P}_\tau(\pi) \leq M$. Since any entry of U exceeds the corresponding entry of L at most by ϵ, therefore, by the definition of the ergodic coefficient, $\rho(\tilde{P}_\tau(\pi_0)) \leq \rho + \epsilon m/2$ and $\rho(\tilde{P}_\tau(\pi)) \leq \rho + \epsilon m/2$ hold, where ρ is the upper bound on $\rho(L)$. Thus, we can take $\rho_0 = \rho + \epsilon m/2$. With these role assignments we obtain from Lemma 1

$$\|\tilde{\pi}_0\tilde{P}_1(\pi_0)\ldots\tilde{P}_t(\pi_0) - \tilde{\pi}\tilde{P}_1(\pi)\ldots\tilde{P}_t(\pi)\| \leq (\rho+\epsilon m/2)^t\|\tilde{\pi}_0-\tilde{\pi}\|+\mathcal{E}\sum_{k=0}^{t-1}(\rho+\epsilon m/2)^k$$

where $\mathcal{E} = \max_\tau \|P_\tau(\pi_0) - P_\tau(\pi_0)\|$ and the norms are as in Lemma 1. Taking (7) and (8) into account yields

$$\|\tilde{\pi}_t - \tilde{\pi}\| = \sum_{i=1}^{m} |\pi_t(A_i) - \pi(A_i)| \leq (\rho + \epsilon m/2)^t\|\tilde{\pi}_0 - \tilde{\pi}\| + \mathcal{E}\sum_{k=0}^{t-1}(\rho + \epsilon m/2)^k. \tag{9}$$

Thus, it only remains to estimate $\|\tilde{\pi}_0 - \tilde{\pi}\|$ and $\mathcal{E}$. Given that $\tilde{\pi}_0, \tilde{\pi}$ are both stochastic vectors, we have $\|\tilde{\pi}_0 - \tilde{\pi}\| \leq \|\tilde{\pi}_0\| + \|\tilde{\pi}\| \leq 2$. Further,

$$\mathcal{E} = \max_\tau \|P_\tau(\pi_0) - P_\tau(\pi)\| = \max_\tau \max_i \sum_{j=1}^{m} |p_\tau^{(\pi_0)}(i, j) - p_\tau^{(\pi)}(i, j)| \leq \epsilon m,$$

since (5) holds for any considered π_0 (including π), and, by the definition of ϵ-lumpability, $u_{ij} - l_{ij} \leq \epsilon$. Substituting the estimations into (9), we obtain

$$\sum_{i=1}^{m} \left| \pi_t(A_i) - \pi(A_i) \right| \le 2(\rho + \epsilon m/2)^t + \epsilon m \sum_{k=0}^{t-1} (\rho + \epsilon m/2)^k$$

$$= 2(\rho + \epsilon m/2)^t + \epsilon m \frac{1 - (\rho + \epsilon m/2)^t}{1 - \rho - \epsilon m/2}$$

proving the Theorem.

If the chain is lumpable in the ordinary sense, then we get a "cleaner" result. Let $\tilde{\pi}_t$ be the state distribution of the lumped chain after t steps and let $\tilde{\pi}$ be its stationary distribution. For concise description let us apply a frequently used distance concept among probability distributions. If p, q are two discrete probability distributions on the same set S, then their *total variation distance* $D_{TV}(p, q)$ is defined as

$$D_{TV}(p, q) = \frac{1}{2} \sum_{x \in S} |p(x) - q(x)|.$$

It is well known that $0 \le D_{TV}(p, q) \le 1$ holds for any two probability distributions. It is also clear from the definition of the ergodic coefficient that it is just the maximum total variation distance between any two row vectors.

Note that (ordinary) lumpability is the special case of ϵ-lumpability with $\epsilon = 0$. Therefore, we immediately obtain the following corollary.

Corollary 1. *If the Markov chain in Theorem 2 is lumpable (i.e., $\epsilon = 0$), then in the lumped chain for any $t = 0, 1, 2, \ldots$ the following holds:*

$$D_{TV}(\tilde{\pi}_t, \tilde{\pi}) \le \rho^t$$

where $\rho = \rho(\tilde{P})$ is the ergodic coefficient of the transition matrix $\tilde{P}$ of the lumped chain.

Proof. Take $\epsilon = 0$ in Theorem 2.

4   An Example

Let us consider the following situation. Let $\mathcal{M}$ be a Markov chain with a huge state space S. Assume we want to estimate the stationary measure $\pi(A)$ of a subset $A \subseteq S$. A practical example of such a situation is to estimate the probability that there is at least one blocked link in a loss network (for information on loss networks see, e.g., [5]). Of course, we can also consider other events, e.g., at most a given percentage of traffic is blocked.

In many cases we are unable to directly compute $\pi(A)$. This task frequently has enormous complexity, for the theoretical background see [9]. Then a natural way to obtain an estimation of $\pi(A)$ is simulation. That is, we run the chain from some initial state, stop it after t steps and check out whether the stopping state is in A or not. Repeating this experiment a large enough number of times, the relative frequency of ending up in A will give a good estimation of the measure of $\pi_t(A)$ (conditioned on the initial state). If t is chosen such that π_t is close enough to the stationary distribution π for any initial state, then we also obtain a good estimation for $\pi(A)$. This is the core idea of the Markov Chain Monte Carlo approach.

Unfortunately, Markov chains with huge state space often converge extremely slowly. Therefore, we may not get close enough to π after a reasonable number of steps. In such a case our result can do a good service, at least when the chain satisfies some special requirements. As an example, let us consider the following case.

Assume the set $A \subseteq S$ is "regular" in the sense that for any state $x \in A$ the probability to move out of A in the next step is *approximately* the same. Similarly, if $x \notin A$, then moving into A in the next step has approximately the same probability from any $x \notin A$. Formally, assume there are values p_0, q_0, ϵ, such that the following conditions hold:

- If $x \in A$ then $p_0 \leq p(x, \bar{A}) \leq p_0 + \epsilon$ where $\bar{A} = S - A$.
- If $x \in \bar{A}$ then $q_0 \leq p(x, A) \leq q_0 + \epsilon$.
- The numbers p_0, q_0, ϵ satisify $p_0 + \epsilon < 1$, $q_0 + \epsilon < 1$ and $0 < p_0 + q_0 < 1$.

Let us apply Theorem 2 for this situation. The parameters will be as follows: $m = 2$,

$$L = \begin{bmatrix} 1 - p_0 - \epsilon & p_0 \\ q_0 & 1 - q_0 - \epsilon \end{bmatrix} \qquad U = \begin{bmatrix} 1 - p_0 & p_0 + \epsilon \\ q_0 + \epsilon & 1 - q_0 \end{bmatrix}.$$

Furthermore, we can take $\rho = 1 - p_0 - q_0 - \epsilon$. Then we obtain from Theorem 2, expressing the estimation in terms of the total variation distance:

$$D_{TV}(\tilde{\pi}_t, \tilde{\pi}) \leq (1 - p_0 - q_0)^t + \epsilon \frac{1 - (1 - p_0 - q_0)^t}{p_0 + q_0}$$

where the distributions $\tilde{\pi}_t, \tilde{\pi}$ are over the sets of the partition $(A, \bar{A})$, not on the original state space. Note that in our case we actually have $D_{TV}(\tilde{\pi}_t, \tilde{\pi}) = |\pi_t(A) - \pi(A)|$, due to the fact that $|\pi_t(A) - \pi(A)| = |\pi_t(\bar{A}) - \pi(\bar{A})|$. Therefore, we obtain the estimation directly for the set A:

$$|\pi_t(A) - \pi(A)| \leq (1 - p_0 - q_0)^t + \epsilon \frac{1 - (1 - p_0 - q_0)^t}{p_0 + q_0}.$$

If $p_0 + q_0$ is not extremely small, then the term $(1 - p_0 - q_0)^t$ will quickly vanish, so after a reasonable number of steps we reach a distribution π_t from *any* initial state, such that $|\pi_t(A) - \pi(A)|$ is bounded approximately by $\epsilon/(p_0 + q_0)$. For a numerical example let us take $p_0 + q_0 = 1/2$. In this case after $t = 100$ steps we obtain the estimation

$$|\pi_t(A) - \pi(A)| \leq 2^{-100} + \epsilon \frac{1 - 2^{-100}}{1/2} \approx 2\epsilon.$$

Note that we do not have to know the actual value of p_0, q_0 to get a good estimation. We only need that $p_0 + q_0$ is not so small that the term $(1 - p_0 - q_0)^t$ would converge too slowly to 0. If we have any lower bound $a \leq p_0 + q_0$, then we can directly estimate the number of steps needed to get to stationarity within $\sim \epsilon/a$ error.

If the original chain does not satisfy the condition of ϵ-lumpabibity with a reasonably small ϵ, then it is worth trying the chain generated by k-step transitions of the original one, with some appropriate value of k. This usually has a "smoothing effect" and increases the chance for ϵ-lumpabibity with small ϵ. (Note that if ϵ is not small, then ϵ-lumpabibity is not a restrictive requirement, but then our bound becomes too lose with growing ϵ.)

5 Conclusion

We have analyzed the convergence rate of quasi-lumpable Markov Chains. The result is a new bound on the rate at which the aggregated state distribution approaches its limit in such chains. We have also demonstrated that in certain cases this can lead to a significantly accelerated way of estimating the measure of certain subsets in Markov chains with huge state space.

References

1. T. Dayar and W.J. Stewart, "Quasi Lumpability, Lower Bounding Coupling Matrices, and Nearly Completely Decomposable Markov Chains", *SIAM J. Matrix Anal. Appl.*, 18(1997/2), pp. 482-498.
2. G. Franceschinis and R.R. Muntz, "Bounds for Quasi-Lumpable Markov Chains", *Performance Evaluation*, 20(1994) pp. 223-243.
3. D.J. Hartfiel, *Markov Set-Chains*, Lecture Notes in Mathematics 1695, Springer-Verlag, 1998.
4. D.J. Hartfiel, "Results on Limiting Sets of Markov Set-Chains", *Linear Algebra and its Applications*, 195(1993), pp. 155-163.
5. F.P. Kelly, "Loss Networks", *Annals of Applied Probability*, Vol. 1, No. 3, 1991, pp. 319-378.
6. J.G. Kemeny and J.L. Snell, *Finite Markov Chains*, Van Nostrand Reinhold, New York, 1960. (Later editions: Springer, 1976, 1983)
7. M. Kijima, *Markov Processes for Stochastic Modeling*, Chapman & Hall, 1997.
8. C. P.-C. Lee, G. H. Golub and S. A. Zenios, "A Fast Two-Stage Algorithm for Computing PageRank and Its Extensions", Technical Report SCCM-2003-15, Scientific Computation and Computational Mathematics, Stanford University, Stanford, CA, 2003.
9. G. Louth, M. Mitzenmacher and F.P. Kelly, "Computational Complexity of Loss Networks", *Theoretical Computer Science*, 125(1994), pp. 45-59.
10. A. Sinclair, *Algorithms for Random Generation and Counting*, Birkhäuser, Boston 1993.

Applying the UML Class Diagram
in the Performance Analysis

Ahmad Alsaadi

Department of Informatics and Computers Engineering
University of Damascus, Syria
`ahmad.alsaadi@gmx.de`

Abstract. This paper covers the performance parameters for an object=
oriented software system: The number of classes in the class diagram of
this system, the number of attributes and methods in each class, their data
types, the multiplicities of single classes, the number of relationships in
this diagram, the types and multiplicities of relationships, the lengths of
access paths, and the allocation of methods and attributes to classes. A
performance analysis is described. It treats a class diagram, which must
be in attendance at each analysis because used dynamic diagrams must
be consistent with it, and encloses these parameters. It is based on an approach which enables one to predict the performance values of response
time, throughput and utilization, for use cases that can operate on databases related to this diagram.

Keywords: class, relationship, class diagram, database, performance
analysis.

1 Introduction

A class diagram illustrates classes and interfaces, and relationships between them.
It contains the statics and dynamics of its software system, and can be schemes for
(object-oriented) databases at the same time. Thus, this diagram can be applied
to conduct a performance analysis. From a performance viewpoint, the structure
of a class diagram influences the behavior in this diagram. It encloses parameters
such as: The *number of classes*, the *number of attributes and methods* in a class,
their *data types* for example set, *multiplicities of classes*, the *number of diagram
relationships*, their *multiplicities*, *types* for instance relationships between classes
and part classes or subclasses, *lengths of access paths*, and *distribution of methods
and attributes* to classes. Most of these parameters, expounded in the next section,
in particular multiplicities and types of relationships and cardinalities of object
collections are included in Data Integrity Constraints (DICs), which are checked
when data is updated in databases [8]. All parameters can be so adjusted that the
performance quality of a software system is ensured. Both terms "class diagram"
and "UML class diagram" refer to the same.

This paper describes a performance analysis for an object-oriented software
system in which the class diagram of this system, i.e. its parameters, is treated.

A. Horváth and M. Telek (Eds.): EPEW 2006, LNCS 4054, pp. 148–165, 2006.
© Springer-Verlag Berlin Heidelberg 2006

An approach, which is adopted and partially explained in [1], considers how these parameters are applied. It requires the UML documents of the class diagram including the description of the behavior within it (collaborations) and the deployment diagram. The use case diagram and sequence diagrams are used to present this behavior. In fact, these diagrams are *extra*, very useful delineations for the dynamics, and they must be *consistent* with the class diagram to lead an analysis that produces correct results [25], [18].

The approach delivers, for use cases that can operate on databases related to the class diagram, the performance values of response times, throughput, and utilization of components of computer system. It consists of a number of activities: (I) Defining the workload intensities, or arrival rates, of use cases and setting up the performance requirements, or objectives, of them; (II) Defining the statistics of the class diagram; (III) Annotating the (DICs) in use cases with performance information; (IV) Deducing the Execution Graphs (EGs) for use cases from their sequence diagrams; (V) Deriving the Queueing Network Model (QNM) of computer system from the deployment diagram and instantiating the EGs with information from this diagram; and (VI) Deducing, parameterizing, and evaluating the QN performance models of use cases by using analytic approaches. The performance requirements and performance values are compared. If requirements are not met, the class and/or the deployment diagram must be changed and the performance analysis has to be repeated.

This analysis of the performance is conducted on a developing software system for a book store system. One of the most performance critical use cases that frequently transports a lot of data between the main and secondary storages is chosen and analyzed. Because its performance values are small, it is twice redesigned in accordance with the class diagram and studied, in subsection 4.2.

Section 2 explores the class diagram for an analysis of the performance. Section 3 describes this analysis, while section 4 demonstrates it on a software system in the design phase. Section 5 surveys existing works to manage the performance by means of UML diagrams, and the last section contains conclusions.

2   The Performative UML Class Diagram

A class is set of objects which have the same features (attributes), behaviors (methods), connections to other objects (reference attributes), and semantics (meaning). A relationship is a connection between model parts, such as actors, classes, and objects [19]. A class diagram is a graph, the nodes of which present classes and interfaces, and the edges of which express relationships. It can model a system from a static and dynamic viewpoint. This diagram manages both classes and interfaces, and it is necessary for further making and maintaining a software system. As interface operations are realized in classes, class diagrams with only classes as well as binary relationships are considered in this paper.

Subsection 2.1 discusses the performance parameters which are inherent in a class diagram. Subsection 2.2 gives an overview about the behavior in this diagram.

2.1   Performance Parameters of a Class Diagram

The performance parameters, or factors, of a class diagram have trade-offs between themselves. Some of them have to be stated for the performance analysis of behaviors if they are unknown, while other already given parameters are involved in this analysis. If these parameters are changed, a class diagram is redesigned, and conversely.

2.1.1   Number of Classes

Concerning databases the objects of a class are put in one or many data files and managed by one or many index files. Disregarding index files, many classes map to a number of data files. This number should not be much smaller than the number of the classes, because it indicates that, data is clustered or unified very much and, hence, system performance will be bad. On the other hand, big number of data files can, among other things, increase the volume of index data and the management information of these files and their index files, and also causes more accesses to databases or secondary storages than it will be needed. Consequently, the *number of the classes* and *of data files* have not to be much different. That is, an increase of class number produces an increase of file number. If a software system is not changed, the first number can be varied by de-, normalizing, unifying, or splitting classes, and the second number, by clustering, partitioning, or replicating files [21], [1].

2.1.2   Number of the Attributes in a Class

The volume of a data object of a class is contingent on the number of the attributes in this class. Many attributes in a class can mean that a class is connected to a number of other classes and, thus, is repeatedly accessed. This performance factor can be modified either by reassigning attributes to classes or building or destroying links between classes.

2.1.3   Number of the Methods in a Class

Methods, including those methods which realize interface operations, can be seen as special attributes in classes. Therefore, the number of methods in a class affects the volume of a data object of this class. Many methods in a class can mean that this class is frequently accessed. This parameter is changeable by distributing methods to classes.

2.1.4   Data Type of an Attribute or a Method

The type of an attribute in a class can be simple, such as *int* and *string*. It has a size of some bytes. An attribute can have a complex data type, like a class, list, or set of objects. This type has a bigness of many bytes. The size of a data type of an attribute influences the volume of a data object, and the volume of its index record in the case of databases.

2.1.5   Multiplicity of a Class

That is the number of the objects which a class can have in a class diagram [3]. The multiplicity of a class should agree with the multiplicities at the ends

of relationships attached to it. In databases the extension of a class is the set
of objects of this class over the time [20]. This statical parameter controls the
cardinality of a class extension and, thus, the volume of a data file and its ac-
companied index file(s). It can be altered by manipulating objects of classes.
In UML this parameter is commented as a number in the upper right corner
inside the notation of a class, while the cardinality of an extension can be annotated by using *tagged value* or *note* outside the notation of a class [3], as shown
in Fig. 3.

2.1.6 Multiplicity of a Relationship End

In UML this parameter is simply drawn at the ends of relationships. It gives
number of objects of a class which are connected to an end. Multiplicities are
expressed in form of single number, list or range of numbers, or lower/upper
bounds of numbers. In respect to schemes of databases this factor expresses
a data integrity constraint, as discussed in subsections 2.2, 3.3, and 4.2.3. If
it is not constant and a relationship is not *restricted* [3], it can be varied by
updating objects and their connections (in object collections at ends of links),
as demonstrated in subsection 4.3.

2.1.7 Type of a Relationship

The connection type affects the performance values of use cases, because it expresses a data integrity constraint. If databases are dealt with, this paper only
considers the following types of relationships: (I) Association with its further
specification as an aggregation or a composition of objects; (II) Inheritance with
its kinds single or multiple, and their further descriptions as complete or incomplete and as disjoint or overlapping. The types of relationships can be changed
in a class diagram, for example by delegation from multiple inheritance to aggregation [19].

2.1.8 Length of an Access Path

That is the number of relationships on an access path which connects two classes
in a class diagram and on which reference attributes in classes are visible to
their neighboring classes and relationships are navigable in the direction to
the accessed class [3], as illustrated in subsection 4.1.1. Obviously, long access
paths cause extra processing times. This parameter can be modified by building
new or destroying existing relationships, de-, normalizing, unifying, or splitting
classes.

2.1.9 Number of Relationships

This factor refers to both explicit and implicit relationships in a class diagram.
The more there are relationships between classes, the shorter access paths are
from a class to another. On the contrary, many relationships, such as deep
inheritance, aggregation, or composition hierarchies and big number of successor classes, produce much processing, to check the specifications of these
relationships in the case of databases. Generally, the more classes a class

diagram includes, the more relationships this diagram exhibits. Big number of classes and small number of relationships generate long access paths in a class diagram.

2.1.10   Allocation of Methods and Attributes to Classes

The location of methods in classes influences the performance values of use cases. Methods of classes have to be accessed along relationships and then executed. This parameter has to do with lengths of access paths between client and server classes [2]. The same is for attributes.

2.2   Behavior Within the Class Diagram

The behavior of a software system is specified by use cases, and their performance is to analyze. Use cases, which can contain database transactions, are defined and implemented as methods, that is collaborations, in classes of a class diagram or in special classes called for example *Collection*. This Technique, based on object-oriented concepts, is presently applied in some Object-Oriented DataBase Management Systems (OODBMSs), such as *GemStone* which has developed an object-oriented database language GemStone Smalltalk and *ObjectStore* [8], [5], [9]. Because use cases which manipulate data in databases can include the realization of data integrity, data integrity constraints are debated in the following paragraph.

Data integrity constraints are defined and specified in the analysis phase of a development process of a software system. They are inherent in class diagrams. With respect to object-oriented databases, they can be divided into the following types [20], [8], [9], [10], [5].

1. Domain constraints: An example is the *not null* constraint for attributes, that is, *null* values are not valid for these attributes.
2. Primary key constraints: A group of attributes of a class is chosen as a key. Their values must uniquely identify objects of this class and contain no null part values [20].
3. Cardinality constraints: Lower and/or upper bounds or (lists of) single values are set for multiplicities of relationships and, for cardinalities of attributes data types of which are complex such as set.
4. Aggregation and composition constraints: They concern with objects taking part in aggregations and compositions as well as associations. For example, it is to forbid to delete an object which is referenced by other objects from a database.
5. Inheritance constraints: There is a series of constraints that are related to this type. An *inclusion* constraint requests that the extension of a subclass is a (real) subset of the extension of its class (which is abstract), and a *disjointness* constraint ensures that intersection of all extensions of the subclasses of a class is equal to the empty set. A *covering* constraint forces that the union of all extensions of the subclasses of a class is equal to the extension of this class which is abstract. Other constraints from this kind are class *migration*, class *membership*, and role *change* constraint [20].

3   Performance Analysis

In this section, an approach to a performance analysis of an object-oriented software system is elucidated. It requires the UML documents of the class diagram including descriptions of collaborations within it and the deployment diagram. It predicts for those collaborations the performance values of response times, throughput, utilization of computer components, and consequently, detects the bottle necks in these components. Useful diagrams are the use case diagram and sequence diagrams of single use cases. The first can be obtained from the functional requirements. The other diagrams are different forms for collaborations in the class diagram. The approach, run by performance analyst, handles dynamic diagrams which have no asynchronous interactions, and it is based on product-form QNs. It combines a number of steps discussed in [1], [11], [22], [13] [14], [4].

The approach is supported by QN-based performance tools, such as SPE.ED [23], ObjecTime [16], or QSolver/1 [13], which are integrable into software production environments. The use of UML tools, e.g. Together or Rational Rose, aids the consistency between the class diagram and other UML dynamic diagrams.

3.1   Defining the Workload Intensities and Establishing the Performance Objectives

The workload intensities, that is number of the calls of a use case in a time unit or transactions per second (tps), and the calling probabilities of use cases, by the users of a software system, are stated. If there is a system, workload intensities are measured. For early software descriptions they can be estimated based on experience [26]. Calling probabilities can be determined from system measuring if system exists, user-level software sketches, or also estimates close to practice, as achieved in subsections 4.2.1 and 4.1.2.

Then, the performance objectives of use cases, like response times, are set up, as seen by the stakeholders of a software system [24]. They should be quantitative and measurable. For each of workload intensities, calling probabilities, and performance objectives comments can be made on a use case diagram in the form of UML tagged values, notes, or expressions of the Object Constraint Language (OCL) [3].

3.2   Defining the Statistics of the Class Diagram

The demands on components of a computer system are determined for database transactions or use cases. The physical design document of a database is dealt with. This contains: Specifications of hardware, like Hard Disk (HD) devices; DBMS characteristics including access path techniques, e.g. B-Trees, Bitmaps, or Hashing; optimization plans of use cases; information about design decisions such as data clustering; and information about data and index files and their statistics, like (average) volumes. For a use case the number of the accesses to a database depends on its optimization plan, number of the entered data files, and decisions of the design. For an access to a database number of the accesses to an HD device is reckoned over used access path techniques, which are very good regarded in the literature, and the remaining contents of this document [6], [12], [21].

If there is no available information about the data and index files and their statistics, the logical or conceptual design document of a database is processed. The latter consists of the performative class diagram. The average volume of a database can be defined thus: Firstly, the persistent class sub-diagram is converted into an equivalent class sub-diagram which only includes one type of relationships, binary associations, and OCL constraints [1].

Secondly, the following actions are achieved and the data is put on that sub-diagram: (I) Define the average cardinality for each single class extension; (II) Define the average multiplicities at both ends for each single association.

If system exists, data is measured. If not, it can be acquired from user-level descriptions, multiplicities on the sub-diagram, data of problem domains, or estimates based on experience. The average cardinalities of extensions must agree with the average multiplicities of associations, or of classes. In the case of complete inheritance, the sum of the average cardinalities of the extensions of subclasses must be equal to the average cardinality of the extension of abstract class.

Finally, the average volume of a data file and an index file is counted, by multiplying the average cardinality of a class extension and the (average) volume of an object of this class or index record together. (Average) object and record volume have also to be calculated from sums of sizes of data types of attributes and methods in a class and an index record, or to be assessed if data types or number of attributes and methods are still unknown.

3.3   Annotating the DICs with Performance Information

The realization of data integrity constraints, by collaborations in the performative class diagram, is concerned. The *cardinality* constraints are involved in all other types of constraints: They must be always met, after those types were tested. Their numbers as well as frequent checks influence a system performance. Comments on these constraints are made in this manner: One begins with a certain class and navigates in the converted sub-diagram to other classes. Each association end which lies in the navigation direction is annotated with performance information that should be conformable with the original multiplicity of this association, as demonstrated in subsection 4.2.3. If system exists, this data is measured. Otherwise, it can be obtained from user-level software descriptions or estimates related to practice. Performance data of the other constraints' types are presented by the performance factors in the last section. For example, in the case of inheritance this data is number of the subclasses of a class.

The data integrity constraints of a database system are specified in the sequence diagram(s) of use cases which manipulate data. For the consistency between the class diagram and those extra and helpful diagrams, this performance data is also depicted onto them [25], [18], as done in subsection 4.3.

3.4   Deducing the Execution Graphs for Use Cases

An Execution Graph is similar to a UML activity diagram: Its nodes hold software components or workloads, and its edges display the processing sequence of these components. There are many algorithms in the literature [11], [22], [4] to derive EGs from software specifications.

The algorithm described in [4] builds the EG for a use case. It infers an EG for each sequence diagram of a use case, and then adds the calling probabilities of each diagram by users to its EG. Shortly, the algorithm maps every interaction in a sequence diagram into a basic node in which the name of this interaction, the sender, and the receiver design component are noted. According to the control flow in this sequence diagram, it connects an existing node with a new node by a pending arrow, cycle, branching, fork, or join node.

3.5   Deriving the QNM of Computer System and Instantiating EGs

A deployment diagram supplies the analysis with data about the hardware configuration of the (future) computer system on which a (developing) software system should run [3]. There exists a lot of approaches in the literature [11], [22], [13] to build QNs for computer systems. The approach illustrated in [22] can be applied to data of a deployment diagram. It is chosen to complete this step. In brief, it identifies components of a computer system, e.g. CPUs and HD devices, which are key to the performance of this computer system, and represents them by queueing service centers. It then joints these centers to each other by the way their computer components interact with others.

A deployment diagram displays the components of a software design and their distribution on the components of a computer system [3]. For this reason, it provides the analysis with data about communication times between computer components. In order to instantiate an EG agreeably with a deployment diagram, this data is added to it in this way: For each node in an EG the sender and receiver design component are replaced by the communication time between their places. When this process has finished, it results in another graph which is very similar to the original EG. It is called an EG *instance* according to the involved deployment diagram [4], as shown in subsection 4.2.4.

3.6   Deducing, Parameterizing, and Evaluating the QN Performance Models

The EG instances of use cases are further processed. For an EG instance the subsequent activities are completed: Firstly, natural numbers and probabilities, for the users of its use case, are assessed, and are then written on its cyclic nodes and at the edges of its branching or fork nodes respectively. This data is gathered from subsection 3.3, system measurements if possible, user-level software descriptions, or assessments based on experience.

Secondly, for each node in this EG instance which has an interaction the demands on service centers of the QNM, or the number of the machine instructions executed by components of the attended computer system, are determined. This data is collected from subsections 3.2, 3.3, and [22]. Finally, simple arithmetical algorithms are applied to this EG instance, to calculate its demands on those centers, that is the *demand vector* of its use case.

On the condition that there is only one user and no competition with other users on the service centers, the processing time of a use case is computed as follows: Each component of the demand vector is multiplied by the (average) service time of its service center. Processing time is equal to the total sum of all products. If this time is less than the time of the objective of a use case, the performance analysis continues, as done in subsection 4.2.5.

The demand vector of a use case is put together with the QNM, to deduce the subnet or *QN performance model* of this use case [22], [13]. Then, this model is parameterized with information from the deployment diagram such as CPU

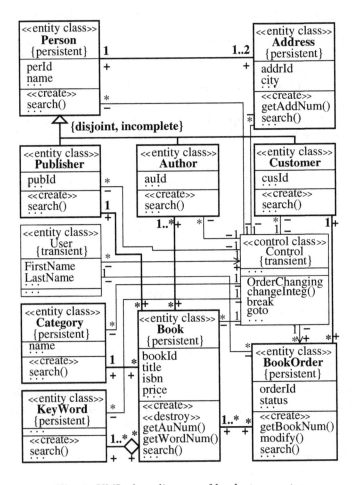

Fig. 1. UML class diagram of book store system

size and speed, from the demand vector, and from workload intensities. It is evaluated by using analytic approaches or performance tools.

4   Case Study: Book Store System

A software design for a book store system will be studied. This system offers many services, and users call them, for instance to get information, order books, or possibly change their orders.

Subsection 4.1 introduces a specification for a book store system. It explains a class diagram, a sequence diagram of a collaboration which realizes a use case or service, and a deployment diagram of a computer system. Subsection 4.2 leads the performance analysis, and subsection 4.3 argues design choices for this use case.

4.1   The Book Store Specification

4.1.1   The Class Diagram

Fig. 1 presents a class diagram for a book store system: It comprises nine persistent classes (in bold) which are linked by ten binary relationships of different types, that is associations e.g. amid the classes *Book* and *Category*; an aggregation of the classes *Book* and *KeyWord*; and both disjoint and incomplete inheritance between the concrete class *Person* and the subclasses *Publisher*, *Author*, and *Customer*.

It contains two transient classes *User* and *Control* to model the users of a book store and to steer interactions between the classes respectively, and a boundary class which has links with the classes and is ignored for the sake of the diagram complexity. It is assumed that class *User* only has access rights to methods of class *Control*; *Control*, to attributes and methods of *BookOrder*; reference attributes in persistent classes are visible to neighboring persistent classes; and the relationships between these classes are navigable. As can be seen, the diagram is early in maturing, why the specifications of its classes are still unfinished.

4.1.2   The Use Case, Sequence, and Deployment Diagram

The use case diagram of this software system holds many use cases, from which a performance critical use case *Order Changing* will be treated. Customers who have ordered items from the store can later alter their commissions, until a time limit and once at most. They can request additional books, remove items from their orders, and/or exchange books for others.

For the simplicity, the use case diagram is reduced to a diagram with this use case. Thus, *Order Changing* has a calling probability of one. It is supposed that customers alter their orders before the time limit at one time. Fig. 2 presents a sequence diagram for this use case: For a user (customer) who has to type into a new version for his/her old request again, a new object of the class *BookOrder* is created. The interaction *changeInteg()* checks the data integrity of this object, and *modify()* manipulates an existing book order if the data integrity of the new object is fulfilled.

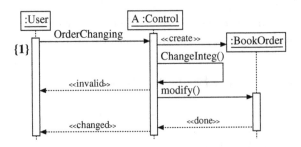

Fig. 2. Sequence diagram of *Order Changing*

For the diagram of *changeInteg()* it exists two variants: The first, similar to a diagram in [1], is not given for limited place, but its EG instance. The second is presented later. The deployment diagram, of a node in a shared-nothing system, consists of one CPU device with frequency of 2 GHz and very large memory and one 4 GB HD device with access time of 16.43 msec. It is also illustrated in [1].

4.2   Performance Analysis

The steps of the performance analysis are carried out for use case *Order Changing*. It is assumed that all databases are opened and all transactions are compiled.

4.2.1   Defining the Workload Intensities and Establishing the Performance Objectives

Estimates that are related to practice are assigned to workload intensity λ: $\lambda = 0.05, 0.1, \ldots$ tps as in Fig. 5. It is requested that the response time R should not exceed five seconds: $R \leq 5$ secs.

4.2.2   Defining the Statistics of the Class Diagram

The persistent class sub-diagram in Fig. 1 is converted into an equivalent class sub-diagram which only includes binary associations and OCL constraints and which is fully discussed in [1]. Fig. 3 presents this diagram: It shows the defined, average multiplicities of associations and cardinalities of class extensions (in normal), and is found that one access to any database requires one access to the HD device.

4.2.3   Annotating the DICs with Performance Information

The cardinality constraints for a revised order are concerned, since further constraint types (primary key constraints) are already annotated, when performance factors (extension and key size) are stated, or not given. Starting with class *BookOrder* in the scheme of book order database in Fig. 3, comments for performance information (values in bold) are made on the multiplicities of association ends which one reaches in the navigation to other classes. They are estimated to be equal to the information *already existing* in the book order database.

As explained in subsection 3.4, the EG of *Order Changing* is constructed. It is shown by its instance in Fig. 4A and 4B, which is alike.

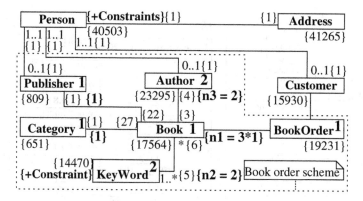

Fig. 3. Equivalent UML class diagram for book store system

4.2.4   Deriving the QNM of Computer System and Instantiating the EG

The CPU and HD device in the deployment diagram are mapped to an M/M/1/1-PS CPU and M/M/1/1-FCFS HD queueing service center respectively. The network which links these centers matches the logical communication network between their devices.

Fig. 4A presents an EG instance for *Order Changing* that is tailored to the deployment diagram. The expanded node *Loop_Books* (in bold) is refined by Fig. 4B. As the design components (GUI, OODBMS, and *Order Changing*) are located on the same CPU memory, the communication times between them are very small and negligible [7]. Each node comprises two pieces of data: The name of an interaction and the communication time for it.

4.2.5   Deducing, Parameterizing, and Evaluating the QN Performance Model

Probabilities for users, approximated from the practice, are assigned to the edges of branching nodes in figures 4A and 4B, and numbers, taken from subsection 4.2.3, are put in the cyclic nodes of Fig. 4B. Assuming that the average rate of one high-level instruction to machine instructions is 1:20, using the information gained in subsections 4.2.2 and 4.2.3, and using estimates from similar software systems in [22], [6], [12], the average demands on CPU and HD device are determined for each node of figures 4A and 4B, including the processing overhead. Node or interaction *modify()* has a demand vector of (1,110,000; 44) and the demand vectors of the remaining interactions are summarized in [1].

The demand vector of *Order Changing* is calculated from figures 4A, 4B, and demand vectors of their nodes. As the processing time T is $T \approx 0.57$ sec. < 5 sec., the performance analysis pursues. The queueing subnet associated with this use case is constructed by combining its demand vector with the QNM of the computer system. Fig. 4C presents it: It is an open QN, because the customers change their orders and leave the system.

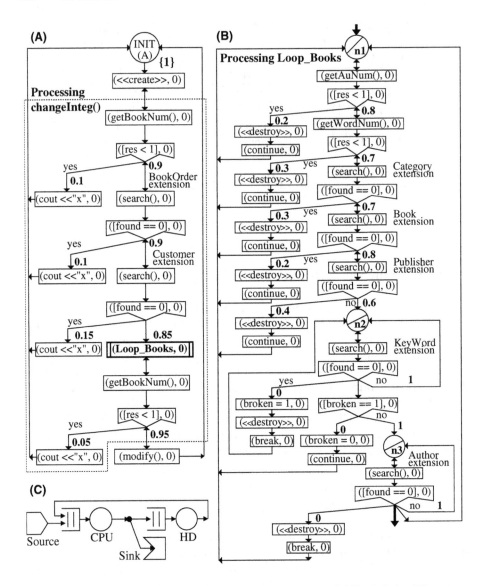

Fig. 4. EG instance (A and B) and QN performance model (C) of *Order Changing*

This QN performance model is then parameterized with information from the deployment diagram, the demand vector, and subsection 4.2.1. For the simplicity, it is assumed that there is only one kind of job *Order Changing* routing in the system. By typing the performance model into a tool like QSolver/1, the values of response times can be computed. Fig. 5 graphically presents them: The upper curve shows an (exponential) increase of the response time $R1$, over the workload intensity λ. As can be seen, the maximal achievable workload intensity $\lambda1$ which yet fulfills the performance requirement is by 1.54 tps, $\lambda1 \approx 1.54$ tps. It is also the

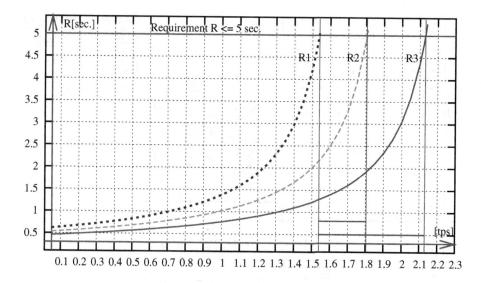

Fig. 5. Response times of *Order Changing*'s redesigns

maximal delivered system throughput $X1$, $X1 = \lambda1$. The HD utilization averages about 90%. Hence, the HD device is a bottle neck in the system.

4.3 Redesigns of Use Case *Order Changing*

Obviously, the design of *Order Changing* requires many demands on devices of the computer system, especially on the hard disk device. Fig. 6 presents another architecture for the method *changeInteg()*: The cardinalities of object collections — that is, books, keywords, and authors — in Fig. 1 are initially tested. Then the *existence* of the part objects of a revised order in both book and customer database is checked by traversing this figure in the visit series *BookOrder, Customer, Book*, and so on, as drawn in Fig. 6, to invoke method *search()*.

The analysis is again conducted: Both the performance objective and statistics of the class diagram are the same as before. Also, the performance data on Fig. 3 and 6 is identical. The EG of the new designed use case is done. It is instantiated agreeably to the deployment diagram. Its instance is analogous to figures 4A and 4B, and on it the same comments of information are made. It is assumed that probability of errors caused by *cardinality* and *existence* test is equal distributed: $P([res < 1]) = 0.05 \div 2 = 0.025$ after the second and third call of *getBookNum()* (in bold) in Fig. 6 (Cf. Fig. 4A). The demand vector is calculated for this instance and the performance model is followed. The latter is the same as Fig. 4C. It is parameterized and evaluated. The middle curve in Fig 5 shows the response time $R2$ of the second design. The maximal workload intensity $\lambda2$ is by 1.805 tps, $\lambda2 \approx 1.805$ tps, and the HD utilization averages about 90%. As a result, the new design has increased the system throughput by $\Delta X1 = \Delta\lambda1 = \lambda2 - \lambda1 \approx 0.265$ tps.

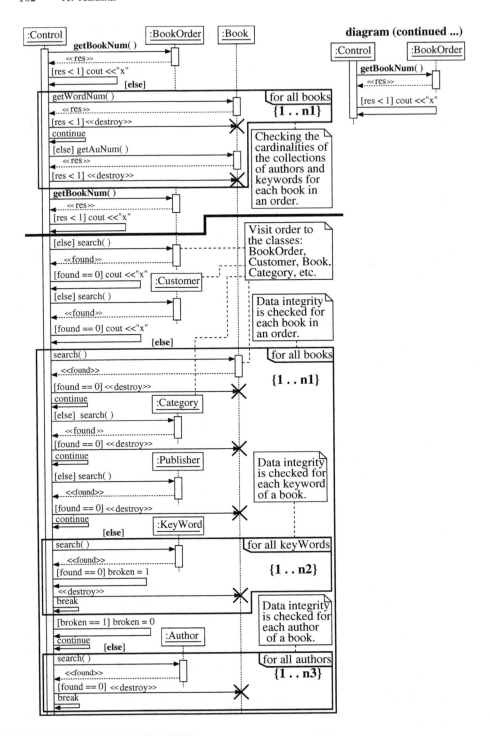

Fig. 6. Sequence diagram of *changeInteg()*

Taking that the previous design has not sufficiently raised λ and other physical design choices do not notably adjust λ too, the class diagram is treated. The multiplicities at the ends to class *KeyWord* and *Author* (for one book in book order scheme in Fig. 3) are varied, and also performance data from $n2 = 2$ to $n2 = 1$ and $n3 = 2$ to $n3 = 1$. The altered performance data is put on Fig. 6 for consistency between both diagrams. The analysis is repeated anew: The lower curve in Fig. 5 shows the response time $R3$ of the third design. The workload intensity $\lambda3$ is by 2.14 tps, $\lambda3 \approx 2.14$ tps, and the HD utilization is about 90%. As a result, the throughput is enhanced by $\Delta X2 = \Delta\lambda2 = \lambda3 - \lambda1 \approx 0.60$ tps, that is 2160 transactions per an hour.

There are three ways, to further extend the performance values. After which the performance analysis has to be repeated.

- The first is a further redesign the class diagram in Fig. 1 and its collaboration in Fig. 6. For example, the classes *Category* and *Publisher* in both book and book order database can be unified to build one class *PubCate*. This varies the performance factors *number of classes* and *number of relationships*.
- The second is an alteration of the deployment diagram. One or more HD devices have to be added to the computer system, or the existing HD device has to be replaced by a new HD device which is quicker or by many HD devices. Problems that are related with this way are discussed in [22].
- The third is a combination of the two ways above.

5   Related Works

On the area of performance engineering there exists many works about UML diagrams. Most of them apply helpful, dynamic diagrams, like [4] which deduces QN performance models for use case and sequence diagrams and [15] which infers petri net performance models for the last diagrams via state transition diagrams.

A further work [17] uses the class diagram. Precisely, it analyzes the *space* performance for an existing software component in the context of a software application. As the speed performance analysis here, this work treats parameters of the class diagram to complete an analysis of the performance. It consists of three steps. (I) Gathering Data: The software engineer collects information about the memory allocation and deallocation of every object and the sizes of each; (II) Annotating Structural Information: Dynamic information is depicted onto the class diagram, as done in subsection 3.2; and (III) Using the Annotated Structure for Prediction: The engineer selects a particular class for memory projecting, and then uses it to predict the memory size which will be allocated by a component. Elementary arithmetical operations are carried out, as explained in subsection 3.2 and [1]. On the one hand, the approach in [17] deals with software components already developed, and deduces their class diagrams from their codes by reverse transformations. Alternatively, the analysis in this paper addresses class diagrams which are already given and which can be in evolving states, that is at early design stages or incomplete. Regardless of transient or persistent diagrams, a space performance analysis is done in subsections 3.2 and 4.2.2.

6 Conclusions

A performance analysis for an object-oriented software system is shown. It treats the class diagram of this system, by applying an approach to use cases which can operate on databases related to this diagram. A performance critical use case is studied. It includes a data alteration in a database. Use cases which have no accesses to databases can be handled too. The analysis supports decisions as to number of classes, such as "design a subclass as a part of a class diagram" or "build its extention from superclasses by queries or use cases".

The use or integration of the class diagram into an analysis of the performance conveys the following benefits.

- Besides the correspondence between the deployment diagram — of a computer system and (developing) software system — and the QNM of this computer system, it saves the consistency between the class diagram and used dynamic diagrams. Thus, it yields right execution graphs and manages an analysis that delivers correct results.
- In addition to the redesign of an architecture of a behavior, the class diagram provides all other performance parameters (Cf. section 2.1) to tune the performance of this behavior.
- Leading the space performance analysis at the same time and finding a compromise between both speed and space performance analysis for a software system on a computer system.

Acknowledgement. I would like to thank the committee for comments on this work.

References

1. Ahmad Alsaadi. A Performance Analysis Approach Based on the UML Class Diagram. In *Proceedings of the Fourth International Workshop on Software and Performance* (WOSP 2004), pages 254-260, Redwood Shores, California, USA, January 14-16, 2004.
2. Booch, G.: Object-Oriented Analysis and Design, With Applications. 2nd edn. Benjamin/Cummings Publishing Company (1994)
3. Booch, G., Rumbaugh, J., Jacobson, I.: The Unified Modeling Language User Guide, Covers UML 2.0. 2nd edn. Addison Wesley (May 2005)
4. Cortellessa, V., Mirandola, R.: Deriving a Queueing Network Based Performance Model from UML-Diagrams. In: Proceedings of the Second International Workshop on Software and Performance (WOSP 2000), pages 58-70. Ottawa, Canada (September 17-20, 2000)
5. Geppert, A.: Objektrelationale und objekt-orientierte Datenbankkonzepte und -systeme [Object-Relational and -Oriented Database Concepts and Systems]. Erste Auflage. Dpunkt.verlag (2002)
6. Härder, T., Rahm, E.: Datenbanksysteme, Konzepte und Techniken der Implementierung [Database Systems. Concepts and Techniques of the Implementation]. Zweite, überarbeitete Auflage. Springer-Verlag (2001)

7. Hennessy, J.L., Patterson, D.A.: Computer Architecture, A Quantitative Approach. 2nd edn. Morgan Kaufmann Publishers, Inc. (1996)
8. Heuer, A.: Objektorientierte Datenbanken, Konzepte, Modelle, Standards und Systeme [Object-Oriented Databases, Concepts, Models, Standards, and Systems]. Zweite aktualisierte und erweiterte Ausgabe. Addison Wesley (1997)
9. Khoshafian, S.: Object-Oriented Databases. John Wiley & Sons, Inc. (1993)
10. Khoshafian, S., Abnous, R.: Object Orientation. 2nd edn. John Wiley & Sons, Inc. (1995)
11. Lazowska, E.D., Zahorjan, J., Graham, G.S., Kenneth, C.S.: Quantitative System Performance, Computer System Analysis Using Queueing Network Models. Prentice-Hall, Inc., Englewood Cliffs, New Jersey (1984)
12. Lockemann, P.C., Schmidt, J.W. (eds): Informatik-Handbücher: Datenbankhandbuch [Informatics Handbooks: Database Handbook]. Springer-Verlag (1987)
13. Menascé, D.A., Almeida, V.A.F., Dowdy, L.W.: Capacity Planning and Performance Modeling, From Mainframes to Client-Server Systems. Prentice=Hall, Inc., Englewood Cliffs, New Jersey (1994)
14. Menascé, D.A., Gomaa, H.: On a Language Based Method for Software Performance Engineering of Client/Server Systems. In: Proceedings of the First International Workshop on Software and Performance (WOSP 98), pages 63-69. Santa Fe, New Mexico, USA (October 12-16, 1998)
15. Merseguer, J., Campos, J., Mena, E.: Evaluating Performance on Mobile Agents Software Design. In: Cazorla, D. (ed), Actas de las VIII Jornadas de Concurrencia, pages 291-307, Cuenca, Spain, June 2000. Universidad de Castilla-la Mancha
16. ObjecTime User's Manual. ObjecTime Limited, Kanata, Ontario, Canada (1994)
17. Murphy, G.C., Saenko, E.: Predicting Memory Use from a Class Diagram using Dynamic Information. In: Proceedings of the First International Workshop on Software and Performance (WOSP 98), pages 145-151. Santa Fe, New Mexico, USA (October 12-16, 1998)
18. Petriu, D.C., Sun, Y.: Consistent Behaviour Representation in Activity and Sequence Diagrams. In: Evans, A., Kent, S., Selic, B. (eds): "UML" 2000 -The Unified Modeling Language. Advancing the Standard. LNCS, Vol. 1939, pages 369-382. Springer-Verlag (2000)
19. Rumbaugh, J., Blaha, M., Premerlani, W., Eddy, F., Lorensen, W.: Object=Oriented Modeling and Design. Prentice-Hall, Inc., Englewood Cliffs, New Jersey (1991)
20. Saake, G., Türker, C., Schmitt, I.: Objektdatenbanken [Object Databases]. International Thomson Publishing (1997)
21. Saake, G., Heuer, A.: Datenbanken: Implementierungstechniken [Databases: Implementation Techniques]. Erste Auflage. MITP-Verlag GmBH (1999)
22. Smith, C.U.: Performance Engineering of Software Systems. Addison Wesley (1990)
23. Smith, C.U., Williams, L.G.: Performance Engineering Evaluation of Object=Oriented Systems with SPE.ED. In: Marie, R., et al. (eds): Computer Performance Evaluation: Modelling Techniques and Tools. LNCS, Vol. 1245, pages 135-154. Springer Verlag (1997)
24. Sommerville, I.: Software Engineering. 6th edn. Addison Wesley (2001)
25. Tsiolakis, A., Ehrig, H.: Consistency Analysis of UML Class and Sequence Diagrams using Attributed Graph Grammars. In: Ehrig, H., Taentzer, G. (eds): Actas de GRATAR 2000, pages 77-86. TU Berlin, Informe técnico 2000-2 (March 2000)
26. Woodside, C.M.: Software Performance Evaluation by Models. In: Haring, G., Lindemann, C., Reiser, M. (eds): Performance Evaluation: Origins and Directions. LNCS, Vol. 1769, pages 283-304. Springer-Verlag (2000)

Dependability Evaluation of Web Service-Based Processes[*]

László Gönczy[1], Silvano Chiaradonna[2], Felicita Di Giandomenico[2],
András Pataricza[1], Andrea Bondavalli[3], and Tamás Bartha[1]

[1] DMIS, Budapest University of Technology and Economics
Magyar Tudósok krt. 2. H-1117, Budapest, Hungary
gonczy@mit.bme.hu
[2] ISTI-CNR, Via G. Moruzzi 1, I-56124 Pisa, Italy
+39 50 315 2904
{silvano.chiaradonna, felicita.digiandomenico}@isti.cnr.it
[3] DSI - Universita' di Firenze, Viale Morgagni 65, I-50134 Firenze, Italy
+39 55 479 6776
bondavalli@unifi.it

Abstract. As Web service-based system integration recently became the main-stream approach to create composite services, the dependability of such systems becomes more and more crucial. Therefore, extensions of the common service composition techniques are urgently needed in order to cover dependability aspects and a core concept for the dependability estimation of the target composite service. Since Web services-based workflows fit into the class of systems composed of multiple phases, this paper attempts to apply methodologies and tools for dependability analysis of Multiple Phased Systems (MPS) to this emerging category of dependability critical systems. The paper shows how this dependability analysis constitutes a very useful support to the service provider in choosing the most appropriate service alternatives to build up its own composite service.

1 Introduction

Recently, the main paradigm of creating large scale information systems is shifting more and more towards integrating services instead of integrating components as in traditional technologies. Open standards like Web Service Description Language (WSDL) assure system interoperability. This integration and development paradigm is called Service Oriented Architecture (SOA). The top level description of a SOA process describes the main business logic and it is usually very close to the traditional business process models (BPM). Recent development tools provide a quite powerful support for functional service integration but they lack the support of the description and analysis of the non-functional aspects in the system. However, service level

---

[*] This work was partially supported by the HIDENETS European project (IST-FP6-STREP-26979) and the "Quality of Service and Dependable Computer Networks" Project of the Italian-Hungarian Intergovernmental S&T Cooperation Programme.

A. Horváth and M. Telek (Eds.): EPEW 2006, LNCS 4054, pp. 166–180, 2006.

integration raises new problems as the service provider is composing its main services from elementary services as building blocks without having a complete control over them. Thus, the result of the main service may be invalidated by simple faults and errors in imported services. Dependability analysis has to focus on creating a system-wide dependability model of the component models and evaluating the impact of the faults in the individual components, including the identification of dependability bottlenecks and the sensitivity analysis of the overall system to the components' dependability characteristics [1].

Based on the observation that Web services-based workflows fit into the class of systems composed of multiple operational phases characterized by potentially different requirements and goals, the paper attempts to apply methodologies and tools for dependability analysis based on the paradigm of Multiple Phased Systems (MPS, [2], [6], [7]) to this emerging category of dependability critical systems. A methodology for transforming workflow description of composite Web services into an MPS description is proposed, and, once such a description is derived, appropriate tools for MPS modeling and evaluation are applied to quantitatively assess specified dependability indicators. Hereby we use the DEEM tool to describe dependability models and to evaluate the indicators.

This paper is organized as follows. Section 2 describes the Web service flows and exposes the need for evaluating dependability indicators and discusses the related work. Section 3 introduces the MPS paradigm and the DEEM tool for dependability analysis. Section 4 discusses the possible ways of combining Web service flows as an implementation-close description of processes running in a distributed environment and MPS as a dependability modeling paradigm. Section 5 describes the model transformations performed in the VIATRA 2 framework [5] which enables a (semi-) automatic transformation of business processes (such as those built of Web services) to formal analytical models (e.g. Deterministic and Stochastic Petri Nets). Section 6 illustrates the methodology by a case study. Section 7 concludes the paper and summarizes further research directions.

2 Dependability Aspects of Web Service Flows

Present BPM tools (e.g. [26]) enable performance analysis/simulation with the restriction that all resources are available. Therefore, no faulty states can be modeled in a consistent way, failure rates and repair times cannot be considered during the analysis and no dependability analysis can be performed on the model. Similarly, there is a lack of error handling, despite the fact that some languages (for instance, Business Process Execution Language [8]) can handle exceptions. A BPEL exception handling routine, however, may contain only compensation actions which try to eliminate the effect of an uncommitted transaction, transaction time-outs, non-atomic operations etc.

The service-based approach to system integration raises the problem of defining Service Level Agreements [9] (SLA) between the provider and user of the main service. In this context, SLAs are used to describe the required quantitative parameters of a service, related to a particular client or class of clients. In general, an SLA contains measurement objectives, their guaranteed values, a measurement methodology and some goals and obligations for the participating parties. An SLA can be attached to all service invocations, described as simple activities in a BPM, although no unified formalization of such documents exists.

As the service level of the system depends on external providers, a standardized description of the QoS parameters of Web services is needed in order to have a consistent view of the QoS at the level of composed services. Several descriptions of the QoS parameters of Web services were proposed, e.g. in [11], [12], and [13], however, no single, standardized description format was generally accepted. Accordingly, in the current paper, no specific syntax will be assumed on the service quality description, but merely only those core concepts which can be found in an arbitrary QoS definition will be referred.

To illustrate the importance of dependability analysis of Service Oriented Architecture, consider a sample process of three simple steps: receiving a request, forwarding it to an external partner ("outsourcing") and then returning the answer to the client. The first and the last activities use internal resources (e.g. a Web server) having known performance and dependability characteristics. The second activity is however deployed on an external system, therefore its resource usage is unknown, it is described only by its Service Level Agreement parameters, for instance, "AverageResponseTime" etc. The provider of the main service has to estimate the guaranteed QoS parameters of his service, for instance the failure rate, which depends on the failure rates of the internal resources and the failure rate of the external service over which he has no control.

Fig. 1. A sample process with external method invocation

The model based analysis of a process necessitates additional information to the basic functionality of the process, such as failure rates of components, required and guaranteed response times, availability, repair times (for instance, time interval between retrying to invoke a service), etc. Non-functional design patterns such as Recovery Block should also be considered, e.g. in case of a failure, the invocation of the fastest service can be followed by calling a slower but more robust variant. The system dependability model [14] has to be created from rather different engineering models. The external service is described only by a black box model, describing the functional interface, performance and dependability-related quantitative parameters while the internal services have to be extracted from a model indicating both the functionality and the deployment to resources, extended by the non functional parameters. A uniform system-wide model has to be derived from these engineering models for the further analysis.

Available extensions of BPM lack a support of the usage of dependability parameters and fault tolerance patterns in the model. There are, however, numerous evolving standards, specifications and research in this field such as [17]. XML-based description languages such as WS-Reliability[16], WS-BaseFaults [18] can describe the characteristics of a certain endpoint, i.e. a Web service or a port/method of a Web service. These descriptions can be associated with WSDL files [19].

As the actual description language is irrelevant from the analysis point of view, a general description language is adopted among the several emerging languages and technologies such as Web Service Level Agreements (WSLA) which contains language elements for at least a subset of the performance and dependability characteristics. As this language is quite flexible and extensible, we propose to use this for the description of non-functional parameters, as this way the external services and the internal resources could be characterized using the same description, using Service Level Agreements. A typical SLA contains the objectives to be measured, such as the transactional throughput of a web server or the response time of a remote web service, the measurement algorithm (e.g. how to compose an average measure), the fee of the service and the punishments related to violating the requirements. Guaranteed values of SLA parameters can be negotiated with the client. After such a negotiation, a complex process can be composed based on elements having well-defined QoS guarantees. The process of this negotiation is out of the scope of this paper; several ideas are discussed in [21], [22]. In our research the emphasis is on the evaluation of the process models extended with the dependability description. Hereby we suppose a WSLA-like description for the resources and the services.

Evaluation of Web Service compositions has been addressed in the literature by using Petri Net-based techniques ([29], [31]), Timed Automata [30], non-deterministic automata [32] or some kind of pi-calculus [31], [33]. PEPA models are also used to derivate quantitative characteristics of the systems and are the basis of SLA evaluation [28]. However, to our best knowledge, none of these were applied directly on a high-level (for instance, BPM) description to perform quantitative dependability analysis without the need to create a lower level model of the system, only basic verification is fully automatized.

The availability of a versatile and highly efficient tool dealing with dependability analysis of Multiple Phased Systems, combined with the appropriateness to include web-service based processes in the category of MPS systems as shown in the sequel, motivated the choices at the basis of our work.

3   Dependability Modeling: Multiple Phased Systems and DEEM

This paper elaborates on characterizing Web services-based workflows as Multiple-Phased Systems for the purpose of dependability analysis. In this section, a brief overview of MPS is provided, together with a short description of the tool DEEM for the dependability analysis of MPS.

Multiple-Phased Systems (MPS) is a class of systems whose operational life can be partitioned in a set of disjoint periods, called "phases". During each phase, MPS execute tasks, which may be completely different from those performed within other phases. The performance and dependability requirements of MPS (such as throughput, response time, availability, etc.) can be utterly different from one phase to another. The configuration of MPS may change over time, in accordance with performance and dependability requirements of the phase being currently executed, or simply to be more resilient to an hazardous external environment. As the so-called MPS goal may change over time, the sequence of phases of which the MPS execution is composed (the execution of a given workflow) may depend on the state (such as success/failure) of previous phases. Phased Mission Systems (PMS) and Scheduled Maintenance Systems (SMS) are two typical subtypes of MPS. Examples of MPS can be found in various application domains, such as nuclear, aerospace, telecommunications, transportation, electronics, and many other industrial fields. Because of their deployment in several critical application domains, MPS have been widely investigated, and their dependability analysis has been the object of several research studies ([2], [3], [4], [6], [7], the complete expose of the literature can be found in [2]).

Recently, a dependability modeling and evaluation tool, DEEM, specifically tailored for MPS, has been developed at the University of Florence, and ISTI-CNR [4]. DEEM relies upon Deterministic and Stochastic Petri Nets (DSPN) as the modeling formalism, and on Markov Regenerative Processes (MRGP) for the model solution [2]. When compared to existing general-purpose tools based on similar formalisms, DEEM offers advantages on both the modeling side (sub-models neatly model the phase-dependent behaviors of MPS), and on the evaluation side (a specialized algorithm allows a considerable reduction of the solution cost and time).

The rich set of modeling features provides DEEM with a two-level modeling approach in which two logically separate parts are used to represent MPS models. One is the SystemNet (SN), which represents the resource states and the failure/repair behavior of system components for each phase, and the other is the PhaseNet (PhN), which represents the execution of the various phases, as illustrated later in Figure 6. Each net is made dependent on the other one by marking-dependent predicates which modify transition rates, enabling conditions, transition probabilities, multiplicity functions, etc., to model the specific MPS features.

In DEEM, very general dependability measures for the MPS evaluation can be defined by a reward function. Among the measures assessable through such approach are the probability of successful mission completion, the relative impact of each single phase on the overall dependability figures, and the amount of useful work that can be carried out within the mission. The main motivation of using DEEM was that –as it was shown in [2]– it is a versatile and highly efficient tool for dependability modeling and evaluation of MPS systems.

4   Combining BPM as a Modeling Language and MPS as a Dependability Analysis Paradigm

As it was discussed earlier in Sect. 2., BPM models can be extended to capture non-functional parameters of the system. Therefore, an approach is needed which exploits the possibility of modeling multiple states of a resource. The modeling methodology and the evaluation procedure implemented in DEEM allow to describe the flow models of the web service systems and to analyze their dependability attributes, as shown in the next subsections.

4.1   Considering Business Process Flows as MPS

Processes in the SOA context can be considered as Multiple Phased Systems in a natural way. The two layer-representation of Multiple Phased Systems corresponds exactly to the logic of workflow-like integrated component services. The upper layer corresponds to the workflow sequence consisting of the sub-service elements while the detailed model may be used to describe the individual component services. Remind that the possibility of splitting the description into functional and non-functional aspects allows the natural expression of different parameterization of the invocation of the services and data-dependent branching in the main workflow. To illustrate the modeling issues of a business process, a more detailed view of the process in Fig.1. is presented, as shown in Figure 2.

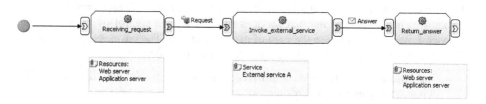

Fig. 2. Sample business process and the underlying resources

The "Receiving request" and "Return answer" activities are executed locally, i.e. on controllable and observable internal resources. Resource parameters can be modeled in a standard way using the General Resource Model UML [20] profile of the OMG. The resource faults and their effects can also be described by using the notations defined in this profile as it was shown in [10], [15]. The "Invoke external service" activity corresponds to a Web service invocation, therefore the quantitative parameters of this activity can be derived from the SLA descriptions of the service as pointed out in Sect. 2.

The dynamics of the business process flow can be treated as a Multiple Phased System in the following way. The phases (partitions of system operation) are the tasks of the BPM, unless consecutive tasks use the same internal resource. This way the context of the operation (the environment of the mission) will be different for each phase. The resource parameters –appearing in SystemNet if modeled in DEEM– such as failure rates, repair times, number of identical resources (e.g. the number of possible retransmissions of a request or the number of Web servers) may depend on the operation context, thus on the actual phase. The mission goal can change over the time and the execution of the process (i.e. the mission goal) may depend on the result of previous phases and the system state. For instance, if validating a credit card does not terminate within a predefined timeout, then a flight ticket reservation cannot be confirmed, but is saved as a conditional reservation.

The chosen method to evaluate the dependability of the web service systems is describing the model in BPM and transforming it to a MPS model, since the basic description language –in which the process is built– is easy to use, a wide range of tools are available, and an implementation skeleton (i.e. the workflow control description) can be generated directly from the model after passing the dependability analysis. Moreover, BPM activities can be converted into phases of a MPS in a quite natural way while the opposite direction (i.e. generating the skeleton of a control flow from a MPS model) raises several questions as many activities can be described in one phase, if their dependability parameters are the same. Using model transformations instead of describing the model in a meta-language brings the benefit of easy implementation of additional transformations (for instance, model checking based on qualitative properties of the mode) as the model is stored in the format of the graph transformation tool. The transformation tool also enables the generation of practically any type of output (which can be further the basis of a runtime validation).

The basic BPM model should be extended with some information about the required behavior of components (basic activities), such as maximum response time, maximum number of timeouts in a given time interval, guaranteed rate of good answers for a prefixed number of requests, availability, etc. All these characteristics can be derived from the characteristics of the resources and the software implementation (if known) in the case of internal services (those we have control over) or from the Service Level Agreements in the case of external service. The business process model can be transformed to a MPS according to the following rules:

- The different activities will be different phases in PhaseNet with different goals, dependability metrics and resources.
- The performance and dependability characteristics of resources and services will determine the SystemNet parameters such as transition rate, initial marking, etc.
- The dependencies between PhaseNet and SystemNet are given by the task-resource bindings and SLAs of the (both internal and external) services.
- The measurements of a MPS analysis are determined by the "business measures" of the BPM, i.e. the QoS parameters of the main service.

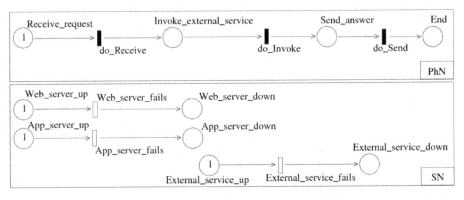

Fig. 3. The sample process seen as a MPS system and modeled in DEEM

Figure 3 shows the sample process as a Multiple Phased System. Note that the parameters of the DSPN are derived from the BPM parameters based on the resource descriptions and SLAs. The expected durations of the timed transitions of the Phase-Net correspond to the estimated execution time for activities of the business process. For instance, the expected duration of the transition "do_Receive" results from the average execution time of "Receive request" activity while the expected duration of the transition "do_Invoke" is derived from the average response time of the external service, described in the corresponding SLA. Error manifestation is expected to happen at the invocation of an operation using a resource. Resource faults inducing errors are modeled by the timed transitions of the SystemNet while the enabling conditions of these transitions model the resource allocation.

For instance, the transition "Web server fails" is enabled during the phases which correspond to tasks using the web server while the transition rate corresponds to the expected failure rate of a server during a typical transaction. These parameters are represented in the IBM WBI as the "description" of the resources (since the definition of failure rates of resources is not supported by the present BPM tool). For external services, such as "External service" in this example, the failure rate is derived from the Service Level Agreement, also using a textual field in the modeling tool. The main difference between the internal resource usage and the external service invocation is that in the former case, multiple resources can be used simultaneously and a fault in any of them prohibits the proper service while in the latter case only a single service and −at most− one resource, namely the application server is used.

5 Model Transformations with VIATRA2

As it was mentioned in Sect. 4., the dependability indicators of business processes can be evaluated if they are transformed into a MPS model. The model transformation-based analysis of business process descriptions consists of the steps shown in Figure 4.

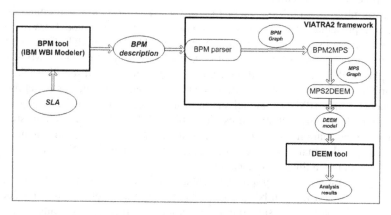

Fig. 4. Transformation of business processes

Using model transformations for the analysis of high-level system models is part of the Model Driven Architecture (MDA) concept. The motivation for using model transformations in the VIATRA (Visual Automated Model Transformations) framework was the *extensibility* of the transformation engine by additional parsers and plugins which enable the decoupling of the format of the source model and the target analysis platform.

First, the engineering model of the functionality −enriched by dependability parameters− is taken to be analyzed by formal methods. This model will be generated by a BPM tool [26] and transformed by the VIATRA2 framework into a DEEM model. To build a mathematical model from the high level business description in an automated way, the BPM is parsed into a graph representation ("BPM Graph"). In our case, this will be the inner representation language of the VIATRA2 tool, which is a public domain model transformation framework, developed at BUTE [23]. It is now part of the Eclipse GMT project [5]. In the VIATRA2, graph pattern matching [24] is controlled by Abstract State Machines [25].

Then, graph transformations are performed upon this parsed model in order to generate a graph which represents the relevant elements of the system in the target paradigm ("MPS Graph"). In this case, the target paradigm is MPS and the target model representation format is that of the DEEM tool. However, as it will be discussed later, the transformation itself was implemented in two steps. Once the model can be read by the target analysis tool, a precise analysis method (in this case, the Markov Regenerative Process-based dependability evaluation) can be performed.

The transformations were implemented with the VIATRA2 model transformation framework. The automatic generation of a DEEM model consists of three basic steps:

1. Importing the XML files which contain the description of different aspects of the BPM model ("BPM description"), such as the basic process model and the actual values of the variables which determine the runtime behavior of the system, e.g. the probabilities of paths to be followed after decisions. This step was implemented using the built-in BPM parser component of the VIATRA2 framework, which creates an inner graph representation –in the VPML language of the tool– of the business process ("BPM Graph").

2. Transforming the graph representation of the BPM structures and concepts into a graph representation of a multiple phased system. The model transformation ("bpm2mps") itself is implemented in this step. The metamodel of a general MPS description contains the elements of a DSPN-based representation of MPS, such as the places, the transitions and the arcs of the SystemNet and the PhaseNet ("MPS Graph"). The transformation is described by precondition patterns matching to the concepts of the BPM metamodel and the corresponding postcondition patterns give the equivalent Petri Net structures, describing a Phase Mission System still in the graph representation language. As this transformation is based on a generic MPS metamodel, the analysis tool can be replaced by another Petri Net based tool without any change in this transformation.

3. Code generation: once a graph representation of the MPS is available, the text file in the DEEM format can be generated by a simple transformation ("mps2deem"). This transformation is designed to take a graph, in which the elements are stored in a tree structure and references between them describe the logical connections, and generate a text file ("DEEM model"). The main reason of the separation of model transformation and the code generation is twofold; first, this way the changes in the tool representation format (or even the replacement of the DEEM by another analysis tool) can be easily tracked and do not interfere with algorithm of the transformation of the main concepts. Therefore, the transformations are maintainable. Second, since the DEEM representation is a flat format, the whole graph tree is needed for the code generation, and therefore this step cannot be started before the entire model transformation is finished.

In order to analyze business processes with DEEM ("Analysis results"), the two transformations ("bpm2mps" and "mps2deem") were implemented in the VIATRA2 framework. At the moment there are some limitations on BPM elements due to the BPM parser of the framework, but anyway they do not affect the essence of the methodology.

6 Case Study

Consider an insurance company with a database containing client data (e.g. previous accidents) wanting to provide a premium calculator service which receives client data and returns an estimated insurance fee for the given person. Consider that this company wants to interact with other companies to complete its knowledge about a client's insurance record. This interaction is done via Web service interface; the partners provide similar premium calculator services.

The clients of such an application are employees of the company, individual brokers, other companies, registered users, etc. The company implements this functionality as a Web service to support communication between heterogeneous, loosely-coupled systems. The company wants to assure QoS parameters for the clients. Therefore, its own resources and services have to match several expectations just as the external services.

There are different types of clients with different QoS requirements against the premium calculator service. For instance, a client with a "Golden value" contract (another insurance company) may have different expectations against the system than a registered user accessing the service from a home PC.

Requests which mean a big risk (a calculation for an insurance of big amount or for a client with missing personal data) have to be checked by other partners to eliminate the chance of failure or cheating. On the other hand, different partner companies offer their calculator services (which are external activities in the process flow) for different prices.

The measures of interest are –among others– the following:

- The probability that a client request fails (for different types of clients).
- Performability metrics which show the cost of dependability, i.e. which external services to invoke at given QoS parameters and price. Requests of different client types, of course, can be forwarded to different external partners in order to assure the required QoS at a reasonable price.

Finally, sensitivity analysis is required to evaluate the effect of component failure rates on above measures.

6.1 The Example Model in BPM

This section describes the high-level BPM model of the example. The concrete modeling tool is IBM WBI Modeler which, on the one hand, supports the modeling of resources (in this case, the quantitative parameters of the services) and, on the other hand, has a BPEL export feature.

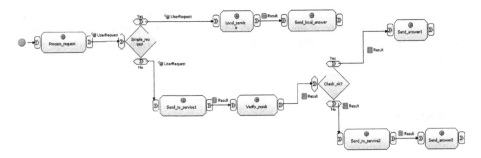

Fig. 5. The example in IBM WBI modeler

The rounded rectangles represent the internal and external activities. Parameters of the resources and the services are stored in the model repository but are not visualized. To comply with the BPEL standard, internal activities can also be accessed via a SOAP interface, but their QoS parameters depend on resources with known characteristics.

6.2 The Example Model as an MPS

This section describes the MPS model of the example business flow, showing the general method of transforming a BPM to a MPS. The system can be considered as a MPS in the following way.

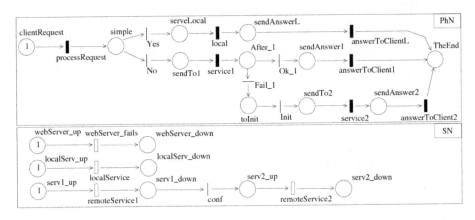

Fig. 6. The MPS model of the example

The Web server is modeled in the SystemNet (the lower partition of Fig. 6) which can be reconfigured according to that actual phase. The Web server can fail with a failure rate which is the parameter of the "webServer_fails" transition. This motivates the usage of the same topology (places and transitions) for representing all resources; the transition rates may change over time, according to the actual phase.

The first phase of the system is receiving a message from the client. This corresponds to the first activity of the business process. The second phase is upon a decision; whether the request can be served locally (in this case, no remote web service is invoked) or it needs to be sent to a remote partner. In the latter case, the answer is verified against some basic requirements, for instance, the presence and the consistency of all required data fields are checked.

If additional information is needed, the request is sent to a backup service, provided by another partner, and built upon another database. The first activity of the workflow ("Process request") is the only element of a sequence of internal service invocations. Therefore, it is the first phase of the system. The length of the phase will be represented by a timed transition (processRequest in Fig. 6) with a transition duration determined by the length of the task in the business process. During this phase, the system can fail if the internal resource, in this case the Web server, crashes.

The next phase is selected according to the user type; the simple calculations are served locally while the difficult calculations, e.g. those of users with missing data or big value of insurance, are sent to external partners. In this version, the "Recovery Block" pattern is implemented in a service oriented environment, which could be called "Recovery Block-like Service Invocations". This means the invocation of a primary service, and if the answer is not acceptable –for instance, some user record is empty– then the invocation of a backup service.

The parameters of external service invocations (modeled by phase "service1" and "service2") are determined by the SLAs. The failure rate of the services comes from the UpTimeRatio parameter from the SLA (which is represented in the BPM tool as a resource parameter of the services which represent the remote partners). The possible reconfiguration of the system, i.e. the resending of the request to the "backup service", is represented by the transition "conf" in the SystemNet.

6.3 Dependability Analysis Results

To illustrate how dependability analysis constitutes a support to the provider of the composed service, we answer the questions "What is the probability of the failure of a client request?" and "Which is the most appropriate external service provider from the set of available providers?".

In a real scenario, the parameters of the services and resources are described by Service Level Agreements. As our aim is to present a methodology for the evaluation of dependability indicators, we used some sample values based on a measurement performed against public domain web services, such as the web service interface of google [27]. Hereby we suppose ten available service alternatives for Service1, which have their parameters described in Table 1 (considering the same response time). Please remember that these do not have realistic meanings, but have been chosen just to illustrate the possibilities of such an analysis. Due to the space problems, we do not include a table with the fix parameters used for the evaluations (e.g., the costs in the reward measure, the duration of the phases, etc.).

Table 1. Parameters of services in the example

Service alternatives	1.	2.	3.	4.	5.	6.	7.	8.	9.	10.
Failure rate	0.010	0.012	0.017	0.020	0.025	0.030	0.040	0.042	0.048	0.070
Service price	14.0	13.5	13.3	13.0	12.8	12.6	12.5	12.2	12.0	11.5

The aim of this analysis is at determining the impact of the price and dependability characteristics of an external web service on the probability of the failure of a client request and on the income of the composite service. This income is the fee that a client pays for the service minus the sum of the prices of the invoked local and external services. As the client receives a compensation for every failed request, this value has to be considered as a penalty. The measures of interest are defined in DEEM as

```
probServiceFail = IF ( MARK(webServer_down)=1 OR
MARK(localServ_down)=1 OR MARK(serv1_down)=1 OR
MARK(serv2_down)=1 ) THEN (1) ELSE (0) //failure prob

ServiceReward = [VAR(ClientFee) -
VAR(serv1Price)*FUN(serv1Succ) -
VAR(serv2Price)*FUN(serv2Succ)-
VAR(localPrice)*FUN(localServSucc)]*

(1-FUN(serviceFail)) -
FUN(serviceFail)*VAR(servicePenalty) //service reward
```

The results of the analysis is shown in Fig. 7.

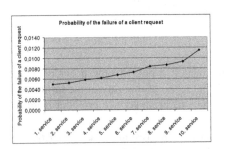
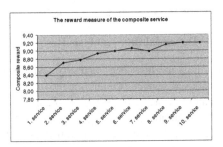

Fig. 7. Results of the dependability analysis

Based on dependability aspects only, 1.service is obviously the best choice as the number of failed requests has a minimum for this service. However, if the services are evaluated against the performability measure, then 10.service seems to be optimal as it has the highest reward value. If both aspects are considered, 9.service should be chosen instead, as it has almost as good performability measure as that of 10.service with a significantly lower probability of failure of a client request.

7 Conclusions

We presented a methodology for transforming higher level models of Service Oriented Architectures into a formal description in order to perform dependability analysis. Based on the observation that Web services-based workflows fit within the Multiple Phased Systems, model transformations were implemented in the VIATRA2 framework to perform precise mathematical analysis. Business process descriptions extended with quantitative parameters taken from SLAs were transformed, by using semi-automated transformations, into a precise mathematical model, a formal description of a Multiple Phased System, which can be solved by the dependability evaluation tool DEEM.

The current research direction is to extend the proposed methodology to analyze high level models described in BPEL and XML-based Web service description languages to provide a dependability analysis for a wider toolset. This way, a really platform (and vendor) independent analysis framework can be established. SLA-driven synthesis of web service compositions is another important research direction.

References

1. M. Martinello. Availability modeling and evaluation of web-based services –A pragmatic approach. PhD Thesis. LAAS-CNRS, 2005.
2. I. Mura, A. Bondavalli, X. Zang, and K. S. Trivedi, "Dependability modelling and evaluation of phased mission systems: a DSPN approach," in IEEE DCCA-7 - 7th IFIP Int. Conference on Dependable Computing for Critical Applications, San Jose, CA, USA, 1999, pp. 299–318.
3. I. Mura and A. Bondavalli, "Markov regenerative stochastic Petri nets to model and evaluate phased mission systems dependability," IEEE Transactions on Computers, vol. 50, no. 12, pp. 1337–1351, 2001.
4. A. Bondavalli, S. Chiaradonna, F. Di Giandomenico, and I. Mura. Dependability modeling and evaluation of ultiple-phased systems, using DEEM. IEEE Transactions on Reliability, 53(4):509-522, 2004.
5. The VIATRA2 Model Transformation Framework, Generative Model Transformer Project, The Eclipse Foundation. http://eclipse.org/gmt/
6. M. Smotherman and K. Zemoudeh, "A non-homogeneous Markov model for phased-mission reliability analysis," IEEE Transactions on Reliability, vol. 38, no. 5, pp. 585–590, 1989.
7. M. Alam and U. M. Al-Saggaf, "Quantitative reliability evaluation of repairable phased-mission systems using Markov approach," IEEE Transactions on Reliability, vol. R-35, no. 5, pp. 498–503, 1986.
8. Specification: Business Process Execution Language for Web Services Version 1.1, May 2003. http://www-128.ibm.com/developerworks/library/ws-bpel/
9. D. Menasce, V. A. F. Almeida. Capacity Planning for Web Services: Metrics, Models, and Methods. Prentice Hall, 2001.
10. I. Majzik, A. Pataricza, and A. Bondavalli. Stochastic dependability analysis of system architecture based on UML models. In R. De Lemos, C. Gacek, and A. Romanovsky, editors, Architecting Dependable Systems, LNCS 2677, pp. 219-244. Springer-Verlag, Berlin, Heidelberg, New York, 2003.

11. Web Service Level Agreements Project. http://www.research.ibm.com/wsla/
12. Web Services Flow Language (WSFL 1.0) - Appendix C: Endpoint Property Extensibility Elements. IBM Software Group, 2001.
13. V. Tosic, B. Paguerk, K.Patel. WSOL – A Language for the Formal Specification of Various Constraints and Classes of Service for Web Services. Research Report, Carleton University, 2002
14. A. Avizienis, J.C. Laprie, B. Randell, C. Landwehr. Basic Concepts and Taxonomy of Dependable and Secure Computing IEEE Transactions on Dependable and Secure Computing, Vol.1, N.1, pp.11-33, 2004
15. A. Pataricza: From the General Resource Model to a General Fault Modeling Paradigm? Workshop on Crititcal Systems Development with UML at UML 2002, Dresden, Germany
16. WS–Reliability. OASIS Standard
    http://docs.oasis-open.org/wsrm/ws-reliability/v1.1/wsrm-ws_reliability-1.1-spec-os.pdf
17. A. Graziano, S. Russo, V. Vecchio, P. Foster,Metadata models for QoS-aware information management systems. In Proc. of SEKE 2002, Ischia, Italy, 2002.
18. Web Services Base Faults. Oasis.
    http://docs.oasis-open.org/wsrf/2004/06/wsrf-WS-BaseFaults-1.2-draft-02.pdf
19. Web Service Description Language 1.1. W3C.org. http://www.w3.org/TR/wsdl
20. OMG Group, General Resource Model (GRM), URL: http://www.omg.com
21. L. Zeng, B. Benatallah, M. Dumas. Quality Driven Web Services Composition. In Proceedings of WWW2003, May 20-24, 2003, Budapest, Hungary.
22. S. Ran. A model for web services discovery with QoS. ACM SIGecom Exchanges, Vol. 4., N.1, pp. 1-10. ACM Press, 2003.
23. D. Varró, G. Varró, A. Pataricza, "Designing the Automatic Transformation of Visual Languages," Science of Computer Programming, 44:205-227 2002.
24. H. Ehrig, G. Engels, H.-J. Kreowski, and G. Rozenberg (eds.). Handbook on Graph Grammars and Computing by Graph Transformation, vol. 2: Applications, Languages and Tools, World Scientific, 1999.
25. E. Börger and R. Stark. Abstract State Machines. A method for High-Level System Design and Analysis. Springer-Verlag, 2003.
26. IBM Corporation. WebSphere Business Integrator 5.1
    http://www-06.ibm.com/software/integration/
27. Google Web API (beta). http://www.google.com/apis/index.html
28. J.T. Bradley, N.J. Dingle, S.T. Gilmore, W.J. Knottenbelt. Derivation of Passage-time Densities in PEPA Models using ipc: the Imperial PEPA Compiler. In Proc. of MASCOTS'03, Orlando, USA, 2003, pp. 344.351.
29. C. Ouyang, E. Verbeek, W.M.P. van der Aalst, S. Breutel, M. Dumas, A.H.M. ter Hoftstede WofBPEL: A Tool for Automated Analysis of BPEL Processes. In. Proc. of ICSOC 2005, Amsterdam, The Netherlands. 2005. pp. 484-489.
30. R. Kazhamiakin, P. Pandya, M. Pistore. Modelling and Analysis of Time-related Properties in Web Service Compositions. In Proc. of WESC'05, Amsterdam, The Netherlands, 2005.
31. W. M.P. van der Aalst, M. Dumas, A.H.M ter Hofstede, N. Russell, P. Wohed, H. M. W. Verbeek. Life After BPEL?. In Proc. of WS-FM, Versailles, France. 2005. pp 35-50.
32. J. Koehler, G. Tirenni, S. Kumaran, From Business Process Model to Consistent Implementation: A Case for Formal Verification Methods, EDOC, Lausanne, Switzerland, 2002, pp. 96-106.
33. R. Milner. Communicating and Mobile Systems: The Pi-Calculus. Cambridge University Press, Cambridge, UK, 1999.

Improving the Performance of IEEE 802.11e with an Advanced Scheduling Heuristic

Burak Simsek and Katinka Wolter

Institut für Informatik, HU Berlin
Unter den Linden 6, 10009 Berlin
simsek@informatik.hu-berlin.de, wolter@informatik.hu-berlin.de

Abstract. The new standard IEEE 802.11e targets at enhancing the legacy 802.11 so that QoS management over WLAN standards becomes possible. This is done by the introduction of two new functions, the enhanced distributed channel access (EDCA) and the hybrid coordination function controlled channel access (HCCA) for offering diffserv and intserv functionalities. The efficient coordination of both functions plays a crucial role in terms of the performance of 802.11e. In this paper we propose a new method for the calculation of the service interval by using the send rates of different traffic streams and suggest an advanced way to determine which one of the functions for which kind of streams to deploy. We show that despite its simplicity the proposed methods decrease packet delay and loss rates significantly and increases the number of streams having acceptable QoS levels.

1 Introduction

802.11 standards are among the most prominent wireless communication technologies for daily use. However the lack of quality of service support on 802.11 does not allow sufficient protection for real time traffic for which there is a high demand on the customer side. In order to overcome this problem, the IEEE 802.11e task group developed an amendment to the legacy 802.11 standard. The amendment targets at enhancing the legacy 802.11 medium access control so that real time traffic can be offered using WLAN devices within acceptable quality of service levels.

The most dominant enhancement in 802.11 medium access control (MAC) is the introduction of the hybrid coordination function (HCF) which consists of two sub functions, the enhanced distributed channel access (EDCA) and the HCF controlled channel access (HCCA). As the 802.11e standard is new, most of the relevant studies made so far include performance analysis and the improvement suggestions for the new functions EDCA and HCCA [1, 2, 3]. In these studies, it was shown that although the new standard improves the WLAN performance substantially, only a very careful fine tuning of the parameters of these functions results high QoS levels. In our previous study [4], we also showed that especially the maximum service interval (maximum allowed time between transmissions of two successive packets belonging to a specific traffic stream) and the amount

A. Horváth and M. Telek (Eds.): EPEW 2006, LNCS 4054, pp. 181–195, 2006.
© Springer-Verlag Berlin Heidelberg 2006

of time reserved for HCCA affect the QoS that one may expect using 802.11e. The correct choice of these parameters boosts system performance drastically. Although the effects of the service interval choice and the time reserved for HCCA were shown to be significantly high in [4], no method was proposed for a proper selection of these parameters.

In this paper we analyze mathematically the effect of the service interval choice on the delay and loss rates of the traffic being served within HCCA and correspondingly propose methods for choosing service interval length leading to significant performance improvements. We also propose an admission control algorithm which is an enhanced version of the reference admission control of 802.11e. Within the proposed admission control algorithm, we differentiate between uplink, downlink and bidirectional traffic. We figure out in which cases these different traffic types should be assigned to which one of the two sub functions (EDCA and HCCA) of the hybrid coordination function. We show that the cooperation and so the performance of 802.11e in terms of offered QoS can be significantly increased when using this control mechanism and the service interval selection method. To the best of the authors' knowledge there is no study which deals with the service interval selection problem and a corresponding admission control procedure although it is one of the most effective parameters of 802.11e in terms of satisfying QoS requirements [4].

The rest of the paper is organized as follows. In the second section the functioning of HCCA is summarized in order to give background information about 802.11e. In the third section a short literature review is given. In the fourth section we analyze the relationship between service interval and the QoS metrics. Fifth section presents the validation of mathematical analysis with simulation results. In the sixth section we draw the conclusions.

2 Background

The IEEE 802.11e task group enhanced the legacy WLAN standard with two well known QoS mechanisms. These mechanisms are called differentiated services (diffserv) and integrated services (intserv). Diffserv mechanism is setup in the way that access points can serve multiple traffic classes with different QoS requirements. Instead of priorities, intserv is based on the individual QoS requirements of the stations. The hybrid coordination function of 802.11e uses EDCA for diffserv and HCCA for intserv. Depending on the load of the network, hybrid coordination function determines respectively at what time which one of these functions to use. An example to successive deployment of EDCA and HCCA can be seen in figure 1.

Basically the HCCA is an asynchronous real time scheduler. For cases where there are strict delay and loss constraints, the stations inform the access point that they must be included in the HCCA scheduler. In order to do this, they give detailed information about the traffic stream within a management frame called TSPEC. TSPEC includes information like nominal MAC service data unit (MSDU) size, mean data rate, suspension interval, delay, surplus bandwidth

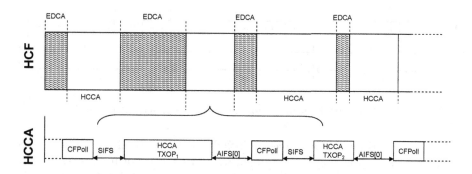

Fig. 1. An illustration of HCF, HCCA and EDCA

allowance and maximum service interval. This information is used to decide on accepting the incoming requests for being included in the schedule of HCCA or not. If a stream is accepted to the HCCA schedule, then a time interval for that specific stream is reserved in the schedule. This time interval is called the HCCA transmission opportunity (HCCA TXOP). The usage of HCCA TXOP is summarized in Fig. 1. Stations are informed about the reserved TXOP with a frame called CFPoll frame after the channel is sensed to be idle for a time period which is called the arbitration inter frame space (AIFS). In fact AIFS is different for all traffic priorities. For this reason the arbitration interframe space of the access point is denoted as AIFS[0] within Fig. 1. The station receiving the CFPoll sends its frames after waiting for a short inter frame space (SIFS). During a TXOP only the station which received the CFPoll can send its frames. This period is also called the contention free period, because only the stations who receive HCCA TXOP are allowed to transmit any packets.

In real time schedulers one of the most common and most important parameters used for building the schedule is the deadline. The HCCA reference scheduler uses the maximum service intervals that are given by the stations for this purpose. Maximum service intervals define the maximum amount of time that is allowed between transmissions of two successive frames of a specific stream. For the sake of simplicity, the reference scheduler proposes a cyclic schedule which cycles through a path of TXOPs determined at the beginning of a beacon period (See Fig. 2). This cycling is delineated as follows. A beacon period is defined as the time between two beacon frames where a beacon frame is a management frame used to advertise general information regarding the access point to all surrounding stations periodically. The reference scheduler selects a number as its service interval which is smaller than the smallest maximum service interval given by the stations and which is a submultiple of the beacon interval. In this way it makes sure that all of the maximum service intervals (in other words 'due dates') are taken into account. HCCA calculates TXOPs needed by each one of the stations during one service interval. The same TXOPs are distributed to the stations during each of the following service intervals until a new set of TXOPs is determined. This cyclic procedure is illustrated within Fig. 2 where

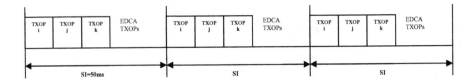

Fig. 2. TXOP distribution for three streams named as i,j and k

three different traffic streams receive TXOPs at the beginning of each service interval. As seen from Fig. 2 the time in which HCCA is not used is reserved to EDCA. For more information about the functioning of EDCA please refer to [5].

3   Literature Review

Due to the long lasting ratification of 802.11e, one can find many studies for the optimization of EDCA and HCCA. To the best of the authors' knowledge, in all these studies, except the one from Ramos et al. [6], EDCA and HCCA were dealt with separately. Banchs et al. [7] introduced an admission control algorithm based on an analytical model for the throughput performance of 802.11e using EDCA, where they dynamically adapt the contention windows of each priority level, as new traffic associates with an access point. On the other hand Xiao [8] presented an enhancement suggestion by introducing "TXOP Budgets" to each access category. In this way, they protect voice and video traffic from the best effort traffic. Kim and Suh [9] and Gao et al. [10] instead use the physical transmission rates of the stations in order to prevent unfairness because of distance at the cost of lower throughput.

For HCCA, the studies concentrate more on the protection of voice and video traffic. Ma et al. [11] use the talkspurt-silence alternation characteristics in order not to reserve time in the HCCA scheduler for a voice stream when it is silent. Ansel et al. [12] and Fan et al. [13] introduce algorithms for dealing with variable bit rate traffic (VBR), as it is one of the main problems of HCCA. As a result of these studies the recommended TXOP calculation of 802.11e was changed so that VBR is also supported. [12] uses exponential smoothing for estimating queue length information of VBR traffic and reassigns TXOPs in case of deviation from the ideal queue length. [13] makes the redistribution of TXOPs by calculating VBR traffic drop rates with a trade-off between the packet loss performance and the number of admitted flows.

Different than EDCA and HCCA performance analysis, in [4] we evaluated the quality of the QBSS load element of 802.11e in terms of an information element for solving the candidate access point selection. It was shown that the complexity of the cooperation of EDCA and HCCA avoids having reliable information for estimating the QoS that a traffic stream can receive after associating with an access point. The service interval and the amount of time reserved for HCCA plays a crucial role in this problem. Taking this result as the basis, we tried to find out the optimum choice of service interval length and the amount of time reserved for HCCA. This paper is devoted to present the results of our studies for increasing 802.11e system performance by adapting a new service interval selection mechanism and time reservation policy for HCCA.

4   Service Interval and the QoS Metrics

A service interval starts with the distribution of TXOPs which are determined as follows: Let N_i be the number of packets arriving within a service interval SI, p_i is the application data rate and L_i is the nominal MSDU size of the traffic stream (TS) in TS queue i, then :

$$N_i = \lceil \frac{p_i * SI}{L_i} \rceil. \tag{1}$$

TXOPs for different traffic streams are assigned as follows:

$$TXOP_i = max(\frac{N_i * L_i}{R_i} + O, \frac{M}{R_i} + O), \tag{2}$$

which is the maximum time needed to transmit N frames of size L with data rate R and time needed to send one maximum size MSDU (M) plus overheads. The hybrid coordinator sends the so called CFPoll frames to the stations which includes the information about the assigned TXOP. As given in Fig. 1, the station receiving CFPoll sends its packets after waiting SIFS (short inter frame space) long. In case there is no packet to be transmitted or the excess TXOP is not needed any more, the station sends QoS NULL packet so that next station in the schedule can transmit its packets. For the usage of the given TXOPs there are three possible cases:

- TXOP is used completely, so that there is no free time to send QoS NULL packet at the end
- TXOP is used partially and a QoS NULL packet is sent following a QoS DATA
- TXOP is not used and a QoS NULL packet is sent directly

   Although first case is the ideal case, it is not the most usual one because TXOP reservation mechanism rounds up the expected number of packets during a service interval (See eq. (1)). For this reason, there is most of the times unused TXOP for any stream. The expected ratio of unused TXOPs can be given as follows. For a stream with a send rate of x and a service interval length of x+y where y is a positive number, the average number of TXOPs that are not used during a service interval is:

$$NU_{small} = (\frac{N_i}{x + y} - \frac{1}{x}) * (x + y). \tag{3}$$

For a stream with a send rate of z which is greater than or equal to the service interval (x+y), the average number of TXOPs that are not used is:

$$NU_{big} = (\frac{1}{x + y} - \frac{1}{z}) * (x + y). \tag{4}$$

Then the average time used by HCCA during one service interval is:

$$HCCA[y] = Lost[y] + Used[y], \qquad (5)$$

where

$$Lost[y] = (\frac{1}{x+y} - \frac{1}{z}) * n_i * nothing_i + (\frac{N_i}{x+y} - \frac{1}{x}) * n_j * nothing_j) * (x+y), \quad (6)$$

$$Used[y] = n_i * TXOP_i * \frac{x+y}{x} + n_j * TXOP_j * \frac{x+y}{z}. \qquad (7)$$

For the sake of simplicity we assume that there are only two types of streams, one having a send rate smaller than the service interval and the other one bigger than the service interval. n_i and n_j are the numbers of traffic streams of the first and the second types and $nothing_i$ and $nothing_j$ are the lengths of the times needed for sending QoS NULL frames with the overheads.

As long as there is enough time reserved in the scheduler for any traffic, packet losses should not occur for that traffic. For this reason, in such cases the length of the service interval and so the lost time because of extra TXOP does not play a role in the packet loss rate. However Lost[y] is decreasing in y. Hence, any reduction in the lost time will result lower packet loss rates within a congested channel. We can then estimate the necessary increment in the length of the service interval for a new traffic by finding the increment in the unused time within HCCA scheduler:

$$r * (x+y+k) - HCCA[x+y+k] - (r * (x+y) - HCCA[x+y]) = TXOP_{new}, \quad (8)$$

where r is the maximum percentage of time that can be reserved for HCCA scheduler within a service interval and k the required increment in the service interval length, so that new stream can be served using HCCA. Rather long algebra gives the following solution for k:

$$\frac{TXOP_{new} * x * z}{r * x * z - z * n_i * (T_i - nothing_i) - x * n_j * (T_j - nothing_j)} = k, \qquad (9)$$

where T_i is the time needed to send one MSDU plus overheads. Although this equation is harder to solve if there are more than two types of traffic streams to consider, the problem could be reduced to the first priority streams in such cases.

Average delay for the packets is also independent of the lost time, since TXOP distribution is cyclic and the order of TXOP distribution is the same for each service interval. As seen from Fig. 2, the average length between two TXOPs of any specific traffic is the addition of the expected time spent for HCCA plus the remaining time for EDCA. This length is equal to the service interval length. Consequently the average time between two TXOPs of any stream is always equal to the service interval length.

Average delay caused by this service interval is increasing in the length of the service interval and dependent on the number of common divisors of the send rate and the service interval. The simple logic behind this fact is the wasted time

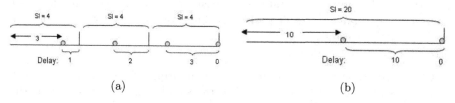

(a)   (b)

Fig. 3. Delay caused by 4ms and 20ms SIs to packets with interarrival rates of 3ms and 10ms

because of the asynchronous occurences of the TXOPs and the packet arrivals. In the worst case they have no common divisors. A simple example is illustrated in Fig. 3(a) where the service interval length is 4ms and the send rate is 3 ms. Here, the first packet waits for 1ms to be sent, the second packet waits for 2ms, the third packet 3ms and the last packet is sent directly. Consequently, packets experience delays from 0 to service interval minus one (Here from zero to 3ms). Hence, the average delay is the addition of the integers from 1 to service interval minus one divided by the number of packets experiencing these delays, which is equal to the length of the service interval. This gives the average delay as (SI-1)/2. This implies the fact that each increment in the service interval length also increases the delay of the packets as much as half of this increment. Hence service interval should be kept as small as possible.

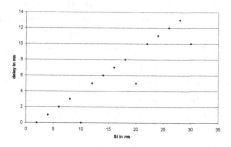

Fig. 4. Delay caused by different SIs to a packet with a interarrival rate of 10ms

The best case scenario is where the interarrival rate or the service interval is a divisor of the other. In this case, if the service interval is longer than the interarrival rate, average delay is (SI-interarrival rate)/2. Fig. 4 illustrates the case where interarrival rate is equal to 10ms. As seen from Fig. 4, we are indifferent between choosing a service interval which is one more than any multiple of the interarrival rate and the next multiple of the interarrival rate. This implies the following point: if we need extra time for a new stream, then we can increase the service interval length to the next multiple without increasing the expected delay. This is achieved by synchronizing TXOPs distributions with the packet arrival times as much as possible. In case there are more than one interarrival rate, decision should be made using delay constraints of the streams. However using the smallest interarrival rate as the basic rate would make sense for most cases, since the number of sent packets is the most for the stream having the smallest interarrival rate.

To summarize our findings:

- Choose the smallest comman multiple/submultiple of the interarrival rates, which is also greater than or equal to the smallest interarrival rate, as the service interval length.
- If we have to increase the service interval length because of a new stream, then we choose the next multiple of the interarrival rates which is also greater than the result of the equation (9).

These two points are used during our simulations in section 6 to select the appropriate service interval.

5   Assigning Traffic Streams to HCCA and EDCA

So far we analyzed the effect of the service interval to loss and delay of the traffic streams served within HCCA. In this section we clarify which type of traffic should be assigned to HCCA during admission control processes.

The access point accesses the channel like a station when using EDCA. Having only as much channel access chance as a station with the load of all stations impairs downlink traffic drastically. In case the TXOP given to access point for any priority is not enough, then especially the interface queue length increases substantially leading to high delay and even loss rates. For this reason it is reasonable to protect the downlink traffic during HCCA, and only if there is remaining time in the HCCA scheduler reserve it for the uplink traffic. However it can be shown using simple calculations that as long as the overhead for sending the needed amount of packets using HCCA is higher, it makes no sense to reserve time for uplink traffic in the scheduler within a congested channel. If we describe the total time usage (TT) within a service interval as:

$$TT = \sum_{j=1}^{3}\sum_{i=1}^{j} N_{j,i} * p_{j,i} + \sum_{j=1}^{3}\sum_{i=1}^{j} ((\frac{SI}{x_{j,i}} - N_{j,i}) * q_{j,i}) + B, \qquad (10)$$

where $N_{j,i}$ is the number of packets from the ith stream of the jth priority allowed to be transmitted using HCCA, $p_{j,i}$ is the amount of time needed to send one packet during HCCA and respectively $q_{j,i}$ is the time needed during EDCA, $x_{j,i}$ is the interarrival rate and B is the time used by traffic which did not request any HCCA TXOP, which was rejected by the HCCA scheduler and the background traffic. The summation is done over three priorities, since background traffic does not receive HCCA TXOP. Using this equation one can find the effect of reserving TXOP for an additional packet:

$$\partial_{N_{j,i}} TT = \sum_{j=1}^{3}\sum_{i=1}^{j} p_{j,i} - \sum_{j=1}^{3}\sum_{i=1}^{j} q_{j,i}. \qquad (11)$$

As seen, the slope of the total time usage with respect to $N_{j,i}$ is dependent on the packet transmission times required for EDCA and HCCA. If the time needed to send the same packet during HCCA is longer than the time needed to send the same packet during EDCA, than reserving time in the HCCA for this packet causes more channel utilization because of the increasing TT (total time usage). The time needed to send one packet during HCCA and EDCA can be illustrated as follows:

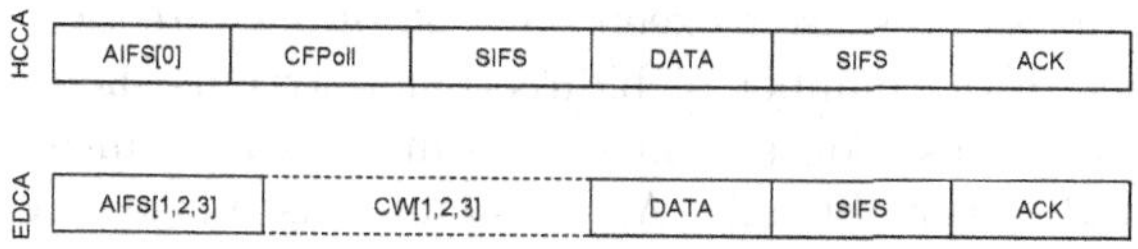

Fig. 5. Comparison of packet transmission times with EDCA and HCCA

In Fig. 5 each block represents the time needed for different actions. AIFS[0] is the length of the arbitration inter frame space used by the access point. CFPoll is the time needed to send one CFPoll frame, ACK is the time needed to send the acknowledgment, and CW is the contention window length. We include AIFS and CW of the first three priorities as the fourth priority uses only EDCA for its transmissions. If we compare both cases, we see that the difference of the times needed by HCCA and EDCA to send the same packet is AIFS[0]+ CFPoll + SIFS <> AIFS[1,2,3]+CW[1,2,3]. The assignment of the lengths of arbitration inter frame spaces is described in the standard as follows:

$$AIFS[AC] = AIFSN[AC] * slotTime + SIFS, \qquad (12)$$

where AIFSN[AC] is a number greater than or equal to 2 for all access categories (AC) of non access point stations and greater or equal to one for access points. If we assume that the AIFSN for the access point is one and for three of the access categories 2,3 and 4, then in the worst case the difference of the time needed by HCCA and EDCA is 3slotTimes + CW[3] <> CFPoll+ SIFS. Within a congested channel with low service interval values, which is the case with the above defined service interval selection criteria, it is not trivial to assume that the 'next' access category that is going to send its packets has a backoff timer of length 1 time slot. Considering this, 4slotTimes < CFPoll + SIFS will be true for most of the usual configurations of the parameters of 802.11e. One could argue the fact that CFPoll can be piggybacked on a QoS DATA frame so that the QAP does not have to wait extra AIFS long. However, in such cases the physical transmission rate of QoS DATA frame is reduced to a basic rate, which is the smallest of the maximum physical transmission rates of all the associated stations. If there is one station away from the QAP or a station using 802.11b instead of 802.11g, this would increase the time needed for sending QoS DATA even further. For this reason, piggybacking is not a solution to the mentioned problem. Hence it makes sense not to reserve time during HCCA for uplink traffic. This is true even if the time needed by HCCA is shorter than the time needed by EDCA, since there is an upper bound for the time reserved to HCCA. In a crowded network reserving time for uplink traffic within HCCA degrades the performance of downlink traffic because there is not enough time to reserve TXOPs to all downlink streams. Additionally reserving more TXOPs in the HCCA scheduler results losing more time during a service interval as explained in the previous section. We can reduce this lost time by distributing less TXOPs to the uplink traffic.

An exception to this argument is the bidirectional traffic. If the traffic is bidirectional, it makes no sense to keep the QoS of one direction good, ignoring the other. Therefore the number of bidirectional streams should be optimized regarding both directions. Consequently there must be a balance between HCCA and EDCA for bidirectional traffic. Access point must make sure that expected time in EDCA is sufficient for the packets of the bidirectional traffic which are not being served within HCCA.

To summarize:

- Reserve time of HCCA first of all for downlink traffic.
- Even if there is remaining time in the HCCA scheduler, we are better off if we do not reserve TXOPs for uplink traffic in case there is a high congestion probability. This is true as long as we do not have strict service level agreements for such traffic.
- It does not make sense to reserve time for bidirectional traffic in case the requirements of one direction cannot be fulfilled.

Taking these into account, we developed an admission control mechanism which consists of following constraints:

$$\sum_{j=1}^{3}\sum_{i=1}^{j}((\frac{a_{j,i} * (1 + b_{j,i}) * SI}{s_{j,i}} - x_{j,i}) * q_{j,i}) + \sum_{j=1}^{3}\sum_{i=1}^{j} x_{j,i} * p_{j,i} + B \leq SI, \quad (13)$$

$$a_{j,i} \geq x_{j,i}, \quad (14)$$

$$\sum_{j=1}^{3}\sum_{i=1}^{j} x_{j,i} * p_{j,i} \leq HCCAlimit, \quad (15)$$

$$x_{j,i} \ \epsilon \ downlink, \quad (16)$$

$$a_{j,i} \ \epsilon 0, 1, \quad (17)$$

where k is the number of streams in the scheduler, $b_{j,i}$ is the binary for bidirectional traffic and $a_{j,i}$ determines if the stream is accepted by the HCCA scheduler or not. Constraints (13) and (14) make sure that bidirectional streams receive TXOPs for uplink and downlink in case they are accepted and the total amount of time reserved for HCCA TXOPs plus the time used by uncontrolled traffic is smaller than the selected service interval. Constraint (15) makes sure that the time reserved for HCCA is less than the maximum amount of time allowed and last constraint reserves HCCA TXOPs only to downlink traffic. If the incoming streams satisfy all the above defined constraints, then they are accepted to the HCCA scheduler. This admission control mechanism is used within our simulation runs in the following section.

6 Simulation

6.1 Simulation Environment

In order to show the effect of the service interval choice in different traffic situations we run simulations using an updated and slightly corrected version of ns2 network simulator for 802.11e developed by [14]. Within the simulation environment, there is one access point and different number of stations of each priority. Each station uses only one type of traffic. There are a total of 6 types of traffic during simulations. These are given as follows:

1. First priority, bidirectional constant bit rate (CBR) traffic using UDP with a packet size of 160 bytes and sample intervals (interarrival rate) of 5,8,10,15, ..,35 ms. (1st access category)
2. First priority, bidirectional constant bit rate (CBR) traffic using UDP with a constant voice payload of 64 Kbps and interarrival rate of 10,20 and 30 ms. (1st access category)
3. First priority, bidirectional constant bit rate (CBR) traffic using UDP with a constant voice payload of 8 Kbps and interarrival rates of 10,20, 30 ms. (1st access category)
4. Second priority CBR traffic using UDP with a packet size 1280 bytes and interarrival rate of 5, 10, 20, 30ms.(2nd access category)
5. Bidirectional interactive traffic using TCP with a packet size of 1100 bytes and exponentially distributed arrival rates having an average of 50ms on time, 30ms off time and sending rate of 60Kbits/s during on times corresponding to an average of 10Kbytes/s. This complies with the interactive traffic definition of 3GPP TS 22.105 [15] and ITU G.1010 [16]. (3rd access category)
6. VBR Background traffic using TCP with a packet size of 1200 bytes and exponentially distributed inter arrival times having an average of 1000ms off and 200ms on times with a sending rate of 100Kbits/s corresponding to low load 11Kbytes/s traffic. (4th access category)

The first three traffic types are defined to simulate voice traffic. The first traffic type targets at showing the effects of changing interarrival rates without caring for the existence of a corresponding voice codec being used in the internet. The second and third types represent the codecs G.711 and G.729 correspondingly as defined in Cisco Call Manager [17]. These three types of voice packets cover most of the used codec formats in the internet [18]. The second priority is defined for video traffic with different qualities which also comprises most of the video codecs being used in the internet [19]. Third and fourth traffic types are defined to simulate normal hot spot user behaviour as given in [20]. As a result, the results presented in the following sections are representative for most of the traffic combinations being used currently. Additionally the 802.11e specific parameters are given in table 1.

Table 1. List of Simulation Parameters

Bandwidth	11Mbps
PLCPTransmissionrate	1 Mbps
RTSThreshold	$3000\mu s$
ShortRetryLimit	7
LongRetryLimit	4
slotTime	$9\mu s$
AIFS(1,2,3,4)	$1, 2, 6, 12$
CWmin(1,2,3,4)	$7, 15, 15, 31$
CWMax(1,2,3,4)	$15, 31, 255, 525$

6.2   Simulation Results

The results presented in this section are the average results where we used up to 13 background, 13 interactive, 5 video and 14 voice streams with a changing ratio of the maximum amount of time reserved to HCCA (from 14% to 82%). In each run, voice streams are selected from the defined three types of first priority traffic randomly. In case not otherwise stated, the largest 99% confidence interval is within 20% of the given results. For each service interval and voice stream count combination we evaluated 4225 runs.

The results of our simulations mostly coincide with the findings presented in the previous section. As seen in Fig. 6(a), choosing different service intervals has no effect on the packet loss rate of high priority traffic. The differences between the loss rates at different service intervals are either statistically insignificant or ignorably small. We also observe an increasing delay for high priority traffic in SI as shown in Fig. 6(b). However the experienced average delay during our simulations is less than the theoretical delay which is nearly equal to the half of the service interval. A linear regression of the simulation results gives a slope of 0.22 with an R^2 value of 0.24. The R^2 value shows the goodness of fit and is calculated as:

$$R^2 = 1 - \frac{SSE}{SST} \tag{18}$$

where SSE is the sum squared error and SST is the total variance in the data. As R^2 approaches 1 the regression approaches a perfect fit. The fit is not perfect in our case, since we also used service intervals which are multiples of the inter-arrival rates. This introduces a deviation to the expected delay. Additionally, we could not show that choosing a common multiple of the interarrival rates as the service interval length decreases the average delay as explained in section 4. In fact with service intervals 25ms, 30ms and 40ms this effect is observable. However this is not true for service interval values 20ms and 50ms. This may be due to some minor implementation errors in the network simulator ns2.

On the other hand simulation runs in which we used an admission control mechanism by implementing the findings of the previous section proved to be very efficient in terms of channel reservation. As seen from Fig. 7(a), if we distribute TXOPs to the uplink traffic, then unacceptable loss rates occur starting

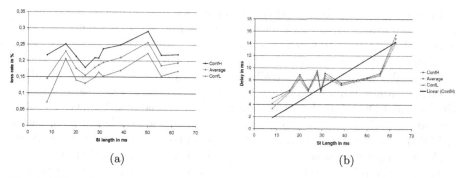

Fig. 6. Effect of service interval choice on delay and loss rate. ConfH and ConfL illustrate the 99% confidence interval levels.

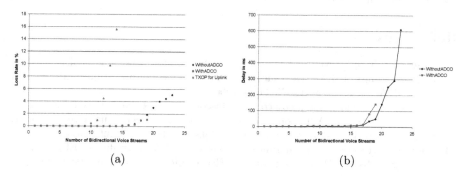

Fig. 7. Comparison of delay and loss rates of 1st priority traffic with different admission control mechanisms

with the 12th bidirectional voice stream. However this number grows up to 18 if only downlink traffic receives TXOPs. On the other hand using the admission control mechanism which combines the findings of the previous section does not allow more than 19 voice streams. For the 19th stream the service interval is increased using equation (9)and the effect of this increment can be seen in Fig. 7(a) where the loss rate is about the half of the case without the admission control mechanism. However this happens at the cost of more delay as seen in Fig. 7(b). As seen, the admission control algorithm does not allow delay more than 150ms.

7   Conclusion

Research activities on the upcoming standard 802.11e show that WLAN will be able to satisfy high QoS expectations of different applications much more than we can reach currently. 802.11e does this by offering both diffserv and intserv mechanisms at the same time in a comprehensive manner. However only an efficient cooperation of these two mechanisms makes sure that the resultant QoS levels are as high as expected.

In this paper we studied the effects of the service interval on the delay and loss rate of high priority traffic. We showed that, with a clever choice of the service interval it is possible to reach much higher QoS levels. Using these results we suggested very simple changes in the recommended way of calculating service intervals. We also divided the traffic into four categories as uplink, downlink, bidirectional and unidirectional traffic and assigned these traffic categories into HCCA and EDCA based on their transmission procedures. We showed using simulation analysis that the suggested methods enable an efficient cooperation of EDCA and HCCA by maximizing the numbers of streams that can be offered for higher priority streams and keeping the QoS within acceptable limits.

We are currently working on developing novel ways for making autonomous decisions by the hybrid coordinator so that the usage of EDCA and HCCA are optimized dynamically without being dependent on the scheduling algorithms used by different vendors.

References

1. Ansel, P., Ni, Q., Turletti, T.: An Efficient Scheduling Scheme for IEEE 802.11e. In: Proceedings of IEEE Workshop on Modelling and Optimization in Mobile, Ad Hoc and Wireless Networks (WiOpt). (2004)
2. Boggia, G., Camarda, P., Grieco, L., Mascolo, S.: Feedback Based Bandwidth Allocation with Call Admission Control for Providing Delay Guarantees in IEEE 802.11e Networks. Computer Communications (28(3)) (2005) 325–337
3. Choi, S.: Protection and Guarantee for Voice and Video Traffic in IEEE 802.11e Wireless LANs. In: Proceedings of the IEEE Conference on Computer Communications. (2004)
4. Simsek, B., Wolter, K., Coskun, H.: Analysis of the QBSS Load Element Parameters of 802.11e for a priori Estimation of Service Quality. International Journal of Simulation: Systems, Science and Technology, Special Issue: Performance Engineering of Computer and Communication Systems (2006)
5. IEEE: *802.11E-2005 IEEE Standard for Information technologyTelecommunications and information exchange between systemsLocal and metropolitan area networksSpecific requirements Part 11: Wireless LAN Medium Access Control (MAC) and Physical Layer (PHY) specifications: Amendment 8: Medium Access Control (MAC) Quality of Service Enhancements* (2005)
6. Ramos, N., Panigrahi, D., Dey, S.: Dynamic Adaptation Policies to Improve Quality of Service of Multimedia Applications in WLAN Networks. In: Proceedings of BroadWIM. (2004)
7. Banchs, A., Costa, X., Qiao, D.: Providing Throughput Guarantees in IEEE 802.11e Wireless LANs. In: Proceedings of the International Teletraffic Congress. (2003)
8. Xiao, Y.: An Analysis for Differentiated Services in IEEE 802.11 and IEEE 802.11e Wireless LANs. In: Proceedings of ICDCS. (2004) 32–39
9. Kim, E., Suh, Y.: ATXOP: An Adaptive TXOP Based on the Data Rate to Guarantee Fairness for IEEE 802.11e Wireless LANs. In: proceedings of IEEE Vehicular Technology Conference. (2004)
10. Gao, D., Cai, J., Zhang, L.: Physical Rate Based Admission Control for HCCA in IEEE 802.11e WLANs. In: Proceedings of the 19th International Conference on Advanced Information Networking and Applications (AINA'05). (2005)

11. Ma, X., Zhu, Y., Niu, Z.: Dynamic Polling Management for QoS Differentiation in IEEE 802.11e Wireless LANs. In: Proceedings of the 10th IEEE Asia-Pacific Conference on Communications. (2004)
12. Ansel, P., Ni, Q., Turletti, T.:   FHCF: An Efficient Scheduling Scheme for IEEE 802.11e. In: ACM/Kluwer Journal on Mobile Networks and Applications (MONET), Special Issue on Modelling and Optimization in Wireless and Mobile Networks. (2005)
13. Fan, W., Gao, D., Tsang, D., Bensaou, B.: Admission Control for Variable Bit Rate traffic in IEEE 802.11e WLANs. In: Proceedings of the 13th IEEE Workshop on Local and Metropolitan Area Networks (LANMAN) SF Bay area. (2004)
14. Ni, Q., Turletti, T., Dabbous, W.:   IEEE 802.11e NS2 Implementation, http://www-sop.inria.fr/planete/qni/fhcf/ (2004)
15. 3GPP: 3GPP TS 22.105 V6.3.0 . Technical report, Third Generation Partnership Project (2005)
16. ITU: ITU-T G.1010, End-user Multimedia QoS Categories . Technical report, International Telecommunications Union (2001)
17. Cisco: (Cisco Call Manager, http://www.cisco.com/warp/public/788/pkt-voice-general/$bwidth\_consume$.html)
18. Stohll, G., Kozamernik, F.: EBU Listening Tests on Internet Audio Codecs. Technical report, EBU (2000)
19. Kozamernik, F.: Media Streaming Over the Internet an Overview of Delivery Technologies. Technical report, EBU (2002)
20. Na, C.: IEEE 802.11 Wireless LAN Traffic Analysis: A Cross-layer Approach. PhD thesis, The University of Texas at Austin (2005)

Worst Case Analysis of Batch Arrivals with the Increasing Convex Ordering[*]

Ana Bušić[1], Jean-Michel Fourneau[1], and Nihal Pekergin[1,2]

[1] PRiSM, Université de Versailles Saint-Quentin-en-Yvelines,
45, Av. des Etats-Unis, 78035 Versailles, France
[2] Centre Marin Mersenne, Université Paris 1, 75013 Paris, France

Abstract. We consider a finite buffer queue with one deterministic server fed by packets arriving in batches. We assume that we are not able to fully describe the batch distribution: only the maximal size and the average number of packets are supposed known. Indeed, these two quantities are simple to measure in a real system. We additionally allow the batch distribution to be state dependent. We analyze the worst case distribution of the queue length and the expectation of lost packets per slot. We show that the increasing convex ordering provides tight bounds for such a system.

1 Introduction

In the case when we do not have complete information but some qualitative and quantitative information, a quite natural approach in many fields of applied probability consists in finding an extremal distribution. For instance, in reliability modelling, one can compute the worst case Increasing Failure Rate distribution knowing the first moment (for the definitions and method see Barlow and Proschan [2, p. 113]).

In Performance Evaluation such a method has received less attention. The major exception are the $(max, +)$ linear equations which naturally arise when one models Stochastic Event Graphs, a subset of Petri Nets (see the book by Baccelli et al. [1] for a considerable survey on these topics). Most of the results obtained in this book can be generalized to models exhibiting stochastic linear recurrence equations in some semirings: for instance (min, max) semiring or $(min, +)$ semiring. These results are based on the properties of the semirings: when we consider more complex algebraic structures most results do not apply any more.

A completely different idea was recently proposed by P. Buchholz [5]. The main assumption is that the modellers do not know the real transition probabilities. Thus, one wants to model a system by a family of Markov chains where the transition probabilities belong to an interval. One has to derive the worst case (or the best case) for all the matrices in the set. The theoretical arguments rely on Courtois's polyhedral approach. The algorithms are very accurate as the

[*] This work was supported by project *Sure-Paths* from ACI and the French "programme blanc" project *SMS*.

A. Horváth and M. Telek (Eds.): EPEW 2006, LNCS 4054, pp. 196–210, 2006.
© Springer-Verlag Berlin Heidelberg 2006

bounds can be reached by a matrix in the set. Unfortunately the complexity is quite high. Very recently a similar problem was solved independently by Haddad and Moreaux [9]. Again one has to find the best and the worst matrices in a set. However, Haddad and Moreaux's approach is based on strong stochastic ordering (st-ordering). The algorithm is simpler but the bounds are generally less accurate. To the best of our knowledge, the two approaches have not been compared on some benchmarking problems.

Our approach combines some of these ideas. We analyze a finite buffer queue with a deterministic service fed by a batch process. The batch distribution can be state dependant. We assume that we know the maximal batch size and the average number of packets in a batch. Note that both quantities are simple to obtain from the specifications of a system or from simple measurements. The maximal size of the batch is the number of inputs in a slotted system and the mean batch size is easily related to the load. A natural question when we analyze such a system is to find the worst batch distribution when we compute the distribution of the queue size, its average, or the average packet loss. Even if the system exhibits a simple evolution equation, the analysis is quite difficult. Indeed, due to the buffer finiteness this equation is based on three operators: max, $+$, and min, and the theory developed in [1] does not apply.

The infinite buffer case has already been studied by several authors [10, 11]. In that case the model has an evolution equation on max and $+$ operators and the analysis is in general much simpler. Unfortunately, the finite buffer case introduces min operator and the underlying monotonicity disappears on the boundary of the state space.

We consider here a different approach based on Markov chains rather than evolution equations. We design an upper bounding monotone chain for the considered system in the sense of the increasing convex order (icx-order). This order is known for a long time [13] but only recently an algorithmic derivation of icx-monotone chains has been proposed [4]. The main advantage of this order is that it is possible to obtain a bound with the same mean as the initial distribution. Such a property is very important here to obtain tight bounds. This property is not valid with the usual st-ordering. Indeed, if X is smaller than Y in the sense of the st-order and if the expectation of X is equal to the expectation of Y, then X equals Y.

The problem we consider is related to the dimensioning of finite buffer in systems with fixed size packets: for instance ATM [14] or optical packet networks like ROM [8]. Such systems are slotted, thus discrete time chains provide natural models. The time slot is the service time and arrivals occur in batches of packets. The maximum batch size is the number of wavelengths in the optical transmission part of the network. The real distribution of batches is unknown and the traffic can be state-dependent. Instead of trying to give more and more details on the traffic, we try to derive a more pessimistic traffic. This traffic will be used to dimension the buffer. Hence our approach is quite different from the traditional traffic engineering approach.

The remaining of the paper is as follows. In Sect. 2 we briefly introduce the icx-order and the useful results proved in [13] and [4]. We also describe the worst case batch distribution in the sence of the icx-order. In Sect. 3 we construct an upper bounding icx-monotone Markov chain for a Batch/D/1/N queue where only the maximal and the average batch size are known, and we show that this chain provides a worst case bound for the queue length. We additionally show how we can use this bound to derive bounds on the number of lost packets. Finally in Sect. 4 we present some numerical results.

2   Some Preliminaries on Stochastic Bounds and the Icx-Worst Case Batch Distribution

In this section we first give some basic definitions and theorems of the stochastic comparison. We refer to [13] for proofs and further details. Then we consider a batch distribution whose average is known and we recall the worst case (largest) distribution for the icx-ordering [15].

2.1   Stochastic Comparison Under the Icx Order

Definition 1. *Let X and Y be two random variables taking values on a totally ordered space $\mathcal{E}$. Then we say that X is smaller than Y in the increasing convex sense (icx),*

$$X \preceq_{icx} Y \text{ if } E(f(X)) \leq E(f(Y)), \text{ for all increasing and convex functions } f,$$

whenever the expectations exist.

In the case of a finite state space $\mathcal{E} = \{0, \ldots, N\}$, we have the following characterization of icx-comparison of two random variables.

Proposition 1. *Let X and Y be two random variables with probability vectors $p = (p_i)_{i=0}^{N}$ and $q = (q_i)_{i=0}^{N}$ ($p_i = P(X = i)$ and $q_i = P(Y = i)$, $\forall i$). Then,*

$$X \preceq_{icx} Y \iff \sum_{k=i}^{N}(k - i + 1)\, p_k \leq \sum_{k=i}^{N}(k - i + 1)\, q_k, \; \forall i \in \{1, \ldots, N\}.$$

Recall that the usual strong stochastic order (st) is generated by the family of all increasing functions. Obviously, $X \preceq_{st} Y$ implies $X \preceq_{icx} Y$, as the family of all increasing functions is larger. Characterization of the st-comparison on a finite space $\mathcal{E} = \{0, \ldots, N\}$ is given by

$$X \preceq_{st} Y \iff \sum_{k=i}^{N} p_k \leq \sum_{k=i}^{N} q_k, \; \forall i \in \{1, \ldots, N\}.$$

Example 1. Let us consider $\mathcal{E} = \{0, \ldots, 3\}$, and let

$$x = (0.5, 0.1, 0.1, 0.3), \; y = (0.3, 0.3, 0.1, 0.3), \text{ and } z = (0.3, 0.2, 0.4, 0.1)$$

be probability vectors on $\mathcal{E}$. Then $x \preceq_{st} y$ and, therefore, $x \preceq_{icx} y$. The vectors x and z are not icx-comparable (and, consequently, not st-comparable), as $x_3 = 0.3 > 0.1 = z_3$, but $x_1 + 2x_2 + 3x_3 = 1.2 < 1.3 = z_1 + 2z_2 + 3z_3$. Finally, vectors y and z are not st-comparable, but $z \preceq_{icx} y$.

The stochastic comparison can be also defined on a process level.

Definition 2. *Let $\{X_k\}_{k\geq0}$ and $\{Y_k\}_{k\geq0}$ be two homogeneous Markov chains. Then,*

$$\{X_k\} \preceq_{icx} \{Y_k\}, \text{ if } X_k \preceq_{icx} Y_k, \text{ for all } k \geq 0.$$

Let us now introduce the comparison and the monotonicity property for stochastic matrices. It is shown in Theorem 5.2.11. of [13, p.186] that comparison and monotonicity of the transition matrices of homogeneous discrete time Markov chains yield sufficient conditions to stochastically compare the underlying chains. Notice that Definitions 2, 3, 4, and Theorem 1 are also valid for the st-order.

Definition 3. *Let $\mathbf{P}$ and $\mathbf{Q}$ be two stochastic matrices. We say that $\mathbf{P} \preceq_{icx} \mathbf{Q}$ if*

$$P_{i,*} \preceq_{icx} Q_{i,*}, \quad \forall i \in \{0,\dots,N\}$$

where $P_{i,*}$ denotes the ith row of matrix $\mathbf{P}$.

Definition 4. *A stochastic matrix $\mathbf{P}$ is said to be icx-monotone if for any probability vectors p and q,*

$$p \preceq_{icx} q \implies p\mathbf{P} \preceq_{icx} q\mathbf{P}.$$

Theorem 1. *Two homogeneous Markov chains $\{X_k\}_{k\geq0}$ and $\{Y_k\}_{k\geq0}$ with the transition matrices $\mathbf{P}$ and $\mathbf{Q}$ satisfy $\{X_k\} \preceq_{icx} \{Y_k\}$, if*

- *$X_0 \preceq_{icx} Y_0$,*
- *$\mathbf{P} \preceq_{icx} \mathbf{Q}$*
- *at least one of matrices $\mathbf{P}$ or $\mathbf{Q}$ is icx-monotone.*

Definition 4 is not very useful in practical applications. We give here the algebraic characterization of icx-comparison for the finite space case. We refer to [3, 4] for the proof. Characterization for the icx-monotonicity for $\mathcal{E} = \mathbb{Z}$ can be found in [12].

Let $\mathbf{P}$ be a stochastic matrix taking values on $\mathcal{E} = \{0,\dots,N\}$. Let us first introduce the following notations:

$$\begin{aligned}\phi_{i,j}(\mathbf{P}) &= \sum_{k=j}^{N}(k-j+1)P_{i,k}, &&0 \leq i \leq N,\ 0 \leq j \leq N,\\ \Delta_{i,j}(\mathbf{P}) &= P_{i,j} - P_{i-1,j}, &&1 \leq i \leq N,\ 0 \leq j \leq N.\end{aligned}$$

We will denote by $\phi(\mathbf{P})$ the matrix $\phi(\mathbf{P}) = (\phi_{i,j}(\mathbf{P}))_{i,j=0}^{N}$.

Proposition 2. *A stochastic matrix $\mathbf{P}$ taking values on $\mathcal{E} = \{0,\dots,N\}$ is icx-monotone if and only if the vector*

$$\phi_{*,j}(\mathbf{P}) = (\phi_{i,j}(\mathbf{P}))_{i=0}^{N} \text{ is increasing and convex, for all } j \in \{1,\dots,N\},$$

i.e.

$$\phi_{1,j}(\mathbf{P}) \geq \phi_{0,j}(\mathbf{P}) \text{ and } \phi_{i+1,j}(\mathbf{P}) + \phi_{i-1,j}(\mathbf{P}) \geq 2\phi_{i,j}(\mathbf{P}),$$

for all $i \in \{1,\dots,N-1\}$, $j \in \{1,\dots,N\}$. Notice that the vector $\phi_{*,j}(\mathbf{P})$ is increasing and convex if and only if the vector $\Delta_{*,j}(\phi(\mathbf{P}))$ is non-negative and increasing.

Example 2. Let us consider the two matrices

$$\mathbf{P} = \begin{pmatrix} 0.2 \ 0.5 \ 0.3 \\ 0.3 \ 0.3 \ 0.4 \\ 0.2 \ 0.3 \ 0.5 \end{pmatrix} \text{ and } \mathbf{Q} = \begin{pmatrix} 0.5 \ 0.4 \ 0.1 \\ 0.3 \ 0.3 \ 0.4 \\ 0.1 \ 0.4 \ 0.5 \end{pmatrix}.$$

Using Proposition 2 it can be easily shown that the matrix $\mathbf{P}$ is icx-monotone, while the matrix $\mathbf{Q}$ is not.

2.2   Icx-Worst Case Batch Distribution

We now study the existence and description of the worst case distribution within the family of all distributions with the same mean. Formally, let $\mathcal{F}_\alpha$ be the family of all probability distributions on the space $\mathcal{E} = \{0, \ldots, N\}$ having the same mean α. This family admits a greatest distribution under the icx-order.

Proposition 3. *The distribution* $q = (1 - \frac{\alpha}{N}, 0, \ldots, 0, \frac{\alpha}{N})$ *satisfies*

$$q \in \mathcal{F}_\alpha \text{ and } p \preceq_{icx} q, \text{ for all } p \in \mathcal{F}_\alpha.$$

See Theorem 2.A.9 of [15] for a proof.

Note that the family $\mathcal{F}_\alpha$ does not admit a greatest element under the st-order. Indeed, if for two random variables X and Y, $Y \preceq_{st} X$ and $E(X) = E(Y)$, then X and Y have the same distribution (see Theorem 1.2.9. of [13, p.5]).

In the next section we consider a finite capacity single server queue with batch arrivals and we are interested in queue length worst case analysis. Distribution q from Proposition 3 will be used to model the unknown batch distribution of a given mean, thus we will refer to it in the following shortly as to "the worst case batch".

Finally, it is worthy to remark that this distribution q is also an icx-bound for batch distributions whose mean is smaller than α.

3   Worst Case Analysis of a Batch/D/1/N Queue

We consider a finite capacity queue with a single server. The queue capacity is N. The service is deterministic and equals to one time slot. The queue is fed by a batch arrival process. We do not assume that the batch arrivals are i.i.d., for instance they can be state dependent. We suppose that we know the maximal size K of the batch. More precisely, let $A_i = (a_0^{(i)}, \ldots, a_K^{(i)})$ denote the distribution of the batch arrivals at state i. The exact values of $a_k^{(i)}$ $(0 \leq k \leq K)$ are unknown. We only know the mean batch size $\alpha = E(A_i)$. In order to have the mean load less than 1, we assume that $\alpha < 1$. Note that the maximum batch size is generally determined from the underlying physical system. For instance, in the case of optical networks the batch size is upper bounded by the number of wavelengths. Both parameters α and K are quite simple to measure or obtain from specifications.

3.1   Upper Bound for the Queue Length

We suppose that $K << N$ and that $0 < \alpha < 1$. We are interested in upper bounding the queue length of an arbitrary Batch/D/1/N queue with the maximal batch size equal to K and the mean batch size equal to α.

First step consists in finding the transition matrix $\mathbf{P}$ such that

$$\mathbf{R} \preceq_{icx} \mathbf{P},$$

for each transition matrix $\mathbf{R}$ of a Batch/D/1/N queue with the maximal batch size equal to K and the mean batch size equal to (or smaller than) α. From the description of icx-worst case batch in the previous section, we easily get:

$$\mathbf{P} = \begin{cases} P_{0,0} = 1 - \frac{\alpha}{K} & P_{0,K} = \frac{\alpha}{K} \\ i = 1, \ldots, N - K + 1 : & P_{i,i-1} = \left(1 - \frac{\alpha}{K}\right) & P_{i,i+K-1} = \frac{\alpha}{K} \\ i = N - K + 2, \ldots, N - 1 : & P_{i,i-1} = \left(1 - \frac{\alpha}{N-i+1}\right) & P_{i,N} = \frac{\alpha}{N-i+1} \\ P_{N,N-1} = (1 - \alpha) & P_{N,N} = \alpha \end{cases}$$

Notice that the rows $i = N - K + 2, \ldots, N$ are obtained by taking the worst case batch (Proposition 3) with the mean batch size equal to α and the maximal batch size equal to $N - i + 1$ (and not K), since we need to assure the icx-comparison of the unknown matrix $\mathbf{R}$ and the matrix $\mathbf{P}$, i.e. $\mathbf{R}_{i,*} \preceq_{icx} \mathbf{P}_{i,*}$, for all i. We want to emphasize that the matrix $\mathbf{P}$ actually belongs to the family of queues we want to bound. However, this matrix is not icx-monotone so we cannot directly apply Theorem 1.

Now we apply to $\mathbf{P}$ a linear transform which does not modify the steady-state distribution,

$$\mathbf{Q} = \delta \mathbf{P} + (1 - \delta)\mathbf{Id},$$

where δ is a real constant, $0 < \delta < 1$. This transform was shown to improve the accuracy for st-bounds [6]. Here it has a crucial role as it allows to move some probability mass to the diagonal elements (see (3) and the proof of Theorem 2).

$$\mathbf{Q} = \begin{cases} Q_{0,0} = 1 - \delta\frac{\alpha}{K} & Q_{0,K} = \delta\frac{\alpha}{K} \\ i = 1, \ldots, N - K + 1 : \\ Q_{i,i-1} = \delta(1 - \frac{\alpha}{K}) & Q_{i,i} = 1 - \delta & Q_{i,i+K-1} = \delta\frac{\alpha}{K} \\ i = N - K + 2, \ldots, N - 1 : \\ Q_{i,i-1} = \delta(1 - \frac{\alpha}{N-i+1}) & Q_{i,i} = 1 - \delta & Q_{i,N} = \delta\frac{\alpha}{N-i+1} \\ Q_{N,N-1} = \delta(1 - \alpha) & Q_{N,N} = 1 - \delta + \delta\alpha \end{cases} \tag{1}$$

Finally, we define the matrix $\mathbf{B}$ as follows:

$$\mathbf{B} = \begin{cases} B_{0,0} = 1 - \delta\frac{\alpha}{K} & B_{0,K} = \delta\frac{\alpha}{K} \\ i = 1, \ldots, N - K + 1 : \\ B_{i,i-1} = \delta(1 - \frac{\alpha}{K}) & B_{i,i} = 1 - \delta & B_{i,i+K-1} = \delta\frac{\alpha}{K} \\ i = N - K + 2, \ldots, N - 1 : \\ B_{i,i-1} = f_i & B_{i,i} = e_i & B_{i,N} = \delta\frac{\alpha}{K}(i - N + K) \\ B_{N,N-1} = \delta(1 - \alpha) & B_{N,N} = 1 - \delta + \delta\alpha \end{cases} \tag{2}$$

where $e_i = 1 - \delta + \delta\alpha - (N - i + 1)B_{i,N}$ and $f_i = 1 - e_i - B_{i,N}$.

This matrix $\mathbf{B}$ will be used to derive the worst case bounds for the underlying system. The proof of the following theorem is given in Appendix.

Theorem 2. *Suppose that*

$$\delta \leq \frac{1}{1 + \alpha U}, \tag{3}$$

where $U = \max_{r=2...K-1} \frac{r(K-r+1)}{K}$. *Then,*

1. **B** *is a stochastic matrix.*
2. **B** *is irreducible.*
3. $\mathbf{Q} \preceq_{icx} \mathbf{B}$.
4. **B** *is icx-monotone.*

Now $\mathbf{Q} \preceq_{icx} \mathbf{B}$ gives $\delta \mathbf{R} + (1 - \delta)\mathbf{Id} \preceq_{icx} \mathbf{B}$, for each transition matrix $\mathbf{R}$ of a Batch/D/1/N queue with the mean batch size smaller or equal to α. Note that **B** is also icx-monotone. Therefore, it follows from Theorem 1 that

$$\pi_{\delta \mathbf{R}+(1-\delta)\mathbf{Id}} \preceq_{icx} \pi_{\mathbf{B}},$$

where $\pi_{\mathbf{A}}$ denotes the steady-state distribution, provided that it exists, of a Markov chain with the transition matrix $\mathbf{A}$. Since $\delta \mathbf{R} + (1 - \delta)\mathbf{Id}$ and $\mathbf{R}$ have the same steady-state distribution, the matrix **B** provides an upper bound for the steady-state queue length distribution of a queue given by matrix $\mathbf{R}$, i.e.

$$\pi_{\mathbf{R}} \preceq_{icx} \pi_{\mathbf{B}}.$$

3.2 Deriving Bounds on Lost Packets

The bounds on the queue length we obtained in Sect. 3.1 can be also used to compute the bounds on the average number of lost packets per slot. As we consider the icx-order, we must prove that the rewards describing the mean number of lost packets are increasing and convex. Unfortunately they are not in general, thus we upper bound the rewards by an increasing and convex function. Recall that we do not know the real batch distribution.

Let us remind that we consider the state dependant batches, where $A_i = (a_0^{(i)}, \ldots, a_K^{(i)}) \in \mathcal{F}_\alpha$ denotes the distribution of batch arrivals in state i. Let us define a reward g, with $g(i)$ equal to the mean number of lost packets in state i,

$$g(i) = \begin{cases} 0, & 0 \leq i \leq N - K + 1 \\ \sum_{k=0}^{K} P(A_i = k)(i - 1 + k - N)^+, & N - K + 2 \leq i \leq N. \end{cases}$$

Proposition 4. *The reward g is upper bounded by the increasing and convex function h,*

$$h(i) = \begin{cases} 0, & 0 \leq i \leq N - K + 1 \\ r\frac{\alpha}{K}, & i = N - K + 1 + r, \ 1 \leq r \leq K - 1. \end{cases}$$

Proof. From $A_i \in \mathcal{F}_\alpha$ and Proposition 3 it follows that

$$A_i \preceq_{icx} q = (1 - \frac{\alpha}{K}, 0, \ldots, 0, \frac{\alpha}{K}), \tag{4}$$

for all $i \in \{0, \ldots, N\}$. On the other hand, for $i = N - K + 1 + r$,

$$g(i) = \sum_{k=0}^{K} a_k^{(i)} (i - 1 + k - N)^+ = \sum_{k=K-r+1}^{K} a_k^{(i)} (k - K + r),$$

for all $r \in \{1, \ldots, K - 1\}$. Now from (4) and Proposition 1 it follows that

$$g(i) = \sum_{k=K-r+1}^{K} a_k^{(i)} (k - K + r) \leq \sum_{k=K-r+1}^{K} q_k (k - K + r),$$

for all $i = N - K + 1 + r$, $r \in \{1, \ldots, K - 1\}$. Notice that only the last term of the right side in the above equation is strictly positive, thus

$$g(i) \leq r \frac{\alpha}{K} = h(i),$$

for all $i = N - K + 1 + r$, $r \in \{1, \ldots, K - 1\}$, and, therefore, $g \leq h$.   □

Finally we can bound the average number of lost packets per slot by the expectation of the reward h on the steady state distribution of matrix $\mathbf{B}$.

4   Numerical Results

As the matrices considered here are very small (up to one thousand states) we use GTH [7], a direct elimination algorithm which is known to be very accurate. First we show that the monotonicity constraints we impose on matrix $\mathbf{B}$ does not have a very important effect on the accuracy of the bound. Recall that the matrix $\mathbf{B}$ was constructed in three steps. First we found the matrix $\mathbf{P}$, the largest transition matrix in the sense of icx-order. There exists a state dependent batch which allows to reach this largest batch matrix. Then we compute matrix $\mathbf{Q}$ which has the same steady state distribution as $\mathbf{P}$. Finally, matrix $\mathbf{B}$ is built from $\mathbf{Q}$ to prove the monotone icx-bound at the steady state. Only the last step of the method can add some perturbation. Tables 1 and 2 illustrate the quality of the bound.

In Table 1 we report the average queue length. Clearly the relative errors are not very large when the load is light or moderate. At heavy load ($\alpha > 0.95$) they are still smaller than 0.5%.

Let us know consider the probability that the queue is full (Table 2). The bounds are now less accurate, especially when the load is light. Even though the relative errors are significant, the probabilities are very small and the absolute errors are not so important. So we advocate that the bounds are tight. The analysis provides a bound which is very close to one matrix in the feasible set. We give in Figure 1 the evolution of the average queue length for the bound when we change the load or the maximum batch size.

Now we consider a state dependent batch. We assume that the queue has some kind of back-pressure mechanism. When the queue size is large, a signal is sent to the sources of traffic to avoid congestion. We assume that this mechanism

Table 1. Comparison of the mean queue length at the steady-state between the "largest-batch" queue (**P**) and the monotone upper bound (**B**) for $N = 1000$

	K=10			K=100		
α	P	B	rel. error	P	B	rel. error
0.5	5.000e+00	5.000e+00	<1.0e-15	5.000e+01	5.000e+01	5.292e-06
0.8	1.880e+01	1.880e+01	<1.0e-15	1.962e+02	1.965e+02	1.708e-03
0.9	4.140e+01	4.140e+01	1.602e-12	3.909e+02	3.924e+02	3.895e-03
0.95	8.645e+01	8.645e+01	4.452e-08	6.038e+02	6.060e+02	3.585e-03
0.99	3.984e+02	3.984e+02	1.670e-05	8.990e+02	8.999e+02	1.085e-03

Table 2. Comparison of $\pi(N)$ at the steady-state between the "largest-batch" queue (**P**) and the monotone upper bound (**B**) for $N = 1000$

	K=10			K=100		
α	P	B	rel. error	P	B	rel. error
0.5	1.375e-60	2.667e-60	9.404e-01	4.169e-07	3.299e-06	6.913e+00
0.8	1.646e-21	2.265e-21	3.759e-01	5.589e-03	1.341e-02	1.400e+00
0.9	9.240e-11	1.094e-10	1.838e-01	8.069e-02	1.261e-01	5.624e-01
0.95	1.154e-05	1.258e-05	9.056e-02	2.889e-01	3.619e-01	2.527e-01
0.99	1.057e-01	1.076e-01	1.788e-02	7.820e-01	8.184e-01	4.648e-02

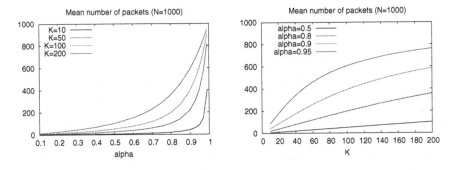

Fig. 1. Upper bounds for the mean number of packets for $N = 1000$

changes the variability of the traffic. The traffic still has the same average but the variability of the batch is now smaller. Typically a traffic shaper can have this effect. More formally we assume that the back-pressure signal is sent when the queue size is larger than 80% of the buffer size. We also assume that the signal instantaneously acts upon the source and that the effect ends when the queue size becomes smaller than the threshold. The batch distribution is the worst batch introduced in Sect. 2 when the queue size is small. When the queue becomes larger than the threshold we assume that the maximal batch size is now 2. Remember that the average batch size is still the same. We present in Table 3 the numerical results for the average number of packets in the queue.

Table 3. Comparison of the mean queue length at the steady-state between the state dependant "back-pressure mechanism batch" (**S**) and the monotone upper bound (**B**) for $N = 1000$

	K=10			K=100		
α	S	B	rel. error	S	B	rel. error
0.5	5.000e+00	5.000e+00	<1.0e-15	5.000e+01	5.000e+01	2.755e-05
0.8	1.880e+01	1.880e+01	<1.0e-15	1.935e+02	1.965e+02	1.526e-02
0.9	4.140e+01	4.140e+01	8.916e-09	3.690e+02	3.924e+02	6.346e-02
0.95	8.644e+01	8.645e+01	9.122e-05	5.453e+02	6.060e+02	1.113e-01
0.99	3.780e+02	3.984e+02	5.396e-02	7.946e+02	8.999e+02	1.325e-01

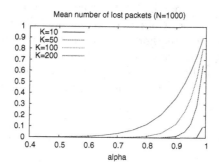

Fig. 2. Upper bounds for the mean number of lost packets

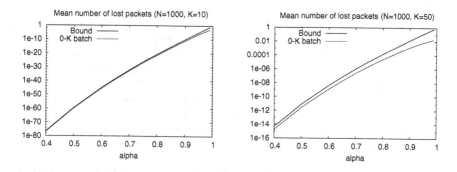

Fig. 3. Exact values and for the mean number of lost packets for "0-K" batch compared to the bound

We compute the exact solution and the bound to check the accuracy of the approach for a large buffer ($N = 1000$). As expected, the bound is very accurate at light load for small and large values of K. At heavy load the relative errors are larger but it is still a good estimate.

Let us now consider the average number of lost packets per slot. We give in Figure 2 the evolution of the mean number of lost packets for the bound as a function of the load. In Figure 3 we compare this bound to the exact mean number of lost packets for the queue with the i.i.d. batch $(1 - \frac{\alpha}{K}, 0, \ldots, 0, \frac{\alpha}{K})$ ("0-K" batch). The approach is acceptable when the load is relatively light. At extremely heavy load (i.e. larger than 0.9) the bounds on the lost packets are not accurate.

5 Conclusion

In this paper, we have shown how we can provide a worst case analysis of a finite buffer queue with deterministic service and batch arrivals when the detailed description of the arrival process is not available. The approach is based on the derivation of a worst case matrix which is larger than the matrix in the set and which is also icx-monotone. Note that to the best of our knowledge it is not easy to apply the coupling method here because we use the icx-ordering rather than the st-ordering. We expect that such a method will help to dimension networking components because it is more and more difficult to really model the traffic characteristics and the worst case analysis is certainly a useful tool in the context of traffic engineering.

References

1. F. Baccelli, G. Cohen, G. J. Olsder, and J.-P. Quadrat. *Synchronization and Linearity: An Algebra for Discrete Event Systems.* Willey, New York, 1992.
2. R. E. Barlow and F. Proschan. *Statistical Theory of Reliability and Life Testing.* Holt, Rinehart and Winston, New York, 1975.
3. M. Ben Mamoun. *Encadrements stochastiques et évaluation de performances des réseaux.* PhD thesis, Université de Versailles Saint-Quentin-en-Yvelines, 2002.
4. M. Ben Mamoun, A. Busic, J.-M. Fourneau, and N. Pekergin. Increasing convex monotone Markov chains: Theory, algorithm and applications. Accepted for Markov Anniversary Meeting, June 2006, Charleston, SC.
5. P. Buchholz. An improved method for bounding stationary measures of finite Markov processes. *Performance Evaluation*, 62:349–365, 2005.
6. T. Dayar, J.-M. Fourneau, and N. Pekergin. Transforming stochastic matrices for stochastic comparison with the st-order. *RAIRO Operations Research*, 37:85–97, 2003.
7. W.K. Grasman, M.I. Taksar, and D.P. Heyman. Regenerative analysis and steady-state distributions for Markov chains. *Oper. Res.*, 13:1107–1116, 1985.
8. P. Gravey, S. Gosselin, C. Guillemot, D. Chiaroni, N. Le Sauze, A. Jourdan, E. Dotaro, D. Barth, P. Berthomé, C. Laforest, S. Vial, T. Atmaca, G. Hébuterne, H. El Biaze, R. Laalaoua, E. Gangloff, and I. Kotuliak. Multiservice optical network: Main concepts and first achievements of the ROM program. *Journal of Ligthwave Technology*, 19:23–31, 2001.
9. S. Haddad and P. Moreaux. Sub-stochastic matrix analysis for bounds computation: Theoretical results. To appear in European Journal of Operational Research.
10. A. Hordijk. Comparison of queues with different discrete-time arrival processes. *Probability in the Engineering and Informational Sciences*, 15:1–14, 2001.

11. G. Koole, M. Nuyens, and R. Righter. The effect of service time variability on maximum queue lengths in $M^X/G/1$ queues. *Journal of Applied Probability*, 42(3): 883–891, 2005.

12. H. Li and M. Shaked. Stochastic convexity and concavity of Markov processes. *Mathematics of Operations Research*, 19(2):477–493, 1994.

13. A. Muller and D. Stoyan. *Comparison Methods for Stochastic Models and Risks*. Wiley, New York, NY, 2002.

14. M. de Prycker. *Asynchronous transfer mode (2nd ed.): solution for broadband ISDN*. Ellis Horwood, Upper Saddle River, NJ, USA, 1993.

15. M. Shaked and J. G. Shantikumar. *Stochastic Orders and their Applications*. Academic Press, San Diego, CA, 1994.

Appendix

In this appendix we give the proof of Theorem 2. Let us first show some properties of diagonal and lower triangular entries of matrices $\mathbf{Q}$ and $\mathbf{B}$.

Lemma 1. *The diagonal entries of matrix* $\phi(\mathbf{Q})$ *have a constant value for all* $i > 0$. *Moreover, the diagonal of matrix* $\phi(\mathbf{B})$ *is equal to the diagonal of matrix* $\phi(\mathbf{Q})$,

$$\phi_{i,i}(\mathbf{B}) = \phi_{i,i}(\mathbf{Q}) = \begin{cases} 1 + \delta\alpha, & i = 0, \\ 1 - \delta + \delta\alpha, & \text{for all } i > 0. \end{cases}$$

Proof. Follows directly from the definitions of matrices $\mathbf{Q}$ and $\mathbf{B}$ (equations (1) and (2)). □

Lemma 2. *The lower triangle entries of matrices* $\phi(\mathbf{Q})$ *and* $\phi(\mathbf{B})$ *have the same values,*

$$\phi_{i,j}(\mathbf{Q}) = \phi_{i,j}(\mathbf{B}) = 1 - \delta + \delta\alpha + (i - j), \ j < i.$$

Proof. Notice that, for $0 \leq i \leq N$, $0 \leq j \leq N - 1$,

$$\phi_{i,j}(\mathbf{P}) = \phi_{i,j+1}(\mathbf{P}) + \sum_{k=j}^{N} P_{i,k}. \tag{5}$$

The statement of the corollary follows directly from Lemma 1, (5), and the fact that $\sum_{k=j}^{N} Q_{i,k} = \sum_{k=j}^{N} P_{i,k} = 1$, for all i, j such that $j < i$. □

Proof of Theorem 2.

1) $\mathbf{B}$ *is a stochastic matrix.* Notice that rows $0, \ldots, N - K + 1$ and row N are the same for matrices $\mathbf{Q}$ and $\mathbf{B}$. For a row $i = N - K + r$, where $2 \leq r \leq K - 1$, we have $0 < \frac{r}{K} < 1$ and $B_{i,N} = \delta\alpha\frac{r}{K}$, thus

$$0 < B_{i,N} < 1, \ i = N - K + 2, \ldots, N - 1. \tag{6}$$

It remains us to show that

$$B_{i,i} = e_i \geq 0 \text{ and } e_i + B_{i,N} \leq 1, \ i = N - K + 2, \ldots, N - 1.$$

Then $B_{i,i-1} = f_i \geq 0$ and $\sum_{j=0}^{N} B_{i,j} = 1$, $i = N - K + 2, \ldots, N - 1$. For a row $i = N - K + r$, where $2 \leq r \leq K - 1$, we have

$$e_i = 1 - \delta + \delta\alpha - \delta\alpha\frac{r(K - r + 1)}{K} \geq 1 - \delta + \delta\alpha - \delta\alpha U. \tag{7}$$

Now from (3) and $\delta\alpha > 0$ it follows that $B_{i,i} = e_i > 0$, $i = N - K + 2, \ldots, N - 1$.
   For a row $i = N - K + r$, where $2 \leq r \leq K - 1$,

$$e_i + B_{i,N} = 1 - \delta(1 - \alpha) - \delta\alpha\frac{r(K - r)}{K} < 1, \tag{8}$$

since $0 < \alpha < 1$. Thus,

$$B_{i,i-1} = f_i = 1 - e_i - B_{i,N} > 0, \quad i = N - K + 2, \ldots, N - 1, \tag{9}$$

and $\mathbf{B}$ is a stochastic matrix.

   2) $\mathbf{B}$ *is irreducible.* Follows easily from (2) and the fact that $0 < \alpha, \delta < 1$.

   3) $\mathbf{Q} \preceq_{icx} \mathbf{B}$, i.e. $\phi_{i,j}(\mathbf{Q}) \leq \phi_{i,j}(\mathbf{B})$, $i = 0, \ldots, N$, $j = 1, \ldots, N$. We need to consider only the rows $i = N - K + 2, \ldots, N - 1$, as the remaining ones are the same for both matrices. Furthermore, from Lemmas 1 and 2 it follows that

$$\phi_{i,j}(\mathbf{Q}) = \phi_{i,j}(\mathbf{B}), \quad j \leq i.$$

On the other hand, from the definition of matrices $\mathbf{Q}$ and $\mathbf{B}$ we have $\phi_{i,j}(\mathbf{Q}) = (N - j + 1)Q_{i,N}$ and $\phi_{i,j}(\mathbf{B}) = (N - j + 1)B_{i,N}$, $N - K + 2 \leq i < j < N$. Therefore, we need only to verify that

$$\phi_{i,N}(\mathbf{Q}) \leq \phi_{i,N}(\mathbf{B}), \quad N - K + 2 \leq i \leq N - 1.$$

For a row $i = N - K + r$, $2 \leq r \leq K - 1$, we have

$$\phi_{i,N}(\mathbf{Q}) \leq \phi_{i,N}(\mathbf{B}) \Leftrightarrow Q_{i,N} \leq B_{i,N}$$
$$\Leftrightarrow \frac{1}{K - r + 1} \leq \frac{1}{K}r$$
$$\Leftrightarrow r^2 - (K + 1)r + K \leq 0$$

The above second order equation has two real roots: 1 and K. Thus, for $r = 2, \ldots, K - 1$, $r^2 - (K + 1)r + K < 0$. Therefore, $\mathbf{Q} \preceq_{icx} \mathbf{B}$.

   4) $\mathbf{B}$ *is icx-monotone.* After Proposition 2 this is equivalent to show that $\phi_{*,j}(\mathbf{B})$ is an increasing and convex vector, i.e. that $\Delta_{*,j}(\phi(\mathbf{B}))$ is a non-negative and increasing vector for all $j = 1, \ldots, N$.

   We will consider the partition of matrix $\phi(\mathbf{B})$ into the following zones:

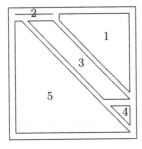

1. $i = 0$, $K + 1 \leq j \leq N$ and
   $1 \leq i \leq N - K$, $i + K \leq j \leq N$
2. $i = 0$, $0 \leq j \leq K$
3. $1 \leq i \leq N - K + 1$, $i + 1 \leq j \leq i + K - 1$
4. $N - K + 2 \leq i \leq N - 1$, $i + 1 \leq j \leq N$
5. $1 \leq i \leq N$, $0 \leq j \leq i$

Matrix $\phi(\mathbf{B})$ can be then written as follows:

Zone 1 : $\phi_{i,j}(\mathbf{B}) = 0$,

Zone 2 : $\phi_{0,0}(\mathbf{B}) = \delta(1 + \alpha)$, $\phi_{0,j}(\mathbf{B}) = (K - j + 1)\delta\frac{\alpha}{K}$, $1 \leq j \leq K$,

Zone 3 : $\phi_{i,j}(\mathbf{B}) = (i + K - j)\delta\frac{\alpha}{K}$, $\qquad\qquad\qquad\qquad\qquad$ (10)

Zone 4 : $\phi_{i,j}(\mathbf{B}) = (i - N + K)(N - j + 1)\delta\frac{\alpha}{K}$, $\qquad\qquad$ (11)

Zone 5 : (Lemmas 1 and 2)

$$\phi_{i,j}(\mathbf{B}) = 1 - \delta + \delta\alpha + (i - j). \qquad\qquad\qquad (12)$$

Zone 1 is trivial as $\phi_{*,j}(\mathbf{B})$ has a constant value 0 within this zone for all j. Notice that for an arbitrary column $\phi_{*,j}(\mathbf{B})$, inside of zones 3, 4, and 5 we have a linear increase:

$$\Delta_{i,j}(\phi(\mathbf{B})) = \delta\frac{\alpha}{K}, \text{ for all } (i - 1, j), (i, j) \text{ in zone 3,} \qquad (13)$$

$$\Delta_{i,j}(\phi(\mathbf{B})) = (N - j + 1)\delta\frac{\alpha}{K}, \text{ for all } (i - 1, j), (i, j) \text{ in zone 4,} \qquad (14)$$

$$\Delta_{i,j}(\phi(\mathbf{B})) = 1, \text{ for all } (i - 1, j), (i, j) \text{ in zone 5.} \qquad (15)$$

Notice that $\delta\frac{\alpha}{K} \leq (N - j + 1)\delta\frac{\alpha}{K}$, since $j \leq N$. Furthermore, inside of zone 4 we have $j \geq i + 1 \geq N - K + 3$. Thus, $(N - j + 1)\delta\frac{\alpha}{K} \leq \delta\alpha\frac{K-3}{K} < 1$, as $\delta\alpha < 1$.

For all j, $1 \leq j \leq N$, column $\Delta_{*,j}(\phi(\mathbf{B}))$ has thus a constant, non-negative value within each of the zones 1, 3, 4, and 5. Additionally, those constants are increasing with the respect of the number of the zone. Notice that the zones are ordered in such a way that each column j crosses the zones in increasing order with respect to the row index.

Some special care has to be done at the boundaries between different zones. We illustrate the procedure on the example of boundaries $3 - 4$ and $4 - 5$. The proof for other boundaries is simpler and it is omitted due to the lack of space.

Boundary $3 - 4$. We have to show that

$$\Delta_{N-K+1,j}(\phi(\mathbf{B})) \leq \Delta_{N-K+2,j}(\phi(\mathbf{B})) \leq \Delta_{N-K+3,j}(\phi(\mathbf{B})), \qquad (16)$$

for all $N - K + 3 \leq j \leq N$. From (13) for $j < N$, $\phi_{N-K+1,N}(\mathbf{B}) = \delta\frac{\alpha}{K}$, and $\phi_{N-K,N}(\mathbf{B}) = 0$ it follows that $\Delta_{N-K+1,j}(\phi(\mathbf{B})) = \delta\frac{\alpha}{K}$, $N - K + 3 \leq j \leq N$. Equations (11) for $(N - K + 2, j)$ and (10) for $(N - K + 1, j)$ imply

$$\Delta_{N-K+2,j}(\phi(\mathbf{B})) = (N - j + 1)\delta\frac{\alpha}{K}, \quad N - K + 3 \leq j \leq N.$$

Thus, the left inequality in (16) holds.

Equation (14) implies $\Delta_{N-K+3,j}(\phi(\mathbf{B})) = (N-j+1)\delta\frac{\alpha}{K}$, $N-K+4 \leq j \leq N$. Thus, the right inequality in (16) holds for $N - K + 4 \leq j \leq N$. It remains us to show $\Delta_{N-K+2,N-K+3}(\phi(\mathbf{B})) \leq \Delta_{N-K+3,N-K+3}(\phi(\mathbf{B}))$. Equations (12) for $(N - K + 3, N - K + 3)$ and (11) for $(N - K + 2, N - K + 3)$ imply $\Delta_{N-K+3,N-K+3}(\phi(\mathbf{B})) = 1 - \delta + \delta\alpha - 2(K - 2)\delta\frac{\alpha}{K}$. Therefore,

$$\Delta_{N-K+2,N-K+3}(\phi(\mathbf{B})) \leq \Delta_{N-K+3,N-K+3}(\phi(\mathbf{B}))$$
$$\Leftrightarrow 1 - \delta + \delta\alpha - \delta\alpha\frac{3(K - 2)}{K} \geq 0.$$

Proposition hypothesis (3) implies $\delta(1+\alpha\frac{3(K-2)}{K}) \leq 1$. Thus, the right inequality in (16) holds also for $j = N - K + 3$.

Boundary $4 - 5$. We have to show that

$$\Delta_{i-1,i}(\phi(\mathbf{B})) \leq \Delta_{i,i}(\phi(\mathbf{B})), \quad N - K + 3 \leq i \leq N, \text{ and} \quad (17)$$
$$\Delta_{i,i}(\phi(\mathbf{B})) \leq \Delta_{i+1,i}(\phi(\mathbf{B})), \quad N - K + 3 \leq i \leq N - 1. \quad (18)$$

From (11) for $(N - K + 2, N - K + 3)$, (10) for $(N - K + 1, N - K + 3)$, and (14) for $i > N - K + 3$, it follows that

$$\Delta_{i-1,i}(\phi(\mathbf{B})) = (N - i + 1)\delta\frac{\alpha}{K}, \quad N - K + 3 \leq i \leq N.$$

Equations (12) for (i, i), (11) for $(i - 1, i)$, and (15) give

$$\Delta_{i,i}(\phi(\mathbf{B})) = 1 - \delta + \delta\alpha - (i - 1 - N + K)(N - i + 1)\delta\frac{\alpha}{K},$$
$$N - K + 3 \leq i \leq N,$$
$$\Delta_{i+1,i}(\phi(\mathbf{B})) = 1, \quad N - K + 3 \leq i \leq N - 1.$$

Since $\alpha < 1$ and $(i - N + K)(N - i) > 0$, $N - K + 3 \leq i \leq N - 1$, (18) holds.

In order to show (17), we have to show that

$$1 - \delta + \delta\alpha - (i - N + K)(N - i + 1)\delta\frac{\alpha}{K} \geq 0, \quad N - K + 3 \leq i \leq N. \quad (19)$$

Notice that, for $N - K + 3 \leq i \leq N - 1$, the left side of the above equation is equal to $B_{i,i} = e_i$ (see (7)), and we have already proved that, under the hypothesis of the proposition, $e_i \geq 0, N - K + 2 \leq i \leq N - 1$. It remains us to show (19) for $i = N$. We have

$$1 - \delta + \delta\alpha - K\delta\frac{\alpha}{K} = 1 - \delta \geq 0.$$

Thus, (18) holds for all i, $N - K + 3 \leq i \leq N$. $\qquad\square$

The Impact of Buffer Finiteness on the Loss Rate in a Priority Queueing System

Jeroen Van Velthoven, Benny Van Houdt*, and Chris Blondia

University of Antwerp, Middelheimlaan 1, B-2020 Antwerpen, Belgium

Abstract. This paper discusses five different ways to approximate the loss rate in a fundamental two class priority system, where each class has its own finite capacity buffer, as well as an exact approach. We identify the type of error one can expect by assuming that one, or both buffers are of infinite size. Furthermore, we investigate whether asymptotic based results can achieve the same level of accuracy as those based on the actual steady state probabilities. Three novel priority queueing models are introduced and efficient algorithms, relying on matrix analytic methods, are developed within this context. A comparative study based on numerical examples is also included.

Keywords: Buffer finiteness, priority queues, loss rate, matrix analytic methods, generating functions.

1 Introduction

The study of priority queues has a long history and is often motivated by their common occurrence in communication networks [16, 17, 3, 4, 8], where they can be used to model Random Access Memory (RAM) buffers and in service part logistics [14, 15]. One of the key performance measures of such a buffer is the loss rate induced by their finite capacity as this strongly affects the network performance. From an analytical point of view, dealing with finite capacity queues is often more troublesome compared to infinite size buffers. Therefore, it is a common practice to analyze the infinite capacity system first and afterward to apply a heuristic method to obtain an estimate of the loss probability for the finite capacity problem (e.g., the probability of having more than C customers in the infinite case is frequently used as an approximation to the loss rate in a finite capacity C setting [6]).

Although this approach has been shown to be fruitful for many queueing systems, more recent results may question such an approach when applied to the (low priority) loss rate in priority queueing system. More specifically, in [2, 10, 16, 17] it is shown that the tail behavior of the low priority buffer occupation might be nongeometric when both the low and high priority buffer is of infinite capacity. Earlier results (e.g., [5]), however, have shown that one typically has geometric tails when the high priority buffer capacity is finite

---

* B. Van Houdt is a post-doctoral fellow of the FWO-Flanders.

A. Horváth and M. Telek (Eds.): EPEW 2006, LNCS 4054, pp. 211–225, 2006.

(and arbitrarily large). One does not expect a substantial difference between having an infinite or a very large finite buffer for the high priority traffic (i.e., any simulation run attains some finite maximum queue length). As such, the correspondence between the infinite and finite capacity C system should grow as C increases. However, the tail behavior of both systems, for any finite C, follows a very different regime, implying that blindly trusting upon asymptotic results may lead to substantial errors. The opposite modeling approach, where infinite size queueing systems are studied by truncation to accomplish a numerical evaluation, also exists [3, 4], further motivating our interest in this subject.

The objective of this paper lies in identifying the approaches that may cause poor estimates. To achieve this goal, we will analyze a fundamental discrete-time queueing system with two priority classes, where each priority class has its own waiting room. To study the impact of the buffer finiteness, we introduce three novel discrete time queueing models with batch arrivals: one to analyze the system where both queues (low and high priority) are finite and two models that evaluate the systems where either one of the buffers is finite. The arrival process considered allows correlation between the number of arrivals of each priority class. There is, however, no correlation between the number of arrivals during consecutive time slots. We further assume a deterministic service time of one time slot for all packets. Although this model is a rather restrictive one, it allows us to isolate the impact of assuming one (or two) infinite size buffers on the accuracy of the loss rate obtained.

A variety of matrix analytic techniques are exploited to assess the (estimated) loss rate for each of the three models with at least one finite capacity buffer. Especially useful is the observation that the system with two finite capacity buffers can be captured by the paradigm developed in [7] for an M/G/1-type Markov chain with some regenerative structure, as well as the explicit knowledge of the G matrix appearing in the M/G/1-type Markov chain for the finite capacity high priority buffer. For the setup where both queues are of infinite size we can rely on existing results involving generating functions [17] to obtain numerical results. In case the low priority traffic has an infinite size capacity buffer, we develop two estimates for the loss rate: one based on a numerical evaluation of the steady state probabilities and another that uses an asymptotic description of the tail behavior. This leads to a total of six different approaches to gather the loss rate of a system with two finite buffers (including five approximations).

Notice, although the methods developed in [3] are closely related to the model with an infinite high and finite low capacity buffer, they do not apply directly as batch arrivals are not considered in [3]. Finally, some of the solution techniques can be adapted such that they still apply to a more general setting (i.e., more general service times).

2 System Characteristics

We consider a discrete-time single-server multi-class queueing system with a priority scheduling discipline. We consider a system with two priority classes, denoted as the high (class-1) and the low (class-2) priority class. The arrival process is chosen as in [10, 16, 17] and is characterized by the probabilities

$$a(i_1, i_2) \overset{\Delta}{=} Prob[a_1 = i_1, a_2 = i_2], \tag{1}$$

where a_j denotes the number of arriving packets of class-j during a time slot. The corresponding joint probability generating function is given by

$$A(z_1, z_2) \overset{\Delta}{=} E\left[z_1^{a_1} z_2^{a_2}\right] = \sum_{i_1=0}^{\infty} \sum_{i_2=0}^{\infty} a(i_1, i_2) z_1^{i_1} z_2^{i_2}. \tag{2}$$

Notice that the number of arrivals from different classes in one slot can be correlated. There is however no correlation between the number of arrivals during consecutive time slots. For further use, let $a_1(i) = \sum_{i_2=0}^{\infty} a(i, i_2)$, $a_2(i) = \sum_{i_1=0}^{\infty} a(i_1, i)$, $a_1^*(i) = \sum_{k=i}^{\infty} a_1(k)$ and $a_2^*(i) = \sum_{k=i}^{\infty} a_2(k)$. The class-$i$ arrival rate λ_i equals $\sum_{k=1}^{\infty} a_i^*(k)$.

We assume a deterministic service time of one time slot for all the packets. Although this assumption is rather strong, it allows us to isolate the impact of assuming one (or two) infinite size buffers on the accuracy of the loss rate obtained. There are two buffers, one for the high and one for the low priority traffic. If an arriving packet finds the server busy, it joins the appropriate buffer. The class-1 packets have priority over these of class-2 and within each class the service discipline is assumed to be First Come First Served. Therefore, when a packet completes its service, the class-1 packet with the longest waiting time will be served. If there are no high priority packets available, the oldest low priority packet is selected for service.

In the next sections, we discuss four different cases, where the buffer size of the two buffers is either finite or infinite. For each situation, we determine the steady state probabilities of the system contents distribution, which can, among others be used to calculate loss probability of the class-2 packets. In each of these models, all events such as arrivals, service completions and packet losses are assumed to occur at instants immediately after the discrete time epochs. We further assume that departures occur before arrivals.

3 Finite High Priority Buffer

Let us first discuss the above-mentioned queueing system provided that the class-1 buffer is finite, with a capacity H, and the class-2 buffer is infinite. We can model this system using an M/G/1-type Markov chain represented by the following transition matrix:

$$P = \begin{bmatrix} B_0 & B_1 & B_2 & B_3 & \dots \\ A_0 & A_1 & A_2 & A_3 & \dots \\ 0 & A_0 & A_1 & A_2 & \dots \\ 0 & 0 & A_0 & A_1 & \dots \\ \vdots & \vdots & \vdots & \vdots & \ddots \end{bmatrix}. \tag{3}$$

We denote the states of this Markov chain as $\langle i, j \rangle$, where the level $i \geq 0$ denotes the number of low priority packets in the queueing system and $j = 0, \ldots, H+1$ reflects the number of high priority packets. An expression for the $(H+2) \times (H+2)$ matrices A_i $(i = 0, 1, \ldots)$ is given first. A transition to a lower level can only occur, if there are no high priority packets present in the system, otherwise such a packet is served, preventing any low priority packet from leaving the system. As a consequence only the first row of the matrix A_0 contains non-zero probabilities. A second condition in order to have a transition to a lower level is that no low priority packets arrive during the current time slot. Hence,

$$A_0 = e_1(a(0,0), a(1,0), a(2,0), \ldots, a^*(H+1,0)), \tag{4}$$

where $a^*(i, j) = \sum_{k=i}^{\infty} a(k, j)$ and e_1 is a column vector with all its entries equal to zero, except for the first which equals one. The transitions from state $\langle i, j \rangle$ to state $\langle i+k, j' \rangle$ are covered by the matrix A_{k+1}, for $i \geq 1$ and $k \geq 0$. We distinguish two cases: $j = 0$ and $j > 0$. In the first case, a low priority packet is in service; hence, $k+1$ low priority packets need to arrive in order to get a transition to level $i+k$. In the latter case, a class-1 packet occupies the server. A transition to level $i+k$ thus occurs if k class-2 packets arrive. This yields,

$$A_{k+1} = \begin{bmatrix} a(0, k+1) & a(1, k+1) & a(2, k+1) & \cdots & a^*(H+1, k+1) \\ a(0, k) & a(1, k) & a(2, k) & \cdots & a^*(H+1, k) \\ 0 & a(0, k) & a(1, k) & \cdots & a^*(H, k) \\ \vdots & \ddots & \ddots & \ddots & \vdots \\ 0 & \cdots & 0 & a(0, k) & a^*(1, k) \end{bmatrix}. \tag{5}$$

Finally, the matrix B_k contains the probabilities of having a transition from level zero to level k. Level zero corresponds to having zero class-2 packets in the system, implying that k low priority packets must arrive to enter a level k state, for $k \geq 0$,

$$B_k = \begin{bmatrix} a(0, k) & a(1, k) & a(2, k) & \cdots & a^*(H+1, k) \\ a(0, k) & a(1, k) & a(2, k) & \cdots & a^*(H+1, k) \\ 0 & a(0, k) & a(1, k) & \cdots & a^*(H, k) \\ \vdots & \ddots & \ddots & \ddots & \vdots \\ 0 & \cdots & 0 & a(0, k) & a^*(1, k) \end{bmatrix}. \tag{6}$$

To calculate the steady state vector $x = (x_0, x_1, x_2, \ldots)$, with x_k a $1 \times (H+2)$ vector for $k \geq 0$, of P, i.e., the joint system contents distribution, Ramaswami's formula [13, 12, 11] can be used. This formula requires x_0 and a (stochastic) matrix G, being the smallest nonnegative solution of $G = \sum_{k=0}^{\infty} A_k G^k$, as its input. The (j, k)-th entry of this matrix represents the probability that, starting from state $\langle i+1, j \rangle$, the Markov chain visits the set of states $\{\langle i, 0 \rangle, \ldots, \langle i, H+1 \rangle\}$ the first time by entering the state $\langle i, k \rangle$. Finding G is often by far the bottleneck when computing the invariant vector of an M/G/1-type MC. However, in this setup, a transition to a lower level can only occur when there are no high priority packets in the system and there is no arrival of low priority traffic at the current time instant. As a consequence, all the rows of G are identical and can be given explicitly by the vector $\alpha = (a(0,0), a(1,0), a(2,0), \ldots, a^*(H+1,0))/a^*(0,0)$. Notice that $G^k = G = e\alpha$ for $k > 0$ and $g = \alpha$, where g is the unique solution of $gG = g$, with $ge = 1$ and e a column vector of ones. Combining [12, Chapter 3] and the structure of the A_k and B_k matrices with these properties, the following algorithm to compute x can be devised:

Algorithm 3.1: [H/∞]

1. Input: the probabilities $a(i_1, i_2)$ for $0 \leq i_1$ and $0 \leq i_2$, concerning the arrival process and the capacity H of the buffer for the high priority traffic.
2. Determine the matrices A_k and B_k ($k \geq 0$) using Eqn. (4), (5) and (6).
3. Calculate $\rho = \pi\beta$, where π is the vector representing the stationary distribution of the stochastic matrix $A = \sum_{k=0}^{\infty} A_k$ and $\beta = (1+\lambda_2)e - e_1$.
4. Next, set $\tilde{\kappa}_1 = \psi_2 + (B_1 + a_2^*(2)e\alpha)(I - A_1 - a_2^*(1)e\alpha + a_2(1)e_1\alpha)^{-1}\psi_1$, where I is the identity matrix of the appropriate dimension. The vectors ψ_1 and ψ_2 are given by the following expressions:

$$\psi_1 = (I - A_0 - A_1)(I - e\alpha)(I - A + (e - \beta)\alpha)^{-1}e$$
$$+(1-\rho)^{-1}a_2(0)e_1,$$
$$\psi_2 = (B - B_0 - B_1)(I - e\alpha)(I - A + (e - \beta)\alpha)^{-1}e$$
$$+(1-\rho)^{-1}(\lambda_2 - \rho + a_2(0))e,$$

   where $B = \sum_{k=0}^{\infty} B_k$.
5. The vector x_0 containing the steady state probabilities that there are no low priority packets in the system, is given by $x_0 = (\kappa\tilde{\kappa}_1)^{-1}\kappa$ with κ the invariant probability vector of $K = B_0 + (I - B_0)e\alpha$.
6. Finally, the following recursion is used to calculate the remaining vectors x_i of the steady state distribution:

$$x_i = \left(x_0\bar{B}_i + \sum_{j=1}^{i-1} x_j\bar{A}_{i+1-j}\right)(I - \bar{A}_1)^{-1}, \qquad i > 0. \qquad (7)$$

In this expression we have $\bar{A}_k = A_k + (a_2^*(k)e - a_2(k)e_1)\alpha$ and $\bar{B}_k = B_k + a_2^*(k+1)e\alpha$, for $k \geq 0$.

Notice, the matrices A_k, B_k, $\bar{A}_k$, $\bar{B}_k$, etc. are fully characterized by their first (or first two) rows; hence, there is no need to store more than one (two) rows for each of these matrices.

In this section, we assumed an infinite size low priority buffer. In practice, buffers are finite and some low priority losses can occur. To estimate the loss probability of the class-2 packets, given the maximum capacity L of the corresponding buffer, we can use the following standard approach in queueing[1]. This

---

[1] High priority buffers are usually dimensioned such that hardly any losses occur, therefore, we focus on the low priority packets.

approach approximates the packet loss in a finite size L buffer, by the expected value of $\max(0,\text{number of packets waiting} -L)$ in an infinite size system:

$$P_{loss} \approx \sum_{k=L+1}^{\infty} (k-L)x_k e - x_{L+1}(0), \tag{8}$$

where $x_{L+1} = (x_{L+1}(0), x_{L+1}(1), \ldots, x_{L+1}(H))$. The accuracy of this estimate is studied in Section 7. Apart from computing the steady state vector $x = (x_0, x_1, x_2, \ldots)$ in an exact manner via Algorithm 3.1, we can also rely on a theorem by Falkenberg [5, Theorem 3.5], that describes the tail behavior of an M/G/1-type MC, to approximate x_k for k large. This theorem states that the tail will typically decay geometrically, with parameter τ. This parameter is the solution $\tau > 1$ to $\xi \left(\sum_{k=0}^{\infty} A_k z^k \right) = z$, with $\xi(X)$ representing the Perron-Frobenius eigenvalue of the matrix X, and can be computed by a simple bisection algorithm. By plugging the approximated x_k values in (8), we find an alternative estimate for the class-2 loss probability. We will refer to this approach as the H/∞_t approach (as opposed to the H/∞ approach of Algorithm 3.1).

4   Finite Low Priority Buffer

Consider the same system as in Section 3, but with an infinite buffer for the high priority traffic and a finite one of size L for the low priority traffic. As before, we start by setting up an M/G/1-type Markov chain to describe the system. The transition matrix of this Markov chain is given by

$$P = \begin{bmatrix} B_0 & B_1 & B_2 & B_3 & \cdots \\ C_0 & A_1 & A_2 & A_3 & \cdots \\ 0 & A_0 & A_1 & A_2 & \cdots \\ 0 & 0 & A_0 & A_1 & \cdots \\ \vdots & \vdots & \vdots & \vdots & \ddots \end{bmatrix}, \tag{9}$$

with A_k $(k \geq 0)$ an $(L+1) \times (L+1)$ matrix, B_k $(k > 0)$ an $(L+2) \times (L+1)$ matrix, B_0 an $(L+2) \times (L+2)$ matrix and C_0 an $(L+1) \times (L+2)$ matrix. The different dimensions originate from the fact that there can be $L+1$ low priority packets in the system only if there are no packets of high priority present. Within a level, the states of this Markov chain correspond to the number of low priority packets; thus, level zero contains one additional state. Arguments similar to the one presented in Section 3 yield the following expressions:

$$A_k = \begin{bmatrix} a(k,0) & a(k,1) & \cdots & \bar{a}(k,L) \\ 0 & a(k,0) & \cdots & \bar{a}(k,L-1) \\ \vdots & \ddots & \ddots & \vdots \\ 0 & \cdots & 0 & \bar{a}(k,0) \end{bmatrix}, \quad k \geq 0, \tag{10}$$

$$B_0 = \begin{bmatrix} a(0,0) & a(0,1) & a(0,2) & \cdots & \bar{a}(0,L+1) \\ a(0,0) & a(0,1) & a(0,2) & \cdots & \bar{a}(0,L+1) \\ 0 & a(0,0) & a(0,1) & \cdots & \bar{a}(0,L) \\ \vdots & \ddots & \ddots & \ddots & \vdots \\ 0 & \cdots & 0 & a(0,0) & \bar{a}(0,1) \end{bmatrix}, \tag{11}$$

$$B_k = \begin{bmatrix} a(k,0) & a(k,1) & \cdots & \bar{a}(k,L) \\ a(k,0) & a(k,1) & \cdots & \bar{a}(k,L) \\ 0 & a(k,0) & \cdots & \bar{a}(k,L-1) \\ \vdots & \ddots & \ddots & \vdots \\ 0 & \cdots & 0 & \bar{a}(k,0) \end{bmatrix}, \quad k > 0 \tag{12}$$

and

$$C_0 = \begin{bmatrix} a(0,0) & a(0,1) & a(0,2) & \cdots & \bar{a}(0,L+1) \\ 0 & a(0,0) & a(0,1) & \cdots & \bar{a}(0,L) \\ \vdots & \ddots & \ddots & \ddots & \vdots \\ 0 & \cdots & 0 & a(0,0) & \bar{a}(0,1) \end{bmatrix}, \tag{13}$$

where $\bar{a}(i,j) = \sum_{k=j}^{\infty} a(i,k)$. Given these expressions, we only need to find x_0 and the matrix G before we can apply Ramaswami's formula to compute $x = (x_0, x_1, \ldots)$. For this setup, there is no explicit expression for G. However, various iterative algorithms can be used to compute G. A low memory implementation can be achieved using the following basic scheme: $G_0 = I, G_n = \sum_{k=0}^{\infty} A_k G_{n-1}^k$. The time needed to execute one iteration can be reduced by observing that only the first row has to be calculated for the entire matrix to be known. That is, the matrix G_n is a triangular matrix with the following structure (due to the probabilistic interpretation of G) :

$$G_n = \begin{bmatrix} G(0) & G(1) & \cdots & G(L) \\ 0 & G(0) & \ddots & G^*(L-1) \\ \vdots & \ddots & \ddots & \vdots \\ 0 & \cdots & 0 & G^*(0) \end{bmatrix},$$

where $G^*(i) = \sum_{k=i}^{L} G(k)$. Hence, the steady state vector of the stochastic matrix G is given by $g = (0, 0, \ldots, 1)$. Similarly, as $A = \sum_k A_k$ is also triangular, its invariant vector $\pi = (0, 0, \ldots, 1)$ as well. Furthermore, the matrices A_k, B_k and $C_0 (k \geq 0)$ can be represented by their first row and both $A_k e$ and $B_k e$ equal $a_1(k)e$ (for $k \geq 0$). This leads to the following simplifications: $\beta = \lambda_1 e$, $\rho = \lambda_1$, $\psi_1 = \psi_2 = a_1(0)(1 - \lambda_1)^{-1} e$ and $\tilde{\kappa}_1 = (1 - \lambda_1)^{-1} e$. These expression can be obtained from [12, Chapter 3] by noticing that $(I - A + (e - \beta)g)^{-1} e = \sum_{k=0}^{\infty} (A - (e - \beta)g)^k e = \sum_{k=0}^{\infty} \lambda_1^k e = (1 - \lambda_1)^{-1} e$. Therefore, the following algorithm can be used to compute $x = (x_0, x_1, x_2, \ldots)$:

Algorithm 4.1: [∞/L]

1. Input: the probabilities $a(i_1, i_2)$ for $0 \leq i_1$ and $0 \leq i_2$, concerning the arrival process and the capacity L of the buffer for the class-2 traffic.
2. Determine the matrices A_k, B_k $(k \geq 0)$ and C_0 using the Eqn. (10), (11), (12) and (13).
3. Set $x_0 = (\kappa \tilde{\kappa}_1)^{-1}\kappa = (1 - \lambda_1)\kappa$ with κ the invariant probability vector of the matrix K:

$$K = B_0 + \left(\sum_{k=1}^{\infty} B_k G^{k-1} \right) \left(I - \sum_{k=1}^{\infty} A_k G^{k-1} \right)^{-1} C_0.$$

4. Finally, we can use the following iteration to calculate the other vectors of the steady state distribution:

$$x_i = \left(x_0 \bar{B}_i + \sum_{j=1}^{i-1} x_j \bar{A}_{i+1-j} \right) (I - \bar{A}_1)^{-1}, \qquad i > 0, \qquad (14)$$

where $\bar{A}_k = \sum_{i=k}^{\infty} A_i G^{i-k}$ and $\bar{B}_k = \sum_{i=k}^{\infty} B_i G^{i-k}$, for $k \geq 0$.

As A_k, B_k and G are fully characterized by their first row, so are the $\bar{A}_k$ and $\bar{B}_k$ matrices, allowing a significant reduction in the computing time and storage space needed to implement Ramaswami's formula (i.e., (14)). Having found the steady state probabilities, $x_j(k)$ denotes the steady state probability of having j high and k low priority packets in the system. Define $\bar{a}^*(i, j) = \sum_{k=i}^{\infty} \sum_{l=j}^{\infty} a(k, l)$.

Let us now take a look at the calculation of the loss rate of class-2 packets. Low priority packets are lost when the buffer has reached its maximum capacity upon their arrival. This happens in the following two cases:

- The system contains $j = 0, 1$ class-1 packets, i class-2 packets (for $0 \leq i \leq L + 1 - j$) and (a) at least one high and $L + 1 - [i - \bar{\jmath}]^+$ low priority packets arrive (where $[x]^+ = \max(0, x)$ and $\bar{\jmath} = j + 1 \mod 2$) or (b) no high and at least $L + 2 - [i - \bar{\jmath}]^+$ low priority packets arrive. Notice, $[i - \bar{\jmath}]^+$ represents the number of class-2 packets left behind by the possible departure and seen by the new arrivals. The expected number of losses due to these cases corresponds to

$$\sum_{j=0}^{1} \sum_{i=0}^{L+1-j} x_j(i) \left(\sum_{k=L+1-[i-\bar{\jmath}]^+}^{\infty} \bar{a}^*(1, k) + \sum_{k=L+2-[i-\bar{\jmath}]^+}^{\infty} \bar{a}(0, k) \right).$$

- There are j $(j > 1)$ class-1, i $(0 \leq i \leq L)$ class-2 packets and more than $L - i$ low priority packets arrive. The expected number of losses caused by these cases equals $\sum_{j=2}^{\infty} \sum_{i=0}^{L} x_j(i) \left(\sum_{k=L+1-i}^{\infty} \bar{a}_2^*(k) \right)$.

The loss rate of the class-2 traffic can now be calculated by taking the sum of these two expressions. We expect that this approach provides us with a more accurate estimation than the one presented in the previous section, keeping in mind that the high priority queue is typically dimensioned sufficiently large such that hardly any losses occur. In Section 7 we will give some numerical examples in which both approaches are compared.

5   Two Finite Buffers

This section focuses on the system with both a finite, size L low and finite, size H high priority traffic buffer. In practice, all buffers are finite, thus the results obtained in this section are the most relevant. The system state, captured by the number of low and high priority customers in the queue, can be described by a Markov chain with the following transition matrix P:

$$
P =
\begin{bmatrix}
B_0 & B_1 & \dots & B_{L-1} & D_L & C_L \\
A_0 & A_1 & \dots & A_{L-1} & D_{L-1} & C_{L-1} \\
0 & A_0 & \ddots & A_{L-2} & D_{L-2} & C_{L-2} \\
\vdots & \ddots & \ddots & \vdots & \vdots & \vdots \\
\vdots & & \ddots & A_0 & D_0 & C_0 \\
0 & & \dots\dots & 0 & F & E
\end{bmatrix}.
\tag{15}
$$

As in Section 3, the states are labeled as $\langle i, j \rangle$, with i and j reflecting the number of low and high priority customers, respectively. Notice that the states $\langle L + 1, j \rangle$ can only be reached if $j = 0$. Otherwise, a high priority customer will occupy the server, leaving only L buffer places available for the low priority traffic. As a consequence C_i $(0 \leq i \leq L)$ are column vectors, F is a row vector, and E is a scalar.

In many applications, the dimension of the buffer for the class-1 traffic is significantly smaller than the class-2 buffer. Keeping this in mind, choosing the representation above allows us to work with relatively smaller matrices then would be the case when the order of both variables would be switched. Moreover, this choice also causes P to have a useful regenerative structure. The expressions for the matrices A_k and B_k $(0 \leq k < L)$ are identical to those given in Section 3 and as a consequence the matrix $G = e\alpha$, being the smallest nonnegative solution to $G = \sum_{i=0}^{\infty} A_i G^i$, is again known explicitly.

Let us now determine the expressions for the matrices C_k, D_k, E and F. First, the matrix C_k $(0 \leq k \leq L)$ contains the probabilities of having a transition to level $L + 1$, which can only occur when there are no high priority packets in the system during the next time slot. Meaning, C_k is a column vector, the first two entries of which only differ form zero:

$$
C_L =
\begin{bmatrix}
\bar{a}(0, L+1) \\
\bar{a}(0, L+1) \\
0 \\
\vdots \\
0
\end{bmatrix}
\quad \text{and } C_k =
\begin{bmatrix}
\bar{a}(0, k+2) \\
\bar{a}(0, k+1) \\
0 \\
\vdots \\
0
\end{bmatrix}, \ 0 \leq k < L.
\tag{16}
$$

A similar argument can be used to find

$$E = \bar{a}(0,1) \tag{17}$$

The transitions to level L are described by D_k $(0 \le k \le L)$ and F, and can be written as:

$$D_L = \begin{bmatrix} a(0,L) & \bar{a}(1,L) & \bar{a}(2,L) & \cdots & \bar{a}^*(H,L) \\ a(0,L) & \bar{a}(1,L) & \bar{a}(2,L) & \cdots & \bar{a}^*(H,L) \\ 0 & \bar{a}(0,L) & \bar{a}(1,L) & \cdots & \bar{a}^*(H-1,L) \\ \vdots & \ddots & \ddots & \ddots & \vdots \\ 0 & \cdots & 0 & \bar{a}(0,L) & \bar{a}^*(1,L) \end{bmatrix}, \tag{18}$$

$$D_k = \begin{bmatrix} a(0,k+1) & \bar{a}(1,k+1) & \bar{a}(2,k+1) & \cdots & \bar{a}^*(H,k+1) \\ a(0,k) & \bar{a}(1,k) & \bar{a}(2,k) & \cdots & \bar{a}^*(H,k) \\ 0 & \bar{a}(0,k) & \bar{a}(1,k) & \cdots & \bar{a}^*(H-1,k) \\ \vdots & \ddots & \ddots & \ddots & \vdots \\ 0 & \cdots & 0 & \bar{a}(0,k) & \bar{a}^*(1,k) \end{bmatrix} \tag{19}$$

and

$$F = (a(0,0), \bar{a}(1,0), \bar{a}(2,0), \ldots, \bar{a}^*(H,0)), \tag{20}$$

Now that we have derived an expression for the building blocks of the transition matrix P, we are in a position to calculate its steady state distribution $x = (x_0, x_1, \ldots, x_{L+1})$. P is a downward skip-free finite transition matrix with a special regenerative structure, in [7, Theorem 4.1] Ishizaki introduced an efficient algorithm (similar to Ramaswami's formula) to compute the steady state vector of such a matrix P. Applying this algorithm to our setting and using the same notations as in Section 3, we can calculate the steady state probabilities by means of the following set of equations:

Algorithm 5.1: [H/L]

1. Input: the probabilities $a(i_1, i_2)$ for $0 \le i_1$ and $0 \le i_2$, concerning the arrival process and both buffer capacities L and H.
2. Determine the matrices A_k, B_k $(0 \le k \le L-1)$, C_k, D_k $(0 \le k \le L)$, E and F using Eqns. (4–6) and (16–20).
3. Let x_0 be the stochastic solution of $x_0 = x_0 K$, where $K = B_0 + (I - B_0)e\alpha$.
4. Set $x_i = \left(x_0 \bar{B}_i + \sum_{k=1}^{i-1} x_k \bar{A}_{i-k+1} \right) (I - \bar{A}_{i,1})^{-1}$ for $i = 1, \ldots, L-1$, where the matrices $\bar{A}_k$ and $\bar{B}_k$ were defined in step 6 of Algorithm 3.1.
5. Let $x_L = \left(\sum_{k=0}^{L-1} x_k (D_{L-k} + C_{L-k}F^*) \right) (I - \bar{D}_0)^{-1}$, where $F^* = F/(Fe)$ and $\bar{D}_0 = D_0 + C_0 F^*$.
6. Compute $x_{L+1} = \left(\sum_{i=0}^{N} x_i C_{L-i} \right) (1 - E)^{-1}$.
7. Normalize $x = (x_0, x_1, \ldots, x_{L+1})$ such that $\sum_{i=0}^{L+1} x_i e = 1$.

Observe that we compute $(x_0, \ldots, x_{L-1})$ in exactly the same way as in Section 3, except that x_0 is not normalized. Normalization occurs after computing x_L and x_{L+1}. Thus, obtaining results for the system with two finite buffers is almost computationally equivalent to solving the finite/infinite system. This is exceptional as finite buffer systems typically demand more computational power. Using these steady state probabilities, the loss probability of the class-2 packets can be calculated in the same way as in Section 4.

6 Two Infinite Buffers

To analyze the system where both buffers are of infinite size, we can rely on some existing results in the literature. From [17], it follows that the probability generating function $Q_2(z)$ of the number of class-2 packets waiting in the queue can be written as

$$Q_2(z) = (1 - \lambda)\frac{(z - 1)(Y(z) - 1)}{(z - Y(z))(A(1, z) - 1)}, \tag{21}$$

where $Y(z)$ is implicitly defined by $Y(z) = A(Y(z), z)$. From Rouché's theorem, it can be seen that there is exactly one solution for $Y(z)$, with $|Y(z)| \leq 1$ for $|z| < 1$. There are two approaches to retrieve an estimate for the class-2 loss probability from (21). The first involves a numerical inversion of the generating function to obtain an approximation for the distribution of the number of class-2 packets present in the buffer. The inversion is realized using a discrete Fourier transform method (DFT), where a damping parameter $0 < r < 1$ is used [1]. We make use of a damping parameter such that when evaluating $Q_2(z)$ at $r\omega_N^s$, where ω_N^s for $s = 0, \ldots, N - 1$ are the N-th roots of unity, $Y(z)$ is uniquely defined by Rouché's theorem as $|r\omega_N^s| < 1$. This leads to the following algorithm:

Algorithm 6.1: $[\infty/\infty]$

1. Input: the probabilities $a(i_1, i_2)$ for $0 \leq i_1$ and $0 \leq i_2$, concerning the arrival process.
2. Evaluate $Q_2(z)$ at $r\omega_N^s$, where ω_N^s for $s = 0, \ldots, N - 1$ are the N-th roots of unity (where N is a power of 2 sufficiently large). This entails that we have to determine the unique solution of $Y(z) = A(Y(z), z)$, with $|Y(z)| < 1$, for each $z = r\omega_N^s$.
3. Compute q_k, for $k = 0, \ldots, N - 1$, via the inverse DFT. The values q_k can be used as an approximation to the probability of having k buffered class-2 packets.

In [9], it is argued that as long as enough numerical precision is used, the desired probabilities can be obtained to any given accuracy. Therefore, it is advised to use a software package that supports high numerical precision when implementing this algorithm (e.g., Maple or Mathematica). The class-2 loss probability can be estimated as $P_{loss} \approx \sum_{k=L+1}^{\infty}(k - L)q_k$.

A second approach is to rely on the tail behavior of (21) to get an alternate approximation q'_k for the probability of having k class-2 packets buffered. A description of the tail behavior of interest can be found easily from [17, Eqn. (21)]. The key in generating numerical results from these expressions is the computation of the real numbers $z_T > 1$ and $z_B > 1$: these numbers are the solutions to $A(z, z) = z$ and $A^{(1)}(Y(z), z) = 1$ (where $A^{(1)}(z_1, z_2)$ is the first partial derivative of $A(z_1, z_2)$), respectively. As $A(z, z)$ is a convex function with $A(1, 1) = 1$ and $\left. \frac{dA(z,z)}{dz} \right|_{z=1} < 1$ (otherwise the system would be unstable), we can apply a simple bisection algorithm to find z_T. For z_B we can use the following algorithm:

Algorithm 6.2: $[\infty/\infty_t]$

1. Set $z_{2:min} = 1$ and $z_{2:max} = 2$. Determine $z_1 > 1$ via a bisection algorithm such that $A^{(1)}(z_1, z_{2:max}) = 1$. As long as $A(z_1, z_{2:max})$ is less than z_1, increase $z_{2:min}$ and $z_{2:max}$ by one.
2. Let $z_{2:new} = (z_{2:min} + z_{2:max})/2$. Determine $z_1 > 1$ via a bisection algorithm such that $A^{(1)}(z_1, z_{2:new}) = 1$. If $z_1 < A(z_1, z_{2:new})$, assign $z_{2:new}$ to $z_{2:max}$, else $z_{2:min} = z_{2:new}$. Repeat step 2 until $z_{2:max} - z_{2:min} < 10^{-14}$.

For details on how to compute an approximation q'_k given z_T and z_B we refer to [17].

7   Numerical Examples

In this section we will compare the discussed approaches to estimate the loss probability of the low priority traffic. Let us first describe the arrival process under consideration. The number of arrivals during one time slot is bounded by N and is generated by a Bernoulli process with rate λ_T/N, where an arriving packet belongs to class-j $(j = 1, 2)$, with a probability λ_j/λ_T (with $\lambda_1 + \lambda_2 = \lambda_T$). This arrival process is characterized by the joint probability generating function

$$A(z_1, z_2) = \left(1 + \sum_{j=1}^{2} \frac{\lambda_j}{N}(z_j - 1) \right)^N . \tag{22}$$

It was also used in [16] where a non-blocking output-queueing switch with N inlets and N outlets was given as a possible application.

More specifically, we assume the maximum number of simultaneously arriving packets to be 16. The probability that a class-1 packet arrives is fixed throughout this section at $\lambda_1 = 0.4$, while the buffer for the high priority traffic has a size $H = 25$ packets. By dimensioning the high priority buffer like this, the probability that a class-1 packet is dropped due to buffer overflow is in the order of 10^{-20}. Figure 1(a) represents, for each of the discussed approaches, the loss rate of the class-2 packets where the corresponding buffer has a size $L = 20$ packets and $\lambda_2 = 0.1, \ldots, 0.4$.

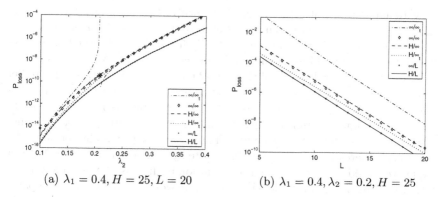

(a) $\lambda_1 = 0.4, H = 25, L = 20$ (b) $\lambda_1 = 0.4, \lambda_2 = 0.2, H = 25$

Fig. 1. Comparison of the loss rate of low priority packets for each of the six approaches

The exact results obtained via the system with two finite buffers, is denoted by the full line. It can be seen that the ∞/L results are very accurate, meaning there is no harm in assuming an infinite size high priority buffer. The other four approximation approaches give rise to higher loss probabilities. This difference is caused by the heuristic calculation used to estimate the loss probability. Whenever an infinite buffer is used for the low priority traffic, the estimate for the loss probability is based on the probability that the number of packets in the buffer exceeds L. In general, this causes an overestimation as packets that would be dropped earlier by the finite capacity system may still reside in the infinite buffer setup when the next arrival(s) occur.

In case both queues are assumed to be infinite, we observe some poor results around $\lambda_2 = 0.21$ for the ∞/∞_t approach, which relies on the asymptotic tail behavior of the class-2 queue. This is caused by the fact that the tail transition point is situated at $p_t = 0.208060765$: for $\lambda_2 \leq p_t$ the tail is nongeometric, whereas for $\lambda_2 > p_t$, we have a geometric tail. When $\lambda_2 < p_t$, the asymptotic regime is dominated by a branch point, whereas for $\lambda_2 > p_t$ there exists a dominant pole. When we approach the transition point, the domination becomes

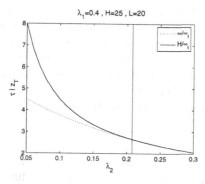

Fig. 2. Comparison of the coefficient for the tail approaches

less severe and significant errors occur as shown in this example. The loss rate obtained for $\lambda_2 = p_t$ is quite accurate as indicated by the star on the plot.

Figure 1(b) illustrates the influence of the buffer capacity for the low priority traffic on the loss probability of this traffic in the case where $\lambda_2 = 0.2$. As could be expected, the loss probability of the class-2 packets decreases when this buffer becomes larger. If we compare the different approaches, we notice the same behavior as in Figure 1(a). Because taking $\lambda_2 = 0.2$ brings us relatively close to the transition point, a significant error is introduced by assuming both queues infinite and relying on the tail behavior. That is, the loss probability obtained by this approach overestimates the actual loss rate by a factor of 100 to 1000. If, for example, we would use the ∞/∞_t approximation to dimension the class-2 buffer such that the loss probability is less than 10^{-5}, we would need a buffer of 14 packets, whereas a buffer of only 8 packets suffices if we consider the H/L approach.

In Figure 2 we compare the two approaches based on the tail behavior of the low priority queue. In fact, the full line represents the geometric decay parameter in function of the arrival rate λ_2 of the low priority traffic. The dotted line represents the parameter z_T, described in algorithm 6.2. On the figure, the transition point is indicated by the vertical line. As mentioned before, on the left of this line the tail for the class-2 queue obtained by algorithm 6.2 is nongeometric, whereas on the right of the transition point the tails are geometric. It can be noticed that the values indicated by the two curves, converge to the same value as λ_2 reaches the transition point.

8   Conclusions

In this paper we have studied the influence of buffer finiteness on the low priority loss probability in a queueing system with two priority classes. Three novel discrete time queueing models with at least one finite capacity buffer were introduced, together with efficient solution techniques that rely on matrix analytic methods. Six different approaches to estimate the low priority loss rate were discussed and compared.

The most accurate approximation results were generated by the approach in which only the high priority traffic is considered as infinite. Moreover, given that the size of the high priority buffer is chosen sufficiently large, the distinction with exact results is negligible. When the low priority queue was assumed to be infinite, we observed an overestimated loss rate. Relying on the actual steady state probabilities or the asymptotic tail behavior seemed to make little difference if the high priority queue was finite. However, in case both queues are infinite very inaccurate loss probability were observed when we made use of the asymptotic tail behavior, especially in the area near the transition point.

References

1. J. Abate and W. Whitt. The Fourier-series method for inverting transforms of probability distributions. *Queueing Systems*, 10:5–88, 1992.
2. J. Abate and W. Whitt. Asymptotics for M/G/1 low-priority waiting-time tail probabilities. *Queueing Systems*, 25:173–233, 1997.

3. A.S. Alfa. Matrix-geometric solution of discrete time MAP/PH/1 priority queue. *Naval Research Logistics*, 45:23–50, 1998.
4. A.S. Alfa, B. Liu, and Q.M. HE. Discrete-time analysis of MAP/PH/1 multiclass general preemptive priority queue. *Naval Research Logistics*, 50:662–682, 2003.
5. E. Falkenberg. On the asymptotic behaviour of the stationary distribution of Markov chains of M/G/1-type. *Stochastic Models*, 10(1):75–97, 1994.
6. A. György and T. Borsos. Estimates on the packet loss ratio via queue tail probabilities. In *IEEE Globecom*, San Antonio, TX, USA, Nov 2001.
7. F. Ishizaki. Numerical method for discrete-time finite-buffer queues with some regenerative structure. *Stochastic Models*, 18(1):25–39, 2002.
8. K.P. Sapna Isotupa and David A. Stanford. An infinite-phase quasi-birth-and-death model for the non-preemptive priority M/PH/1 queue. *Stochastic Models*, 18(3):387–424, 2002.
9. N.K. Kim and M.L. Chaudry. Numerical inversion of generating functions: a computational experience. Manuscript, 2005.
10. K. Laevens and H. Bruneel. Discrete-time multiserver queues with priorities. *Performance Evaluation*, 33(4):249–275, 1998.
11. B. Meini. An improved FFT-based version of Ramaswami's formula. *Stochastic Models*, 13:223–238, 1997.
12. M.F. Neuts. *Structured Stochastic Matrices of M/G/1 type and their applications*. Marcel Dekker, Inc., New York and Basel, 1989.
13. V. Ramaswami. A stable recursion for the steady state vector in Markov chains of M/G/1 type. *Commun. Statist.-Stochastic Models*, 4:183–188, 1988.
14. A. Sleptchenko, A. van Harten, and M.C. van der Heijden. An exact analysis of the multi-class M/M/k priority queue with partial blocking. *Stochastic Models*, 19(4):527–548, 2003.
15. A. Sleptchenko, A. van Harten, and M.C. van der Heijden. An exact solution for the state probabilities of the multi-class, multi-server queue with preemptive priorities. *Queueing Systems*, 50(1):81–107, 2005.
16. J. Walraevens, B. Steyaert, and H. Bruneel. Performance analysis of a single-server ATM queue with a priority scheduling. *Computers & Operations Research*, 30(12):1807–1829, 2003.
17. J. Walraevens, B. Steyaert, and H. Bruneel. A packet switch with a priority scheduling discipline: Performance analysis. *Telecommunication Systems*, 28(1):53–77, 2005.

Experimental Analysis of the Correlation of HTTP GET Invocations

Philipp Reinecke[1], Aad P.A. van Moorsel[2], and Katinka Wolter[1]

[1] Humboldt-Universität zu Berlin
Institut für Informatik
Berlin, Germany
{preineck, wolter}@informatik.hu-berlin.de
[2] University of Newcastle upon Tyne
School of Computing Science
Newcastle upon Tyne, United Kingdom
aad.vanmoorsel@ncl.ac.uk

Abstract. In this paper we experimentally investigate if optimal retry times can be determined based on models that assume independence of successive tries. We do this using data obtained for HTTP GET. This data provides application-perceived timing characteristics for the various phases of web page download, including response times for TCP connection set-ups and individual object downloads. The data consists of pairs of consecutive downloads for over one thousand randomly chosen URLs. Our analysis shows that correlation exists for normally completed invocations, but is remarkably low for relatively slow downloads. This implies that for typical situations in which retries are applied, models relying on the independence assumption are appropriate.

1 Introduction

When a computing job or task does not complete in a reasonable time, it makes common sense to retry it. Examples are plentiful: clicking the browser refresh button, retry of TCP connection attempts at expiration of the retransmission timer, reboot of machines if jobs do not complete ('rejuvenation'), preemptive restarting of a randomised algorithm using a different seed, etc.

In concrete terms, a retry makes sense if a new try takes less time to complete than the ongoing attempt would have taken. If we assume that the completion times of consecutive tries are independent and identically distributed and that no time penalty is incurred when issuing a retry, it can be shown that retries improve the overall mean completion time when the completion time distribution is of a particular type, most notably heavy-tailed, bi-modal or log-normal [9]. Since we know from existing experimental work (e.g., [5]) that Internet response times fit such distributions, Internet applications potentially respond positively to retries.

However, the above reasoning assumes independent identically distributed tries, an assumption that may not necessarily hold. Hence, models that determine optimal retry times based on the independence assumption [2, 4, 5, 9] may

A. Horváth and M. Telek (Eds.): EPEW 2006, LNCS 4054, pp. 226–237, 2006.

not necessarily be appropriate either. To analyse if and to what extend the independence assumption holds for Internet applications, we conducted experiments and collected data for consecutive HTTP GET invocations. This paper reports on the analyses of the correlation characteristics of this data. To the best of our knowledge such data capturing and analysis has not been done before (compare for instance the surveyed experimental work in [3]). In earlier work [6], we analysed HTTP GET invocations, but did not possess the detailed data for subsequent requests to the same URL we use in this paper.[1]

Our experiments capture data for many consecutive downloads from individual URLs, always executed in pairs. This allows us to investigate correlation between consecutive attempts as well as to determine the distribution of completion time. We collected data for various phases of the download of a web page, distinguishing TCP connection set-up, time until the first data has been received, intermediate 'stalling' times and the overall download time of an object. We are interested in these detailed metrics because they potentially provide clues on when to initiate a retry. We only obtained data for metrics that are visible at the application level, since we are interested in investigating retries that could be introduced in an Internet application such as a browser or a software agent.

We gained the following insights from the analysis in this paper. On the one hand, if we consider all samples, the correlation between subsequent tries is surprisingly low, irrespective of the considered phase in a web page download. On the other hand, if we only consider attempts that complete 'fast' (that is, within a small deviation of the average), the correlation is considerable. We conclude from this that the independence assumption is reasonable for model-based optimisation of retry times, *provided one limits retries to times at which completions can be considered slower than normal.* Clearly, this corresponds to the case in which one would want to consider retries to begin with. We also study the correlation between different phases of the same download, and conclude that these typically exhibit very low correlation. This makes it difficult to make use of knowledge of earlier phases of the download to predict the remaining download time (as has been utilised in [7] for retries of database queries).

We now first describe our experiment set-up and its underlying system model, as well as the metrics we observed. We present the collected data in Sect. 3, followed by the statistical analysis.

2 Experiment Design and Execution

Figure 1 depicts response times of HTTP GET invocations as an application perceives it. The figure shows the various phases during the download of a

---

[1] The data used in [6] contains completion times for TCP connection set-up, images, objects and complete web pages for three experiments using 56,000 randomly selected URLs. However, it lacks data for subsequent tries over long periods of time. We have made available on the web [1] both the data set used in [6] and the one used in this paper.

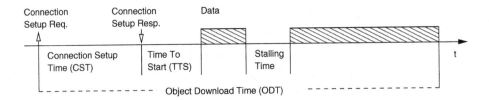

Fig. 1. Metrics and measurement points during the download task

single object (such as a page or an image) and denotes the metrics used in our experiments.

We call the overall time spent downloading the Object Download Time (ODT), which is comprised of:

- Connection Set-up Time (CST): the time for the TCP connection set-up
- Time To Start (TTS): the time between sending the GET request and receiving the first data
- the time consumed by actual data transfer (we do not collect this time explicitly)
- Longest Stalling Time (LST): the length of possible stalling periods during the download, of which we record the longest

These metrics allow us to assess the performance of a download in three distinct phases:

Connection Set-Up Time: In TCP, connection set-up is accomplished by a three-way-handshake and error handling procedures involving the Retransmission Timeout (RTO) timer. From the application's point of view, this task corresponds to calling a `connect()` function, and waiting for this call to return the connection. The application has no means to infer the state of the connection set-up, and thus the performance of this whole process is described by a single metric, namely its length.

Time To Start: The client proceeds by sending its request over the connection. The network transports the request data to the server, which generates an answer and sends it back to the client. At the transport layer, the connection's receive and send windows are adjusted to accommodate for network characteristics ('slow start'). At the application level a new server instance may have to be started on the server, and content has to be prepared and sent out. As with connection set-up, the intricacies of this phase remain hidden from the client application, since it cannot observe whether its request actually reached the server, was processed, nor whether a reply was sent back. Instead, it encounters a period of inactivity between sending the request and receiving the first chunk of data.

Longest Stalling Time: During the download, various factors (e.g., network or server congestion) may lead to periods of temporary stalling. In these periods, no new data is available to the application when it polls the socket (done at 20 ms intervals, see below). We always track the longest such interval. If there was no stalling period, LST will be zero.

Object Download Time: Together, CST, TTS, LST, other stalling intervals, and the length of periods in which data arrives add up to the Object Download Time. That is, ODT is the time it takes from initiating the download until the object is available to the application.

2.1   Experiments

To conduct our experiments we implemented a Java client that repeatedly downloads web pages from a set of hosts and measures the above-mentioned performance indicators. The client issues GET / HTTP/1.0 requests to a web server, and the ODT metric then corresponds to the time it takes to download the web server's root document (e.g., index.html) without any images or other objects that might otherwise be included.

To obtain a sample, the client chooses a URL at random. We randomise the order in which we visit servers to decrease the likelihood of introducing substantial dependencies between ordered requests to different machines. The Java client then downloads the host's root document twice in a row, with a 20 ms pause in between. The pairs of samples thus obtained allow us to study correlation between subsequent requests. All our samples have a 20 ms granularity, because the client polls a TCP socket for new data at 20 ms intervals.

The initial list of URLs was determined in two passes. First, to create a reasonably random set of live URLs, we fed words from a large word list into the Google search engine and extracted the links (the first 100) from the results. In earlier experiments we used all of the resulting 56,000 URLs. In the current experiment, we reduced the list by randomly drawing 2000 entries for detailed investigation. As failing hosts may stall the experiments, any URL that produces fatal errors or exceeded certain time thresholds (24 s for CST, 60 s for TTS, and 1200 s for ODT) was automatically removed from the list. Due to this mechanism, our list shrank, and the data presented in the next section stems therefore from 725 unique URLs, each yielding a large number of samples (at least 1000).

The experiments were run on two Linux PCs connected to the Internet using 768kbit ADSL dial-up with the same ISP. On the first, a 2.0 GHz PC, the experiment ran for 22 days, on the second, a 1.6 GHz PC, we collected samples for 10 days. The experiments faced three interruptions (interrupted dial-up connection, etc.), and we accounted for these interruptions in our analysis in such a way that they did not influence the results.

3   Results

Table 1 gives an overview of the results for the metrics defined in Sect. 2. The first and second trial are denoted by subscripts 1 and 2, respectively. Note that for Time To Start and Object Download Time the second attempt is typically faster than the first. Most likely the second request benefits from work already

Table 1. Overview of data set characteristics for the 725 URLs analysed. All times are given in milliseconds.

	CST_1	CST_2	TTS_1	TTS_2	LST_1	LST_2	ODT_1	ODT_2
First data set (22.09.2004, 6:44 – 14.10.2004, 15:48; 816397 samples)								
mean	178.9	180.4	311.2	295.6	62.9	62.3	721.7	704.7
median	160	160	180	180	0	0	440	440
std. deviation	301.9	229.6	1663.5	1627.9	404.9	427.5	1918.6	2280.8
CoV	1.687	1.273	5.345	5.507	6.437	6.862	2.658	3.236
minimum	0	20	40	0	0	0	0	40
maximum	23700	24000	58440	60020	197480	309000	317700	1201880
Second data set (07.10.2004, 11:36 – 17.10.2004, 20:04; 212805 samples)								
mean	174.6	173.4	293.9	279.0	63.7	62.4	1382.4	1347.2
median	160	160	180	180	0	0	840	840
std. deviation	320.3	250.4	1576.6	1545.0	264.3	201.9	3547.126	6242.9
CoV	1.834	1.444	5.364	5.537	4.15	3.235	2.566	4.634
minimum	20	20	20	0	0	0	320	340
maximum	21440	24000	57880	60020	57420	26760	274940	2420360

done for the previous one, e.g., the server might re-use the server instance that handled the first attempt and could also serve cached data. However, this effect is not very large, and close to negligible if we consider the median (at 20 ms granularity).

It is worth mentioning that all sampled metrics have a coefficient of variation (CoV, which is defined as the standard deviation divided by the expectation of the considered metric) greater than one, indicating high variability. This holds especially true for TTS and the Longest Stalling Time. The high variability of TTS can most likely be explained by the dependence of TTS on network conditions, the server, the client's operating system state, etc. The high CoV value for LST may be explained by the fact that it is a maximum value and is therefore rather unpredictable.

In interpreting our results it is important to understand the working of TCP's retry mechanism. During connection set-up, TCP initiates a retry when the RTO times out. RTO first expires after 3000 ms and doubles after every expiration, i.e., RTO expires and TCP re-attempts to set up a connection 3, 9, 21, 45 and 93 seconds after the initial attempt. The consequence of this mechanism on the download time can be observed very well in Fig. 3, as we explain in Sect. 3.1.

We note that in our experiments about 0.3 percent of all TCP connection set-up attempts experienced one or more RTO expiries, i.e., CST > 3000 ms (this is not directly visible in the table). In earlier experiments [6] we found that the IP-level failure percentage for TCP connection set-up is close to 0.6 percent. The difference can probably be explained by our method of selecting URLs, which tends to favour less failure-prone hosts.

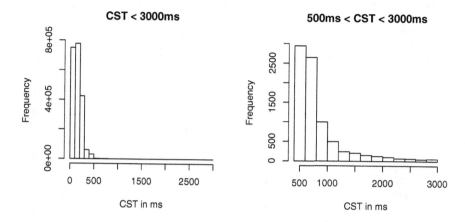

Fig. 2. Histograms for all CST < 3000 from both sets

Figure 2 illustrates the distribution of CSTs for attempts without RTO expiration, with the right side graph zooming in on the left. The histogram in Fig. 2 suggests that for non-failed connection set-ups, CSTs for random URLs have quite a high variance and frequently exhibit a relatively long completion time. This may be interesting in its own right, but also bodes well for issuing restarts, as was also found in [5, 8]. The question remains, however, whether consecutive connection set-up times are independent, an issue we will study now.

3.1   Correlation

Various models that are used to determine the optimal retry time rely on the assumption that subsequent tries exhibit independent and identically distributed (iid) completion times. If the iid assumption is true, then correlation will be zero. In other words, if correlation is high, we conclude that the independence assumption is not valid. Therefore we now analyse the correlation characteristics of our data. The analysis presented here is based solely on data from the first data set, but we found that both sets lead to similar conclusions regarding correlation.

A first visual indication of the degree to which consecutive downloads are correlated is given by the scatter plots in Fig. 3 and Fig. 4, for the CST and ODT metric, respectively. Scatter plots of consecutive attempts show the correlation between the first and second attempt by plotting the duration of the former against that of the latter. For points close to the diagonal the first and the second download experienced roughly equal completion times, and therefore indicate strong correlation. Points far off the diagonal signal low correlation. Data points below the diagonal of the scatter plot could have benefitted from a retry, since the second attempt would have taken less time than the first. Points above the diagonal would not have benefitted from a retry.

Figure 3 depicts connection set-up times. The importance of TCP's RTO timeout values shows quite clearly through clusters of samples just above 3000 ms

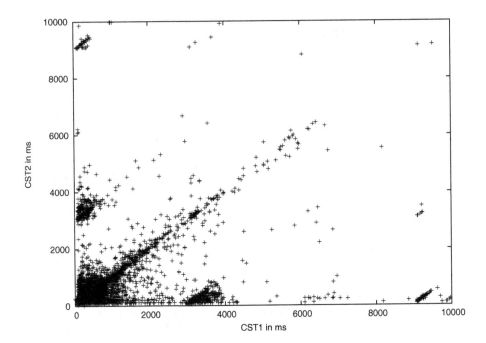

Fig. 3. Scatter plot for CST1 and CST2. TCP's RTO values are clearly visible in the clusters in the off-diagonals around 3000ms and 9000ms on each axis.

and 9000 ms near both axes. Since these two clusters are far from the diagonal, they indicate low correlation between consecutive connection set-ups. However, note that these clusters (indicating low correlation) correspond to cases in which one of the two connection set-up attempts experienced failures on the IP level. In cases where both connection set-ups succeed without an RTO expiry (that is, both CST_1 and CST_2 are below 3000 ms), the samples more strongly gravitate towards the diagonal, indicating substantial correlation.

The clusters caused by the RTO time out values are still faintly visible in the scatter plot for ODT_1 and ODT_2 (Fig. 4). However, this picture is much more diffuse, as could already have been expected based on the coefficient of variation values in (Tab. 1) (the ODT coefficient of variation is double that for CST). Together, these two observations suggest that, while delays introduced by the RTO mechanism may have a strong influence on the ODT, the additional factors affecting this metric can change the pattern of observed ODTs considerably.

Although they provide a strong visual insight into the amount of correlation, the scatter plots do not objectively quantify the degree to which observations are actually correlated for a given set of URLs. To this end, we study the distribution of correlation coefficients per URL, as shown in the histograms in Fig. 5 until Fig. 7. That is, we split the data set by URLs and for every URL treat the (thousand or more) observations for each metric M from the first and the second attempt as resulting from two random variables M_1 and M_2. We then compute

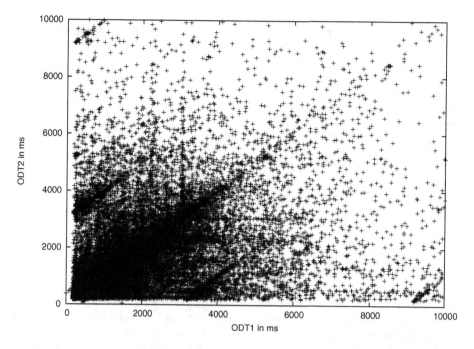

Fig. 4. Scatter plot for ODT1 and ODT2

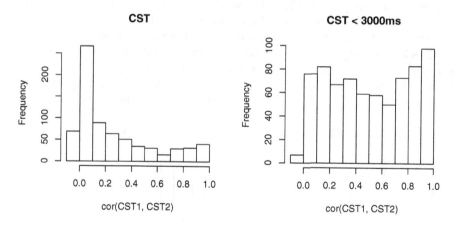

Fig. 5. Histograms of correlation coefficients for (CST_1, CST_2)

$Cor(M_1, M_2)$ for each URL and display the distribution of $Cor(M_1, M_2)$ over all URLs. Figure 5, for instance, shows that if we consider CST, close to 300 URLs have correlation in the range between 0.0 and 0.1.

In our discussion of the scatter plots, we already touched upon the difference in correlation of 'failed' attempts (i.e., failed on the IP level) and 'fast' attempts. This issue can be studied quantitatively by comparing the left and right hand

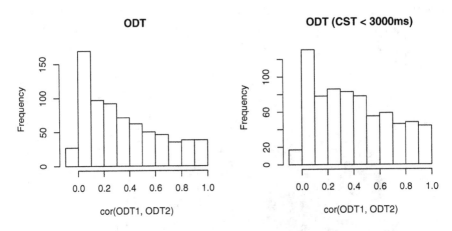

Fig. 6. Histograms of correlation coefficients for (ODT_1, ODT_2)

bar chart in Fig. 5. The left hand side, where we consider all attempts, shows low correlation, whereas the right hand side indicates high correlation if we consider only pairs that were successful (CST below 3000 ms) in both tries. This indicates that the independence assumption is only valid in the 'failed' case, not for the common situation of normally succeeding attempts. So, even though successful completion times may be distributed according to a distribution that is amenable to retries (log-normal, heavy-tail), this does not imply that retries do indeed pay off because the independence assumption is probably invalid. However, when one considers higher retry times, retries at those times are not highly correlated, and models based on the independence assumption are likely to be valid.

This difference between correlation for 'failed' and successful attempts can also be observed for ODTs in Fig. 6, although here there remains a larger portion

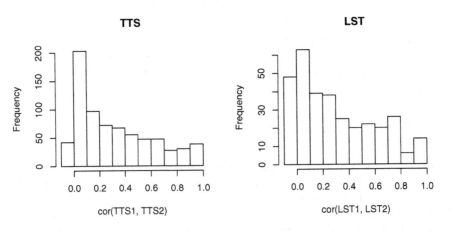

Fig. 7. Histograms of correlation coefficients for (TTS_1, TTS_2) and (LST_1, LST_2)

of URLs with low correlation. The latter may find its explanation in the low correlation for TTS and LST, as seen in Fig. 7. The time-to-start values of the first and the second attempt seem often, but not always, uncorrelated, as can be seen in Fig. 7 on the left, while the longest stalling time often is long (or short) again upon the second try, if it was long (or short) before, as can be seen in Fig. 7 on the right.

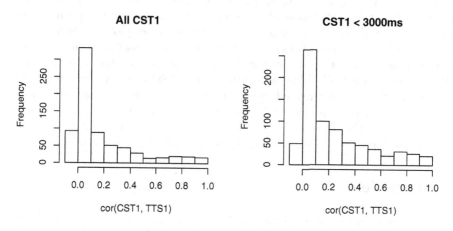

Fig. 8. Histogram of correlation coefficients for (CST_1, TTS_1)

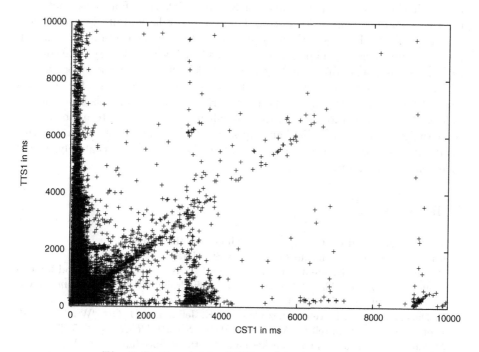

Fig. 9. Scatter plot for CST1 and TTS1, zoomed in

Cross-Measure Correlation. A final point of interest is the correlation between various phases of the download. If correlation exists, samples for one metric M may be used to predict the completion time of a subsequent metric M' within the same download (along the lines of [7]).

Figure 8 is just one example for the likelihood of such correlation, namely that between connection set-up time and time to start. It shows that correlation is relatively low, and similar behaviour exists between the other phases. This makes it difficult to exploit possible inter-phase dependence for computing retry times. Figure 9 illustrates the fact further. In this scatter plot we observe that there is no obvious relation between CST and TTS; TTS may take on any value when the connection set-up was very fast, and vice versa. The cluster for values of TTS close to zero at CST values of 3000 ms and at 9000 ms signify that retries of connection set-ups do not make large TTS more likely. The diagonal, indicating positive correlation, is pronounced only for small values of both metrics, and, in particular, for CST< 3000. This latter observation indicates that inter-phase dependencies may be exploitable only in the absence of packet loss.

4   Conclusions

In this paper we have analysed empirical data sampled using HTTP GET. We have investigated correlation patterns in the data and found high correlation when using data from connections that were successfully set up straight away, i.e., with Connection Set-up Times of less than 3000 ms. For these, not only the corresponding Connection Set-up Times are correlated, but also the Object Download Times. However, when considering data from connections that 'failed' (i.e., Connection Set-up Time greater than 3000 ms), we found very little correlation. The consequence of our finding is that models that rely on the independence of successive tries will not likely be useful to determine retry times for fast tries (even if their distribution is amenable to retries). However, models based on the independence assumption *are* appropriate when one wants to determine optimal retry times for slower or 'failed' attempts. Since retries are most relevant in this latter situation, this validates the use of optimisation models that rely on the independence assumption.

References

1. The data discussed in this paper is available from the web site
   http://homepages.cs.ncl.ac.uk/aad.vanmoorsel/data.
2. H. Alt, L. Guibas, K. Mehlhorn, R. Karp and A. Wigderson, "A Method for Obtaining Randomized Algorithms with Small Tail Probabilities," *Algorithmica*, Vol. 16, Nr. 4/5, pp. 543–547, 1996.
3. F. Donelson Smith, F. Hernandez Campos, K. Jeffay and D. Ott "What TCP/IP Protocol Headers Can tell Us About The Web," *SIGMETRICS*, pp. 245–256, 2001.
4. M. Luby, A. Sinclair and D. Zuckerman, "Optimal Speedup of Las Vegas Algorithms," *Israel Symposium on Theory of Computing Systems,* pp. 128–133, 1993.

5. S. M. Maurer and B. A. Huberman, "Restart strategies and Internet congestion," in *Journal of Economic Dynamics and Control,* vol. 25, pp. 641–654, 2001.
6. P. Reinecke, A. van Moorsel and K. Wolter, "A Measurement Study of the Interplay between Application Level Restart and Transport Protocol," in *Springer Verlag Lecture Notes in Computer Science 3335, International Service Availability Symposium: Revised Selected Papers,* M. Malek, M. Reitenspiess and J. Kaiser (Eds.), pp. 86–100, 2005.
7. Y. Ruan, E. Horvitz and H. Kautz, "Restart Policies with Dependence among Runs: A Dynamic Programming Approach," in *Proceedings of the Eight International Conference on Principles and Practice of Constraint Programming,* Ithaca, NY, 2002.
8. M. Schroeder and L. Boro, "Does the Restart Method Work? Preliminary Results on Efficiency Improvements for Interactions of Web-Agents," in *Proceedings of the Workshop on Infrastructure for Agents, MAS, and Scalable MAS at the Conference Autonomous Agents 2001,* T. Wagner and O. Rana (Eds.), Springer Verlag, 2001.
9. A. van Moorsel and K. Wolter, "Analysis and Algorithms for Restart," *Proceedings of International Conference on Quantitative Evaluation of Systems,* Twente, Netherlands, pp. 195–204, 2004.

Author Index

Lecture Notes in Computer Science

For information about Vols. 1–3956

please contact your bookseller or Springer

Vol. 3998: T. Calamoneri, I. Finocchi, G.F. Italiano (Eds.), Algorithms and Complexity. XII, 394 pages. 2006.

Vol. 3997: W. Grieskamp, C. Weise (Eds.), Formal Approaches to Software Testing. XII, 219 pages. 2006.

Vol. 3996: A. Keller, J.-P. Martin-Flatin (Eds.), Self-Managed Networks, Systems, and Services. X, 185 pages. 2006.

Vol. 3995: G. Müller (Ed.), Emerging Trends in Information and Communication Security. XX, 524 pages. 2006.

Vol. 3994: V.N. Alexandrov, G.D. van Albada, P.M.A. Sloot, J. Dongarra (Eds.), Computational Science – ICCS 2006, Part IV. XXXV, 1096 pages. 2006.

Vol. 3993: V.N. Alexandrov, G.D. van Albada, P.M.A. Sloot, J. Dongarra (Eds.), Computational Science – ICCS 2006, Part III. XXXVI, 1136 pages. 2006.

Vol. 3992: V.N. Alexandrov, G.D. van Albada, P.M.A. Sloot, J. Dongarra (Eds.), Computational Science – ICCS 2006, Part II. XXXV, 1122 pages. 2006.

Vol. 3991: V.N. Alexandrov, G.D. van Albada, P.M.A. Sloot, J. Dongarra (Eds.), Computational Science – ICCS 2006, Part I. LXXXI, 1096 pages. 2006.

Vol. 3990: J. C. Beck, B.M. Smith (Eds.), Integration of AI and OR Techniques in Constraint Programming for Combinatorial Optimization Problems. X, 301 pages. 2006.

Vol. 3989: J. Zhou, M. Yung, F. Bao, Applied Cryptography and Network Security. XIV, 488 pages. 2006.

Vol. 3987: M. Hazas, J. Krumm, T. Strang (Eds.), Location- and Context-Awareness. X, 289 pages. 2006.

Vol. 3986: K. Stølen, W.H. Winsborough, F. Martinelli, F. Massacci (Eds.), Trust Management. XIV, 474 pages. 2006.

Vol. 3984: M. Gavrilova, O. Gervasi, V. Kumar, C.J. K. Tan, D. Taniar, A. Laganà, Y. Mun, H. Choo (Eds.), Computational Science and Its Applications - ICCSA 2006, Part V. XXV, 1045 pages. 2006.

Vol. 3983: M. Gavrilova, O. Gervasi, V. Kumar, C.J. K. Tan, D. Taniar, A. Laganà, Y. Mun, H. Choo (Eds.), Computational Science and Its Applications - ICCSA 2006, Part IV. XXVI, 1191 pages. 2006.

Vol. 3982: M. Gavrilova, O. Gervasi, V. Kumar, C.J. K. Tan, D. Taniar, A. Laganà, Y. Mun, H. Choo (Eds.), Computational Science and Its Applications - ICCSA 2006, Part III. XXV, 1243 pages. 2006.

Vol. 3981: M. Gavrilova, O. Gervasi, V. Kumar, C.J. K. Tan, D. Taniar, A. Laganà, Y. Mun, H. Choo (Eds.), Computational Science and Its Applications - ICCSA 2006, Part II. XXVI, 1255 pages. 2006.

Vol. 3980: M. Gavrilova, O. Gervasi, V. Kumar, C.J. K. Tan, D. Taniar, A. Laganà, Y. Mun, H. Choo (Eds.), Computational Science and Its Applications - ICCSA 2006, Part I. LXXV, 1199 pages. 2006.

Vol. 3979: T.S. Huang, N. Sebe, M.S. Lew, V. Pavlović, M. Kölsch, A. Galata, B. Kisačanin (Eds.), Computer Vision in Human-Computer Interaction. XII, 121 pages. 2006.

Vol. 3978: B. Hnich, M. Carlsson, F. Fages, F. Rossi (Eds.), Recent Advances in Constraints. VIII, 179 pages. 2006. (Sublibrary LNAI).

Vol. 3977: N. Fuhr, M. Lalmas, S. Malik, G. Kazai (Eds.), Advances in XML Information Retrieval and Evaluation. XII, 556 pages. 2006.

Vol. 3976: F. Boavida, T. Plagemann, B. Stiller, C. Westphal, E. Monteiro (Eds.), Networking 2006. Networking Technologies, Services, and Protocols; Performance of Computer and Communication Networks; Mobile and Wireless Communications Systems. XXVI, 1276 pages. 2006.

Vol. 3975: S. Mehrotra, D.D. Zeng, H. Chen, B.M. Thuraisingham, F.-Y. Wang (Eds.), Intelligence and Security Informatics. XXII, 772 pages. 2006.

Vol. 3973: J. Wang, Z. Yi, J.M. Zurada, B.-L. Lu, H. Yin (Eds.), Advances in Neural Networks - ISNN 2006, Part III. XXIX, 1402 pages. 2006.

Vol. 3972: J. Wang, Z. Yi, J.M. Zurada, B.-L. Lu, H. Yin (Eds.), Advances in Neural Networks - ISNN 2006, Part II. XXVII, 1444 pages. 2006.

Vol. 3971: J. Wang, Z. Yi, J.M. Zurada, B.-L. Lu, H. Yin (Eds.), Advances in Neural Networks - ISNN 2006, Part I. LXVII, 1442 pages. 2006.

Vol. 3970: T. Braun, G. Carle, S. Fahmy, Y. Koucheryavy (Eds.), Wired/Wireless Internet Communications. XIV, 350 pages. 2006.

Vol. 3969: Ø. Ytrehus (Ed.), Coding and Cryptography. XI, 443 pages. 2006.

Vol. 3968: K.P. Fishkin, B. Schiele, P. Nixon, A. Quigley (Eds.), Pervasive Computing. XV, 402 pages. 2006.

Vol. 3967: D. Grigoriev, J. Harrison, E.A. Hirsch (Eds.), Computer Science – Theory and Applications. XVI, 684 pages. 2006.

Vol. 3966: Q. Wang, D. Pfahl, D.M. Raffo, P. Wernick (Eds.), Software Process Change. XIV, 356 pages. 2006.

Vol. 3965: M. Bernardo, A. Cimatti (Eds.), Formal Methods for Hardware Verification. VII, 243 pages. 2006.

Vol. 3964: M. Ü. Uyar, A.Y. Duale, M.A. Fecko (Eds.), Testing of Communicating Systems. XI, 373 pages. 2006.

Vol. 3963: O. Dikenelli, M.-P. Gleizes, A. Ricci (Eds.), Engineering Societies in the Agents World VI. XII, 303 pages. 2006. (Sublibrary LNAI).

Vol. 3962: W. IJsselsteijn, Y. de Kort, C. Midden, B. Eggen, E. van den Hoven (Eds.), Persuasive Technology. XII, 216 pages. 2006.

Vol. 3960: R. Vieira, P. Quaresma, M.d.G.V. Nunes, N.J. Mamede, C. Oliveira, M.C. Dias (Eds.), Computational Processing of the Portuguese Language. XII, 274 pages. 2006. (Sublibrary LNAI).

Vol. 3959: J.-Y. Cai, S. B. Cooper, A. Li (Eds.), Theory and Applications of Models of Computation. XV, 794 pages. 2006.

Vol. 3958: M. Yung, Y. Dodis, A. Kiayias, T. Malkin (Eds.), Public Key Cryptography - PKC 2006. XIV, 543 pages. 2006.